columns

Smyth & Helwys Publishing, Inc.
6316 Peake Road
Macon, Georgia 31210-3960
1-800-747-3016
©2004 by Smyth & Helwys Publishing
All rights reserved.
Printed in the United States of America.

The paper used in this publication meets the minimum requirements of
American National Standard for Information Sciences—
Permanence of Paper for Printed Library Materials.
ANSI Z39.48–1984. (alk. paper)

Library of Congress Cataloging-in-Publication Data

Dilday, Russell H.
Columns : glimpses of a seminary under assault / by Russell H. Dilday.

p. cm.
ISBN 1-57312-443-5 (pbk–alk. paper)

1. Southwestern Baptist Theological Seminary.
2. Baptists–Doctrines. 3. Fundamentalism.
4. Dilday, Russell H. 5. Theological seminary presidents–Texas.
I. Title.

BV4070.S86D55 2004
230'.07'3617645315–dc22

2004022080

Russell H. Dilday

Glimpses of a Seminary Under Assault

SMYTH&HELWYS

PUBLISHING, INCORPORATED · MACON, GEORGIA

Contents

Preface

As the president of Southwestern Baptist Theological Seminary for sixteen years, I received numerous letters. "I'm honored to be a Southwestern graduate," people commented. "I'm proud to be a part of the Southwestern family." "I appreciate Southwestern because those days were growing times in my personal walk with the Lord." "Southwestern was a special blessing." "Thanks, Southwestern, for a quality education." "I'm forever indebted to Southwestern." "I love Southwestern and will always love those who instructed me." "Thanks to Southwestern for continuing to share the good news of the gospel of Jesus Christ."

I, too, shared these feelings for Southwestern. I first came to the campus as a student in fall 1952. My wife Betty and I graduated from Baylor University in May, got married in August, and then moved to a duplex at 4093 Sandage in Fort Worth and began classes the next week. Three weeks later I was called to be the pastor of the Antelope Baptist Church in Jack County, Texas—my first pastorate. For eight years I attended classes, served as pastor, worked at secular jobs, and taught adjunctly at Southwestern. Betty taught school to help pay our expenses until our first child was born in 1955.

When I graduated from Southwestern in 1960 with a doctorate in philosophy of religion, I continued to serve as pastor of Baptist churches for eighteen more years in Texas and Georgia. I didn't have much contact with the Seminary during those years, other than attending alumni luncheons at the state and national Baptist conventions. It was then that I reminisced with colleagues about the preparation, inspiration, and hard work the Seminary had given us. I always felt a sense of loyalty and thankfulness, and we made modest gifts when various alumni campaigns were launched.

In the mid-1970s I was invited back to Southwestern as the speaker for its pastors' conference and faculty retreat. In God's timing I was again linked with the school that had profoundly influenced my life. When the presidential search committee asked me to accept the presidency in October 1977, I was overwhelmed with the privilege and challenge of helping equip ministers of the gospel in the school I had always cherished.

In order to keep more than 35,000 alumni aware of the Seminary's accomplishments and opportunities, I wrote a column each month, which I included in our newsletter, *Southwestern News*. From 1978, when I began my tenure as president, until 1994, when fundamentalists on the board of trustees fired me, thousands of alumni, donors, and friends of the Seminary across the world read these columns.

Recently, in researching data for a book on my personal experiences in the Baptist controversy of the past 25 years, I read again my original copies of those 146 president's columns. (My book of reflections and lessons related to the SBC controversy is titled *Higher Ground* and will be released in 2005.) Obviously, at the time of writing, I had no intention of linking these columns together, nor did I try to relate the themes month by month. But in reading them again as a group, I was struck by how well they tell the story of the joys, accomplishments, and disappointments we experienced and how the Seminary family worked together to keep Southwestern "lashed to the cross."

Aided by a timeline of key events that occurred in the Southern Baptist Convention and on Southwestern's campus each year, these columns speak for themselves. They become a remarkable and sometimes sad chronicle of how the fundamentalist takeover of the SBC from 1978 to 1994 ultimately undermined the world's largest seminary and the "jewel of Baptist theological education."

The "Key Events" page preceding each chapter includes:

(1) Notable occurrences during that year both in the Southern Baptist Convention and the Seminary.

(2) Names of key leaders—fundamentalists and mainstream Baptists who were invited to speak on campus. This demonstrates the open inclusiveness characteristic of Southwestern.

(3) Fundamentalists who invited the president to preach in their churches, especially during the early years of my administration. The hundreds of traditional churches in which I was privileged to preach are not included.

(4) Speaking engagements across the convention where I addressed issues in the controversy and attempted to correct misconceptions and false accusations against Southwestern.

(5) Details of events, in some instances, in order to give background for better understanding of the columns.

(6) My assessment each year of the changing makeup of the Seminary board of trustees as a result of the takeover of the appointment process. The reader can track the progress of the organized effort to control the Seminary by choosing trustees who were loyal supporters of the takeover.

As you read the columns, noting the context in which each one was written, you have a window through which to view life on the campus. Some of you were there and will remember. Others of you have read about the events and heard reports from faculty and students. I hope reflecting on these years again will renew your appreciation for the Southwestern of yesterday, will highlight dangers to avoid in future models of ministry training, and will clarify some of the mystery of how such a great school could be captured and pillaged.

Introduction

In the light of recent world events swirling around Islamic extremists, the term "fundamentalism" has become a household word with negative connotations. A fundamentalist is one with extremist, fanatical views. Convinced that their position is the only right one, fundamentalists are confrontational and argumentative, demonizing anyone who differs. Reflecting a hidden insecurity, fundamentalists try to control others, forcing them into conformity. In furthering their cause, the end often justifies the means.

At one time among Baptists the term had a positive implication. A fundamentalist was someone committed to the fundamentals of the faith. But today, the term "fundamentalism" suggests a mind-set that is narrow, self-righteous, smug, judgmental, rigid, angry, combative, negative, critical, sanctimonious, and hypocritical. Whether it is political fundamentalism or philosophical fundamentalism, Islamic fundamentalism or Baptist fundamentalism, these same characteristics will likely be shared.

I encountered this negative fundamentalist mind-set among the individuals who conspired over the last twenty-five years to seize control of the Southern Baptist Convention. Let me be clear that, in vigorously opposing their assault, I was not against conservative theology or unsympathetic with the desire to keep our Baptist denomination rooted in orthodox biblical faith. My disagreement was always aimed at the fundamentalist spirit, the secular political methodology of the takeover party, their disregard for authentic Baptist principles, the exaggeration of their accusations, and the twisting of the Scriptures they claimed to believe. This clarification may help future Baptists answer the question, "Why were those who opposed the so-called 'conservative resurgence' in the SBC so bothered?"

I served as president of Southwestern Baptist Theological Seminary from 1978 to 1994. It was not only the largest seminary in the world, but one of the best. In 1990, *Christianity Today* released a poll of its readers ranking the effectiveness of American seminaries. Southwestern Seminary was ranked "number 1 among the top 33 graduate theological schools in the nation." To imagine this great institution, built and supported by the sacrifices of faithful Baptists over ninety years, threatened by a fundamentalist assault was unthinkable. That's why I and others are so bothered. That's why I and others vigorously opposed what the leaders of the takeover euphemistically call a "conservative resurgence." In the effort to defend Southwestern Seminary, I encountered firsthand the attitude, the politics, the disregard for Baptist principles, the exaggerations, the misinterpretation of the Bible, and other evils of Baptist fundamentalism.

The Grinches Who Stole the Convention and Southwestern Seminary

At about the time I assumed the presidency of Southwestern in 1978, Paige Patterson, a Dallas minister, and Paul Pressler, a Houston judge, launched their successful scheme to capture control of the SBC in order to reshape it according to their vision. Arousing false fears that the Southern Baptist Convention was slipping into theological liberalism, they set up a precinct-style political organization throughout the South to "turn the convention back to the Bible." The plan was simple: send messengers (delegates in their view) to the annual meeting of the SBC with instructions to elect their handpicked fundamentalist candidate as president. That president would then appoint like-minded committees that in turn would fill the vacancies on the boards of the various convention agencies and seminaries with fundamentalist trustees. In about ten years, each institution would then be in the hands of the Patterson/Pressler faction.

Pressler crudely described this strategy as "going for the jugular." In response to criticism of his remark, Pressler explained, "I was only speaking metaphorically." (I would hope so!) He and Patterson stirred up the anger and fervor of their troops by ridiculing current trustees as "rubber stamps and dumb bunnies," suggesting that people serving on boards like Southwestern Seminary were inept pawns of the administration. The trustees, they claimed, didn't think for themselves, but blindly did the bidding of the president and faculty. Their lack of courage permitted widespread "liberalism" to flourish in the six SBC theological seminaries. These accusations were not only blatantly untrue, but insults to capable men and women who were unselfishly helping Southwestern achieve its best days.

The Southern Baptist Convention's longstanding system for electing trustees for institutions like Southwestern Seminary was based on openness and trust. The Committee on Boards (appointed by the Committee on Committees, in turn appointed by the president of the SBC) had the responsibility of selecting for Southwestern's board a trustee from each Baptist state convention. Additional "local" trustees were named from Texas. Trustees could serve two five-year terms and could not be reelected until they had been off the board for at least a year. This system served Baptists well until it was manipulated by the well-organized and well-financed fundamentalist coalition.

In the days before the Patterson/Pressler party took over the procedure, I and other seminary presidents would be invited to make suggestions to the committee about the kind of board members the schools needed. Unless the committee specifically asked for it, this invitation did not include offering names of individuals, only qualities and expertise that would be helpful. However, after the takeover, we were excluded from any input and were not even told who the nominees were until a few days before their election at the annual meeting of the SBC in June.

When I was elected president in November 1977, thirty-four diverse but cooperative trustees served on Southwestern's board. All but one were men, and about half of them were pastors or church staff ministers. Educators, bankers, pastors, musicians, missionaries, business owners, and physicians—they had been chosen from their respective states because they had qualifications and expertise that could strengthen the Seminary. What a privilege it was to work with these trustees on behalf of Baptists to make Southwestern what we believed the Lord wanted it to be!

Admittedly, there were a few on the board who might have been classified as fundamentalists. Their input, representing one segment of our diverse Baptist family, was welcomed in trustee deliberations, but they couldn't dominate or control decisions.

At the board meeting in October 1977 when the presidential search committee recommended my election, one of the fundamentalist trustees, a Dallas lawyer and a member of the First Baptist Church there, led an abortive effort to turn down the committee's recommendation and elect his brother-in-law instead.

Even though he had lobbied hard, his substitute motion failed with only a half-dozen affirmative votes. My election was then affirmed as "unanimous."

One year later, when I named John Newport as vice president of academic affairs and provost of Southwestern, this same trustee was angry that I didn't name his brother-in-law to that position. Frequently, at the end of trustee meetings, his personal resentment would come out. He would refer to some comment I'd made and with vitriolic anger accuse me of speaking out against the takeover effort. When his twelve years on the board ended in 1987 (filling an unexpired term of two years and two more five-year terms) the Seminary family was relieved that this "troublemaker" had finally rotated off the board. But, after a brief reprieve, we were shocked that the Patterson/Pressler organization reappointed him in 1992 for what would be another ten years. It was no surprise that this same Dallas attorney led the conspiracy to fire the president in 1994.

But even with a half-dozen fundamentalists on the board, my first few years with the trustees were a productive time of cooperative teamwork, the kind churches expected of their trustees and administrators. However, as the Patterson/Pressler scheme for taking over the SBC institutions moved into high gear, we began to receive trustees of a different kind. Instead of being chosen for qualifications or expertise that could strengthen the Seminary, this new breed was picked solely on the basis of their loyalty to the fundamentalist party and their willingness to carry out the takeover agenda. Only one or two rare exceptions slipped through the cracks of the Patterson/Pressler network undetected.

These party loyalists resented the accusation that Pressler or Patterson had screened them for appointment, even rebuking me in one meeting for implying as much. Instead, they publicly contended that their appointments were God's will for the Seminary. However, this issue was settled when one trustee was bold enough to say, "Let's be honest, guys. If you say Paige Patterson and Paul Pressler had nothing to do with our appointment to this board, you're either lying or incredibly naïve." He went on to describe how one Texas Baptist layman who was being nominated did not please Pressler and was therefore arbitrarily cut from the nomination list. Often described as "Mr. Southwestern," this man had given much of his life to the Seminary, but he was not one of their party loyalists, so the trustee telling the account was named in his place. The courageous trustee said, "It was only after I was interviewed by the judge and met his approval that I was nominated for the board."

Thankfully, throughout my sixteen years as president, there were always capable, traditional Baptists on the board who resisted the fundamentalist tide. But after 1985, these traditional Baptists were the minority at Southwestern. By 1994, when I was fired, there remained only eight who vocally denounced the effort. One left before the vote was taken; seven voted against it. Now in full control, the Patterson/Pressler trustees have drastically changed the nature and character of the school. As Jerry Falwell (pastor of Thomas Road Baptist Church in Lynchburg, Virginia, which was an independent Baptist congregation before joining the SBC in recent years) boasted recently, "All six Southern Baptist seminaries are now thoroughly fundamentalist." In a celebration held in conjunction with the Indianapolis convention meeting, Falwell declared to the gathering of fundamentalist leaders, "I was not a Southern Baptist when you guys hijacked it, but I joined soon after." Falwell made his first appearance in Southwestern's chapel in fall 2004, making a politically-charged address that received national press in midst of the presidential election campaign.

Political Loyalty, Not Character

At times, moral character took a back seat to political loyalty as a criterion for election, and people with questionable reputations were nominated to Southwestern's trustee board.

For example, just before an annual meeting of the SBC, a woman called me to complain about one of the ministers who was to be nominated. "He's had affairs with women in his church. Here's the name and phone number of one woman who will confirm his adultery." I explained that I had no power to influence the appointments, but I'd do what I could. I called the nominee, a pastor, and told him about the woman's phone call. "It was just a misunderstanding," he said, "It's all been cleared up. There's nothing to it."

The young pastor was elected at the SBC meeting and later became a leading conspirator in my dismissal. In a press interview following my firing, he publicly ridiculed me for not accepting the financial "buy out" the board had offered if I resigned quietly, left immediately, and no longer criticized the fundamentalist takeover. He said, "If I'd been offered that much money, I'd have taken it!" A few years later, while serving as chair of Southwestern Seminary's board of trustees, he made media headlines when a group of women in his Texas congregation sued him, accusing him of sexual misconduct. His church dismissed him, and he resigned from the board.

In a similar vein, a Texas lawyer was on the list of those to be elected to our board at an upcoming SBC meeting. When his name surfaced, Baptists in Fort Worth and across the state called to warn me. He was an extremist and a disgrace to the legal profession, and besides that, it was widely reported that he had had an affair with a secretary.

I called the man, suggesting that since his election would be challenged at the convention, and since it would be embarrassing to his family and the Seminary when the accusations were made public, it would be best for him and the Seminary if he withdrew his name. He vehemently denied the charges and was angry with me for trying to intimidate him.

His pastor, who later became one of the most strident fundamentalists on our board, came to my office with the lawyer to complain about my actions. With Bibles in hand, they charged me with everything from slander to blatant manipulation. After explaining that I was acting on the reports of his professional colleagues and was suggesting he withdraw in the interest of all concerned, they stormed angrily from the office. Just before the SBC meeting, I learned that the lawyer had declined to be nominated.

Weeks later, this same lawyer came to my office to tell me that in a revival at his church, the Holy Spirit had convicted him. He had publicly confessed his misdeeds—including the affair. Now he wanted to confess that he had lied to me and was sorry. After listening to some of the sordid details, I told him I was glad he had gotten right with the Lord. We prayed, and I never saw him again.

His pastor, however, still resented my intervention in his election and my opposition to the Patterson/Pressler takeover. As a new trustee himself, this pastor became a leading instigator in my dismissal in 1994 and was later elected chair of Southwestern's trustees.

Additional evidence of the questionable character of some who were elected to the Seminary board concerns another attorney. Following a worship service in a large Baptist church where I had preached, two law partners, members of the church, introduced themselves. They said, "That fellow who's giving you all the trouble on the Seminary board ought to be in the penitentiary. He was our law partner, and he misappropriated money from the firm. We fired him, but we should have sent him to jail. If you want us to, we'll come to one of your meetings and tell the trustees what kind of person they're dealing with." I thanked them but never followed up on their offer.

There was another fundamentalist on our board, a high-profile denominational leader who eventually served as chair. A longtime friend and Southwestern graduate was particularly upset that this high-profile leader was appointed to the board. He told me that when this man was pastor of a church in the state where my friend served, he was inappropriately involved with a young woman in the membership. He said, "I have her name, the details, and her permission to expose him. It's not right that people like that are in charge of my seminary." It was tempting to use his information, but I decided to withhold it.

In March 1994, during the meeting of the board at which I was fired, one of our students approached a trustee from his church and asked, "Is the rumor we're hearing true? Are you and the board going to fire Dr. Dilday at this meeting?" The trustee, who helped plan the firing strategy, responded, "Not in a million years! It's just a rumor." The next day, after the vote to dismiss was announced, the student made a beeline to the trustee and asked, "What happened? You told me you weren't going to fire Dr. Dilday." The trustee grinned at the student and replied, "Didn't you see me wink when I told you that?" and walked away. This casual disregard for the truth and ethical behavior was shockingly prevalent among fundamentalists on the board.

Political Loyalty, Not Competence

For the most part, the fundamentalists Patterson and Pressler placed on the board were inexperienced, anti-institution, even anti-education. They were people with limited experience, resources, or expertise to govern a graduate theological seminary. Some of them accepted the trusteeship not as a solemn responsibility, but as a personal benefit, an honor with perks. It was their turn to share in the "big-time" of denominational privilege. It was not unusual for the Seminary to receive requests from a board member to bring family members and stay at the hotel for a few more days at Seminary expense.

From time to time, new trustees would request personal stationery and business cards engraved with their names and the title "Trustee, Southwestern Seminary." This was their time to be in the limelight and call the shots. Such requests, unheard of until now—and certainly not in order—were not granted.

Some had little or no formal education. That alone would not disqualify a person from serving on the board. My own father was a self-taught leader with no college degree, but he believed in education and promoted it enthusiastically in our family and in his ministry. These trustees, though, not only had limited education, but they didn't believe in it. They publicly voiced their suspicion that too much education would dilute a minister's zeal for the Lord—even destroy his faith. On several occasions, one new trustee boasted, "I thank the Lord every day that he didn't let me go to the seminary." Each time, loud "amens" echoed from others on the board. Ironically, here were people elected to govern a highly respected Baptist seminary that awarded accredited master's and doctor's degrees, but they had no appreciation for education in general and mistrust of the scholarly work of Southwestern in particular!

Most blindly accepted the fundamentalist claim that the seminaries were bureaucracies of highly paid liberal intellectuals who were leading the denomination away from the Bible. A large number of them had never been on Southwestern's campus, or to any seminary campus for that matter. Most of them doubted that a graduate school could be both scholarly and biblically sound.

One board member called me from a western state to complain about what he called a printed "syllable" (*sic*) one of our professors was using in his classes. He said, "That 'syllable' talks about criticizing the Bible. We won't stand for teachers who criticize the Bible." The "syllable" (syllabus) to which he objected included a section on biblical criticism, a positive term scholars—including conservative biblical scholars—use for a literary study of the Bible.

Clearly, most of the fundamentalist trustees believed their primary responsibility as soldiers in the takeover campaign was to uncover something wrong with the Seminary. They became what E. Y. Mullins at the beginning of the twentieth century called "smelling committees on fishing expeditions for supposed liberalism." At his first meeting, a newly elected trustee, pastor of a small church in Oklahoma, asked to meet with Vice President John Newport and me. He said, "The boys up in Oklahoma put me on this board to root out all the liberalism here at Southwestern, and I need your help. I'm not sure how to go about it. What should I do?" Dr. Newport and I tried to take him seriously, explaining how he could sit in on classes, read the books, talk to professors, question students, etc. and make up his own mind. After a few meetings, he stood up and reported to the board, "I can't find nothing wrong with this seminary." In a day when compliments from board members were increasingly rare, his endorsement was actually somewhat gratifying!

We had another trustee from North Carolina who, even though he had no legal credentials, would regularly introduce his comments by claiming, "I'm a lawyer, and I suggest . . . ." When we mailed out reports before the meeting of the board, he would go through them with a critical eye to catch what he thought were errors or matters he considered suspicious. Instead of calling my office to clear up his concerns, he would wait until the meeting and then make a speech. Customarily, he would say, "Dr. Dilday doesn't think we read all this material, but I read every word. I'm a lawyer, and on page fourteen I want you to notice . . . ." It was always, without exception, a misunderstanding on his part, but that never discouraged him from repeating this same procedure at nearly every meeting.

On one occasion, after his usual introduction, "Dr. Dilday doesn't think we read all this material, but I'm a lawyer and I read every word," he added, "In the budget Dr. Dilday mailed to us there's a line item in every division called 'Convention Expense.' The president is obviously spending Cooperative Program mission money to send his faculty and staff to the SBC to vote his way. He's trying to control the convention. We shouldn't spend Cooperative Program money to send Dr. Dilday and the faculty to Southern Baptist Conventions."

Our business officer explained that as an SBC agency, Southwestern was expected to send at least half our faculty and several staff to the convention with the president to make reports, operate the display booth, interview prospective students, and answer messenger questions. That seemed to satisfy most of the board in spite of the North Carolinian's pleas.

The next year, projecting lean revenues, we trimmed the recommended budget accordingly. In deciding what to cut from the expenditures, we asked the faculty and staff for suggestions. Since attending the SBC meeting was becoming less and less enjoyable as a result of the fundamentalist takeover, and since we were allowed little voice in convention decisions, the faculty and staff suggested we cut convention expense to a bare minimum. We did.

Having received the usual material in the mail before the next trustee meeting, the same man—one year later—rose to make his speech. "Dr. Dilday doesn't think we read all this material, but I read every word. I'm a lawyer, and I want you to see what's happening. Notice that every line item labeled 'Convention Expense' has a zero. I've discovered Dr. Dilday is deliberately boycotting the convention and refusing to let his faculty and staff attend."

I couldn't help reminding him that just last year he had argued that Cooperative Program money shouldn't be spent on convention expense. He seemed nonplussed but grudgingly agreed that this deletion might be a good thing after all.

This same trustee, after hearing a report of student loan repayments, offered another astute suggestion. From scholarship funds, Southwestern was able to make small tuition loans of several hundred dollars to qualified students at the beginning of each semester. Most repaid the loan by the end of the semester, so the percentage of collections was good—in the high ninetieth percentile. The few loans we had trouble collecting invariably belonged to students who had dropped out of Southwestern and the ministry altogether. Nevertheless, the trustee repeated his "I'm a lawyer" introduction and then made a motion that we require collateral before granting student loans. One of our vice presidents, knowing the limited resources of most seminarians, responded, "I'm afraid if we did that, we would end up with the ugliest collection of beat-up bicycles in Fort Worth." The suggestion was rejected.

Then there was the evangelistic singer on the board whom we invited to present a solo for a banquet of Fort Worth's leading contributors. He sang one stanza of a hymn and then announced he was going to do something few musicians were able to do. He was going to sing and whistle at the same time. What came out was something close to the sound Donald Duck makes in TV cartoons. It was humiliating to all except the fundamentalist board members, who encouraged their colleague with loud cheers and applause. He was one of the trustees who repeatedly led attacks on Southwestern's music school.

One trustee, a Dallas layman in First Baptist Church, worked hard to get the Seminary to invest its endowment in his oil exploration business. When we told him this was not only unwise financially, but would be an illegal conflict of interest, he promptly resigned so he could still work hard at influencing the board to invest the Seminary's money in his venture. We didn't.

Whereas before, we always had board members with financial and investment experience, under the fundamentalist regime those resources became limited at best. The Texas Baptist Foundation portfolio managers who handled our multimillion-dollar endowment fund became concerned. After an annual review with the business affairs committee of the board, the managers told me, "Your trustees aren't really equipped to appraise investment strategies and advise us. They don't know the difference between an equity and a security." For the most part, the new trustees didn't have the financial acumen to read a financial statement or assist our business office in monetary matters.

This isn't said to ridicule nor belittle them. As a matter of fact, reading financial reports and analyzing investments is not my field either. But the Seminary needed trustees who could handle this. We were forced to get our financial advice from our advisory council members and others outside the board.

It should be noted that others shared my impressions of the incompetence— even the various publics beyond our Baptist family. One example involves the Texas Gridiron Club, organized in 1947 by professional journalists. Each year in Fort Worth, the club sponsors the Gridiron Show and Dinner, a spoof of politics, politicians, and other celebrities. A newspaper, *The Yellow Jaundice*, is produced in conjunction with the annual show and dinner. Local politicians and media stars perform in the show as well as attend it. While governor of Texas, Ann Richards participated in the annual show, as did the Honorable Jim Wright. At each annual affair, the journalists single out the one personality who is "demonstrably deserving of disclaim" and grant that person the annual "Horse Collar Award." For example, one year it was awarded to the new owner of the Dallas Cowboys professional football team for firing beloved coach Tom Landry.

In April 1994 the Texas Gridiron Club presented their Horse Collar Award to the fundamentalist trustees of Southwestern Baptist Theological Seminary. They put an empty chair on the stage, placed the Horse Collar on the chair, and read the following proclamation:

What Cleopatra was to chastity, the trustees of Southwestern Baptist Theological Seminary are to education. This group of fundamentalists has succeeded in doing what even the late Fort Worth Preacher J. Frank Norris couldn't do—they have managed to take the "mental" out of fundamentalism.

The reason for giving the 1994 Horse Collar Award to this group, to quote the chairman of the trustees Ralph Pulley, are "not pertinent. We don't have to have a reason. We have the votes, and we can do it." With that attitude, the trustees at Southwestern kicked out students, faculty, staff, and media on March 9 and within sixty minutes summarily fired Russell H. Dilday, the school's president for sixteen years. They gave no reasons for the firing, and what's more, the coup seems to have been planned for days prior to the meeting.

When the public refused to accept their "not pertinent" response to questions about why Dilday was fired, they decided to find pertinent reasons, none of which seemed very reasonable.

For plunging religion to new depths, and for elevating stupidity to new heights, the Gridiron's Horse Collar Award for 1994 goes to the twenty-seven trustees of Southwestern Baptist Theological Seminary who voted to can Russell Dilday.

Extremism, Not Balance

The following may sound exaggerated, even incredible, but here are incidents revealing the extremism of some trustees appointed by the Patterson/Pressler coalition.

One trustee from a Midwestern state voted in the meetings by putting two pieces of paper in his coat pocket—one read "yes" and the other read "no." When it came time to vote, he would whisper a little prayer, mix up the two pieces of paper, pull one out, and vote on the basis of what was written there. He was proud of this procedure. Just like the casting of lots in Scripture, God was showing him what to do. When he moved to another state and resigned from the board, I realized that I missed him. With him, I at least had a 50 percent chance of a favorable vote—better than I had with most of the others!

The fundamentalist trustees were especially threatened by women in ministry. They let me know they would not allow women to teach in "major subjects" like Bible, theology, and preaching; they could only teach in such subjects as religious education, music, history, or missions. Neither would they elect a person to the faculty who belonged to a church that allowed women to serve as deacons—even if that candidate did not promote this practice.

During a discussion of this issue, one trustee announced proudly, "I believe the Bible teaches that a woman should not teach a man anything." His comment was quoted in the news report of the meeting. The next day, a woman wrote a letter to the editor of the *Fort Worth Star Telegram*: "That man out at the seminary who says a woman shouldn't teach men—I guess his mother was a male, all his aunts were uncles, and all his elementary teachers were men. One thing is sure: whoever taught him didn't do a very good job!"

During repeated attacks on Southwestern's music school, the fundamentalist trustees insisted that the school use only the music that was popular in their churches—no "classical, high-falutin' anthems," just choruses and upbeat songs. One board member explained his simplistic view: "It's easy. Any church that begins its service singing, 'The Lord Is in His Holy Temple' is a liberal church and will die. Any church that begins its service singing, 'Because He Lives' is a conservative church, and it will grow."

Once during a discussion of curriculum, a trustee warned us that we should not teach "liberation theology" at Southwestern. The deans and I explained the difference between teaching about a topic and endorsing or promoting a topic. "We're not endorsing 'liberation theology' here. We're presenting it as one contemporary theological view, showing its strengths and weaknesses in the light of Scripture. Any minister—especially a missionary serving in Latin American cultures—will encounter this approach and needs to understand how to evaluate and critique it. You're not suggesting that we not deal with 'liberation theology,' that we never bring it up, are you?"

"That's exactly what we're saying," responded the trustee. "Liberation theology should never see the light of day in a Southwestern classroom." This attitude was widely held by the board members, but they stopped short of an official mandate, and we managed to include such topics in the curriculum anyway.

There was regular criticism of textbooks used in the Seminary, because some trustees held the mistaken opinion that designating a book as a text meant you were endorsing everything in it. As a result we began to discourage the use of the term "textbook" and suggested faculty include these books in a class reading list along with other works instead.

Conclusion

It seemed the fundamentalist appointments to our board were sometimes chosen from the lowest levels of Baptist life: morally, ethically, spiritually, theologically, and competently. In the mid-1980s, frustrated by the poor quality of those being nominated, all six SBC seminary presidents met with convention president Adrian Rogers, who named the committee that nominated our trustees. We told him our objection was not that they were theologically conservative. "Give us the most conservative board members you want to, but please give us people who know and appreciate theological education, who have qualifications and expertise that can help us." He admitted that recent appointments were often "people I wouldn't let serve on committees in my church." He promised to do what he could to help, but we never saw any indication that he did.

In a sermon on Baptist heritage, James Denison referenced a poll taken in the Dallas/Fort Worth Metroplex reflecting public opinion about Baptists. Respondents were asked to identify the words that came to mind when they thought of Baptists. The answers were words like narrow, self-righteous, judgmental, rigid, combative, negative, critical, sanctimonious, and hypocritical. It seems that the fundamentalist mind-set has so permeated our Baptist family that for many observers it now defines who we are. It also struck me that these were the very qualities of Pharisaism our Lord condemned so passionately in the Gospels.

Maybe there's a message in an incident that took place in October 1989. With their new majority, the fundamentalists on the board led an abortive attempt to fire the president. The chairman called the board into executive session, dismissing faculty, students, alumni, and television and newspaper reporters who were in the gallery. Sensing what was about to happen, Southwestern's alumni president made a brief speech opposing the closed meeting, but the chairman's decision prevailed, and non-trustees began to leave the room—except one student who remained seated. The board chairman said, "Young man, this is a closed meeting. You will have to leave." The student, a tall, lanky Texan in Levis and boots, stood and replied, "Well, sir, I respect your authority, but I've prayed about this, and God told me to stay."

The television cameras of all three Metroplex stations recorded the exchange, and the quote was broadcast that night on the 10:00 news. The fundamentalist board chairman said, "Young man, this is a trustee meeting; God doesn't have anything to do with it!"

1978

New Beginnings

We moved to Fort Worth from our pastorate in Atlanta, Georgia, in January 1978. The term of the former president, Dr. Robert Naylor, was to end July 31, so I had a six-month "overlap" as president-elect to get ready to assume full responsibilities on August 1. First, I enrolled in a six-week advanced management course offered by Emory University at Sea Island, Georgia. In addition to valuable information, the course confirmed most of the "theories" of management and leadership I had developed over the years in pastoral and denominational positions. This course, along with others I took through the American Management Association during my tenure, helped allay the concerns of those who wondered if a preacher could handle the administrative demands of a major institution.

The overlap period also gave me an opportunity to get acquainted with faculty and staff. For one hour in each professor's office, I listened to their spiritual pilgrimage, their theological convictions, and their opinions of what needed to be done to help Southwestern reach its full potential. From those discussions, we developed 101 goals that informed our strategic and long-range planning during the next sixteen years (see Appendix). By 1994, every one of those goals had been met or addressed.

By October 1978, when the board of trustees met, I was ready to present a broad picture of the direction in which we wanted to go. I also recommended a reorganization of the administrative team, the election of John Newport as Vice President for Academic Affairs and Provost and Lloyd Elder as Executive Vice President, and a new policy that the board meetings be open to the public.

It is interesting to note from the following key events in 1978 the variety of speakers we had on campus in these early years before the denominational controversy. For example, we welcomed John Bisagno, W. A. Criswell, and Ken Chafin. They represented the right, left, and center of our traditional Baptist theology.

Key Events in 1978

January

1   • Began duties as president-elect, overlapping with President Robert Naylor until August 1, 1978

8   • Spent six weeks at Emory University's Advanced Management Course at Sea Island, Georgia
           • Had one-hour conference with each professor in his/her office
           • Developed 101 goals for Southwestern based on faculty conferences and my own input—all accomplished by 1994

March

9   • John Bisagno, pastor of First Baptist Church in Houston, spoke in chapel

May

12   • W. A. Criswell, pastor of First Baptist Church in Dallas, spoke at commencement

June

13-15   • Southern Baptist Convention met in Atlanta. I introduced Gov. George Busby (member of our church in Atlanta) to welcome convention to Atlanta.

August

1   • Assumed full duties as president of Southwestern

September

26   • Ken Chafin, pastor of South Main in Houston, preached for Seminary
         revival

October

23-24 • First meeting of Southwestern trustees with new president
       • At my suggestion, board meetings opened to public for first time
       • Elected John Newport Vice President for Academic Affairs and Provost
       • Elected Lloyd Elder as Executive Vice President
25   • Inauguration at Southwestern
       • U.S. Attorney General, Griffin Bell, spoke in chapel
       • Vice President Jesse Northcutt presided in chapel
       • My brother, Don Dilday, pastor of First Baptist Church in Navasota,
         gave invocation in chapel
       • Professor Claude Bass's commissioned anthem with my choice of
         Scripture from Joshua—"God's Command to Joshua"
       • Jesse Fletcher, president of Hardin Simmons, gave inaugural prayer
       • Baker James Cauthen, executive secretary of SBC Foreign Mission
         Board, brought address
       • Bob Denny, executive of Baptist World Alliance, gave benediction
       • Griffin Bell also spoke at luncheon for local leaders
       • Comedian Grady Nutt entertained at student picnic

Note: In the fall meeting of 1978, the thirty-six-member board of trustees had the
following composition: 5 hard-core fundamentalists, 26 traditional mainstream
Baptists, and 5 swing voters.

September 1978: New Beginnings

The Wall Street Journal July 18 issue features an article with headlines "Protestant
Problem—Ministerial Glut Spurs a Scramble for Pulpits." The article discusses a
critical oversupply of preachers and other staff people in the churches of our
country. There are those who are quite concerned about this same crisis in
Southern Baptist life and particularly where Southwestern Seminary is involved.
Are we preparing too many ministers? For the last several semesters we have had
record-breaking enrollments. This fall another milestone is reached with 3,400-
plus enrolled. But our record-breaking enrollments at Southwestern are not
negative but positive.

    God has called and those whom He has called have responded in such
impressive numbers that we are facing a totally new challenge unlike anything we

have ever faced before. Our problem is a "good one"—to provide the best possible training for everyone who enrolls. Forty-four new housing units for married students are now under construction. Extra parking provisions are being made, and when a newly planned library building is completed additional classroom and faculty office spaces will be provided. We are adding faculty and service personnel in order to meet the challenge of record enrollments with a quality educational program, a personal and individual concern for students, and a spiritual vitality on campus.

The problem is not too many students. There's enough lostness in our world to challenge all the graduates we can produce. The bigger challenge is to be certain there are places of service for each graduate to carry out the ministry to which God has called him. Bold Mission Thrust will open new opportunities in overseas missions and in pioneer fields at home. Working with the Foreign Mission Board, the Home Mission Board, as well as state conventions and associations, Southwestern has a responsibility to become more aggressive in bringing together our students and the churches to which God may call them.

I am committed to developing a strong "location" office at the Seminary that might be used of God as a channel for revealing and implementing His will in locating the place of service for those whom He has called and prepared.

Oversupply? No! But rather an abundance of opportunity for which we are grateful.

NEW BEGINNINGS . . . always seem to awaken new commitment and new strength for which we are grateful; but Paul's admission, "Who is sufficient for these things?" reminds us how totally dependent we are upon God's enabling power. The prayers of all Southwestern friends are undergirding the Seminary during these days of new beginnings.

October 1978: Southwestern Board of Trustees

THE SOUTHWESTERN BOARD OF TRUSTEES . . . meets this month (Oct. 23-24). This is the first meeting since I became president. I will have the privilege of making recommendations to the board through its committees concerning administrative reorganization, new personnel, additional faculty appointments, and a major new building program. It will also be my first occasion to outline for the entire board some of my dreams and goals as we look to the future.

We have on the board unusually capable men and women who represent the various states in our convention, and they give unselfishly of their time and attention to the matters that concern us here. You will be reading about their important decisions in the next issue of the *Southwestern News*, but meanwhile please remember the meeting in your prayers.

SOUTHWESTERN'S WORLDWIDE INFLUENCE . . . is seen in the lives of the more than one-half of the missionaries who serve around the planet under the appointment of our two mission boards. But it is shown in other ways too. This month we were privileged to have as our guests on campus seventeen distinguished professors of chemistry from the university system in Mexico. They came to observe the creative teaching methods used here at Southwestern with particular interest in the programmed learning techniques of Dr. LeRoy Ford on the faculty of the School of Religious Education.

The week they spent here gave us an opportunity not only to share our academic experience with them but also to share our Christian experience and the theological bases on which our institution is built. They worshiped for the first time in a Baptist church. They shared a chapel service on campus and hopefully will go back to Mexico with a more open attitude toward the Lord and toward Baptist work in Mexico.

Their visit reminded me again of the fact that our Southwestern faculty continues to maintain a worldwide reputation for academic excellence combined with unparalleled commitment to Jesus Christ and His word.

While I am on that subject of the faculty and staff here at the Seminary, let me express our appreciation to two of these who have recently completed significant anniversaries in their relationship to Southwestern. One is Mrs. Virginia Seelig whose twentieth anniversary here on the faculty was observed a few weeks ago. The other is Mr. James Leitch, Director of the Physical Plant, who on October 1 completed twenty-five years of faithful service here.

I'm glad to be a part of such an outstanding team of Christian leaders.

November 1978: Inauguration

INAUGURATION . . . has an interesting etymology. The "augur" in ancient Rome was an official prophet who foretold events by omens. They would predict the favorable or unfavorable conditions for a certain undertaking by observing the flights of birds in the sky (auspices). So the word "inaugurate" came to mean taking omens before entering upon an important undertaking and hence to consecrate or install.

Inaugural ceremonies were observed at Southwestern October 25, 1978. Their purpose was to give expression to our academic heritage, to reaffirm our basic mission as a seminary, to install a new administration, and to celebrate the blessings of the Heavenly Father upon this enterprise.

ANTICIPATION . . . characterized the ceremonies. There was a measure of prophetic "augury" attempted as we recognized the spiritual indicators of a strong future for Southwestern. Enrollments are high. High school and college students with church-related callings are headed our way for the next eight to ten years. Financial support through the Cooperative Program is strong. Bold Mission Thrust is opening new places for graduates to serve. We have an able faculty with solid theological convictions and biblical faith. A growing spirit of evangelism and missions permeates the campus. It's all a powerful portent of the future that suggests in God's providence our best days are ahead.

REALIZATION . . . in the midst of our dreams brings us face to face with certain serious challenges. Increasing inflationary costs demand additional funding beyond Cooperative Program contributions. This fiscal year Southwestern must raise for operations $3,506,163 in addition to its generous Cooperative Program allocation from the churches. More faculties, classrooms, housing are needed to care for the students. We must be creative in helping our graduates find the places of service God has for them and helping the places of great need around the world locate the trained leadership they need. We must keep our curriculum tuned to the issues of the day so that we produce graduates who are spiritually mature and who know how to do the job they were called to do.

GRATIFICATION . . . is an important part of the experiences of these days. I felt it in Richmond recently when thirty of the forty new Foreign Mission appointees were Southwestern graduates. I sensed it in the inaugural challenge of Dr. Baker James Cauthen to keep our missionary zeal. I experienced it in the evangelistic results we saw on Home Mission fields last summer. I knew it in a church in Oklahoma recently where a pastor and staff—all Southwestern graduates—were fulfilling so well their tasks of ministry.

Being president of Southwestern is an awesome responsibility, but I am grateful God led me to this place. There is no enterprise in the entire world I would rather be a part of in these strategic days.

December 1978: An Evening in the White House

(This column described a memorable evening with President and Mrs. Jimmy Carter celebrating National Bible Week. Religious leaders from across the country were invited to hear a command performance of the Broadway hit *The Gospel of Mark*, a recitation by British actor Alex McCowen. It reminded us how powerful a clearly articulated communication of the Gospels can be.)

1979

Why Southwestern Seminary?

Although there were warning signs earlier, most observers mark 1979 as the beginning of the Southern Baptist controversy. When the convention met in Houston in June, two contradictory events took place. First, there was genuine excitement at the launching of "Bold Mission Thrust," the convention's campaign to reach the entire world with the gospel by the year 2000. Possibly for the first time, all the convention's agencies were working together to accomplish the same bold objective. The inspiring prayer and commitment service on the floor of the Astrodome moved many of us to tears.

But simultaneously, in the skyboxes above the floor and in the hallways outside, the Patterson/Pressler political organization was implementing its ten-year plan to acquire control of the convention's agencies and ultimately its future. There were earlier events that at the time did not seem crucial, but looking back they should have warned us of the storm to come.

One was the widespread popularity of the Bible Conferences sponsored by television evangelist James Robinson in which he and others made frequent swipes at "liberal" seminary professors. The six SBC seminary presidents—Milton Ferguson, Landrum Leavell, Randall Lolley, Duke McCall, Bill Pinson, and I—met with W. A. Criswell at First Baptist Dallas in an attempt to ease the friction and head off the unfounded attacks. Criswell was promoting Robinson's crusade, and we wanted to assure him of our total commitment to the trustworthiness and authority of the Bible. We prayed together and agreed we would each speak at one of Robinson's Bible Conferences and have him speak on our campuses. It was a good faith effort—though unfruitful—to address concerns and stop the growing tensions before the convention met in June.

After Adrian Rogers, the Patterson/Patterson candidate, was elected president of the SBC, we invited him to speak in chapel, dialogue with students, and meet with faculty. He said, "I have always been grateful for Southwestern and frequently recommend students here. There is not one faculty member here whose theology I would question!"

Several of the columns I wrote in 1979 describe the unique characteristics of Southwestern Seminary that position it squarely in the center of traditional Baptist convictions and practice and help answer the question, "Why Southwestern Seminary?"

Key Events in 1979

January
- Opened Recreation Aerobics Center. Largest gift ever received by Seminary—one million dollars from Roy and Myra Slover
- Launched President's Club for fund-raising

May
21   • Spoke at First Baptist Church Dallas Academy Commencement
22   • Met with W. A. Criswell, First Baptist Dallas, in his office with other seminary presidents. Prayed, asked his help to ease tensions developing in the SBC, promised our own commitment to the Bible, and agreed to speak at evangelist James Robison's Bible Conferences and have him on our campuses

June
13   • Southern Baptist Convention met in Houston
     • Adrian Rogers, pastor of Bellevue Baptist in Memphis, elected president over Robert Naylor, Duke McCall, Bill Self, Doug Watterson, Ed Price, 51.36 percent, with Jimmy Allen presiding
     • 15,760 messengers
     • The Patterson/Pressler fundamentalist faction successfully launched its first effort to control the Southern Baptist Convention

- Judge Paul Pressler registered as messenger from a church to which he did not belong
- Pastor's Conference featured Homer Lindsay Jr., Adrian Rogers, W. A. Criswell, Jerry Vines, and Charles Stanley; Criswell endorsed Rogers as SBC president—a new precedent. Fundamentalist Jimmy Draper elected Pastor's Conference president
- Announced successful completion of $8 million fund-raising goal
- Billy Graham met with alumni at Southwestern luncheon
- Three Seminary presidents honored as Southwestern Distinguished Alumni: Randall Lolley, Bill Pinson, and Russell Dilday
- Professor J. Leo Garrett elected by Trustees at called meeting

September

28   • Buckner Fanning, pastor of Trinity Baptist in San Antonio, preached for Seminary revival

October

22   • Fall trustee meeting. Adrian Rogers, new president of SBC, spoke in Chapel, met with faculty. He said, "I have always been grateful for Southwestern and frequently recommend students here. There is not one faculty member here whose theology I would question!"

December

4   • W. A. Criswell preached in chapel "What It Means to Be a Baptist"

Note: In the fall meeting of 1979, the thirty-six-member board of trustees had the following composition: 4 hard-core fundamentalists, 28 traditional mainstream Baptists, and 4 swing voters.

January 1979: Dedication of the "RAC"

(This column announced the dedication of the Recreation Aerobics Center, which not only provided a top-of-the-line exercise and fitness facililty for the use of students, faculty, and staff, but also provided a laboratory for students preparing for a ministry in church recreation in the School of Religious Education.)

February 1979: Compassion

(In light of a number of serious illnesses and deaths among the Southwestern family, this column called attention to the fact that the faculty influenced future ministers not only by their lectures in the classrooms, but by demonstrating how Christians face tragedy and loss. It concluded with this request: Pray for those who, in the midst of teaching others how to share God's word with troubled people, gladly share that word themselves in Christ-like ministries of compassion.)

March 1979

WHEN ROY AND MYRA SLOVER . . . gave the $1 million endowment fund at Southwestern, they invested in the training of Christian workers until Jesus returns. It was a spectacular and impressive example of stewardship for which we are grateful—the largest single gift in the history of the Seminary.

This past week I saw another inspiring example of support for Southwestern. Ed Crawford, Director of Development, introduced me to Mr. Warren Nutt. He had ridden a bus to Fort Worth from Dallas to make a gift to the Seminary. Mr. Nutt had recently retired from a career as a bellman with a Dallas hotel. Having little family himself, he decided to make the Seminary his family by naming Southwestern the beneficiary of his life insurance policy. As we talked about his commitment to the Lord and to the church that led him to make his gift, I was reminded that not only the amount of a contribution, but the motive and sacrifice behind it, mark the quality of Christian stewardship. As Paul said to the Corinthian Christians, "They first gave themselves to the Lord and then to us by the will of God" (2 Corinthians 8:5).

ANOTHER RECORD ENROLLMENT . . . this year with 4,154 students at Southwestern (compared to 4,136 last year) places before us an unprecedented challenge. Our faculty and staff are to be commended for accepting this opportunity and its extra demands with excitement and commitment.

TWO SIGNIFICANT ANNIVERSARIES . . . were observed among our staff recently. On January 1, 1979, Dr. David Garland, Professor of Old Testament, observed his twentieth anniversary of teaching here. Dr. Wayne Evans, Vice President for Business Affairs, observed his twenty-fifth anniversary of employment on February 17. Our congratulations to both of these fine men.

April 1979: Trustee Meetings

SOUTHERN BAPTISTS . . . give direction to Southwestern by electing a board of trustees who are responsible for the institution. There are thirty-six now serving in that capacity from twenty-seven states across the SBC. The entire board meets twice a year (fall and spring) with various committees of the board meeting between sessions when necessary. There are laypeople, pastors, denominational leaders, and educators—all active in Southern Baptist churches and all committed to the success of Southwestern in its purpose "to provide graduate theological education for God-called men and women preparing for Christian ministry."

HAVING JUST COMPLETED THE SPRING MEETING . . . with the board, I am deeply impressed with the quality of our trustees and their willingness to give time to the Seminary. We are all conscious of the awesome responsibilities we have in these exciting days of Bold Mission Thrust, and the board is often in prayer in the midst of their deliberations. The schedule of the meeting is a demanding two days of activities. Some of the results of the recent meetings are described in this issue of the Southwestern News.

While the trustees elect an administration to carry out the day-by-day operations of the Seminary, they are in no sense a "rubber stamp" board. Before decisions are made, issues are thoroughly discussed by the four committees of the board and recommendations are weighed carefully. The board meetings are open so that faculty, students, and interested friends of the Seminary—even the press—may be present. I believe the open and democratic nature of the meetings characterized by discussion, differences of opinion, harmony following a decision, all pervaded by the spirit of prayer is typical of the very best tradition of our Southern Baptist life.

On behalf of the Southwestern family, I want to express appreciation once again to these who continue to serve so effectively. Get acquainted with the trustee from your state, communicate with him or her your interest in the Seminary, and let's join together to pray for all of them in their responsible role. (A list of trustees was included.)

May 1979: God Will Take Care of You

Be not dismayed whate'er betide, God will take care of you!

The Seminary chapel sang these words the other day before Dr. Naylor preached his famous sermon on "The Raven Express" (God's provision for Elijah). It was an appropriate hymn and a timely message for the tense "countdown days" at the end of the spring semester. Final examinations, term papers, Senior Preaching Week, Awards Day, interviews, and graduation—all create the kind of pressures that make the promise of God's care so valuable. This spring 331 men and women whom God has called and who have paid the price of disciplined study receive their degrees and move on to serve all around the world. They are Southwestern's *raison d'etre*—graduates prepared, competent, and ready for ministry.

It's refreshing to hear one of these young couples bubbling with enthusiasm tell of their call to a church, the renovated parsonage, warm welcome, and the stimulating new challenge they have been asked to accept. But there are others who are wondering as graduation approaches, "Where do I go from here?"

We believe the Holy Spirit not only calls men and women to ministry, but that He also leads them to specific places of service in the working out of His will in their lives. But the process by which a new seminary graduate clarifies God's call and locates that place of service is not always an easy one.

"Where do I go from here?" Southwestern is working to do more to help our graduates find the place God would have them serve. By means of assessment, testing, interviews, training, and contact with churches seeking pastors or other ministers, an office here at the Seminary will give full time to this important area.

Meanwhile, even though it is only a partial assistance, we send these graduates out with the assurance of the promise, "Through every day, o'er all the way, God will take care of you."

June 1979: Conservative Seminary

Last year a handwritten letter came from a woman in New Jersey who expressed her desire to give $3,000 to Southwestern. Explaining that she had never seen the Seminary, she pointed out that her impressions of our school were based on the graduates she had met. Her own pastor was a Southwesterner. Other preachers who had met her spiritual needs were from this seminary. She also noted that on a recent trip to the Orient, every missionary she met was a Southwestern graduate. "I have been greatly impressed by Southwestern graduates . . . and want to establish a scholarship for deserving students who need help."

The letter not only reinforced my confidence in Southwestern's future, but it also graphically reminded me that largely our graduates who serve around the world build the reputation of Southwestern. Faculty members ministering in churches across the convention also play an important role in this regard. But on a broader scale, the graduate has the best opportunity to answer the question, "What kind of school is Southwestern?" By the quality of service the alumnus renders in the name of Christ and also by direct and intentional communication, interested publics may hear through them the Southwestern story.

Some are quick to apply labels of "conservative" or "liberal" in evaluating the seminaries today. One person's definition of these labels might be totally different from another's. But to me one measurement of "conservative" means an unashamed commitment to the truth embodied in "The Baptist Faith and Message" adopted by the SBC in 1963. Each faculty member at SW affirms in writing these truths.

To me, conservative means not only believing the Bible to be the inspired word of God but committing one's allegiance to practice and obey the Bible as authority. SW goes beyond an academic teaching of the Scriptures to an emphasis on the practical application of its message.

To me, conservative means involvement in evangelism—actively sharing the gospel in order to bring others to personal faith in Jesus Christ. Based on its longstanding tradition in this area, Southwestern continues to give strong emphasis to evangelism both in academic instruction and in practice by students and faculty.

To me, conservative means involvement in missions—obedience to Christ's commission to make disciples of all nations. Each year the Seminary sends its graduates around the world where one-half of all who serve under appointment of the Home and Foreign Mission Boards are Southwesterners.

To me, conservative means recognizing the local New Testament church as the channel through which baptized believers worship, proclaim, minister, and teach in carrying out the purposes of the Kingdom. Parachurch organizations make contributions, but it is the local congregation that must be given priority as "The Body of Christ." Southwestern has always considered its task to be the training of workers for these churches.

And so, standing in the tradition of Conner, Scarborough, Cauthen, Truett, and others, the Seminary maintains its enthusiastic commitment to biblical theology, evangelism, missions, the local church, and, first of all, to Jesus Christ as Savior and Lord. That explains why letters like the one mentioned above come to Southwestern and why the Seminary continues to attract the largest number of students in the history of theological education.

As an alumnus or friend of the Seminary, help us to accurately convey wherever you go this story of Southwestern.

July/August 1979:
After the Southern Baptist Convention

In spite of the controversies, I have come back from the Southern Baptist Convention in Houston convinced that Southwestern has been reaffirmed by Southern Baptists and that the opportunity before us in Bold Mission Thrust is even greater than ever. My positive feeling is based on several factors:

(1) The warm standing ovation given by the messengers to the seminaries following our report. I cannot remember in any past convention a greater and more manifest expression of support.

(2) The resolution passed by the convention in support of the six seminaries and their faculties.

(3) The best National Alumni Luncheon in my memory with outstanding attendance and spirit indicated and strong support from prior students.

(4) Our trustees, following a called meeting of the board to elect a new faculty member, expressed an enthusiastic endorsement of our faculty.

Add to that the outstanding Missions Rally in the Astrodome in which 1,200 commitments to missions were publicly made. Southern Baptists have a way of pulling together their differences, rejecting peripheral concerns, and getting on with the primary agenda of winning our world to Jesus Christ.

Dr. Billy Graham, who attended our Southwestern Alumni Luncheon in Houston, said, "God has given to our denomination visibility, acceptance, opportunity, leadership, and resources to take the spiritual initiative; and there is no energy crisis with God." I believe Southwestern has a leading role in the Bold Missions drama, and relying on God's power, we are looking forward to fulfilling that role with your help and intercession.

September 1979: Why Southwestern?

WHY SOUTHWESTERN? That question has been answered recently by several groups, resulting in an enforcement of my own convictions about this seminary. I had often heard that Southwestern was born in the heart of God, but the reality of that statement became much clearer to me this last week. At our faculty retreat, Dr. Jesse Northcutt shared with us the remarkable spiritual experience of B. H. Carroll by which the dream of the Seminary first emerged.

He said,

> I was passing through the Panhandle of Texas on a Fort Worth and Denver train on my way to Amarillo to meet my wife and baby. As I looked out over those plains over which in my youth I had chased the buffalo, there arose before me a vision of our Baptist situation in the Southwest. I saw multitudes of our preachers with very limited education, with few books and with small skill in using to the best advantage even the books they had. I saw there in the Southwest many institutions for the professional training of the young teacher, the young lawyer, the young doctor, the young nurse, and the young farmer, but not a single institution dedicated to the specific training of the young Baptist preacher. It weighed upon my soul like the earth on the shoulders of Atlas. It was made

clear to me on that memorable day that, for the highest usefulness of our Baptist people, such an institution was an imperious necessity. From that hour I knew as definitely as I ever knew anything, that God would plant a great school in the Southwest for the training of our young Baptist preachers.

WHY SOUTHWESTERN? The answer too has emerged in the testimonies I heard from faculty members at our retreat that told the group why they came to the Seminary. Story after story pointed to a divine call, conviction of God's will, prayer, circumstances all combining to point their lives in the direction of Southwestern.

WHY SOUTHWESTERN? One answer came from two visitors on our campus this week. They were the parents of a college student whom God had called into the ministry, and they were "checking out" the Seminary on behalf of their son. After an official tour of the Seminary they were pleasantly surprised to learn that because of the Cooperative Program gifts of Southern Baptist churches, the students do not pay tuition but a very small matriculation fee. Having under-written the very expensive tuition bill of their son in college for several years, they could hardly believe that Southern Baptists care enough about the future of church leadership to undergird theological education to such an extent.

Dr. Joel Gregory said in a sermon recently, "While the seminary is not a 'preacher factory,' it might be called a preacher refinery where the gifts of God-called men and women are shaped for effective ministry." Southwestern's existence is more than worthwhile and Southern Baptists have dedicated their resources to this high priority.

In a few days, between 3,000 and 4,000 students will be enrolling for the fall semester. Those students sitting under the instruction of godly scholars are my favorite answer to the question.

WHY SOUTHWESTERN? It came from God and has been sustained through the years by His power and it exists today to fulfill His purpose. With His help, we will keep the Seminary "near to the heart of God."

October 1979

SPIRITUAL FORMATION . . . is the term used in theological education circles to describe the responsibility the Seminary has to provide for the spiritual growth of students as well as their intellectual growth. The annual Seminary "revival week" this year has been more than a perfunctory engagement on the calendar. The timely messages from Dr. Buckner Fanning and the inspired music from Mr. Russell Newport have spoken to us and we have been spiritually renewed.

"Why does a seminary need a revival?" An interested inquirer asked me that question a few days ago. The answer is obvious to those of us on Southwestern's campus. We all are in the process of spiritual growth because God's word commands us to grow (Eph 4:15; 1 Pet 2:2; 2 Pet 3:18). But the tendency to become professional and academic, even in the midst of theological studies, calls for an event aimed at renewal and affirmation. The response this week from students, faculty, and staff to the call for a closer walk with the Lord has been encouraging and has made a valuable contribution to "spiritual formation" here at Southwestern. How thankful we are for these days of genuine revival.

ENCOURAGEMENT . . . has recently come from other sources, too. One is a retired missionary and Southwestern graduate in her nineties who recently designated her will to include the Seminary by establishing an endowment fund to aid students from the country where she served who plan to return there to minister.

Another is a recent graduate who wrote, "Congratulations on reaching $8 million dollars before 1980. Please apply this check to the 'Eight by Eighty' campaign fund. I graduated in July 1978. The debt I owe the seminary cannot be expressed monetarily. Thank you."

Praise God from whom all encouragement comes.

November 1979: My First Year as President

(This column presented the 1978–1979 Annual Report, which also represented a statistical review of my first year as president. Statistics can be found in the Appendix.)

December 1979: Cooperative Giving—Three Churches

THREE CHURCHES . . . came to my attention recently among the many who support Southwestern through generous Cooperative Program giving. The First Baptist Church of Amarillo, Texas (Dr. Winfred Moore, pastor), has adopted its 1980 budget of $2,269,601 with a Cooperative Program Allocation of $400,000. The First Baptist Church of Midland, Texas (Dr. Daniel Vestal, pastor), projects a Cooperative Program budget of 29 percent of their income, which would be a goal of $490,000.

These are apparently new records for any church in the Southern Baptist Convention in total Cooperative Program giving.

The third church is the Central Baptist Church of Jacksonville, Texas (Dr. C.W. Bess, pastor). Their new budget includes a Cooperative Program Allocation of 24 percent of the total receipts of the church, representing about $91,000. This is one of the highest percentages of giving among our churches.

Of course, there are many others who respond every year with worthy mission giving through the SBC CP, but the report of these three came to me personally at a time when an encouraging word was needed! I am moved to say a special word of appreciation to these three churches—and your church also—for keeping the lifeline of seminary support strong and vital as we move into the next decade.

STATE CONVENTIONS . . . meet all across the country during the fall months, and Southwestern is represented in most of them by one of our faculty or staff. I had the privilege of being in New Mexico, Texas, Florida, Illinois, and Northern Plains this year. In every convention, aggressive mission expansion, strong stewardship gains, and encouraging seminary support are indicators that the decade of the eighties will be an unprecedented decade of progress for theological education in the SBC. My faith is strengthened as we make projections in the future.

THANKSGIVING AND CHRISTMAS . . . always come before we are ready for them, and the older one gets the earlier those holidays seem to arrive each year. But what a valuable opportunity they provide to give thanks to the heavenly Father for His bountiful blessings and to celebrate once more the Savior's birth. On behalf of all of the Southwestern family, may I express to you our best wishes and prayer for a joyous holiday?

1980

The Sun Never Sets on the Southwestern Family

During 1980, the Patterson/Pressler organization stepped up the pace of its assault on the Seminary and the larger goal of gaining control of the convention. However, several things happened that seemed to oppose and weaken the fundamentalist position. For one thing, W. A. Criswell publicly rebuked Paige Patterson for using inappropriate methods that he called "those of a different world." He announced that Patterson, then on the staff of First Dallas, would withdraw from denominational politics. Criswell was very supportive of me and Southwestern, inviting me to preach in his absence and to take his place as the preacher for the church's youth choir on their trip to Israel. We attempted to reach out to our critics by having well-known fundamentalists on our campus along with traditional Baptists. In 1980 we had Jimmy Draper, James Robinson, Bailey Smith, Morris Chapman, and Fred Wolf, and we hosted Paul Pressler for a luncheon and dialogue with faculty.

Counterbalancing these constructive efforts, Paul Pressler announced in Lynchburg, Virginia, that the trustees of the seminaries were nothing more than "rubber stamps and dumb bunnies" who were not brave enough to question the administrations. In organized meetings all across the convention territory, he aroused fears among ordinary Baptists by sharing the so-called "examples of liberalism," and encouraged pastors to get involved and to lead their churches to give just enough through the state's Cooperative Program mission funds to qualify for messenger representation at the annual Southern Baptist Conventions.

This was the year we received the first fundamentalist trustees appointed by the Patterson/Pressler political party, namely Hugo Lindquist from Oklahoma and Ken Lilly from Arkansas.

We soon began to receive a growing number of letters from across the country questioning and criticizing certain faculty. For example, Bill Powell accused John Newport of not believing in life after death! He falsely based his accusations on a misreading of Newport's explanation of the difference between the Greek philosophical concept of an innate immortal soul and the biblical concept of bodily resurrection. Similarly, all the other complaints were either misunderstandings and therefore without merit or were old issues that had long ago been dealt with. Nevertheless, the letters, obviously encouraged by and often worded by the Patterson/Pressler organization, continued.

Several columns in 1980 were written to affirm Southwestern's widespread influence in Baptist life and its essential role in fulfilling the Great Commission of our Lord. Others underscored the proper role of trustees in governing an institution like Southwestern.

This was also the year we launched our first five-year plan called "Vision 85."

Key Events in 1980

March

10-12   • Held Bible conference on campus after canceling James Robinson because he broke agreements

17-19   • Spring trustee meeting—Professor Robert Sloan and six others elected

April

11   • Evangelist James Robison in chapel

15   • New Seminary hymn, "Lead on O King Eternal," chosen to replace one that tended to exalt the Seminary instead of its purpose

          • Letters accusing John Newport of liberalism sent to board of trustees from Bill Powell in Georgia

May

22 • W. A. Criswell announces fundamentalist Paige Patterson, president of Criswell College, will withdraw from denominational politics.

June

7-12 • Southern Baptist Convention in St. Louis—Adrian Rogers declined second term

• Evangelist Bailey Smith elected over Richard Jackson and four others—51.67 percent

• 13,844 messengers

July

14-28 • W. A. Criswell asked me to take his place to preach in Israel with First Baptist Church, Dallas, youth choir. Criswell also called me asking for a copy of one of George Truett's sermons for their heritage room.

August

• President Bailey Smith's quote, "God Almighty doesn't hear the prayer of a Jew"

September

12 • Bailey Smith, SBC president, preached in chapel

12-13 • Pressler's comments in Lynchburg, Virginia, about present trustees being "rubber stamps and dumb bunnies." He announced they were "going for the jugular," and advised churches to "give at least enough to the Cooperative Program to be qualified for messenger representation at the convention

October

10 • Richard Jackson, pastor of North Phoenix Baptist, preached for Seminary revival

14 • Morris Chapman, pastor in New Mexico, preached in chapel

20-22 • Fall trustee meeting. Elected Professor Bill Tolar to take Huber Drumwright's position as Dean of the School of Theology

November

17 • Bailey Smith, SBC president, preached in chapel and met with faculty

December

2 • Fred Wolf, pastor in Alabama, preached in chapel

• Invited Judge Paul Pressler for lunch with key faculty

Note: In the fall meeting of 1980, the thirty-six-member board of trustees had the following composition: 5 hard-core fundamentalists, 26 traditional, mainstream Baptists, and 5 swing voters.

January 1980: Affirming Southwestern's Influence

The broad dimensions of Southwestern's influence in the work of our Lord are frequently illustrated in the unique ministries of our graduates.

In an Arkansas church recently I met a new Southwestern graduate serving as minister of education and youth. He told me of his gratifying experience in studying at the Seminary, receiving his MRE degree, being interviewed by the church through our placement program, and ultimately receiving a call to the church staff where he has served for over a year.

In another incident, a letter came from a young woman in Wisconsin who graduated from Southwestern in May 1979. She is involved in her calling as a teacher in a Christian school there and active in a Southern Baptist church. She wrote, "With each new day I realize more fully the precious opportunity I had of studying for three years in a special place. The Godly atmosphere and people at Southwestern will have lifelong benefits in whatever I do and wherever I go. I would like to thank Southern Baptists for providing this type of education and for the financial gifts so freely given. Please pass this expression of thanks on to the Board and the Cooperative Program."

Another letter came from a recent D.Min. graduate who is a pastor of the First Assembly of God Church in a town in Mississippi. He said, "I recently graduated from Southwestern with a D.Min. Degree and want to take time to express my appreciation to the seminary for the education and training I received. I especially appreciate the seminary's openness that allows students from various denominations to attend. I hope that will never change. Please know that this graduate of Southwestern is appreciative and will do whatever I can to channel other students to the seminary."

If the value of Southwestern's role in Bold Mission Thrust needs affirmation, there is adequate reinforcement in these and many other real experiences on the part of our alumni.

Join us in praying that the Lord of the harvest will continue to call laborers to His harvest and that Southwestern Seminary will continue to accept and fulfill its part of the responsibility to train them for services around the world.

February 1980: EEOC Suit

The federal judge who ruled in the Seminary's favor in the recent EEOC suit made some profound statements about Southwestern's purpose in the context of its ministry for the churches of the Southern Baptist Convention. The statements are made more remarkable by the fact that they come from a secular source where such insight would not normally be expected. Let me quote from the court's opinion:

> It cannot be overemphasized that the seminary views a pervasively religious environment as essential to the cultivation of the distinct attitudes and qualities of Baptist ministers and that this view dictates its employment practices as a whole. Employees are not merely hired to perform a task, but must first to last be willing members of the ecclesia. Religious exercise is a virtual condition of employment.
>
> Since all employees, whatever their position, are expected to contribute to a unified religious endeavor and maintain a commitment to spiritual life, religious discipline extends far into their personal lives, not merely to avoid the embarrassment of a notorious lifestyle, but to immerse the students in an atmosphere of intense piety and to provide a model of religious practice to the outside world.
>
> Members of the faculty and administration of a seminary are considered ministers and are hired, assigned, advanced, tenured, evaluated, and terminated on predominately religious criteria. Personal characteristics that evince dedication to Baptist ideals and faithful participation in the activities of the church of which the employee is a member carry equal or greater weight than academic qualifications or scholarship. Recruitment of faculty and administrators is viewed as a divinely guided "spiritual quest" mutually pursued by the seminary and the prospective employee.
>
> The originative power of any religion lies in the institution that schools its ministers, preserving and transmitting dogma in a pure form in the academic sense and endeavoring to animate sterile doctrine into communicable faith. A seminary's function within a particular religion is to replenish the core of faithful who provide its structure, a role even more essential to its mission than served by parochial elementary and secondary schools.

The decision, discussed in an article in this issue of the *Southwestern News*, represents an encouraging affirmation of the principle of the separation of church and state. Moreover, the judge's description of Southwestern's mission reinforces our awareness of the strategic value of quality theological education in the life of our churches.

March 1980: Dr. John Newport

(This column described Dr. John Newport's sermon at Memorial Church, Harvard University, in Boston on February 17, 1980. It was a strong witness for a personal faith in Jesus Christ, a commitment to the local church and its missionary and evangelistic task, and a confidence in the return of our Lord. Southwestern was blessed to have a leader who was known and respected across the academic world. Such occasions as the Harvard address provided an understanding of Southwestern's unique position as a theological institution.)

April 1980: The Duties of Our Board of Trustees

Thirty-three of our thirty-six Southwestern trustees elected by messengers to the SBC from twenty-seven states met in their spring meeting here at the Seminary March 17-19. They are a vital link in the "chain of command" through which the churches of the convention own and operate Southwestern Seminary. They elect an administration to lead the day-by-day operations and, therefore, as trustees they do not actually "run" the school. They do, however, set policies, elect faculty, adopt the budget, approve buildings, promotions, tenure, and new courses, and make scores of other vital decisions. The trustees are not a rubber-stamp group but work closely with the administration. They hammer out solutions to problems and needs that allow the Seminary to more adequately fulfill its mission.

The Academic Affairs Committee of the board, for example, met from 6:30 p.m. to 10:30 p.m. in preparing its recommendations for the board meeting the next day!

This issue of the *Southwestern News* reports on the major features of the meeting related to:

(1) Wise investment and expenditure of mission funds given to the convention.

(2) Election of outstanding people to the faculty whom God has led to the Seminary and who feel called to minister in this way.

(3) Salary increases and new retirement benefits for the faculty and staff.

(4) The launching of a new World Missions/Church Growth Center with Dr. Cal Guy as founding director, as well as approving new courses in missions and church strategy that keep Southwestern on the cutting edge of Bold Mission Thrust.

Each member of the board of trustees gives time, financial support, wisdom, and experience. They also pray. In fact, the opening session of the board meeting was a prayer meeting in which Chairman Kenneth Chafin divided the members into small prayer groups. They prayed for God's guidance and power upon the process of directing the future path of this great institution.

I invite all the Southwestern family to join the board in its prayerful concern and support, claiming the promise of God, "Call unto me and I will answer thee and show thee great and mighty things thou knowest not."

May 1980: The Radio and Television Commission

Southwestern is committed to being on the cutting edge of leadership in theological education. Important evidence of this fact is our recent joint sponsorship of a Radio, Television, and Cable Consultation. In partnership with the Southern Baptist Radio and Television Commission here in Fort Worth, Southwestern hosted a three-day seminar on the broadcast media for pastors and denominational leaders.

Eminent authorities in the field led discussions on such topics as the following:

Bold Missions
The Church Using the Media in the '80s
Media Advertising in the '80s
Sociological Reflections on the Electronic Church
Techniques in Radio and Television Appearances
Lighting and Sound for Broadcasting
The Worship Service on Television
Special Training for the Use of the Media
Writing for Media Use
Bold Mission and Cable/Satellite Use
Audience Response

Our curriculum at Southwestern already includes a number of courses in this area. In fact, our offerings exceed those of most other seminaries, but we are seeing the need and the opportunity for the Seminary to become a center for training Christian workers in communication.

Dr. Jimmy Allen, the president of the Radio and Television Commission, and I are making preliminary plans to harness the resources of these two Southern Baptist Convention agencies to provide here in Fort Worth a unique location for training Southern Baptist students in the use of the media in fulfilling the Great Commission. The "electronic churches" are moving rapidly into this vacuum, but Southern Baptists must not surrender leadership in what may be the most expansive opportunity Christians have ever had to win the world to Jesus.

A second evidence of Southwestern's commitment to leadership is the launching of our World Missions/Church Growth Center. A three-week conference on world missions and church growth is being planned for this October. Dr. Cal Guy, founding director of the center, and the center steering committee are projecting the conference as the first major activity of the new center. You will be hearing more about this later.

It's all good news and we praise the Lord for the exciting new horizons in Southwestern's future.

June 1980: Counseling and Placement

On May 9 I personally shook the hands of 396 graduates as they crossed the platform of the Travis Avenue Baptist Church to receive their diplomas. This is the largest spring graduating class in our 73 years of history. The size of the class indicates the enormous influence and potential our school has for God's kingdom. The students came from 32 states and 5 foreign countries. Fifty-five were women, 289 were married, and about 70 percent already are serving in Christian work or else are in the process of assuming a new place of service.

We are aware of the responsibility the Seminary has to assist all our graduating students, and particularly those who do not have a position, to find the place of ministry God has for them. At a called meeting of our board of trustees in St. Louis in June, a new position, Vice President for Student Affairs, will be recommended for election.

One of the priority responsibilities of that position will be to organize and implement a procedure for vocational counseling and placement. By the time I shake hands with the next spring graduating class, this new procedure should be under way. Our goal is that not one of them would complete their work without ample opportunity to accept a place of service consistent with God's call.

These are urgent and demanding days. The current opportunities for Bold Mission Thrust may not always be ours. We must be about our Father's business.

July/August 1980: How to Judge a Seminary

Jesus gave us the only proper criteria by which we are to make spiritual judgments when He said, "By their fruits, ye shall know them." Competent graduates are the fruit or the product of the Seminary by which we are properly judged.

I have just returned from a trip to the Orient where I saw a graduate of Southwestern's School of Religious Education serving as the president of the Baptist seminary in downtown Kowloon, equipping national pastors to preach Christ to millions of Cantonese on the coast of China.

I met another graduate of Southwestern; this time from our School of Church Music, whose symphony composition in Chinese was performed by the orchestra in the Hong Kong City Hall. Thousands of people on the island of Hong Kong heard through that symphony the simple message, "Jesus loves me, this I know."

In Taiwan I watched a graduate of Southwestern's School of Theology teaching biblical languages to students in the Baptist seminary in Taipei. He speaks English, but he was teaching in Mandarin.

I watched a missionary physician in Macao, who did his seminary work at Southwestern, preparing to spend three weeks in Mainland China with a team of Christian doctors in a cautious first step in that previously forbidden territory.

And then, back in the States, on a Sunday morning I saw two people saved and making public professions of faith in a growing Southern Baptist church led effectively by a pastor and staff, all of whom are graduates of Southwestern.

Multiply in your mind these five personal vignettes by over 3,700, and the impact of Southwestern Seminary through our graduates can be visualized. The Seminary gladly rests its case for judgment and support of our 31,000 graduates and the advice of Jesus, "By their fruits, ye shall know them."

September 1980: Affirmation

Recognition is in order for several members of the Southwestern family: one who is leaving, one who is arriving, and three who have stayed. I would like to affirm:

(1) The Dean of the School of Theology—Dr. Huber Drumwright. Dr. Drumwright assumed his new responsibilities as state executive director in Arkansas on September 1. For seven years he served as dean after a long career as a teacher. Dr. Drumwright's commitment to the Lord and to the Seminary has been convincingly expressed in his service at Southwestern, and he will be greatly missed. Pray for God's leadership as the search procedure leads the election of a

new dean who will guide the 1,838 students and the 47 faculty members in the largest school of theology in the world.

(2) The newly-elected Vice President for Student Affairs—Lawrence Klempnauer. After months of study, planning, and reorganization in the student affairs division at Southwestern, we are grateful for the election of Mr. Klempnauer to this strategic position. He will be responsible for creating a positive environment for learning here on the campus that will enhance the education of our students. His office will become a center for personal counseling, spiritual growth, and vocational guidance and placement—concerns of highest priority at the Seminary.

(3) Distinguished Professors—John Drakeford, Cal Guy, and Boyd Hunt. The Seminary often celebrates the election of new teachers and recognizes those who leave for other places of service, but we should also affirm those who have faithfully invested long years of service and have made distinctive contributions during their tenure. So the Seminary has created a new rank within the faculty titled "Distinguished Professor." In order to be considered for election to the rank, a teacher must have been a member of the elected full-time faculty at Southwestern for a composite of twenty-five years. The teacher's election is based on distinguished service in the classroom and in publication or some other unique achievement or contribution to the Seminary or the denomination.

The trustees in St. Louis chose three who justly deserve this recognition—Dr. John Drakeford, Professor of Psychology and Counseling, teaching since 1954; Dr. Cal Guy, Bottoms Professor of Missions, teaching since 1946; and Dr. Boyd Hunt, Professor of Theology, teaching since 1944. Congratulations!

October 1980: Commitment

OUR CAMPUS REVIVAL . . . calls the entire Seminary—faculty, students, administration, and our families—to renewed commitments to our Lord and to His mission in the world. Through the preaching of Richard Jackson and the music of Mark Blankenship, our attention has been focused again on the centrality of Jesus, moving us to new levels of spiritual growth.

Someone has asked, "Does the seminary need a revival week?" The answer, of course, is an emphatic yes, for it is easy under the pressure of a demanding academic schedule to grow "professional" or to lose sight of the ultimate purpose of theological education. The revival emphasis helps keep us on course and draws us back to spiritual realities. For that we are grateful.

OUR TRUSTEES . . . who will be meeting on campus October 20-22 deserve the enthusiastic affirmation of every Southwesterner. I was troubled by the recent news reports of "convention takeover efforts" that impugn our trustees. The implication was that Seminary trustees are not knowledgeable, not Bible-centered, not Christ-honoring, but rather people who "sit there like a bunch of dummies and rubberstamp everything that is presented to them." The announcement was made by the Patterson/Pressler political organization that plans had been set in motion to replace 60 percent of the trustees in three years by gaining control of the SBC Committee on Committees and the Committee on Boards at Los Angeles, New Orleans, and Pittsburgh annual meetings.

It was suggested by the group that churches should give just enough to the SBC Cooperative Program to qualify for the largest number of messengers who would then go to the convention meeting and help accomplish the takeover. Since I know and work very closely with the men and women on our board and appreciate the Christian commitment and dedication to Southern Baptist life that characterizes them as individuals and as a group, I feel led to make the following comments:

First, the caricature and vilification of dedicated and involved Seminary trustees should be recognized and deplored by all responsible pastors and lay leaders who have elected them through the years.

Second, responsible church leaders should make plans now to become informed about board nominations for trustees and attend the conventions. They must continue to vote for trustees who are devoted to constructive and historic Baptist beliefs.

Third, Baptist people should renew commitment to the Cooperative Program as a channel for missions support. Such generous giving will be in contrast to the hypocrisy of those who would give just enough to gain the maximum number of messengers so they can have their way at the meetings of the Southern Baptist Convention.

Fourth, there is the need for responsible pastors and lay people to undergird Seminary teachers and administrators with prayer and constructive suggestions for continued improvements in service to our Lord and to the purposes of the Southern Baptist Convention.

November 1980: Outline of Vision 85, the Seminary's New Five-year Strategic Plan

(In this column, I presented the first five-year strategic plan during my administration. It was called Vision 85 and included goals and stategies to be accomplished by the year 1985. We chose the following scriptural text: The vision is yet for an appointed time . . . though it tarry, wait for it; because it will surely come, it will not tarry [Hab 2:3].)

December 1980: The Sun Never Sets on the Southwestern Family

This familiar quotation serves as a vivid reminder that more than 31,000 Southwesterners are ministering in the U.S. and 99 other countries around the world. Their life stories are varied and inspiring.

One of these personal dramas came to my attention recently when a musical trade journal carried a story about a musician from the People's Republic of China who would visit the U.S. this spring to attend a music conference. The man's name is Gershom Ma (Ma Geshun) and he is the director of the Shanghai Symphony Orchestra and Chorus as well as a teacher in the Shanghai Conservatory. The article indicated that he was a graduate of Southwestern in Fort Worth, Texas.

I checked with Dr. James McKinney and learned that Gershom Ma finished his master's degree in our School of Church Music in 1950. Because of a complication, Mr. Ma did not receive his diploma, and then the breakdown of diplomatic relations after the communist takeover of China prohibited any further contact with him. Following the Cultural Revolution in China, Gershom Ma is now in a place of significant influence as a noted musician.

I have invited him to stop by Fort Worth in the spring for a visit. It will be our privilege to officially award the diploma to him and to hear a report of these years of Christian witness behind the bamboo curtain.

This distant member of the Southwestern family writes:

Owing to the breakdown of diplomatic relationship between our two countries I did not have contact with you for nearly 30 years. But my mother school is always in my memory. . . .

In addition to other responsibilities I am also conductor of the Shanghai City Chorus Troup and Shanghai Broadcast and TV Station chorus. My ability of work was trained by Southwestern.

. . . I am exceedingly grateful to you for letting me have such an opportunity to express my gratitude.

Yes, the sun never sets on the Southwestern family, nor on the possibility of a continuing Christian influence even in dark days and hostile environments.

1981

Reaching Out to the New— Preserving the Unchanging

As we began to implement some of the goals in "Vision 85," our five-year strategic plan, we saw important new changes on campus in 1981. We broke ground for the construction of the Webb Roberts Building to house the largest theological library in the nation. Plans were also completed for a new music library and classroom wing and for the renovation of space that would be vacated when the new buildings were occupied. We launched the biggest fund-raising campaign in Seminary history: $25 million to pay for the new construction and renovations and for additional endowment. We experienced an upbeat, forward-looking mood that comes with "newness."

Among creative new additions to the curriculum was a Christian Communication Center. In collaboration with the nearby SBC Radio and Television Commission, we introduced courses and onsite training in radio, television, drama, communication arts, religious journalism, and speech—all in the context of ministry.

These exciting new advances, however, did not diminish Southwestern's desire to maintain its traditions as a Christ-centered institution committed to the Bible and to historic Baptist ideals. We wanted to show that a Christian leader could be conservative without being cranky! We wanted to demonstrate that the unchanging truths of our faith could be presented using contemporary and effective methods. The September column quotes James Leo Garrett's reference to another historical situation that seemed to fit Southwestern: "They took the old Baptist motto that the New Testament, and it alone, is the all-sufficient rule of faith and practice and lifted it out of cant, pretense, misuse, littleness, and triviality, and made it mean something."

Life was good on Seminary Hill, and the school was experiencing unprecedented growth both in numbers and effectiveness. There was certainly no need for a "conservative resurgence" on this campus. We were conservative when conservative wasn't cool! As one returning graduate said, "Of course, there have been some changes over the years . . . but even though some of the faces have changed, it's the same seminary that I found as a struggling young student twenty-five years ago. Southwestern still features a conservative, Bible-believing faculty and possesses a fervent evangelistic and missionary spirit . . . some things never change!"

The February column on enrollment is interesting in light of current enrollments in the six SBC seminaries. It was always the plan of the convention for the seminaries to provide graduate theological education, leaving bachelor's level work to the Baptist colleges. Presently, the six SBC seminaries have college programs, and a substantial portion of their enrollments is in this category. If one could calculate the enrollments of their masters and doctors students, it would reveal drastic declines from enrollments in our seminaries before the fundamentalist takeover.

During the years I served at Southwestern, we were training about 50 percent of all the graduate-level students enrolled in our six seminaries, and we did it with only 28 percent of the total Cooperative Program money given to the six seminaries. Southwestern's contribution to the work of the Kingdom and the ministry of Baptist churches was enormous.

Key Events in 1981

March

1   • Preached First Baptist, Wichita Falls

16   • EEOC suit against Southwestern heard in Texas Appeals Court, New Orleans

23-25   • Spring trustee meeting, groundbreaking for library buildings
         • Established Center for Christian Communication Studies

April
21   • Miles Seaborn, pastor in Fort Worth, preached in chapel

May
         • Article in which Adrian Rogers says those opposed to Bailey Smith's election as SBC president are liberals. Similar article by O.S. Hawkins, Fundamentalist pastor in Florida, saying denominational loyalists are liberals.

June
7-11   • SBC met in Los Angeles; Bailey Smith second term over Abner McCall—60.24 percent
         • 13,529 messengers
         • Fundamentalist Ed Young, pastor of Second Baptist, Houston, elected pastors conference president

July
17   • 5th circuit court gives mixed decision on EEOC, but actually a substantial victory for Southwestern. Will appeal to U.S. Supreme Court.
20-24   • Preached at Falls Creek Assembly in Oklahoma

August
23   • Preached Second Baptist, Houston

September
8   • Joel Gregory, pastor of Gambrell St. Baptist, Fort Worth, preached in chapel
29   • Ralph Smith, pastor of Hyde Park Baptist, Austin, preached for Seminary revival
         • Institute for Christian Studies for lay theological education established

October
19-21   • Fall trustee meeting—merger with Mexican Bible Institute (Hispanic Seminary)
         • Launched gerontology program with Baylor
26-27   • Preached at Missouri Baptist Pastor's Conference
28   • Preached Convention Sermon at BGCT in Waco
30   • Southwestern reaccredited for ten years by ATS and SACS

November

4   • Former Dean Huber Drumwright's funeral—Truett Auditorium
17   • Stephen Olford preached in chapel
       • Article in *Texas Monthly*—Paige Patterson: "We have to be Gestapos"

December

15   • Filed appeal with U.S. Supreme Court on EEOC 5th circuit decision

Note: In the fall meeting of 1981, the thirty-six-member board of trustees had the following composition: 5 hard-core fundamentalists, 26 traditional mainstream Baptists, and 5 swing voters.

January 1981: A New Communications Center, a New Library Building, and a New Year

THE NEW CHRISTIAN COMMUNICATIONS CENTER . . . at Southwestern promises to be one of the valuable sources of church leadership training in the coming decades. In cooperation with the Southern Baptist Radio and Television Commission, the center will offer courses on the Seminary campus and onsite training at the commission in such subjects as radio, television, drama, communication arts, religious journalism, speech—all in the context of ministry.

God is calling increasing numbers of people into full-time ministries related to communications media and drama, as well as combination church staff positions and bivocational opportunities. Southwestern is responding to this increasing need with quality training.

A teacher/director will be added to the faculty in the spring of 1981, and the center will be officially launched at a "National Conference on Broadcast Ministries," April 27-29, 1981. This event jointly sponsored by Southwestern and the SBC Radio and TV Commission will bring outstanding media personalities together with pastors and other denominational leaders for in-depth training in the use of radio and television in Bold Mission Thrust.

THE NEW LIBRARY BUILDING . . . at Southwestern will be emerging on the site just east of the present Fleming Library Building. Site preparation has already begun, bids will be returned in February 1981, official groundbreaking ceremonies will be held at the board meeting in March, and the $8.5 million building will be ready for use in the summer of 1983.

VISION 85 . . . is the theme of an effort to secure funding for this major capital project that will house the largest theological library in the U.S. The convention's Cooperative Program capital budget will supply $1.1 million, and the remainder will be sought from foundations and individuals throughout the U.S.

THE NEW YEAR . . . at Southwestern, with the new challenges of Christian training and the new projects in process, reminds us of the confidence we have in the future because of our faith in the One who "maketh all things new."

February 1981: How Seminaries Count Enrollment

Seminary enrollment figures are confusing! I read the recent news release about the enrollments of our six SBC schools and realized again how difficult it is to make accurate comparisons or analyze the numbers. How do seminaries report enrollments?

(1) Fall Head Count Enrollment. Most seminaries have three semesters. Others add "J" terms. At least one of our schools has a new semester each month. But one standard of reporting is to give the total number of people enrolled at the beginning of the fall term, usually in August. The 1980 fall enrollment at Southwestern was 3,684 or 39 percent of the total of those enrolled in all of our schools.

(2) Annual Cumulative Enrollment. The total number of different people enrolled in all the semesters of one year is reported as an annual non-duplicating head count. The cumulative enrollment at Southwestern in the current year (1980–1981) is 4,412, the highest in the school's history. Ten years ago (1970–1971), the cumulative enrollment was 2,171. That's an increase of more than 100 percent.

(3) FTE Enrollment. "Full Time Equivalent" is a term used to describe enrollment based on a count of students on a full-time basis of twenty-four hours per year. The 1979–1980 FTE enrollment at Southwestern was 3,378.

(4) Enrollment by Programs. Each seminary has a variety of educational programs, each enrolling its own category of students. These programs involve master's degree work, doctoral studies, diploma classes, continuing education programs, non-credit courses, courses for auditors, special courses and conferences for wives of students, lay training programs, off-campus programs, international programs, seminary extension programs, and field education courses, as well as practica of various kinds.

For "bragging purposes," a seminary might add up all of the people taking any kind of course offered by the seminary. This means comparisons between the schools run the proverbial risk of comparing apples with oranges. If Southwestern counted all its enrollees as some of the other schools do, we could report nearly 10,000 annually enrolled!

While all of these educational programs are important, the Southern Baptist Convention has given to the seminaries the basic task of training God-called men and women at the graduate level: M.Div., M.R.E., and M.C.M. degrees and a variety of doctoral degrees.

Southwestern is carrying the load for our convention in this basic task—41 percent of all the students enrolled in the master's degree programs of our six seminaries are enrolled at Southwestern. (We provide this major portion of theological education for only 28 percent of the money given to the seminaries from the Cooperative Program.)

Any way you add up these confusing enrollment figures, Southwestern obviously carries the biggest load for the least money. That's a good investment of the mission dollar.

March 1981: Center for Christian Communication Studies

Southwestern has attempted through the years to be on the pioneering frontier of theological education. As new areas of ministry emerge in Southern Baptist churches, the Seminary has tried to respond quickly with training opportunities to meet the need. Evidence of this attempt is seen in the establishment of the World Mission/Church Growth Center, the Christian Recreation Program, Off-campus Centers, the Children's Center, and other innovative programs.

Another in this line of frontier innovations is the new Center for Christian Communication Studies. Jointly sponsored by the Seminary and the SBC Radio & TV Commission, the center will be located at Southwestern and will concentrate and focus on current studies in television, radio, and drama while at the same time adding new curricula and courses of study in the use of media in communicating the gospel. There will be concentrations offered in communications within one of the existing degree programs as well as a new degree in communications specifically targeting bivocational ministry in this field.

In order to meet a growing need for training among church leaders involved in media ministries, the center will also sponsor functional continuing education conferences and seminars.

The facilities and expertise of the Radio and Television Commission will provide a top-of-the-line laboratory setting for "hands-on" training for students and conference participants. In the next few months, we will elect a director/teacher, who will lead the center beginning this summer.

On April 27-29, the Center for Communication Studies will sponsor the National Conference on Broadcast Ministries. Leaders from the field of television and radio will be on the program and conference participants from all over the U.S. will attend. It will officially launch the work of the center and give high visibility to the direction the Seminary is going with this new program.

The system of low-power television stations and the television network called ACTS, proposed by the Radio and TV Commission, will of course open up vast new areas of personnel needs to be met in the next decade. Already students are enrolling at the Seminary who believe God has called them to ministries in media. As the churches begin new avenues of evangelism in the media and as God calls men and women to fill those needs, Southwestern will do its best to provide quality training to equip them to serve.

April 1981: Vision 85

Vision 85 is the name given to the Seminary's efforts to meet its strategic goals by 1985. Vision 85 is a plan as well as a program to raise money to support that plan. The plan includes not only the ongoing objectives at Southwestern, but also the construction of a new library building and remodeling of the present library wing for classroom and office spaces.

The financial goal for Vision 85 is $25 million—the largest financial goal ever attempted at Southwestern—and is divided as follows:

New Library Building	$6,600,000
New Music Library and Education Wing	$1,834,800
Renovation of Present Library and Educational Space	$4,565,200
Seminary Endowment	$12,000,000
Total	**$25,000,000**

In addition to the SBC Cooperative Program capital budget provision of $2 million, the Seminary has already received $1,796,500 in other gifts toward this demanding financial goal.

Proposals have been made to charitable foundations and contacts are being developed with individuals who have potential for major gifts—all in the confidence that God will provide the resources through generous stewards as He has in the past.

At the trustees meeting, March 24, groundbreaking ceremonies for the new library were held. Already construction is under way on the site east of the present Fleming Library building. Completion is estimated in the summer of 1982 when the Seminary staff will move the largest theological library in the U.S. into its new quarters—a valuable resource for the training of God-called men and women in ministry.

Our confidence in the success of Vision 85 is based on the same faith expressed in Habakkuk 2:3, "The vision is yet for an appointed time . . . though it tarry, wait for it because it will surely come, it will not tarry."

The prayers of all Southwesterners are requested for the president, officers, and volunteers of the Seminary who are working to secure these resources.

June 1981: Richard Maples Letter

Dr. Richard Maples, pastor of First Baptist Church, Bryan, Texas, and a graduate of Southwestern, was on campus recently. The next week he wrote about his experience in his church newsletter, and I would like to share with you some of his comments.

This morning I stepped back into history. While visiting on the campus of Southwestern Seminary, Mary Jo and I attended chapel and found ourselves a part of the concluding service of the Spring Mission Emphasis Week. Twenty-five years slipped away and suddenly it was 1956 and I was a freshman divinity student attending my first mission dedication service.

Of course, there have been some changes over the years . . . but even though some of the faces have changed, it is the same seminary that I found as a struggling young student twenty-five years ago. Southwestern still features a conservative, Bible-believing faculty and possesses a fervent evangelistic and missionary spirit. I listened to Roy Fish, an old classmate who is now a professor at the seminary, preach a moving sermon on world missions, watched with tears glistening on my cheeks as fifty or sixty young people committed themselves to go anywhere to preach the gospel and felt it in my soul—some things never change!

Our seminary professors sold out to liberal theology? Never! I am convinced that such charges against the God-called men and women who give their lives to the study and teaching of the scriptures at Southwestern are above contempt.

After the chapel services were concluded we visited with an old friend who is in his first year of teaching on the faculty. We rejoiced over the worship experience, reminisced about our seminary days and mission services of other years, and then he said, "You know, Dick, it's just the same around here as ever. Before coming back to the seminary I couldn't be sure, but it's just the same."

To that I said to him and I say to you, "Amen."

And to that "Amen" I would like to add another.

July/August 1981: Fund-raising

(This column described the president's responsibilities as a fund-raiser. Securng $25 million to pay for the goals of Vision 85 was a daunting task. I outlined the various places around the U.S. where I traveled to speak and solicit contributions. My concluding remarks were, "I am claiming the promise of the prophet, Habakkuk, when God said to him, 'The vision is yet for an appointed time . . . though it tarry, wait for it, because it will surely come, it will not tarry'" [Hab 2:3].)

September 1981: Commitments to Excellence

(This column reflected on the new academic year with new students [825], new faculty [6], new staff [10], and new trustees [5]. New buildings were being completed, and a new maintenance program resulted in an improved appearance on our grounds and in our buildings. New programs of instruction were underway to enable us to better fulfill God's purpose for us. But we continued our historical commitment to the Bible. A quote from an address by Dr. Leo Garrett could well be applied to Southwestern, "They took the old Baptist motto that the New Testament, and it alone, is the all-sufficient rule of faith and practice and lifted it out of cant, pretense, misuse, littleness, and triviality, and made it mean something." Our commitment to the Bible was not just academic and theoretical; it was practical and functional as we seek to obey its authority.)

October 1981: Church Planting Practicum

(In this column, I reinforced Southwestern's plan to enrich classroom learning with direct mission involvement by our students. I reported that fifty-six students helped start twenty-one churches in ten states, Canada, and Mexico during the past summer.)

November 1981: Third Annual Report

(Each fall the president of Southwestern makes a report to the board of trustees showing the status of the Seminary at the conclusion of another academic year. This column pointed out that the full report was printed in a separate brochure.)

December 1981: State Convention Meetings

This is the season when the faculty and administration of Southwestern scatter out across the Southern Baptist Convention to represent the seminary at various state Baptist convention meetings. Some of the representatives are called upon to deliver the official address on theological education, others to preach or bring Bible studies for the convention sessions, while some are there to speak to the annual gathering of Southwestern alumni in that state. It was my privilege to be in Missouri, Louisiana, Mississippi, Alabama, and Texas and the impressions I received in these states matches that of other seminary representatives who reported on their visits:

(1) Southern Baptists all across the nation are reemphasizing the importance of Bold Mission Thrust goals. When controversial issues emerged they were dealt with positively and in a spirit of cooperation. It seems our churches are not willing to be sidetracked from our main purpose of missions and evangelism.

(2) Financial support from churches and conventions through the denomination's Cooperative Program of mission giving is a high priority. In Alabama, for example, an entire evening session was given to recognizing churches with outstanding Cooperative Program giving records and presenting new challenges and goals for both local church and state convention participation. It is my impression that we are at the threshold of a new breakthrough in Cooperative Program advance and that's good news for Southwestern since forty-nine percent of our financial need is supplied by Cooperative Program giving.

(3) All across the nation there is unanimous enthusiasm among Southwestern alumni for the seminary. Again and again sincere and profound appreciation has been expressed for the faculty, the program, and the general emphasis and spirit of Southwestern as it continues to grow stronger year-by-year.

(4) The number of alumni attending the annual state meetings is mushrooming, especially in the Southeast. Two decades ago, in Alabama only a handful of Southwesterners attended the meeting while this year about 140 were at the

dinner meeting. Financial support from alumni is also increasing, as they more clearly understand the importance for our fund raising efforts of a strong percentage of alumni giving.

(5) New students will be enrolling at Southwestern for many years to come. Typical of the experience of other seminary representatives, I am sure, was the opportunity I had to meet and advise potential students from each of the states I visited who were eagerly anticipating their future at the seminary.

The future of Southern Baptist theological education is indeed bright and perhaps brightest of all at Southwestern.

1982

The First Five Years

Having been elected president of Southwestern in fall 1977, I passed the five-year milestone in fall 1982. Major accomplishments during that fifth year capped off a period of impressive seminary growth both in numbers and effectiveness. In 1982 we completed the Tandy Archeological Museum and the campus bookstore, broke ground for the Tarrant Baptist Associational Building on our property, officially named the major buildings on campus, launched a gerontology study program with Baylor University, adopted the Hispanic Baptist Seminary to enhance the training of Latino church leaders, achieved our ten-year accreditation, enrolled a record number of students, and recognized our 20,000th graduate. Southwestern Seminary was widely recognized both for its outstanding quality and its unprecedented size.

The other five Southern Baptist seminaries were also experiencing their best years. In the March column, I point out that Southern Baptists had 10,058 students preparing for ministry in these six schools. This remarkable enrollment is put into perspective when compared with other denominations in 1982.

In 1982, the average seminary enrollment in the U.S. was 263, while Southwestern alone had 4,605 enrolled. Four of the largest five seminaries in the country were Southern Baptist seminaries. Furthermore, in the Seminary

Extension Program operated by the six Southern Baptist schools, another 10,347 were enrolled in seminary courses in 401 extension centers around the country. More than 20,000 men and women, believing God had called them into His ministry, were pursuing studies in our denominational seminaries to equip them to serve.

How ironic that in their efforts to control the convention, the fundamentalist leaders began to attack the seminaries just when these six schools were becoming one of the most valuable resources Southern Baptists—or any other church body—could have.

These were not liberal seminaries! All six of them were committed to the Bible and to our historic Baptists convictions as expressed in strong, conservative confessions of faith. Admittedly, in 1982, there were a few—less than a dozen—of the 400-500 faculty members who held positions to the theological left of most of our Baptist constituents. (None of them was at Southwestern.) But even the most extreme of these would not have been classified as classical theological liberals. In fact, in meetings with seminary leaders from other denominations, they often reminded us that our "worst liberals" would be considered "fundamentalists" in their denominations!

Not one of us who served as Southern Baptist seminary presidents at this time took a casual or cavalier attitude toward a professor whose teaching contradicted our adopted confessions of faith, whether to the theological left or right. These rare circumstances would be corrected forcefully but redemptively in the spirit of Christian charity. Sometimes the corrections did not take place as rapidly or as publicly as fundamentalist critics preferred, but the facts will show that good faith efforts were made to keep our seminaries anchored to our Baptist beliefs. We were keenly aware that Baptist congregations had a right to expect this from the schools that trained their ministers.

Of course, the seminaries were human institutions and therefore not perfect. We had to monitor our programs continually and make needed corrections judicially and without undue publicity. Few observers will be aware, for example, that during my sixteen years at the helm of Southwestern, we had to correct, dismiss, or negotiate the resignation or retirement of half a dozen faculty and eight or nine staff members. Not all the issues were theological; sometimes the problem was moral or spiritual. But they were handled quietly for the most part, without embarrassing the people involved.

My point is that the claims that our seminaries were "overrun with liberals," were "drifting toward liberalism," and were led by people unwilling to make corrections were patently untrue. It is an even greater falsehood to say that this so-called "liberalism" necessitated a political takeover to force a "conservative resurgence."

As the takeover crusade picked up steam, the leaders of the SBC seminaries and agencies made repeated efforts to sit down with Paul Pressler, Paige Patterson, and their followers to respond to their critical attacks and try to settle the issues before more damage was done to our convention. For example, you will notice in the following list of events that in October and November, all-day meetings were held with key leaders from both sides.

On an individual basis, I pursued every opportunity to discuss the concerns with individuals, committees, pastors' conferences, and churches. Furthermore, my book *The Doctrine of Biblical Authority* was published in 1982, and I began a yearlong series of conferences across the country to discuss the book and its topics of authority, inspiration, inerrancy, and interpretation. You will notice too that in more and more of the following editorial columns, I began to address matters directly related to the controversy. (See, for example, the July/August column about the 1982 Southern Baptist Convention meeting.)

Key Events in 1982

February

12   • Met with Randall Lolley, president of Southeastern Seminary, and Bob Witty, founder of Luther Rice Seminary, to consider Witty's suggestion that the six SBC Seminaries acquire Luther Rice Seminary. We were never able to come to an agreement.
     • Broke ground for Tarrant Baptist Association Building on campus

March

22   • Spring trustee meeting
     • Named buildings: B. H. Carroll Memorial Building, which includes Scarborough Hall, Flemming Hall, and Truett Auditorium
     • Dedicated Jim Leitch Physical Plant Building
     • Dedicated Tandy Archeological Museum

April

1   • Supreme Court declines to hear Southwestern's case in the EEOC lawsuit. This lets 5th circuit decision stand, which is mostly a victory for the Seminary
21   • Roy Honeycutt's inauguration at Southern Seminary
26   • In *Newsweek*, Billy Graham says, "the leadership of evangelicalism is no longer in the hands of individuals; it's in the hand of institutions like Southwestern Seminary . . . ."

May

 • Adrian Rogers, SBC president, calls SBC Cooperative Program a "Sacred Cow." Others respond that it is a "Sacred How."

June

16
 • SBC met in New Orleans
 • Jimmy Draper, pastor of FBC Euless, elected over Duke McCall, John Sullivan, and Perry Sanders, 56.97 percent. Draper described as more centrist.
 • 20,456 messengers
 • I was alternate preacher to Bill Hull and read the Scripture text
 • Fred Wolfe, pastor, Alabama, elected Pastor Conference President
 • Called trustee meeting to elect Professor Joel Gregory to faculty

July

 • My article in *Southwestern News* about the June convention. There were actually three conventions!
 • My article in *Southwestern News* suggesting issues in controversy are things like Scientific Creationism, Israel, dispensationalism, abortion, prayer in schools, church/state, denominational style, terminology like inerrancy, women in ministry, Calvinism, pastoral authority, enforced creedalism, and what J. I. Packer's book calls "Carnal Conservatism"

September

2   • Jimmy Draper preached in chapel as SBC president
1   • Richard Jackson preached in chapel
14   • Dedicated new Baptist bookstore on campus
15   • Miles Seaborn preached in chapel
28   • John Bisagno preached fort Seminary revival
     • Established Tandy Archeological Museum through Tandy Corp. gift

October

5   • Met all day at DFW with Jimmy Draper, Paige Patterson, and SBC agency heads. Paige Patterson gave a Four Point Peace Plan.
17   • CBS airs special on Southwestern Seminary
18   • Fall trustee meeting
     • Dedicated Webb Roberts Library, James I. McCord spoke
     • Opened new Baptist bookstore
     • This meeting marked the fifth anniversary of my election as president. Nothing said about this in meeting.

November

12   • Met all day at DFW with Jimmy Draper and others. I presented paper
          on biblical authority
        • O. S. Hawkins preached in chapel. He told Lawrence Klempnauer that
          one of the problems at Southwestern was there were no
          Dispensationalists on the faculty.
18   • Bishop Robinson (Honest to God) in chapel and at our house. (He is
          an avowed theological liberal, but was invited by Professor Russ Bush
          to discuss his conservative views of the early dating of Gospels.)

December

        • Article by Southern Seminary Professor Henlee Barnette suggesting
          that fundamentalist leaders are guilty of celebrityism, success, anti-
          intellectualism, etc.
        • My book *The Doctrine of Biblical Authority* published. I began series of
          conferences across the country on biblical authority.

Note: The 1982 fall meeting of the thirty-six-member board of trustees had the
following composition: 6 hard-core fundamentalists, 25 traditional mainstream
Baptists, and 5 swing voters.

January 1982: Commencement

COMMENCEMENT . . . is in many respects a symbolic event. The name itself
symbolizes the "commencing" of a new phase of service for which educational
preparation has been made. The conferring of degrees is also symbolic since the
"sheepskin" is only a representation of the long and tedious process of study and
research behind it. The ceremony and regalia are also symbolic dramatizations of
the value we give to accomplishments in education. So whether it's a high school
or college, a public or church-related institution, commencement exercises, even
though symbolic, are very important.

But at Southwestern, commencement services have a special quality far
beyond the traditional symbolism typical of the academic world in general. On
December 18 in the sanctuary of the Travis Avenue Baptist Church, 283 men
and women gathered with their families and friends as well as faculty and staff of
the seminary for the Winter Commencement Exercises of 1981. It was first of all
a worship experience. The congregation sang together "Praise the Lord for he is
glorious, never shall his promise fail..." We were led to the Father in prayer by
James Jeffrey and Scott Tatum, both of whom had sons in the graduating class.
Together we read from Philippians 2: "Being confident of this very thing that he

which hath begun a good work in you will perform it until the day of Jesus Christ . . . ." After a beautiful solo, the commencement address was delivered by Dr. James Landes, Executive Secretary of the Baptist General Convention of Texas, who was a last minute substitute for Dr. William Pinson whose mother's death prevented his participation. It was also an occasion of academic pageantry with colorful robes and hoods of the procession symbolizing our seminary's identity as an educational institution.

But the graduates themselves were the central focus of this commencement ceremony—283 from across the United States and other countries as well. Many of them began their seminary work in the same year that I came to be president, in 1978. They move on from Fort Worth to serve churches, conventions, institutions, and missions around the world in ministries that not only will meet the needs of a lost world but also will win many to faith in Jesus Christ.

At this commencement the 20,000th graduate was awarded a degree. We paused in the ceremony to recognize Charles A. Russell from Georgia who received the Master of Divinity degree. He is a graduate of Ouachita Baptist University and is currently serving as pastor of the Calvary Baptist Church in Hamilton, Texas. He too is a symbol, not only of the 282 others in his graduating class, but also of the 38,752 who have either graduated or have attended SW since its beginning.

I am thankful for this and all the other symbols growing out of SW commencement because they remind us clearly that this is the business to which God has called us.

February 1982: Unselfish Contributions

Among the many new impressions I have had since assuming responsibility here at Southwestern, the most moving has been created by the unselfish contributions of generous donors who help meet the financial needs of the seminary.

SBC Cooperative Program money is our lifeline, of course, but about one-half of our operating needs comes from other sources, primarily endowment income, gifts and grants. Each day there is placed on my desk a list of the contributions received the previous day. The deeply moving impressions I have described above come from reviewing that list. Preachers, missionaries, students, professors, laypersons, churches, Sunday School classes, Woman's Missionary Union groups, businesses, corporations, and foundations are listed from all across the United States. One such list included both a $1.00 gift from Washington State, $20,000 from a Texas donor, and $375,000 from a foundation.

Some of the gifts come from personal friends who have encouraged me over the years, others from long-time supporters of Southwestern, still others from persons who have never been here and have only limited knowledge of the seminary. Every gift is important. Without them Southwestern could not continue its work.

In this issue, there is a story about one of these generous supporters—Mrs. Bessie Fleming. She died Christmas Day, 1981, and following the pattern of her generosity during her lifetime, her will also included the seminary. Mrs. Fleming's gifts to the seminary are cumulatively the largest contribution ever received from a single donor.

We will try to acknowledge such generosity and express our thanks, but only the Lord knows the full value of such stewardship. He sees both the $1.00 from Washington and the $375,000 from a foundation. The return on these investments is immeasurable, but it can be visualized in part when in December we saw the 20,000 graduate of Southwestern receive his diploma.

March 1982: Investment of Resources

To one he gave five talents of money, to another two talents, and to another one...the master then returned to settle accounts with them (Matt 25:15-19).

In this passage and others, Jesus made it very clear that we are responsible for the prudent use and investment of the resources He gives us. In order to be wise stewards, we must first know exactly what resources we have. Recently released enrollment figures dramatically remind Southern Baptists of the value of one portion of the Master's treasure which he has entrusted to us—our seminaries.

Southern Baptists have six seminaries with a record cumulative enrollment of 10,058 students. By comparison, and as a way of putting this enrollment in perspective, look at some other figures:

• Roman Catholics have 48 schools with 5,760 enrolled.
• Episcopalians have 9 schools with 1,072 enrolled.
• Lutherans have 7 schools with 1,430 enrolled.
• Presbyterians have 6 schools with 3,208 enrolled.

The average seminary enrollment in the U.S. is 263 while Southwestern alone has 4,605 enrolled. Four of the largest five seminaries in the country are SB seminaries. Furthermore, in the Seminary Extension Program operated by the six Southern Baptist schools, another 10,347 are enrolled in seminary courses in 401 extension centers around the country.

Because of generous Cooperative Program funding, these students receive quality education at the lowest possible cost to them. At Southwestern the matriculation fee is $200 per semester. Compare the annual tuition charges at other evangelical seminaries:

• Asbury Theological Seminary, $2,830
• Dallas Theological Seminary, $3,000
• Fuller Theological Seminary, $3,564
• Gordon-Conwell Theological Seminary, $3,460
• Trinity Evangelical Divinity School, $3,300

The Master certainly will hold all of us as stewards responsible for the wise management of these valuable resources as he calls and sends His servants to be trained.

April 1982: Preaching in Chicago

(Returning from a preaching engagement in Chicago, I reported in this column what Southern Baptists were doing in the metropolitan area. Southwestern also contributed to home mission through its emphasis on bivocational ministry and by the direct involvement of students in "Pioneer Penetration." About 240 students served in 140 home mission churches where they both contributed and learned about the work in these states.)

May 1982: SWBTS Reports to SBC

One of the president's responsibilities at Southwestern is to give an annual report to the Southern Baptist Convention regarding the work of this agency. The report is to be in both written and oral form. I will have about eight minutes on Wednesday, June 16, along with the other five presidents, to report personally to the convention messengers meeting in New Orleans. The written report will be printed in the SBC Book of Reports for distribution to the messengers. I would like to summarize below some of the key elements in that report with a sense of deep gratitude to the Lord for the good year we have had and a commitment on behalf of all of us at Southwestern to lead our seminary to become the school God would have it to be.

Training for Bold Mission Thrust leadership during the 1981–1982 academic year continued to be the major contribution of Southwestern to the worldwide missions efforts of Southern Baptists. According to Southwestern's annual report to the SBC, a record 4,605 students were enrolled during the year, including 1,400 first-time students. The total was a 4.4 percent increase over the previous year and included 1,149 home and foreign mission volunteers.

Southwestern continued to operate off campus centers in Houston and San Antonio, TX, and Shawnee, OK. A record 330 persons were enrolled in these centers. We also participated in new satellite centers being sponsored by the Seminary External Education Division in Nashville.

During the year two important milestones were reached: Robby W. Barrett of Midland, TX, became the 40,000th student to enroll in the seminary's 75-year history when he registered for classes in January 1982.

Charles A. Russell of Jonesboro, AR, was the 20,000th student to receive a degree from Southwestern since its founding in 1908. He received the master of divinity degree in December 1981.

A total of 843 degrees were awarded during the year.

The SBC Cooperative Program contributed $4.9 million to the seminary's record $12 million operating budget. The seminary also reported total endowment of $21.6 million and total assets of $52.5 million.

Six new faculty members were added for the 1981–1982 year, bringing the full-time faculty total to 101. A supplemental teaching force of 55 brought the total to 156 for the year.

Theodore H. Dowell became director of the Marriage and Family Counseling Center. Justice C. Anderson was named director of the World Mission/Church Growth Center.

Two new programs were initiated during the year: A joint gerontology program with Baylor University was begun under the direction of James D. Williams, and the Institute of Christian Studies, non-credit instruction for laypersons, was started in the division of continuing education for ministry.

Trustees approved plans for a merger agreement with Mexican Baptist Bible Institute in San Antonio, TX. The school became Hispanic Baptist Theological Seminary, a component of Southwestern.

Following an eighteen-month self-study, the Association of Theological Schools and the Southern Association of Colleges and Schools reaffirmed the seminary's institutional accreditation for a ten-year period.

A total of $8.8 million has been received in gifts and pledges toward the Vision 85 capital needs and endowment fund raising project. The project includes construction of a new library center, scheduled for completion in August 1982, and $12 million in endowment.

Stanton H. Nash was added to the development staff as director of planned giving. Edwin A. Seale was named director of placement information.

It has been a great year.

June 1982: The Cooperative Program—
A Sacred "How"

COOPERATIVE PROGRAM . . . is a name chosen in 1925 to describe the way Southern Baptist churches would seek to obey the Great Commission of our Lord. When a name is used as frequently as this one has been the last 60 years, it may lose some of its appeal because of over familiarity. But the Cooperative Program is more than a denominational slogan—more than a name. It actually represents our only reason for existence as churches, institutions and as a denomination.

Jesus commanded us to go into all the world and preach the gospel, baptize believers, and teach them. By His example, Jesus also commissioned us to minister and heal and apply the gospel among all the people of the world. The diverse complexity of our world, the availability of expensive new technologies of communication, and the sheer overwhelming numbers of lost men and women call for a cooperative effort—a sharing of resources if churches are to obey our Lord's command.

The Cooperative Program is not then a peripheral, optional, denominational promotion. It is Southern Baptist churches doing what Jesus ordered us to do. Neither is it just a financial plan of giving. The Cooperative Program is rather evangelism, foreign missions, home missions, education, healing, caring, and ministering in the name of Jesus in scores of countries around the world.

Admittedly, the Cooperative Program is not a perfect response to the Great Commission but it is certainly a good one—a workable one. The Cooperative Program has proven to be the most effective missionary strategy our twentieth century Christian world has been able to employ. Considering the alternatives, how better could the churches of this convention do missions than in a cooperative manner?

One of our fundamentalist pastors recently complained that the Cooperative Program was a "sacred cow." But Dr. John Sullivan responded recently, "The Cooperative Program is not a sacred cow—it is a sacred how!"

July/August 1982: SBC Observations

There was a time not too long ago in Southern Baptist history when actions taken at the annual convention on resolutions and motions could be described as representing the majority feeling of the messengers registered that year. This may no longer be true. It seemed to me there were at least three different conventions or "gathering of messengers" at this past annual meeting in New Orleans.

FIRST, there was that group of 17,000 plus who met to elect a president. Two large groups of messengers already committed to two strong candidates were there along with about 3,000 others who have been labeled "swing voters."

The SECOND convention was that smaller group of messengers who stayed for the business sessions in which the vice-presidents were elected and important motions and resolutions were considered. This second "mix" seemed more like the traditional conventions prior to 1978. Not as much political organization was evident, messengers listened to the rationale of motions and nominations, and without predetermined "political loyalties" they voted their conscience on the basis of prayerful consideration. Some were to the left and some were to the right, but primarily this "convention within the convention" was committed to the mainstream positions that have made Southern Baptists a strong, positive missions and evangelistic force.

The THIRD convention was an even smaller group of messengers, only a fraction of the 17,000 who voted in the presidential election earlier, who stayed through to the last business session on Thursday afternoon. This drop-off in attendance on the last afternoon has been customary even legendary. It appeared that the "takeover party" intentionally took advantage of the smaller attendance and encouraged their group to stay over so they would have a clear majority. There was obvious evidence of political organization as blocks of voters with minds already made up sat together and expressed themselves loudly (and sometimes rudely) on the decisions. Issues already decided in the earlier balanced sessions were brought back up for reconsideration with heated debate and loud applause. Resolutions were passed that were heavily weighted toward one side of our Baptist constituency and that drastically contradicted traditional, historic stands Baptists have taken in the past. The real issues were often clouded by emotion and rhetoric. In my opinion, most of the decisions made were not representative of the convention as a whole. They were decisions skewed by a well-planned scheme to take advantage of a vulnerable pattern of Convention attendance.

I suppose the conclusions to be drawn from these personal observations are: (1) Resolutions and motions no longer represent the majority of messengers at an annual meeting but only the majority of those who happen to be in attendance at a the final session. Such a "session majority" would in fact be a very small minority of the total messengers registered. (2) It is increasingly important that messengers stay through to participate in every business session of the convention. (3) The term "messenger" is rapidly giving away to the term "delegate" as a more accurate description of those who are participating in the political party approach to deliberation. I have a feeling this delegate style will be with us for a long time. (4) Conscious of our convention's weaknesses, Southern Baptists need to humbly pray for God's leadership and guidance that we may steer a wise and deliberate course through these difficult days to find and fulfill God's will for us.

SOUTHWESTERN SEMINARY OBSERVATIONS
Southwestern is proud that once again our graduates are well represented among the elected officers of the convention. President Jimmy Draper; First Vice President, John Sullivan; Second Vice President, Gene Garrison; Pastor's Conference President, Fred Wolfe, are all graduates of Southwestern Seminary. In addition, Southwesterners were placed in major positions of leadership in the auxiliary organizations of the convention and on various boards and committees. We will pray for all of them as they lead and guide us during this coming year.

September 1982: World Map on Floor of Rotunda

In 1950 when the seminary dedicated the building now known as the B. H. Carroll Memorial Building, the Southwestern News featured a picture of the world map built into the terrazzo floor beneath the dome of the rotunda. It was pointed out in the article that the map rested on the "exact geographical center of Southwestern's campus" symbolizing the centrality of world missions at the heart of the Seminary.

The geographical center of the campus has shifted somewhat over these thirty-two years as a result of expansion, but the central focus on missions has not shifted. The ultimate purpose of evangelizing the world is behind every decision and action—from maintaining the grounds to planning mission days in chapel, from planning buildings to planning curricula.

If it were somehow possible to calculate the missions contribution of students who have walked across the terrazzo map in the rotunda over these thirty-two years, the sum total would be impressive—persons won to faith in Jesus Christ, New Testament churches started, new evangelism strategies discovered and implemented, teaching, healing, administering around the world. Those student footsteps still cross the terrazzo globe in the B. H. Carroll Memorial Building and the missions beat goes on year after year in cadence with the Great Commission.

Our director of admissions predicts about 4,000 students will enroll this fall at Southwestern compared to 3,837 last fall and 1,435 in the fall of 1950. About 25 percent of these will be mission volunteers. (It is interesting to notice that 18 percent of the students enrolled in 1950 were mission volunteers.) Several hundred others will make missions commitments during the academic year as the urgency of world needs is presented in every classroom.

Under the direction of our World Mission/Church Growth Center an unprecedented number of new courses, degree programs and conferences are being implemented. Hundreds of students are involved in missions and evangelism practica as they learn on the field in the U.S. and overseas.

The evidence seems clear that while the world may be off centered geographically at Southwestern, it still lies at the very center of the Seminary's heart.

October 1982: The Faculty at Southwestern Seminary

Over 100 Southwestern professors met at Salado, TX, August 19-20, for our annual retreat. The time was spent in recreation, fellowship, discussion, and prayer, planned around the theme "Spiritual Formation." Robert Munger from Fuller Seminary in California shared with the faculty Fuller's program of spiritual development. Our faculty discussed various approaches, which might be pursued at Southwestern as we try to strengthen our efforts at spiritual formation in the lives of the students.

But to me the most valuable feature of the retreat was the time spent in small groups for prayer and testimony. It reminded me again that at Southwestern Seminary we have faculty of the highest quality. Their credentials and reputations as scholars are impressive. Because of publication, lectures, and performance, they are being more widely recognized in the broader community of theological education. (For example, Dr. John Newport was guest professor at Princeton Theological Seminary this summer and Dr. Robert Sloan's book is listed in Harper and Row's new *Readers Guide to the Best Evangelical Books.*)

But more important in our Baptist context is the Christian commitment and churchmanship of our faculty. They are dedicated to the high calling of teaching, convinced that the Lord who saved them also has called them to teach and to prepare others for ministry.

This dedication to the Lord, to Southwestern, and to teaching is further evidenced by the fact that many of them stay here through the years even though they are sought in other fields of service. In most cases their financial income would be greater if they accepted the frequent invitations to leave the seminary for other positions. Their commitment is appreciated because the seminary would be weakened if there were among our faculty instability, uneasiness, wistful yearnings for greener pastures, or frequent turnover.

Of course, none of us should ever assume he or she has "arrived," and faculty are continuously upgrading skills and knowledge thanks to a generous sabbatical study leave program at SW. Most of them have earned additional degrees, illustrating again their commitment to the task of teaching and to excellence as their standard.

I agree with Dr. J. Howard Williams, former president of the Seminary, who said,

> The primary function of administration is to enable the faculty to deliver its fullest potential impact on the student body. The school, of course, exists for the student and the primary help to the student must come from the faculty. It is easy to be fond of our faculty as individuals, but it is far more important to so conduct the affairs of the seminary that these devoted friends may be able as servants of the Lord to give their best to this all important work "that the man of God may be perfect, thoroughly furnished unto all good works."

November 1982: Completing Five Years as President

(This column introduced my annual report for the 1981–1982 academic year. The report was printed in a separate brochure.)

December 1982: Summer Mission Practicum

(This column reported on the work of seventy-five students in a summer missions practicum led by Dr. Ebbie Smith. They spent ten weeks in thirteen states starting twenty-three churches, preaching revivals, and winning people to Christ. I also reported that Central Baptist Church in Lawton, Oklahoma, under the leadership of pastor Brad Allen provides scholarships for students at Southwestern. I appealed to other churches to do the same.)

1983

The Heart of Southwestern Is Our Students

Sometimes, in the routine "busyness" of the day-by-day work of the Seminary, it was easy to lose sight of the fact that our main focus should be on the students in our care. During one summer break, when nearly every student had traveled back home or to some mission point, a staff member jokingly said, "It's so wonderfully quiet! We could really have a great seminary if it weren't for all those noisy students!" Recognizing some truth in that humorous statement, we made a special effort in 1983 to focus on the importance of the student body.

With student needs in mind, we built the Atwood II building on the campus of Houston Baptist University for students in our off-campus center there, we remodeled Fleming hall and Scarborough Hall for expanded and improved class-rooms, provided an upgraded dining facility, and reorganized and expanded the Student Affairs division of the administration. More importantly, we revised the curriculum and degree offerings to meet student needs.

We constantly reminded ourselves that we had a unique and humbling opportunity to work with the largest gathering of men and women preparing for ministry in the history of theological education. However, it was not just the unprecedented size of the student body that impressed us, but the incredible range of its diversity. Notice in the May column that this year's students came from every state in the U.S. but four, as well as 33 foreign countries. They had degrees from 550 different colleges and universities, and while 95 percent belonged to 19 different Baptist groups, the rest represented 53 other Christian denominations. Ethnic, gender, and age diversity further enriched the total. What a potential for the spread of the gospel in our country and around the world. Indeed, the heart of Southwestern was our students!

Meanwhile, the fundamentalist plan to assume control of Southwestern continued at a rapid pace. Dallas attorney Ralph Pulley more and more became the point man on our board for the Patterson/Pressler agenda. In 1983, he garnered enough votes to change the way the officers of the board were elected. Five years earlier, we encouraged the board to implement a nominating committee process whereby a vice chair would typically become chair after two years. This provided a more thoughtful, forward-looking continuity. But Pulley wanted to return to the old plan of election from the floor, which made it easier to manipulate the elections to get their people in office.

I continued to confront and address the takeover efforts in a variety of venues, including my columns. The January column, for example, raises a fear that has turned out to be prophetic: "If the debate we are involved in continues long, we may find ourselves as a convention completely out of touch with our primary reason for existence and on a dangerous and expensive detour."

The accuracy of that 1983 prediction is reflected in the comments made by SBC leaders after their 2004 convention meeting in Indianapolis. Jimmy Draper, president of the Baptist Sunday School Board (Lifeway), warned that the convention was battling over trivial issues and had lost its focus. As a result, he said, younger leaders felt left out and had lost interest in denominational matters. Morris Chapman, president of the SBC Executive Committee, warned that in becoming "censorious, exclusivistic, and intolerant," the convention might be headed toward separatism, which he said would be worse than liberalism. He chided his fellow-fundamentalists for leaving good people out and for practicing "politics for the sake of control by a few."

Key Events in 1983

February

14   • Led Biblical Authority conferences in Florence, AL, and Nashville, TN
24   • Carl Henry spoke in chapel
28-29   • Led Biblical Authority Conference in Tucson, AZ

March

1 • Began another round of dialogues in each faculty members office

2 • Led Biblical Authority Conference in OK

10 • Dedicated Tandy Archeological Museum at Southwestern

21 • Trustee meeting—observed seventy-fifth anniversary of Southwestern

• Professor Robert Baker addressed trustees on denominational emphasis

• V.P. Lloyd Elder resigned to take Baptist Sunday School Board position

• Merger with Hispanic Seminary in San Antonio

• Named Lucille Glasscock Mission Center

• Elected Daniel Sanchez, Paul Gritz, Lucien Coleman, Wesley Black, Bruce Leafblad to faculty

23 • John Sullivan, Executive Director of Florida Baptist Convention, spoke in chapel

29 • Led Biblical Authority Conference at First Baptist, Orlando, FL

April

21 • Evangelist Louis Palau spoke in chapel

• Carl Henry lectured at Southwestern

• Broke ground for Atwood II building on HBU campus in Houston to house Southwestern's off-campus center

18 • Led Biblical Authority Conference at Gambrell St. Baptist Church, Fort Worth

May

• Martin Marty lectured at Southwestern. Used term "Baptistification"

June

11 • SBC met in Pittsburgh

• Jimmy Draper elected unopposed

• 13,740 messengers

• Charles Stanley elected Pastors Conference president. He also served as chairman of committee on boards.

July

23 • Led Biblical Authority Conference at Glorieta, NM

September

12 • Led Biblical Authority Conference at First Baptist, Nashville

24 • Led Biblical Authority Conference at Lakeside Baptist Church, Dallas

• Letter from Paul Pressler asking us to have him, Paige Patterson, or Russell Kaemmerling speak at Southwestern

• Remodeled Fleming Hall, Scarborough Hall, and dining facilities

October

10   • Inauguration of President Frank Pollard at Golden Gate Seminary

12   • Dan Yeary, pastor in Florida, preached for Seminary revival

17-19 • Fall trustee meeting

       • Adopted housing provision (deferred compensation) for president; elected Jeter Basden and Hubert Martin as Vice Presidents

       • At end of meeting, as usual, Ralph Pulley brought up new issues. They adopted officer election procedure to bypass nominating committee, which was harder for fundamentalist group to control

Note: In the fall meeting of 1983, the thirty-six-member board of trustees had the following composition: 10 hard-core fundamentalists, 21 traditional mainstream Baptists, and 5 swing voters.

January 1983: A Personal and Denominational Word

A PERSONAL WORD. . . As 1982 comes to a close, a number of personal milestones cannot go unnoticed. One is the fact that I have completed five years as president of Southwestern. At our recent faculty/staff awards luncheon, five-year service awards went to four faculty members, one housing director, one security office, one carpenter, one plumber and one president! It hardly seems possible, but it has been five years and they have been gratifying ones.

Other personal family milestones for which Betty and I recently have been grateful: Robert, our oldest, received the master of divinity degree in December and began work as a writer for the Baptist Joint Committee on Public Affairs in Washington, D.C.; Nancy a public school teacher, was married December 18 to Nolan Duck, a seminary graduate (and student) who is minister of youth at North Richland Hills Baptist Church here in Fort Worth; and Ellen, our youngest, having completed her first year on the Master of Religious Education degree, began work as interim minister of youth at Broadway Baptist Church here in Fort Worth; my parents, Hooper and Opal Dilday, have just moved to Fort Worth where Dad is receiving nursing care and Mom lives close by to look after him.

So much of our personal and family life in addition to vocational responsibilities is vitally connected to Southwestern, and we all feel a growing sense of appreciation for and indebtedness to this great institution as we begin our next five years in Fort Worth.

A DENOMINATIONAL WORD. . . We at Southwestern continue to be greatly concerned about the denomination controversy that threatens the unity and effectiveness of the convention. Recent meetings called by the convention president have brought together some of the outspoken personalities in the controversy as well as leaders of Southern Baptist Convention agencies. The discussions suggest that the issues in the debate are grouped into three categories:

(1) BIBLICAL AUTHORITY: It seems that while, with only·rare exceptions, Baptists hold to the inspiration and authority of the word of God, there is diversity in the vocabulary various Baptists choose to express their belief in the absolute sufficiency of the Scriptures. It seems to me we ought to accept each other's terminology and affirm the fact that nearly all of us as Baptists believe the Bible is the authoritative word of God.

(2) BIBLICAL INTERPRETATION: It is clear from the meetings also that Baptists differ in the way they interpret such teachings as eschatology (last things), the role of women in the church, church/state relationships, etc. This diversity is obvious when one listens to convention debates on resolutions and when one sees the different positions on the same issue taken in state conventions and successive sessions of the Southern Baptist Convention. Only the most unrealistic Baptist would expect us all to agree on all the issues. Our historical tradition has been diversity within unity.

(3) CONVENTION POLITICS: Much of the current debate swirls around such questions as who's going to win? Who's going to control appointments? Who's going to be elected? etc. Political organization has emerged as a recent newcomer to Southern Baptist Convention life. Party loyalty is given high profile creating divisiveness, confrontation, and scrambling for votes. All this tends to detour us from primary convention purposes.

The purpose of the Southern Baptist Convention has always been missions and evangelism and never doctrinal orthodoxy or hermeneutical uniformity. We have been strong because of voluntary cooperation to do missions rather than coerced lock-step doctrinal unanimity. If the debate we are involved in continues long, we may find ourselves as a convention completely out of touch with our primary reason for existence and on a dangerous and expensive detour.

A personal message scribbled on a Christmas card we received said: "May 1983 be a happy and rewarding year for you and may all Southern Baptists— liberals, moderates, conservatives, fundamentalists, neo-fundamentalists, inerrantists and mainstream denominationalists—support and acclaim Southwestern."

I long for the day when we can again affirm the diversity within our unity as a Bible believing convention of Southern Baptist churches and recognizing the pettiness of it all, laugh at ourselves a little bit, and get back to the main task our Lord has given us.

February 1983: Southwestern Seminary Cares

DO WE CARE ABOUT STUDENTS?

That question is raised from time to time at Southwestern—sometimes by a student who feels he has been overlooked, or by faculty members who are sometimes overwhelmed by large enrollments that make it difficult to give personal attention. Sometimes it is asked by a staff member who deals with repeated student demands until patience wears thin and there has been an unfortunate exchange of words. It's a legitimate question to be raised in the world's largest seminary.

Seminary administration is inevitably involved in the major institutional objectives of finances, fund raising, building programs, campus improvements, and denominational concerns, which by virtue of their high priority are given visibility in reports, news releases, and announcements.

Therefore, because of this fact, the impression is given that we are "always talking about money, donors, fund-drive goals, or building programs" and are giving little attention to individual students.

It should be obvious that the seminary would never have survived these 75 years, much less grown to its present position of strength, if enormous measures of energy and time had not been spent in fund raising and institutional promotion. Media exposure, recognitions and promotional efforts are essential to the development programs that generate the financial support SW needs each year. No apology is needed for this—in fact, congratulations to the development personnel is appropriate for the effective work they have done. Their purpose is ultimately "student centered." We are not just building a great institution, but providing the very best we can to individual students who now and in the future will enroll at Southwestern.

While there is always room for improvement, I have been pleased to see abundant evidences on our campus of a sincere and at times sacrificial concern for students:

(1) OPEN DOOR POLICIES make faculty and staff readily available to students.

(2) CREATIVE APPROACHES are taken by professors to get to know and give individual attention to students. Many have students in their homes and provide special office hours for personal conferences.

(3) A NEWLY REORGANIZED AND EXPANDED ORIENTATION PROGRAM, including individual academic counseling helps students get a good start at the seminary.

(4) A NEWLY REORGANIZED STUDENT AFFAIRS DIVISION tries to provide the best possible environment for students while they are here.

(5) THERE IS A PERVASIVE ATTITUDE that the student is first—the reason for our existence at Southwestern.

(6) SPECIAL PRAYER TIMES are held in staff and faculty meetings to intercede on behalf of students facing personal difficulties.

(7) SECOND MILE SERVICES are rendered including trips to the airport, housing assistance, hospital visits, financial help, spiritual counseling and the like which are over and above the call of duty.

Lawrence T. Lowrey, longtime president of Blue Mountain College in Mississippi, had an interesting comment for visitors who came to the campus during the summer when there were no students. He would say, "we are happy to have you at Blue Mountain, but I regret that the college is not here. I can show you some buildings and the campus, but the college has gone home for the summer!" Dr. Lowrey knew that first of all the college is students. That's true here at the seminary, too.

Our record may not be perfect but the intention of the seminary is clear—we do care about students and are striving to translate that concern into daily action.

March 1983: Visiting with Faculty

Five years ago as president-elect of Southwestern, I scheduled an hour's visit in each faculty member's office. There was no agenda except to listen to the professors' concerns for the seminary and their vision of what we ought to be in the future. The majority of them I already knew—former teachers of mine or colleagues with whom I have worked in the ensuing years since I was a student. But others were new to me, so the sessions became valuable opportunities to get acquainted.

Not only did these appointments verify my opinion of this faculty as committed men and women who love the Lord, His word, and His work, but my opinion of them as a group of able scholars was reinforced as well. Since we were about to launch strategic planning for 1980–85, their input was a valuable base for setting the objectives for Vision 85.

Now five years have passed. Most of the goals of Vision 85 are either accomplished or well on their way to achievement by target date. Initial stages of planning for 1985–1990 have begun and once again I am sitting down with each of our teachers to listen.

I have been in the offices of over one-third of our faculty in the past few weeks and my impressions are already forming:

(1) There is a unanimous enthusiasm among the faculty about teaching at Southwestern. They consider their calling a privilege and are optimistic about the future.

(2) There is among them a grateful sense of fulfillment at the progress made during these past five years toward the goals and objectives this seminary has adopted.

(3) They are awed and humbled by the challenge of unprecedented enrollments and the constant pressure to maintain spiritual vitality along with academic excellence.

(4) They would like to help Southwestern assume a place of leadership and influence with a strong, conservative, biblical, evangelistic, missionary, practical, scholarly approach to training ministers and through publications, conferences, and continuing education offer this same kind of leadership to the entire denomination.

It doesn't require the gift of prophesy to predict that with God's help and Southwestern's excellent faculty (including twenty-six new ones who have joined us since 1978) the challenge of the next five years will be met.

April 1983: Moving in the Mainstream of Megatrends

(John Naisbitt's *Megatrends* had become a bestseller, and in this column I listed his trends for the future and pointed out how Southwestern existed to change some trends, but that we must take advantage of other trends as we move into the future. The seminary was doing a great job of keeping up with and capitalizing on:

(1) A shift from an industrial society to an information society.

(2) A parallel growth of "hi-tech/hi-touch."

(3) A shift from national to world interests.

(4) Decentralization of authority, regionalism, participative leadership styles, and networks of people rather than hierarchies of pyramid-like organizations.

(5) Shift of U.S. population from the north to the southwest and Florida.

(6) Shift from "either/or" to multiple options.)

May 1983: Statistics

There are fifty-three denominations represented in our student body including nineteen Baptist groups. After Southern Baptists, the largest denomination represented is Assemblies of God with twenty-nine. The total non-Baptist enrollment at the seminary is only five percent.

Only four states are not represented in this year's enrollment: Nevada, New Hampshire, Rhode Island and the District of Columbia. Five hundred and forty-nine different colleges and universities are represented this year.

There are some trends, which are obvious. One is an increasing number of students coming from state or public colleges and universities and decreases in the number of students coming from Baptist and other church related schools. Economics may be a factor in this trend. We are also seeing older students coming to the seminary after having been in various careers following college. And there is a much more diverse representation of vocational choices as the students come with clearly focused convictions of God's direction in their lives. It is the only place in the world where this many men and women are together on one campus with not only the common experience of salvation through faith in Jesus Christ but convinced of His call into ministry and missions.

No wonder a recent visitor on the campus said, "One feels and senses a spirit here that is not felt anywhere else in the world."

June 1983: Pittsburgh Report

(This column summarized my report to the SBC meeting in Pittsburgh. We used a videotape along with my report to emphasize students. Following an introduction with a helicopter view of the campus showing the new library, the new bookstore, the new plant building, and the Tarrant Association office now under construction, and after a brief look inside the A. Webb Roberts Library featuring the new Tandy Archaeological Museum, the majority of the seven-minute film features brief testimonies of students like the following: There is Ioan Moldavan, a Romanian evangelist who was persecuted and expelled from Romania because of his gospel preaching. Dr. Lydia Girgis is a physician from Egypt whose father was a student at Southwestern in the 1930s and who herself will return to Egypt to continue the work of her preacher father. Charles McGlothlin was the Comptroller at Conoco Oil whom God called to preach at the age of fifty and then guided him to Southwestern to prepare for that calling.

(The tape closed with students singing in a chapel service in Truett Auditorium "To God Be the Glory.")

July/August 1983: Cost of Seminary Underwritten by Southern Baptists

John B. Hancock Jr. graduated from the seminary this past May. He and his wife, Kathy, are foreign mission volunteers. This letter printed in the *Oklahoma Baptist Messenger* is an excellent description from a student's viewpoint of the contributions Southern Baptists make to seminary education.

As I come to the end of my time of preparation and training here at Southwestern and reflect back over the countless blessings I have received from my time here, I am immediately overwhelmed that such an experience has been mine.

I am also mindful that unless so much of the cost of my seminary education had been underwritten by Southern Baptists I would probably have never been able to afford such quality instruction. For example, my tuition for a full class load was $1,234 per semester. However, $633 or 51 percent of this was provided by Cooperative Program funds, $376 or 31 percent was provided by Southwestern, leaving me $225 to pay for the semester. This is 18 percent of the total amount! These figures take on an even more stunning dimension when we realize that seminaries of an equal or even lesser caliber than Southwestern must charge their students as much as five to ten times this amount per semester.

It is no small blessing, Southern Baptists, that you have chosen to give about 4 percent of your Cooperative Program budget to Southwestern to underwrite my education. I am indeed grateful.

I know that I speak for a host of Oklahoma Southwestern students when I say thank you Southern Baptists for making my seminary education a reality financially. Thank you also for your support of Southwestern as it extends the vision of our Lord Jesus Christ to the generations which follow.

September 1983: A New Academic Year

The seminary's seventy-sixth academic year has just begun. At Salado, TX, the faculty spent a few days in prayer, planning, and preparation for the new year. It's called a retreat, but in reality, it is the first event of another demanding and challenging twelve months as we preview new features of the next three semesters.

A new catalog describes new courses that are being offered on new schedules (the result of continued expansion into evening hours, Mondays, and soon with courses on Saturdays!)

Slightly more than 1,000 new students are expected to register for the first time on "the Hill" and at the first chapel they will be officially dubbed "Southwesterners" by the president.

Professors occupy beautiful new offices on the third floor of Fleming Hall where space in the old library has been transformed into a first class facility for a first class faculty. Before this academic year is over, the remaining two floors of Fleming will be completed providing desperately needed classrooms and offices for the World Mission/Church Growth Center, the Continuing Education Center, the Christian Communications Center, Church/Minister Relations and several administrative functions.

In the Naylor Student Center, a new dining area features a new salad, soup and sandwich facility and a newly decorated cafeteria where a greatly improved menu will be offered to students and staff.

But most important of all, let me tell you about some new people who joined the leadership team this fall.

Five new faculty members began their service at Southwestern. They are Wesley Black, instructor in youth education, from the Sunday School Board; Lucien Coleman, professor of adult education, from Southern Seminary; Paul Gritz, instructor in church history, a PhD candidate from Southwestern; Bruce Leafblad, associate professor of church music, from Bethel College and Seminary in St. Paul, MN; and Daniel Sanchez, associate professor of missions, from the Baptist Convention of NY.

A new seminary physician also began his work at the Walsh Medical Center to fill a recent vacancy. He is John Adams, medical missionary from Kenya who is on leave after twenty years of foreign mission service. John and Martha, a missionary nurse, are long-time personal friends who bring to Southwestern not only their medical skills but also a profound commitment to missions and to the seminary's purpose in equipping God-called ministers.

So much is new as we begin the fall semester, but thank God, much of Southwestern life is "old." Faithful personnel who have served here for years will continue their quality work, the spirit of the seminary remains the same unchanging spirit we have all known and appreciated and our commitment to the unchanging truth of the gospel is the same yesterday, today and throughout the 1983–1984 academic year.

October 1983: Cooperative Program Dollar

(This column quoted a testimony from *Royal Service* magazine about the importance of the Cooperative Program in funding the training of ministers in our seminaries.)

November 1983: Annual Report

(The annual report for the 1982–1983 academic year was printed in a separate brochure, and my column for November introduced it.)

December 1983: Degree Terminology

One of the questions raised at state alumni meetings this fall related to the changes in the names of several of our traditional seminary degrees and the adding of new degrees not previously offered in the seminary curriculum. Does this indicate a "trend toward secularization" of seminary degrees?

Not at all. While the curricula of all our degrees is continually being upgraded, the basic theological courses a student must take for a seminary degree remain relatively unchanged. Why the changes then?

(1) ACADEMIC RECOGNITION. In academic circles, certain degrees are more readily recognized as teaching credentials. In the 70s, most seminaries changed the ThD to a PhD degree for that reason. Since the DMin degree has been added to provide for a professional advanced degree, the research and teaching degree was given the title PhD for academic recognition. In part, this explains why the MRE degree was changed to the MA in religious education and why the MCM was changed to the MM degree, but another reason is explained below.

(2) UPGRADING DEGREE LEVEL. For years the basic theological degree was a BD. In reality, this was at least a master's level degree since a bachelor's degree was a requirement for entrance. So in the 70s, most seminaries decided to change the name to MDiv. Recently, the same rationale was used to change the diploma that the seminary gives for non-college graduates to an associate degree. The change from diploma to associate was also approved by the Southern Association of Colleges and Schools.

(3) BIVOCATIONAL REASONS. While the seminary is not in the business of equipping public school teachers, we have discovered that a very effective bivocational ministry is available to people who can teach in public school and at the same time serve as pastor or staff minister in local churches.

Many school districts and foreign governments (such as Brazil) have not recognized the masters' degrees of our seminary graduates as additional preparation for teaching until the terminology of some of our degrees was changed to be more consistent with standard terminology.

Hence, the change from MRE to MA in religious education and the change from MCM to MM, the standard terminology for music teachers. This change already has proven to be a great blessing to foreign missionaries and to many bivocational ministers across the convention. The curricula for these two degrees remain essentially the same even though the terminology is different.

(4) NEW VOCATIONAL NEEDS. Some of the new degrees at Southwestern are created to provide training for church related vocations that have emerged recently in our convention life. The MA in Christian communications is an example. Churches are calling ministers of media and this new degree gives a student not only basic theological courses but also specialized courses in the use of media in ministry.

The new MA in church social services is another example. Also, a student can attend Southwestern and the University of Texas at Arlington and graduate with two degrees, MA/MSSW. Another illustration is the MA in marriage and family counseling certifying a person who is called of God into a ministry of counseling with special emphasis on staff positions in the local church. The MA in missiology is designed only for those missionaries who return on furlough and want additional specialized training.

These and other changes in no way suggest that the seminary is becoming a secular university or is moving away from its traditional purposes. Rather, they illustrate sensitivity on the part of SW to the emerging needs of our churches and denominational mission agencies and the desire of the seminary to be responsible and creative in attempting to meet these needs.

Below is listed all of the degrees now offered at Southwestern:

THEOLOGY: PhD, DMin, MDiv, MAMISS (Master of arts in missiology) ADiv, DipTh (Diploma in Theology, Hispanic Baptist Theological Seminary), CCE (Certificate in Christian Education, HBTS)

RELIGIOUS EDUCATION: EdD, GSRE, MARE, MACOMM, MACSS (Master of arts in church social services), MA/MSSW (Master of arts/Master of science in social work), ARE, (Associate Degree in Religious Education at HBTS) DipCRE (Diploma in Christian education, HBTS).

MUSIC: DMA, MM, MCM, ACM, DipREM (Associate degree in church music and Diploma in religious music at HBTS)

1984

It Is Now Clear

Looking back, I believe 1984 was the year the Patterson/Pressler assault on Southwestern reached its full cruising speed. They had succeeded in planting fifteen hard-core fundamentalists on our board of trustees, but there were still seventeen traditional, mainstream Baptists on the board who would resist them. Four others were "swing voters" who at times would give the fundamentalists a slim majority, and this emboldened them to step up their confrontations.

The heightened intensity of the fundamentalist crusade was also evident in the meeting of the Southern Baptist Convention in Kansas City, which the press labeled the most blatantly political convention in SBC history. I preached the annual sermon titled "Higher Ground," calling on Baptists to:

(1) Turn from the misty flats of forced uniformity to the higher ground of autonomous individualism.

(2) Turn from the muddy swamps of political coercion to the higher ground of spiritual persuasion.

(3) Turn from the barren plains of egotistic self-interest to the higher ground of Christ-like humility.

Back in Fort Worth, I decided it was time to share my concerns and convictions about our denominational conflict with the students. They were confused and anxious about their future in Baptist life, and frequently asked their teachers and me to tell them "what was going on." At my invitation, hundreds of students—some estimated more than 1,000—gathered under the shade of the huge pecan trees on the east lawn of the president's home for a forum on the convention. My presentation was called "It Is Now Clear," and basically what I said is recorded in the July/August column.

Another indicator that the takeover crusade was moving at full steam was the growing hostility at our fall board meeting. Dallas trustee Ralph Pulley instituted what became a regular pattern: waiting until the board meeting was nearly over and then asking for the floor to introduce a complaint. After a speech, he made the following motion: "I move in the best interests of Southwestern, having given the president the benefit of our counsel, that we now instruct him to refrain from overt and public pronouncements concerning and relating to the political activity of the SBC."

It may have been something of a test to see if they could garner a majority vote, but instead, a motion was made and passed by a slim majority to table his motion, and his attempt to silence the president failed. At their next meeting the Southwestern faculty passed the following resolution: "President Dilday has spoken out on the issues facing the SBC. We feel that he has both the right and the responsibility as a denominational leader to make his voice heard. Our president has pointed out real and serious dangers which threaten this seminary, as well as the entire work of the SBC. We share his concern and support his courageous stand."

Ironically, there were other incidents that suggested the Patterson/Pressler drive did not yet have full control. We could still elect faculty—including the election of a woman in the spring meeting—without undue interference from the hardliners. The board even passed a resolution in the fall meeting affirming the faculty. My wife Betty was elected president of the SBC Pastor's Wives Conference. I preached at Second Baptist Church, Houston, where Ed Young was pastor, participated in the celebration of Dr. W.A. Criswell's fortieth anniversary at First Baptist Dallas, and continued to be invited to preach for several Baptist State Conventions.

We also continued reaching out to our critics and attempting to find solutions to the mounting divisions. In August, I participated in dialogues with key Baptist laypeople from the Dallas/Fort Worth area who we thought might influence and discourage the political manuevering of the Patterson/Pressler party. I also had an interesting discussion with Jimmy Draper, who had written an angry letter rebuking me for my convention sermon in Kansas City. He said I had abused the privilege, etc. In September, I participated in what I thought would be a productive meeting of "high level" spokespersons from both sides including Criswell, Pressler, Patterson, Adrian Rogers, Jimmy Draper, and others. The discussion was lively and frank, but it accomplished little.

Key Events in 1984

March
19-21 • Spring trustee meeting—announced record enrollment 5120 in 1983/84 year
   • Announced dedication of Atwood II Building in Houston
   • Elected Winona Elder, Eldridge, Waller, Elley to faculty
   • Named new facility "James R. Leitch Physical Plant Building"
   • James Carter, pastor of University Baptist, Ft. Worth, gave Founders Day address

April
   • Roy Honeycut preached "Holy War" sermon at Southern Seminary

June
11-14 • SBC met in Kansas City; Charles Stanley elected over Grady Cothen and James Sullivan—52.18 percent; Draper presided; 17,101 messengers
13   • I preached "On Higher Ground." First seminary president to preach the convention sermon since E. Y. Mullins in 1901
   • Betty Dilday elected president of SBC Minister's Wives organization
   • Charles Stanley was elected even though he said he had never had time to be involved in the denomination! His church supported non-Southern Baptist Convention missionaries, he did not go to Baptist associational meetings or state conventions, etc.
   • The first vice president had never served as a messenger to an associational meeting, a state convention, or the SBC!
   • Fundamentalists now have floor managers—one for motions and another for resolutions. See quote in the *Dallas Times Herald* story about the convention. "Floor lieutenants were stationed throughout Kansas City's huge, football field shaped auditorium. Patterson or

another leader standing near the platform signaled the party preference for the vote."

- Paul Pressler manipulated his election to SBC Executive Committee
- This convention was called the most blatantly politicized demonstration of Patterson/Pressler party's five-year plan to take over. "It's a different convention," people said.

July
1   • Dean Bruce Corley presented critique of dispensationalism in chapel. "I could not in good conscience abide by the seminary Articles of Faith, the 1963 Baptist Faith and Message, if I were committed to dispensationalism."
3 & 5   • East Lawn gatherings for students to discuss SBC issues. I referenced Corley's chapel address and indicated that one of the issues dividing Baptists was dispensationalism. I said measured by the Baptist Faith and Message, classical dispensationalism would be considered a heresy. Firestorm of criticism erupted from fundamentalist leaders who accused me of saying premillennialism was a heresy!
5   • My article "It Is Now Clear" about SBC controversy printed in Southwestern News. Angered fundamentalists.

August
12   • Preached at Second Baptist Church, Houston
22   • Meetings with Dallas Laymen Dewey Pressley, Alton Reed, et al. to explore ways to stop takeover.

August
      • Meeting with Jimmy Draper to discuss my convention sermon. He had written letter saying the sermon was an "abuse of privilege, etc." At our meeting he said, "I was angry and shouldn't have written the letter."
      • Draper's book on biblical authority released—in response to mine?

September
21   • Dewey Presley, Alton Reid, Darold Morgan, Keith Parks, Bill Pinson, and I with W. A. Criswell, Paige Patterson, Paul Pressler, Jimmy Draper, and Adrian Rogers. Met with group all day discussing SBC controversy.
28   • Ralph Langley, pastor in Alabama, preached for Seminary revival

October

7 • Participated in W. A. Criswell's fortieth anniversary at First Baptist, Dallas

15 • Fall trustee meeting
  • Passed resolution affirming faculty
  • Approved Thad Roberts Chair on basis of David Smith's $500,000 gift
  • Approved PhD in Evangelism
  • Celebrated opening of newly renovated Fleming Hall
  • Executive session. I discussed impact of controversy on the Seminary
  • At end, Ralph Pulley made the following motion: "I move in the best interests of Southwestern, having given the president the benefit of our counsel, that we now instruct him to refrain from overt and public pronouncements concerning and relating to the political activity of the SBC." Second by Hugo Lindquist. Don Wideman moved it be tabled. The motion to table passed.

November

12 • Spoke at Tennessee Convention and pastors conference.

13 • Spoke at Georgia Convention.
  • Southwestern faculty passed resolution: "President Dilday has spoken out on the issues facing the SBC. We feel that he has both the right and the responsibility as a denominational leader to make his voice heard. Our president has pointed out real and serious dangers which threaten this seminary, as well as the entire work of the SBC. We share his concern and support his courageous stand."

15 • Alumni in Georgia passed resolution: "We encourage Dr. Dilday to speak his God-given convictions in matters related to the seminary and the SBC. Fellow Baptists should allow Dilday his personal freedom to speak out as a priest under God."

Note: In the fall meeting of 1984, the thirty-six-member board of trustees had the following composition: 15 hard-core fundamentalists, 17 traditional mainstream Baptists, and 4 swing voters.

January 1984: Dr. Virginia Brubaker

(Since Southwestern was an SBC seminary, I pointed out in this column that 96.3 percent of the students are Southern Baptists. However, the Seminary did minister to 154 from 47 other denominations including Dr. Virginia Brubaker, a missionary serving with the OMS International [formerly Oriental Missionary Society], an interdenominational agency. She came by by office to express gratitude for what Southwestern had meant to her. The quality of the courses, the professors, and the library were complimented, but her strongest words of praise were for the spiritual growth opportunities at the seminary.)

February 3, 1984: Physical Plant

Anderson (IN) College President Robert H. Reardon paid tribute to the physical plant managers on their campus in a recent "President's Corner" column. In that space in his college newspaper, he lauded those who kept the physical plant running and surmised that the resident philosophers and theologians on the faculty often did not realize what skill it took to run a campus. Then he said, "I never have known a philosopher or theologian who ever changed a light bulb."

That certainly is not the case at Southwestern. Our teachers are not "malevolent klutzes" and with down-to-earth practicality they are sensitive to the needs of operating the physical plant. However, the article did point up an important fact. Often we do not recognize the value of those on the seminary staff who change the light bulbs and carry on the other maintenance functions.

That particularly was true recently when a devastating cold wave hit our city. Housing units built for our normal climate here in North Texas were not able to withstand the extended period of near zero temperatures, and you can imagine the disasters that occurred. Gratefully, most of the crises on campus came while the majority of the seminary family was away for Christmas vacation.

Mr. James Leitch, director of bi-vocational training/physical plant, said,

> With the student exodus from the campus for the holidays came the most damaging cold weather we have ever had. Pipes were frozen that have been here since the seminary was established. We were faced with the mammoth job of taking care of 241 vacant housing units where students had gone home. As the pipes were frozen and thawed, this resulted in some 300 work orders for service. Frozen and broken pipes were in many of the Village Apartments, Cowden Hall, Fort Worth Hall—both in plumbing and fire-fighting pipes—Carroll Park and Rosemont apartments. Rosemont Apartments were probably the hardest hit and for most of the week they were without heat and water.

It was late on Christmas Day when we had our own disaster at the president's home on campus. A frozen pipe had broken in the attic and suddenly water was flooding through a wall to the first floor. I had to call Jim Leitch on Christmas Day for help. Even though it was Christmas day, he was there with his crew in a moment—just as he had responded to emergencies all week—and avoided what could have been a very expensive disaster.

All of this has highlighted again the necessity of expressing profound appreciation to these members of our staff. Most of them are seminary graduates who, along with their seminary responsibilities, serve churches in the immediate area as bivocational ministers. They are committed and dedicated craftsmen who could be making far more money in the secular world but who feel God's call to assisting the seminary in this way. Protecting our buildings and grounds, investments from Christian stewards through the years, is certainly a significant calling. These staff members are vital to the operation of our school.

So, at the risk of leaving out the names of some, let me simply say to the following: Jim Leitch, director of physical plant; Harlan Davis, plumbing supervisor; Fred Daniels, plumber; Raul Alvarado, plumber; Tim Leitch, preventative maintenance; Bill King, custodial services; Bill Sullivan, carpentry supervisor; and the security crew. "Congratulations for a job well done during the blizzard of '83 and for all the work you do in the operation of our physical plant."

March 1984: Economic Turbulence of the '80s

The business section of the *Dallas Morning News* is not the usual source for inspiration in writing the president's column. But today it did provide at least a starting point if not outright inspiration. The headlines are not encouraging. In fact, they were a little frightening and depressing:

"A Resurgent Braniff Airlines Limping Back Into Business After Bankruptcy"
"Fast-rising Condominium Empire Collapses"
"Overbuilding of Office Towers Floods Market with Oversupply"
"Suicide-marked Bank Scandal Threatens Community"
"University Struggles with Record Deficit"

This is not exactly the kind of reading that cheers you up for the day. The economic turbulence of the 80s presents the seminary with a challenge and calls for innovative and vigorous strategies in steering a prudent financial course into the future. How can the seminary avoid the calamities described in the headlines above?

Cooperative Program receipts for Southern Baptist Convention mission causes are down this year. In fact, some are predicting that for the first time in remembered history there will be a shortfall in the 1983–1984 Cooperative Program operating budget. It seems certain there will be no capital funds or challenge funds available this year (Southwestern would have received $700,000 for capital projects and $571,598 for operations from challenge funds.)

The Executive Committee is projecting only 2.7 percent increase for the seminaries in next year's operating budget, and now it seems likely that the capital funds planned for 1984–1985 also will have to be postponed.

This has a serious impact on the seminary because one-half of our operating budget comes from the Cooperative Program, and our building and renovation projects depend on these capital funds for completion. Add to this the reduced income we are receiving from endowment funds because of lower interest rates and other economic factors, and the seriousness of the current financial situation is clear.

We have, of course, taken appropriate action to adjust expenditures this year and next to bring them in line with reduced revenues. Student matriculation fees will be increased this next fall, but the greatest help will come from increased gifts and grants from churches, individuals and foundations.

Southwestern's development department, under the leadership of John Seelig, has done an excellent job in fund raising. Our present campaign to raise $25 million by 1985 is on schedule. These efforts to secure the funds needed to keep up with the growth in seminary enrollments and to underwrite new programs and capital projects will become more aggressive than ever, and assistance from the alumni and friends of the seminary is more important now than at any time in our recent past.

Sometimes the question is raised, "Why is the seminary always talking about money?" I hope the information above answers that concern convincingly and motivates all of us who value Southwestern's ministry to pitch in and help. Pray for the students, faculty and administration, and especially for those who lead in development activities. Encourage donors you know to give, and be a part of the financial support yourself. It has been that kind of cooperative support that has seen the seminary through other difficult times in the past.

Of course, our confidence in the future lies not in the efficiency of our plans or people, but in the confidence that this seminary belongs to God and we depend upon His providential guidance to see it through.

April 1984: B. H. Carroll

If he had paid a visit to Southwestern today, B. H. Carroll would know he had not been forgotten. On the way to the campus, he would pass the seminary's B. H. Carroll Apartments and nearby B. H. Carroll School. Entering the north gate, he would see the imposing B.H. Carroll Memorial Building, which displays his portrait and bronze bust in its central rotunda.

Every student and professor, long familiar with his white-bearded features, would recognize and greet him by name. He would be gratified as he sat down in Truett Auditorium to discover that today was "Founders Day," an annual recognition of Southwestern heritage. But imagine his surprise, when glancing at the printed program, Carroll would see his own picture and the topic: "Living in the Lengthened Shadow of B. H. Carroll." Forgotten? Hardly. The moving address by Dr. James Carter—bringing tears to his eyes as it did to ours—would convince him he was remembered.

The surprises would continue in the Student Center where he would be the guest of honor at the annual B. H. Carroll Awards Luncheon. Along with the greats and near-greats of Fort Worth and Dallas, he would applaud the three couples being honored for their contributions to Southwestern: the Jim Cantrells, the Ray Grahams, and the Rufus Higginbothams.

Would B. H. Carroll be surprised at the school he left behind 70 years ago? Yes—at its enrollment of 5,120, at its 12 new buildings, at its renowned faculty, at its vast library collection, at its immense budget. Some of the new courses would bewilder him too: "Computers in the Ministry of the Church," "Urban Strategies in Cross-cultural Missiology," "Televangelism," "Shenckerian Analysis in Church Music." But he would smile, remembering that his visionary proposals were considered bewildering in his day. The remarkable changes would amaze but not faze him.

Other things about modern Southwestern would not surprise Carroll. Expecting to find here the same spirit of evangelism and missions which marked his day, it would be no surprise that over 30 percent of our students are mission volunteers. He would say "Amen" at the report in our trustees' meeting that scores of persons were won to Christ this spring by students in "Pioneer Penetration." It would not surprise him that, while the seminary offers a diverse curriculum with innovative specializations, most of the students—85 percent of them—still take the basic degrees that equip them to be pastors, ministers of education and music, missionaries and evangelists. It would be no surprise that Southwestern teachers are godly, Bible-believing Southern Baptists who combine academic excellence with practicing churchmanship.

What would B. H. Carroll think? He would be grateful that his last advice for Southwestern was still being followed: "Keep the seminary lashed to the cross of Christ."

May 1984: Computer Age on Seminary Hill

My article for this issue of the *Southwestern News* is different, because I'm composing it on my TRS-80 Model 4P computer in my study at home. Even though I'm not technologically inclined, I have learned to tap away at the keyboard and watch the silver letters jog across the screen forming sentences like those in this very paragraph.

It's incredible! Forget correction tape, white correction fluids or erasers, because corrections, deletions and changes can be made in a flash with the punch of a button. Now that I've tried it, I would rather write with the computer than dictate on a cassette recorder. Since I can actually see my words on the screen, I can fiddle with the sentences myself until they're just right, and then print out a perfect copy. No need to wait for the rough draft from the typist to be corrected and then typed again. One step does it all. After printing a copy for my use here at home, I then dial the seminary, Switch on my modem, connect my computer with the seminary's word processor and send my article over the telephone line for printing.

Yes, the computer age has dawned on Seminary Hill! Courses in computer applications for church management are already being taught in our curriculum. Continuing education seminars offered this year discuss how computer technology can be used in ministry. Growing numbers of professors are using personal computers in their disciplines. Our library catalog is "on-line" and accessible from remote locations by persons with microcomputers. We're developing a theological and biblical database similar to other information services around the country. Soon you can "log on" to STABIS (Southwestern's Theological and Biblical Information Service) and transfer directly to your personal computer information on a variety of relevant subjects. A computer laboratory classroom will soon be in place to teach computer techniques. We're convinced the computer is having and will have an enormous impact on the ministry.

In fact, I'm completing a book, *The Micro Computer: A Minister's Personal Resource*, written from the perspective of a person who has known absolutely nothing about computers but has learned to become an enthusiastic user. Its premise is: "If I can learn, you can learn."

While maintaining our primary commitment to the basic tasks of theological education, we want to do everything we can to "redeem" modern technological tools for the Lord in order that our students and, for that matter, all of us may better perform the work to which He has called us.

June 1984: Southwestern Report
to Convention 1983–84

(This column summarized my report before the Kansas City meeting of the SBC, including the fact that annual enrollment of 5,120 was the largest in the history of theological education.)

July/August 1984: It Is Now Clear

Since our meeting in Kansas City, several important facts about the confrontational dissention in our Southern Baptist Convention are now clear.

(1) For several years rumors have circulated that a massive, well-organized political machine was operating with the intent of taking control of the Southern Baptist Convention. The name "Patterson/Pressler Party" has been given to this effort. **IT IS NOW CLEAR** that the rumors were not true. The situation is actually worse than the rumors suggest. There is a powerful machine computerized, national in scope, and aimed at control of the democratic processes of this convention. The leaders of the machine have publicly acknowledged its existence and have boasted about its success. They have stated their goals as "going for the jugular," that is, taking over control of the boards of our agencies and institutions. They have publicly accused our board members of being "dumb bunnies and rubber stamps," and have publicly claimed that they already control the Baptist Sunday School Board and other areas of convention life. One spokesman indicated that when a few more fundamentalists are elected to the seminary boards, "perhaps in five more years, more than 50 percent of the professors will be under pressure from trustees to resign."

The acknowledged leaders of the machine have indicated that their strategy is to elect the president of the Southern Baptist Convention who in turn appoints the committee that names those who eventually nominate board members. Their strategy involves bringing as many messengers as possible to at least the one crucial day of the convention. Hotel and plane reservations are offered to pastors who will attend and bring messengers. They encourage bus and van transportation for others. In some cases hotel expenses and airfares have been paid for by the political organization. Through the use of widely circulated independent newspapers and computerized mail, messengers thus recruited are told how to vote. Sometimes the attacks on persons being considered for the presidency are vicious and inaccurate. The terms "liberal" and "moderate" are used to prejudice messengers against opposing candidates and issues.

Their strategy is to influence the order of business committee and the resolutions committee to schedule decisions they consider crucial on that one day when most of their people have been brought in. (Notice about 17,000 voted for the president on Tuesday and only about 6,000-8,000 voted on the issues of the other days.)

Has there been political activity in our convention before the Patterson/Pressler machine was organized? Yes, but only informal, spontaneous efforts that could in no way be compared to the ambitious techniques or the national scope of the present political organization. Since the Patterson/Pressler machine has emerged, other groups have tried to organize in opposition, but these efforts have been modest and obviously ineffective compared to the massive successes of the fundamentalist organization. This is no longer rumor, innuendo, or hearsay. It is fact. This is now clear and it is deplorable.

(2) **IT IS NOW CLEAR** that the real issue in the debate is not conservative versus liberal theology. While there may have been at the beginning genuine concerns about liberalism in our convention, **IT IS NOW CLEAR** that such concerns are a mask for other interests.

FACT NUMBER ONE: The evidence raised by the Patterson/Pressler machine to prove that the Southern Baptist Convention is "drifting toward liberalism" is too thin to support that claim. For seven years we have asked for specific examples of liberalism and the same half-dozen illustrations are offered. Most of these are marginal at best. Some are out of date, and have already been dealt with by administrators and boards. They do not in the least suggest that Southern Baptists are becoming liberal. If there has been such a drift (and I don't believe there is), the concerns of Southern Baptists, heightened by the controversy, have by now soundly reversed it. The evidence is simply not there.

Southern Baptists are a conservative, Bible-believing people, and our institutions and agencies, while not perfect and while always needing vigilant supervision, are more resolute in staying in the mainstream of Southern Baptist theology than ever before in history and God is blessing them with unprecedented strength.

FACT NUMBER TWO: **IT IS NOW CLEAR** that the issue is not liberal versus conservative theology because leading conservatives with unquestioned orthodoxy are voicing their opposition to the fundamentalist political machine. It is not a matter of conservatives on one side and liberals on the other, but strong conservatives on both sides of this debate. The issue divides itself more accurately along the lines of "the spirit of Southern Baptist cooperation" on one side and "the spirit of independent fundamentalism" on the other. Will we continue to be a convention cooperating to do missions and education, or will we revert to the "society method" with its designated support of favorite benevolences? Remember, it was over the issue of the "convention method" versus the "society method" of doing our work that Southern Baptists separated to become a cooperating convention in 1845.

IT IS NOW CLEAR that the main differences in the debate are related to interpretation of the Bible but not biblical authority. The issue is not "Do you believe the Bible?" but "How do you interpret some of its passages?"

Other issues are: "Who's going to win? Who's going to control the convention? What kind of convention will we be in the future?" This is now clear and it is disturbing.

(3) **IT IS NOW CLEAR** that mainstream Southern Baptists must act to reclaim the convention from the manipulation of political machines and return it to the people. We must restore an open convention and forbid secular politicization from dominating and becoming the pattern of the future. We must shun the blatant power-struggles and redeploy our energies and resources to the priority of obeying our Lord's commission. This is now clear and it is urgent.

September 1984: Wartburg Castle, Eisenach, East Germany

Wartburg Castle, Eisenach, East Germany, majestic fortress of the elector Frederick III. We walked through its ancient rooms remembering the months Martin Luther lived here under Frederick's protection from 1521-22. It's hard not to be impressed when you enter the very room where Luther sat month after month to translate the New Testament into German. A man of deep conviction who said, "Here I stand, I can do no other," Luther is a noble example of a courage that stands by convictions at all costs.

But it was the story of another resident of Wartburg Castle that inspired me the most. "Since you are Baptists," our guide said to our Baptist World Alliance tour group, "I want to show you something we don't usually show regular tourists." She led us across the castle courtyard to the tall stone tower on the castle wall, up ancient steps to a locked door halfway to the top of the tower. Unlocking the door and turning on a light switch, she gathered us around an opening in the floor covered by an iron grate. A light bulb had been suspended into the dungeon 30 feet below. It was not in the comfortable splendor of

Luther's room in the palace above, but here in the dark, dirty dungeon 10 feet in diameter where the other resident of Wartburg Castle had stayed.

His name was Fritz Erbe, a courageous lay leader from nearby Herda. In the mid-16th century (around the time Luther came from Worms to Wartburg), Fritz Erbe was lowered into that terrible hole because he would not give up his Anabaptist convictions. Days stretched into weeks, and months, and then years. Any day Fritz Erbe could have changed his mind. He could have recanted his Baptist convictions and immediately been released—back to daylight, family, to his farm, and freedom. But he didn't. One year, two, four, seven, eight years he was imprisoned until he died there in the dungeon.

He suffered not because he was a Christian, but because he held some of the same basic convictions that we Baptists hold today! (It is no surprise that because of his steadfast courage, half of the residents in his hometown of Herda were converted to Anabaptist belief.)

As I peered into that dark pit, I wondered if there are any Fritz Erbes among us today. Are there those among us who would stay in a horrible dark hole for eight years rather than compromise and surrender our Baptist convictions? Would we die for our faith? I don't suppose we know how courageous we would be until a moment of truth—when we are confronted with the choice.

But in the light of the example of our Baptist forefather Fritz Erbe, I am saddened to see so many today who are willing to surrender and compromise our Baptist heritage so casually. To care so little about the basic tenets of Baptist belief which others have suffered and died to preserve is to me one of the sad travesties of our current denominational conflict.

Oh yes, to stand by those convictions is not always popular. In fact, it may cause you public criticism, rejection by the majority political party, and perhaps a recommendation to another church. But it cost Fritz Erbe his freedom and his life!

Four hundred years later, we're grateful for his persevering courage. Our hope is that years from now other Baptists will be grateful for the courageous convictions of 20th century Southern Baptists who were willing, with God's help, to "keep the faith."

October 1984: The Seminary Is in Hearts of Churches

(In this column I reported how an independent evangelical seminary boasted that their seminary was in the heart of the churches because 2,000 churches provided direct support for their school. Through the Cooperative Program of mission giving, 32,000 Southern Baptist churches had Southwestern in their budgets! Those churches also endorsed and sent us the largest number of students in the history of theological education. These same churches call our graduates as their pastors, ministers, and staff leaders to serve in the increasing range of church vocational positions.

I concluded the column by saying, "It's not bragging. It's a fact! Southwestern is in the hearts of our churches, and we are grateful.")

November 1984: "Do Right and Go Forward"

Southwestern and the other Southern Baptist Convention seminaries have been the targets of criticism during the past few years of denominational controversy. While criticism that is baseless and generalized is unfair and destructive, there nevertheless has emerged from the controversy some positive good.

For one thing, we must acknowledge that no human institution is perfect. Resisting the natural inclination to become defensive, we are learning in this present controversy to listen and to learn from criticism, and to strive for improvement. As a result, we will be a stronger institution.

Secondly, the criticism has encouraged us at Southwestern to re-examine our basic purposes and to reaffirm our unique role in Southern Baptist life.

In a recent interview, Billy Graham was asked who would be the leaders of the evangelical world in the future. He answered, "The next leaders of the evangelical world will not be individuals but institutions—like Southwestern Seminary in Fort Worth, TX." Later I visited with Dr. Graham to ask him about that statement. We talked about the incomparable strength of Southwestern—its size, resources, location, faculty, and heritage. Almost half of the theological students in the Southern Baptist Convention are enrolled here. We have the most advanced and functional theological library in the U.S. We enjoy the healthiest denominational support of any evangelical school. This rare combination of advantages has put us on the threshold of a significant new role of leadership in the evangelical world. While Fuller, Dallas, Gordon-Conwell, Trinity, and other evangelical schools as well as Princeton, Harvard, Chicago, and Yale are making significant contributions, Southwestern is in a position to become the foremost leader in evangelical theological education. This seminary ought to be producing the best publications, research, lectures, and critical insight in the Christian world.

While seeking a balance between the essential task of classroom instruction (the heaviest of any in the world) and scholarly research and publication, we want to see the day when the best book on any theological subject is by a Southwestern author—balanced, biblical, conservative, and scholarly.

Our approach is distinctive:

(1) Southwestern's approach is biblical—not secular or humanistic on the one hand, but on the other hand not "bibliolatrist." We hold the Bible as the perfect word of God, in its proper place in the pattern of authority with the Supremacy of the Father and the Lordship of Christ. We believe the seminary can be committed to scholarship without yielding its commitment to biblical authority.

(2) Southwestern's approach is theologically conservative—not avant-garde or liberal on the one hand, but on the other hand not narrow, brittle, legalistic, anti-intellectual, or as one veteran missionary put it, "feudamentalist."

(3) Southwestern's approach is scholarly—not rationalistic or philosophical on the one hand, but on the other hand not scholastic or pedantic either. We believe faith comes before reason. It is not necessary to build up airtight intellectual arguments before one can believe. Faith is reasonable, but God's truth has nothing to fear from scholarly inquiry or critical thought.

(4) Southwestern's approach is positive and practical—not secluded in the cloistered isolation of esoteric academia on the one hand, but on the other hand not wasting time on negative, polemic, argumentative theological combat. Education at Southwestern is rooted in practice and ought to result in preachers who can preach, ministers who can win souls and build churches and missionaries who can cross cultural barriers with the gospel.

(5) Southwestern's approach is one of open inquiry and critical intellectual examination within the context of faith and revelation. We are not philosophical agnostics who try to approach our task without presuppositions, but neither do we hide our faith behind defensive obscurantism, fearful of examination.

(6) Southwestern's approach is to serve the vast cross section of our people. We will neither turn our backs on our most gifted students, nor design our training exclusively for the intellectual elite. We will take a balanced approach, teaching the average and the brightest, those with limited backgrounds and those whom the Lord has blessed with scholarly research ability.

(7) Southwestern's approach is Christ-centered, evangelistic, global, congregational, denominational, scholarly, and spiritual.

Committed to these distinctives, we will neither be drawn aside by the modernists, liberals, humanists, or secularists on the extreme left, nor will we be intimidated or controlled by the negative, narrow, legalistic, anti-intellectual, independent extremists on the right. Instead, we will claim our biblical heritage in the great Southern Baptist tradition of Carroll, Newman, Goodspeed, Williams, Scarborough, Ray, Conner, and a host of Southwestern scholars who have succeeded them

Our Southwestern spirit was captured accurately by J.B. Gambrell's last message to Southern Baptists. I have used it as the title of this article, "Do Right and Go Forward."

December 1984: The Best Ever State Alumni Meetings

That was the description most often given for the state alumni meetings this fall. As Southern Baptists in the various states met for their annual conventions, the Southwestern family in each state gathered for fellowship and to hear reports from the seminary. In nearly every state the attendance at the alumni gathering was the highest it has ever been, and the spirit and quality of the meetings were "the best ever."

I had the privilege of participating personally in several state meetings, and came away with some impressions that seemed to be characteristic of all the states:

(1) Southwesterners love and appreciate the seminary. All of us are grateful for the years we spent here as students because God used faculty, staff, fellow students, and facilities to strengthen our faith and sharpen our minds and skills for a more effective ministry. That love and appreciation for the seminary is evident when you meet with our alumni across the country.

(2) Southwesterners with new enthusiasm, are supporting the seminary with their prayers and gifts. Never have so many ex-students expressed their prayerful support and given so much of their resources to help the seminary continue in its God-given task. We praise God for this support, especially in the light of serious SBC Cooperative Program shortfalls.

(3) Southwesterners stand in the strong center of Southern Baptist life. They are committed to the Bible, to our denominational heritage, to Southern Baptist mission and evangelism enterprises, and have become, in every state, a vibrant force undergirding the work of the Southern Baptist Convention. Because of that, I am greatly encouraged about the future direction of our denomination. If no one else than the great Southwestern family should stand courageously for mainstream Southern Baptist principles, that would be enough to keep us on track in these troubled days.

(4) Southwesterners believe in the faculty and administration of the seminary and are ready to stand by their school in the midst of criticism and conflict. Standing ovations, resolutions, emotional expressions of affirmation from the state meetings have cheered our hearts here in FW.

Our thanks to all of you out there, and our thanks to God for His enumerable blessings. These days are indeed "the best ever."

1985

The Best of Times— The Worst of Times

In some respects, 1985 brought the "worst of times" in the fundamentalist assault on Southwestern. First, repercussions erupted as fundamentalist leaders, led by Jerry Vines, co-pastor of First Baptist Orlando, Florida, falsely reported remarks I had made to students at the "East Lawn Forum." (See the July/August 1984 column, "It Is Now Clear.")

In the Forum, I referenced a critique of dispensationalism given in a chapel lecture by New Testament Professor Bruce Corley. He pointed out that classical dispensationalism conflicted with several points in the 1963 Baptist Faith and Message confession of faith. Therefore, a classical dispensationalist could not endorse our seminary doctrinal statement. I told the students on the East Lawn, "Measured by the Baptist Faith and Message, dispensational pre-millennialism would be considered a heresy."

In press reports around the country, Jerry Vines led the charge, falsely accusing me of saying, "Pre-millennialism is a heresy." He reminded readers that I had thereby branded famous pre-millennialists like Billy Graham and Adrian Rogers as heretics!

With the help of the editor of the Baptist newspaper in Florida, I set up a meeting at First Baptist, Orlando that included the editor, co-pastors Homer Lindsey, Jr. and Jerry Vines, and myself to correct the false reports. We listened again and again to two audio tapes of my remarks—one an imperfect tape made secretly by a student from Vine's church, and my tape, a clear recording made through the P.A. system at the Forum.

Even after repeated replaying of my words on both tapes, Vines refused to admit he was wrong until Lindsey said, "Brother Jerry, I believe the man has a point. He didn't say, 'Pre-millennialism is a heresy,' he said, 'DISPENSA-TIONAL pre-millennialism is a heresy.'" Vines reluctantly acknowledged the truth, but he never publicly corrected his false accusation.

Second, the spring meeting of the trustees erupted in controversy over a recommendation from the administration that a preaching professor, Farrar Patterson, be dismissed. Carefully following the precise steps outlined in the seminary bylaws and Faculty Manual, I forwarded the recommendation from the dean and the vice-president that the teacher be dismissed for the following reasons: behavior inconsistent with seminary expectations, lack of church involvement, poor quality of academic work, distortion of the truth, insubordination, inappropriate intrusion into administrative affairs, and lack of response to warnings given by supervisors over a period of several years.

Fundamentalist trustees led by Ralph Pulley saw this as an opportunity for embarrassing me and the administrative leaders, and accused me of bringing the motion to fire Patterson because he was a conservative from First Baptist Dallas and disagreed with my opposition to the fundamentalist takeover campaign. Rallying his colleagues on the board, Pulley managed to block the two-thirds vote needed for dismissal by one vote, 19 for—12 against. It was a devastating blow to me, the academic officers, and the faculty committees who had processed the recommendation.

Without my knowledge or involvement, the faculty quickly framed and released a signed endorsement of the president and the administration in recommending Patterson's dismissal.

More than 1,000 students signed a petition endorsing the decision to fire the professor. The staff of the seminary signed their own petition of endorsement. Pulley and later Paul Pressler accused me of manipulating these endorsements, even though they did it without my knowledge. I reminded Pulley that the faculty even solicited fax responses from their fellow teachers on sabbatical leave overseas. Therefore, 100 percent of the faculty except Patterson himself had signed the endorsement. Pulley groused, "Yes, but it took them two weeks!"

Now I was faced with a dilemma: I had recommended the dismissal of a faculty member and the board had declined. Patterson is still on my faculty.

What could I do? I spent time in my workroom in prayer. What were my options? Should I resign? Then, an insight came: he remains on the payroll, but as president, I still control his work assignment. I met with Patterson, explaining that while he had been given a second chance by the board, he would not resume his classroom teaching until he met certain conditions in what I called a "Re-engagement Plan." He must agree to go to church, spend time at his work rather than his personal businesses, refrain from using profanity or telling dirty jokes, etc. He laughed, thinking he had the full support of board, and refused to accept the conditions.

In the following fall meeting of the trustees, Ken Lilly from Arkansas made a motion to remove from the minutes of the spring meeting, my comments listing the reasons for Patterson's firing. This was done, so the minutes did not reveal the serious justifications for the recommendation.

However, when I reported Patterson's refusal to follow my "Re-engagement Plan," they took another vote and sustained the recommendation to dismiss him. A long series of lawsuits and legal steps followed, all settled in Southwestern's favor. None of this would have happened if the fundamentalist trustees had not falsely linked the issue to the convention takeover.

In spite of the "worst of times," 1985 also saw the "best of times." We enjoyed the largest graduation ever in the spring (472), largest number of doctoral graduates in history (24), and the largest fall enrollment (4375). My book *The Personal Computer, a New Tool for Ministry*, was published by Broadman Press, Southwestern received a rousing standing ovation when I made our annual report to the SBC in June, and we had Charles Stanley, the newly-elected president of the SBC to speak in chapel. He surprised everyone by telling us that he endorsed women preachers! He had been saved under the preaching of a woman pastor in the holiness tradition in which he grew up. (However, he said he opposed ordaining women because that would give women authority over men!)

In spite of the controversy, morale on campus was upbeat, positive and grate-ful—except during those weeks surrounding the two meetings of our board of trustees each year. Then a dark cloud of gloomy anxiety engulfed the seminary family. Once the meeting adjourned, Southwestern returned to its normal posi-tive, constructive mood.

Key Events in 1985

January

9-10   • Traveled to Jacksonville, FL, to meet First Baptist co-pastors Jerry
        Vines, Homer Lindsey Jr., and the editor of the *Florida Witness* to clear
        up Vines's false reports about my East Lawn Forum. After listening to
        tapes repeatedly, Lindsey corrected Vines, "Brother Jerry, I believe the
        man has a point." Even though he was wrong, Vines gave no apology

31   • Spoke at Wieuca Rd. Baptist Church, Atlanta, GA, on SBC issues

February

6   • Spoke in Little Rock, AR, on SBC Issues

10   • Spoke at First Baptist Church Longview, TX, on SBC issues and bibli-
        cal authority

14   • J. I. Packer lectured at SW

25-27   • Spoke at Roswell, NM Bible conference on biblical authority

28   • Spoke at First Baptist Church, Little Rock, AR, on SBC issues

March

4   • Spoke on SBC Issues at Abilene, TX

5   • Spoke to Southwestern staff on SBC issues

6   • Met with Indiana State Paper Editor with pastor Bob Latham about
        lies in their paper

11-15   • Gave Stealy lectures at Palm Beach Atlantic College

18   • Spring trustee meeting:
        • Professor Farrar Patterson met with Academic Affairs Committee, then
        motion made to dismiss him. He was officially accused of behavior
        inconsistent with expectations, lack of church involvement, poor qual-
        ity of academic work, insubordination, and inappropriate intrusion
        into administrative affairs, distortion of the truth, and lack of response
        to warnings given by supervisors.
        • Ralph Pulley objected, defended Patterson, and accused us of unfair-
        ness. Written ballot vote was 19-12 for dismissal, one vote short of the
        required two-thirds.
        • Jimmy Draper spoke in chapel

25   • Tim LaHaye spoke at Christian Life Commission seminar on campus

April

2   • Spoke at Spring Baptist Church, Houston, on SBC issues. Surprise, it
        was a fundamentalist meeting! Still well received.

8   • Spoke at Corpus Christi Ministers Association on SBC issues

9 • My book *The Personal Computer: A New Tool for Ministry* presented in chapel by Baptist Sunday School Board

16 • Spoke in Wichita, KS, and Kansas City, MO, on SBC issues

17 • Spoke in St. Louis, MO, on SBC issues

18 • Charles Stanley, SBC President, spoke in chapel. In answer to questions, he endorsed women preachers, indicating he had been saved under the preaching of a woman pastor in the holiness tradition. But he rejected ordination for women because that would "give them authority over men."

21 • Spoke at First Baptist Church, Jonesboro, AR on SBC Issues

22 • Spoke at Jonesboro Ministers Breakfast on SBC issues
   • Spoke at Raleigh, NC, on SBC issues

23 • Spoke at Trinity Baptist Church, San Antonio, TX on SBC issues

25 • Spoke at Charlotte, NC, on SBC issues

26 • Spoke at Ashville, NC, on SBC issues

28 • Spoke at First Baptist Church, Washington DC, on SBC issues

30 • Spoke at First Baptist Church, Shreveport, LA, on SBC issues

May

8 • Spoke at Arlington, TX, Pastor's Conference on SBC issues

10 • Largest commencement in Southwestern history—472 degrees awarded! (Later, May 1987 surpassed it with 503. The largest annual number to date was 967 in 1984–85 year). We also granted the largest number of Doctorates, 24, in our history.

19 • Spoke at Calvary Baptist Church, Little Rock, AR on SBC issues

20 • Spoke at First Baptist Church, Houston, TX, Pastors Conference on SBC issues

24 • Spoke at Southern Seminary Commencement. Faculty presented resolution commending my involvement in opposing the convention takeover

June

1 • Wrote article in the *Southwestern News*, "Authentic Leaders." Fundamentalist Trustees later condemned the article as example of my "political" activity

4 • Spoke at River Oaks Baptist Church on SBC issues

6 • John Bisagno, Pastor First Baptist, Houston, spoke at Southwestern Pastor's Conference on campus
   • SBC met in Dallas. Charles Stanley was reelected over Winford Moore 55.3 percent
   • The largest attendance in history—45,519

- Peace Committee was appointed, Charles Fuller, pastor in Virginia, chairman
- Billy Graham's name used by fundamentalists without his permission to endorse their efforts
- When I gave the Southwestern Seminary Report, the SBC messengers gave a standing ovation

July

24   • Met at Baylor with Herb Reynolds, his faculty, and our faculty to encourage them to wait to start Truett Seminary even though the fundamentalist takeover was threatening Southwestern. We were still hanging on in spite of everything

August

6-11 • Preached at Home Mission Board Week at Glorieta

15   • Largest fall enrollment ever—4375. All time high in Theology—2543.

September

4   • Started visiting with new trustees before the fall meeting: met with Tolbert, Lester, and Baggot, Dice, Malloy, Morris, and Jones

6   • Lunch with Dallas Pastor, Wayne Allen, and legendary trustee, J.T. Luther. Luther's renomination to our board blocked by Paul Pressler and Allen had been named instead with Pressler's approval. Allen promised he was independent and not involved with Pressler's takeover.

October

1-4   • Jess Moody, pastor in CA, preached at Seminary revival

21   • Fall Trustee Meeting. Jimmy Draper requested that the afternoon session be an executive session.
      • They heard my report on the re-engagement plan for Farrar Patterson, and finally agreed to fire him. Motion made by Ken Lilly, AR, seconded by John McKay, TX. It passed 27-2 (2 abstained)
      • Draper nominated Ralph Pulley as chairman., seconded by Ken Lilly, but Drew Gunnells was elected, adding to Pulley's anger.
      • Dedicated the Glasscock World Mission Center.

29   • Spoke at the Missouri Baptist State Convention

November

12-13 • Spoke at the South Carolina Baptist State Convention in Greenville
       • Spoke at Hyde Park Baptist Church Sunday School Convention

Note: In the fall meeting of 1985, the thirty-six-member board of trustees had the following composition: 14 hard-core fundamentalists, 18 traditional mainstream Baptists, and 4 swing voters.

January 1985: "Messenger"—A Definition

mes'sen-ger n. (From Lat. *mittere*, to send.)
One who carries a message or goes on an errand.

That's the Webster definition, but in Southern Baptist language, there's another meaning. A messenger is one elected by a local church that is in "friendly cooperation with this convention and sympathetic with its purposes...and a bona fide contributor to the convention's work."

A messenger is not a delegate. A delegate is elected to carry out an assigned agenda—to vote a certain way. But a messenger is elected to attend the convention meetings and prayerfully vote his or her conscience on the issues before the assembly. This is the democratic method the Southern Baptist Convention has employed through the years to determine the future of its work. Every church has an opportunity to be a part of denominational decisions through its messengers, but unfortunately, not every church exercises that opportunity. In fact, very few of our churches do.

Last year in Kansas City, 81 percent of our churches had no representation whatsoever at the convention! Only 19 percent sent messengers from their churches to vote on important convention business, and 75 percent of those churches had only two messengers—probably the pastor and his wife. That means that grassroots Baptists, the loyal members of our congregations, are having very little say in what the convention does or the direction it takes on critical issues.

This June in Dallas, the Southern Baptist Convention faces its most crucial meeting in recent history. Decisions will be made determining what kind of convention we're going to be. It is urgent that every Southern Baptist Church sends its full quota of messengers to this important meeting.

"What can I do?" That's the question most often asked by Southwestern alumni in these days of denominational struggle. One answer is: "MAKE EVERY EFFORT TO HAVE YOUR CHURCH FULLY REPRESENTED IN DALLAS." Send prayerful, informed, open-minded, spiritually mature men and women who are committed Southern Baptists to help the convention determine its future in God's plan. As a leader, it's the most valuable contribution you can make to your church, your convention, and to Southwestern's future effectiveness as well.

Maybe the Webster definition is applicable to Southern Baptists after all: "A messenger is one who carries a message."

February 1985: Denominational Missions— The Better Way

Mexico City—the world's largest city. Eighteen million persons are compressed into that one metropolitan center creating unimaginable problems. Pollution is out of control; just breathing the air for one day is as unhealthy as smoking two packs of cigarettes. Traffic gridlock occurs regularly, turning thoroughfares into long, frustrating parking lots. Passengers, unable to push their way into already crowded buses, hang onto the outside for a dangerous ride into downtown. So unsolvable are the problems, that the city's motto is ni modo, "no way." The utter futility of their living conditions somehow underscores the spiritual lostness of the population. Mexico City not only needs civic solutions, Mexico City needs Jesus.

We were in that proud, troubled capital a few weeks ago to attend the annual meeting of the Fellowship of Evangelical Seminary Presidents, and to see first-hand what was being done to share Christ with the world's largest city. Among a number of evangelical groups in the city is a non-denominational independent mission society called "Latin American Mission." As a part of the meeting agenda, we learned about the effective work being done by their missionaries, and we were encouraged that so many kindred groups work alongside Southern Baptists in cities like this one.

However, as we met with our Southern Baptist missionaries in Mexico City, I came away more convinced than ever that the denominational approach to world missions is the better way. Our convention's foreign mission program, while not perfect, is superior to the independent, "society" method in a number of ways:

(1) *Accountability* . Many independent missionary entrepreneurs answer to no one. Our denominational program has a clearly defined system of accountability, which continually reviews the work.

(2) *Coordination.* Independent mission projects often overlap with little or no coordination. Our denominational method calls for a "team" approach with well-

planned coordination and balanced, inclusive strategies of evangelism, church planting, social ministries, education, and medicine.

(3) *Cooperation.* Churches who support independent missions must pick and choose which projects to finance. Popular programs with emotional appeal receive greater support than others which may be lesser known, but urgently important. Our denominational Cooperative Program giving provides support for all our mission projects without regard for the popular appeal of eloquent "fund raisers."

(4) *Conviction.* Non-denominational, independent missions must maintain a broad doctrinal position that appeals to a wide range of Christian perspectives. Our denominational program unapologetically maintains loyalty to our Southern Baptist doctrinal distinctives, planting churches with clearly defined biblical characteristics.

(5) *Finances.* Most independent missionaries are responsible for raising their own financial support. Our denominational method provides salary and program support for the missionaries, freeing them to spend their time, not on fund-raising, but on the work of winning people to Jesus.

(6) *Cumulative Experience.* Instead of continually having to "re-invent the wheel," our denominational mission program builds on 140 years of cumulative, unbroken experience to make each generation of mission strategies more effective.

No doubt, there are other advantages, but these are sufficiently convincing to reinforce my conviction that denominational missions is better. Those among us who would reject the cooperative, convention method of world missions for an independent, society method need to study again Southern Baptist history. Long ago, our forefathers chose the convention pathway to obeying the Great Commission, and experience has confirmed it as the better way.

March 1985: Come to Suburban Fort Worth in June—SBC

This column gave me an opportunity to invite alumni from across the convention to return to our campus for a "homecoming event" while they were attending the 1985 SBC. I wrote,

Three months from now, the Southern Baptist Convention will meet in suburban Fort Worth (some call it Dallas). It will be an opportunity for you, especially those who've not been on the campus in years, to visit the seminary while you're in the neighborhood. That's one reason we hope you're making plans now to attend the convention. The other reason we encourage you to come is that messengers will be asked to make decisions, which will vitally affect not only the denomination, but the seminary as well . . . .

At this historic juncture in denominational life, these decisions carry the extra weight of determining such questions as: "What kind of convention will we be?" "Will we remain true to the Bible and our historic Baptist heritage?" "What kind of leaders should we elect?" "Can the issues of the current controversy be settled without threatening the future of our institutions or the effectiveness of our mission programs?" The crucial impact of these decisions during the convention should encourage every Southwesterner to be present and participate.

April 1985: The Worst of Times— The Best of Times

Sometimes in the providence of God, disappointments and blessings arrive simultaneously—the worst and the best together in the same encounter. Easter Sunday reminds us how the miracle of resurrection transformed the dark sadness of the cross in the most joyous experience of history—the empty tomb. By God's power, the worst of times gave way to the best of times.

Southwestern has been through the worst of times in these past few weeks. The seminary family has been saddened, disappointed and concerned as a result of the unfortunate events that have made headlines across the convention. And since the ultimate outcome of these events remains uncertain, we are still burdened about the future of our great institution. But out of these bleak experiences, God is already bringing forth some remarkable blessings.

The adversity is bringing forth an amazing expression of unity and affirmation from Southwesterners everywhere. You have read about the unprecedented unanimity of the faculty who, to a person, has affirmed the administration. The student body has responded with the same overwhelming support. Seminary officers and the administrative staff have publicly expressed their loyalty to Southwestern's leadership. It has been an occasion for all of us to recommit our lives and futures to each other, to the institution and to the Lord who has called us to serve here. There has never been a time when a greater tie of fellowship has bound us together in Christian love.

Add to this an avalanche of mail, telegrams, and calls from alumni, pastors, church staff, and leaders, Southern Baptists from every state, donors and friends in general, and the mounting affirmation of the seminary can only be described as overwhelming. The spirit of discouragement is being replaced by an optimistic mood of mutuality and koinonia. Campus morale is high. The worst of times is giving way to the best of times, and we are grateful.

Betty Dilday, one of my greatest encouragers, wrote this verse of Scripture on a slip of paper and taped it where I would be sure to see it every morning: Let us not lose heart in doing good, for in due times we shall reap if we do not grow weary (Gal 6:9). It's a powerful word from God for the worst of times and the best of times.

May 1985: Defending the Faith on Two Fronts

"As an inerrantist I always have to defend my position on two fronts." This was the testimony of James I. Packer during lectures here a few months ago. Packer is professor of systematic and historical theology at Regent College, Vancouver. He helped compose the definition of biblical inerrancy adopted by the Congress on Inerrancy in Chicago in 1978. He believes biblical infallibility is threatened not only by liberal theology on one side, but just as seriously by extremists who go too far on the other side with their rationalistic, distorted view of inerrancy. So the battle for the Bible must be fought against enemies on two fronts—the left and the right.

Packer's "centrist" position on the inerrancy of Scripture (a position which Gordon Fee calls the "radical middle") is for all practical purposes the position taught here at Southwestern through the years. It should be no surprise then, that we too must defend our convictions on the same two fronts—the extreme left and the extreme right.

As you might expect, most of the pressure against Southwestern's conservative stance has come from the left. Our school has withstood liberal influences through the years and has maintained its strong convictions in the mainstream of Southern Baptist orthodoxy. Even under the glaring searchlight of critical examination during our ongoing denominational debate, Southwestern's reputation as a biblical, conservative, evangelistic institution remains unblemished.

However, in recent days, Southwestern has also had to defend its conservative principles against serious assaults from the extreme right. Some of our critics would like to see our seminary and our convention move beyond conservative theology to an extreme fundamentalism which is equally as dangerous and therefore equally as objectionable as liberalism. This pressure from the right must be resisted just as earnestly as the pressure from the left.

Looking back, it seems clear that this attack on two fronts is not new. Our denominational history often repeats itself. How grateful we ought to be for faculty and administrators in the past who refused to adopt the latest avant-guard liberal philosophies and courageously held our school on course—committed to vigorous biblical scholarship. But shouldn't we also be grateful that those same Southwestern heroes refused to be stampeded by pious-sounding critics from the extreme right who would have destroyed the seminary with their fundamentalist distortions of the truth? Who can forget the vigorous stand seminary leaders took against the Frank Norris movement not many years ago?

We who today enjoy the benefits of a strong convention and a strong seminary owe a great debt to those who spoke out boldly and voted responsibly, maintaining their conservative convictions against pressure from both the right and the left. Surely every one of us who loves this school and has benefited from its teaching is grateful to God for their courageous stand.

Hebrews 13:7 says, Remember your leaders, those who spoke to you the word of God; consider the outcome of their life and imitate their faith. That biblical imperative suggests it is time again for boldness on the part of the Southwestern family to zealously defend our convention and our seminary on both fronts.

June 1985: Authentic Southern Baptist Leaders

In a recent survey, Americans were asked to select current personalities they respected the most as contemporary heroes. At the top of the list were movie stars Clint Eastwood and Eddie Murphy. The survey either suggests we have a serious shortage of respected leadership in our country or else a gross misunderstanding of the identifying characteristics by which great leaders are recognized.

Authentic leadership is an urgent need in our Southern Baptist Convention as well. Southwestern understands the importance of helping its students develop the qualities and skills of Christian leadership in the various ministries to which our Lord has called them. How would you describe authentic Southern Baptist leaders?

(1) Authentic Southern Baptist leaders are those who have a profound, vital faith in Christ, having surrendered to the lordship of Jesus. Authentic leaders do more than speak in pious phrases. They seek to live humble Christ-like lives.

(2) Authentic Southern Baptist leaders are those who take the Bible seriously as the inspired Word of God. Realizing it doesn't need their rationalistic defense, they reverently seek to understand the Bible's message. They readily acknowledge their human limitations and are content to live with the mysteries they do not

understand while diligently seeking to apply the truth the Holy Spirit reveals from the Word.

(3) Authentic Southern Baptist leaders are those who know how to win souls, disciple believers, and build churches—not just to impress their colleagues with records but because they have been called to the task with a brokenhearted concern for lost humanity.

(4) Authentic Southern Baptist leaders are those who are courageous, willing to stand by their convictions at great cost rather than waiting cautiously to see which way the prevailing winds will blow and then safely following the majority.

(5) Authentic Southern Baptist leaders are those who are servants. Their leadership style follows the example of Jesus without regard for self-promotion or personal ambition.

(6) Authentic Southern Baptist leaders are those who have paid the price for adequate preparation. Shortcuts in education are too readily available but authentic leaders want at all cost to offer the Lord the best-prepared instruments they can offer.

(7) Authentic Southern Baptist leaders are those who understand the importance of our Southern Baptist connectionalism. They realize we are at our best when we cooperatively combine our efforts to obey the Great Commission rather than going it alone in independent unilateral efforts. Authentic leaders know we need each other—that we are put here not to see through each other, but to see each other through.

The writer of Hebrews said, Remember your leaders, those who spoke to you the Word of God. Consider the outcome of their lives and imitate their faith.

Remembering the impact of Southern Baptist leaders in the past, Southwestern recommits itself to the task of equipping authentic leaders for the future. Our prayer is:

God give us leaders!

A time like this demands strong minds, great hears, true faith and ready hands.

Leaders whom the lust of office does not kill.

Leaders whom the spoils of office cannot buy.

Leaders who possess opinions and a will.

Leaders who have honor.

Leaders who will not lie.

July/August 1985: The Quality of Endurance

(My July/August column reported on the annual breakfast for graduates preceding commencement. We always asked how many years it took the students to complete their degrees. Traditionally, most were able to finish their studies in two to three years. But there were always others who, for various reasons, took longer. The "prize winner" among the summer graduates worked thirteen years for his diploma! [But that's not even close to the record!]

I also commended faculty and staff who had remained faithful through the years. I said, "They face their share of discouragement, but they don't quit. They're the real performance stars of theological education for Southern Baptists.")

September 1985: Justifying Cooperative Program Support

(Each year in September the Southern Baptist Convention's Executive Committee began planning next year's Cooperative Program budget. The committee asked the Seminary, along with other convention agencies, to report significant accomplishments during the past year as a part of their request for funds. In this column, I summarized the reasons for our request for $8 million that I believed justified this expenditure.)

October 1985: The Seminary Is Missions Too

All of us are enthusiastically grateful for the increasing support in recent years for the work of our Foreign Mission Board and Home Mission Board to the extent that the most recent reports from the Southern Baptist Convention Handbook indicate that 84 cents of every dollar Southern Baptists give to convention causes through Nashville goes to foreign missions and home missions.

In our enthusiasm for the work of these two vital agencies, Southern Baptist Convention support for theological education has declined to a serious degree. This gradual decrease in Cooperative Program support is fostered in party by a growing misconception that the seminaries are not missions. Southern Baptist Convention policies strictly forbid the seminaries from approaching our churches for direct support as the mission boards and state conventions are free to do. And that's as it should be.

The policies also limit the kinds of fund-raising we can do while at the same time mandating that we secure most of our funding for operations and capital needs from gifts outside the Cooperative Program. And that's acceptable also.

But then our lifeline of support—our portion of the Cooperative Program—has steadily been reduced over these past years in order to increase the funding for our mission boards. That decline concerns me greatly, because our six seminaries in general and Southwestern in particular are absolutely vital and essential for Southern Baptist missions.

First, we train all of the foreign and home missionaries Southern Baptists send out. Southwestern is responsible for training about half of them. Through the aggressive programs of our World Mission/Evangelism Center, our faculty specialists, our missions strategy, church growth, and urban methodology, Southwestern provides the finest mission training curriculum available anywhere in the world today.

Second, here at the seminary we call out the called. Our annual missions conference, the regular missions weeks, revivals, and other emphases provide an opportunity for hundreds every year to make their commitments to foreign and home missions service. In addition to that, Pioneer Penetration, church planting practica, and overseas experiences planned for students encourage many others to hear God's call to mission service. At the present time, one-third of our students are mission volunteers.

Third, the seminary provides missionary awareness and orientation for all our students, insuring that each year a new generation of pastors, educators, and musicians graduate from the seminary with a clear conception of what Southern Baptists are doing to reach the world. They know about associational, state and Southern Baptist Convention mission programs. They know about Bold Mission Thrust and the Cooperative Program. They know about our boards, about the Woman's Missionary Union and Baptist Men's organizations. They pray for missions and give to missions as we observe the weeks of prayer, and they are taught the biblical basis and the history of world evangelization.

There may be other defensible reasons for a gradual erosion of Cooperative Program support for the seminaries, but there is certainly no legitimacy to the claim that the seminaries are not missions.

Just two years ago the Cooperative Program supplied 50 percent of the seminary's educational and general budget. This, of course, excludes the auxiliary enterprises on our campus. But this past year the Cooperative Program portion of seminary support dropped to only 44 percent. At the same time the seminary operating budget increased only modestly.

All Southern Baptists need to be challenged to greater support for the work of our two great missions agencies. But let's not forget, Southwestern is missions too.

November 1985: The President's Report

(This column announced the annual report for the 1984–1985 academic year. The report was printed in a separate brochure.)

December 1985: Southwestern's International Students

The officers of our Seminary International Fellowship dropped by the president's office for a visit the other day, reminding me again that the students on our campus from 36 foreign countries are one of Southwestern's most valuable resources. They not only represent enormous potential for world evangelization, but their presence enriches our entire educational experience.

This year's talented and committed officers are representative of the 126 international students enrolled:

Miss Yukling Tang, president, Hong Kong, MA(RE);
Mr. Winston Clemetson, vice president, Jamaica, MDiv;
Mrs. Lorna Wakim (George), secretary, Lebanon, student wife;
Mr. Baek Sung Choi, program chairman, Korea, MA(RE).

The largest foreign contingencies are from Korea, 28; Hong Kong/Taiwan, 27; and Brazil, 9. But we also have students from unusual locations—"far-away places with strange-sounding names"—Marianna, Mauritius, Antigua, and Brunei (incidentally, the international students gave me a globe so I could improve my geographical knowledge!).

We also have students from some of the places where world crises are focused: Beirut, South Africa, Grenada, Central America, and the Philippines. One student is from Mainland China.

Of course, they will eventually return to their homelands to share Christ with their people, but these students are not just waiting for future evangelistic opportunities. They meet with international students from other educational institutions in the Fort Worth area, who for the most part are unbelievers, and have had great success in winning some of them to the Lord. They do translation work for social agencies, business and civic organizations, taking full advantage of the evangelistic opportunities such activities provide them. They assist our churches with international ministries in their communities. All the while coping with the great difficulties of transition into a different culture, financial limitations, and the demands of graduate theological study. You can see why we believe this group of students is a special gift of God to the seminary.

Recently we established an international office in the Division of Student Affairs to assist students from other countries in every way possible. Diane Roberts serves as director. Under her leadership, the office gives assistance in visa problems, housing, program planning for students on campus, community services available to Internationals, ministry of internationals to local churches through special speaking engagements, and student orientation.

The familiar motto is true: "The sun never sets on the Southwestern family." International students and alumni are another providential channel through which the seminary becomes vitally involved in Bold Mission Thrust.

1986

What's Ahead for Southwestern?

The year 1986 marked an interlude in the Southern Baptist battles. The SBC had appointed the Peace Committee which aroused hopes that steps toward reconciliation were being taken. As a kind of "cease fire" settled over the convention while the peace committee completed its work, there was a growing hope that solutions would finally be found to avoid a denominational disaster.

One step the Peace Committee took was to send subcommittees to the seminary campuses to attempt an objective assessment of the situation in the light of the various accusations of theological liberalism. When the subcommittee chaired by Jim Henry from Florida made its visit to Southwestern, they said they were somewhat embarrassed to be there since they had no legitimate concerns about liberalism at our school. Two questions about a couple of concerns were quickly resolved, and the committee left with nothing but praise for Southwestern, its faculty and administrative leadership. It was something like another accreditation of our work which we passed with flying colors.

This growing optimism about the possible ending of the controversy was further reinforced at the meeting of the Peace Committee at Glorieta, New Mexico in October. At the request of the committee, the six seminary presidents agreed to draft a statement of our beliefs about the trustworthiness and authority of the Bible that we would use to guide our schools in the future. "The Glorieta Statement," as it was later named, was a forthright and clear declaration that we not only felt conveyed our individual convictions, but that our faculties could also feel comfortable with as an unofficial guide. (The Glorieta Statement is included in the December, 1987 column and in the Appendix at the end of the book. Although it was a worthy attempt, it did not have the hoped for results.)

In my June column, I described a convention-wide hunger for "biblical leaders" like Joshua who would unselfishly lead us back together and back to the main task of missions and evangelism. I was convinced that Southwestern was in a providential position to lead the way in this grand reconciliation.

Convinced that it was not the issue of biblical authority that divided us, but differences in biblical interpretation, we instituted a new requirement for a course in hermeneutics or biblical interpretation. I even joined Dr. John Newport in co-teaching a class in that important subject.

Things were looking up, and I concluded my last column in 1986 with the prayer that the momentum toward reconciliation would continue and that Southern Baptists would receive the blessed gift of peace this Christmas. I took hope in the fact that Southern Baptists had always been able to disagree agreeably, express our convictions, come to resolutions, and move on to the future stronger and more unified than ever. In the unforgettable words of Richard Jackson's presidential nominating speech, "That's the Baptist way, and I like it!"

Key Events in 1986

January
28-29 • SBC Peace committee visited Southwestern. Jim Henry, Robert Cutino, Bill Poe, Jerry Vines. Chairman indicated they were embarrassed to be there, no complaints, "I sense that our committee feels that Southwestern is solid in every area and at the heart of traditional Southern Baptist history."

March
10   • Spring Trustee meeting
       • Established Drumwright Lectures
       • Gave report of Peace committee visit
16   • Preached at Immanuel Baptist Church, Little Rock, Ark. Met choir member, Governor Bill Clinton.

April
29   • Bill Weber, pastor of Prestonwood Baptist, preached in chapel.

May

24 • Clark Pinnock apologized for fueling inerrancy debate by his support. Now believes term "inerrancy" is not exegetically supported.

June

1 • My article in June *Southwestern News* "Southern Baptists need biblical Leaders" angered fundamentalist trustees.

6-12 • SBC met in Atlanta, GA
• Adrian Rogers elected to a second term (3 years) over Winfred Moore by 54.2 percent. 40,987 messengers
• Adrian Rogers made comment "If we believe that pickles have souls, then the seminaries must teach that pickles have souls . . ."

July

15 • Southwestern's first Oxford University Summer term.

September 18

• Met with SBC Peace Committee and other Seminary Presidents in Atlanta

October

1 • Jess Moody preached for Seminary Revival
13 • Fall Trustee meeting
• Reported on meeting of Seminary Presidents with the Peace Committee and the upcoming meeting in Glorieta with the Peace Committee.
• Ralph Pulley, TX, made a speech and a motion to silence the president, seconded by Hugo Lindquist
• Davis Cooper, CO, made speech about his conservative position and friendship with me and offered the following substitute motion: "That we express our appreciation to the president for the obvious restraint which he has manifested over the last two years and we encourage him to continue this judicious style of leadership."
• T. Bob Davis, TX, mildly rebuked me, but would vote for substitute.
• W. J. Smith, NC, spoke in favor of the substitute motion, calling controversy the work of the devil. He asked the trustees not to bring up things to destroy the good spirit at Southwestern
• Wayne Allen, TX, spoke in favor of the substitute, saying the trustees shouldn't try to run the seminary. He asked me to continue my restrained approach.
• Jimmy Draper, TX, "I voted against substitute. I'm not against the president. I'm for Russell." He accused chairman Cooper of using a

"smooth move" to limit trustees from speaking. He accused me of giving faculty the impression that he was an enemy. He rebuked my comment that if Charles Stanley is elected SBC president, we will lose the seminary. "This is a great seminary. We don't want to fire Russell Dilday and I hope the press will print that."

- Hugo Lindquist, OK spoke: "I Love Russell Dilday. We're friends. I just disagree with some of the things he's doing." He rebuked Newport for saying, "Don't you guys mess things up here at Southwestern . . ."

- C. A. Johnson, AR, "I want to be my own man. There is no takeover." (Later he admitted to me that he felt pressured to vote with them because they got him his church.)

- Bud Funk, NM, "Russell Dilday is real nice, but what is this takeover he talks about? It's just some men pointing out the need to stay conservative. I Don't know much about Southwestern. I don't believe someone whose salary is paid by all Southern Baptist people should take sides on this issue."

- John McKay, TX, "Our discussion was cut off unfairly by the chairman. We avoid each other in different camps and that's O.K. We shouldn't have speakers at seminary that trustees don't endorse. There is a moratorium on conservatives here. Draper spoke here, I know, but we shouldn't have Roy Honeycutt here for commencement."

- Bill Grubbs, TX, criticized Honeycutt's words about "Dark ages and pockets of civility," and my remarks about leadership vacuum. He made a motion that we affirm leaders of SBC and the Peace Committee.

- John McNaughton, TX, complimented the president's leadership and courage and the successful operation of Southwestern.

- I responded: Explained my pilgrimage getting into the debate. Peace Committee advised all participants to cool their rhetoric. I agreed. "In the light of that restraint, I'm surprised at these accusations. There's been nothing controversial in the press until Pulley's motion." I corrected the implication that I was not for keeping Southwestern conservative. "Is there a takeover? Yes. The leaders have admitted it now."

- Bill Grubbs broke in: "We're not in anyone's hip pocket."

- I continued: "The politics are being studied by the Peace Committee. It's not theology." I defended my article. "I've invited conservatives regularly to speak on campus. Adrian Rogers is coming." I defended invitation to Honeycutt to speak as a seminary president. I rebuked them for their secret caucuses and lack of openness.

- John Mckay broke in: "The seminary is not under attack."
- Davis Cooper broke in, complimenting my leadership and called for a vote on the substitute motion. (Approved 19-11, 1 abstained)

October

19-22 • Met at Glorieta, NM with the Peace Committee. Six seminary presidents framed "Glorieta Statement." The Statement gained wide circulation because of its sentence on the Bible, but it contained far more: 7 commitments or affirmations. (The text of the "Glorieta Statement" is found in my column for November, 1986 and in the Addendum)

28 • Spoke at Angleton, TX. Pastor's Conference on SBC Issues

November

3 • Faculty meeting to review Glorieta Statement. Faculty had no problem with it, but Southern and Southeastern Faculties objected strongly

5 • Preached closing message at the Baptist General Convention of Texas

14 • John Bisagno preached in chapel

18 • Adrian Rogers preached in Chapel as President of SBC. Lunch with faculty

19 • Spoke at First Baptist Church Gainesville, TX on biblical Authority

December

11 • Spoke at Deacon's Banquet at Prestonwood Baptist Church
- W. A. Criswell made comment "Pastor rules the church."
- Paul Pressler interviewed on tape about his conversation with reconstructionists Gary North, Son-in-law to J. Rushdoony, main thinker of reconstructionism. Pressler had earlier given written endorsement to series of books printed by Dominion Press affirming reconstructionist writings. This interview was called the "Firestorm Tapes" in which Pressler explained his strategy for taking over SBC.

19 • At Winter Commencement, Southwestern graduated its 25,000th student.

Note: In the fall meeting of 1986, the thirty-six-member board of trustees had the following composition: 14 hard-core fundamentalists, 16 traditional mainstream Baptists, and 6 swing voters.

January 1986: Managing Enrollment

It has never been Southwestern's goal to become the largest seminary in the world. We have that distinction, but not because we have sought it as an institutional objective. In fact, the high enrollments this year have occurred even though efforts have been implemented to manage enrollments by reinforcing admission standards.

Southwestern wants to be sure the students who enroll are qualified persons who ought to be here. So, for the first time, we have personally interviewed more than half of this year's entering students, and eventually will require an interview of all entering students. Our purpose is to help them understand what it means to have a divine call, what serving Christ requires and what the demands of graduate theological education here at Southwestern will be.

Realizing the first appraisal of potential students comes from the churches that send them here, we have improved and enlarged the Church Endorsement Form required of every enrollee. It now calls for a more thorough evaluation of the student's Christian character and potential for ministry.

As a result of these steps, we have delayed or denied admission to more applicants than ever before. Since Southern Baptists are investing $6,976,106 in their training this year, we believe the students who receive that help ought to be those who are properly qualified to receive it.

Another step in achieving our goal of managing enrollment will be instituted next year. The seminary will require of all current students an Annual Certification of Church Membership. The certification will show that the student is not only a member but also an active participant in the church while enrolled at the seminary. The certification forms will be mailed during the spring semester to all students to be completed and returned to the seminary by their respective local churches prior to the fall semester.

We have had the help of the local pastors in the Fort Worth/Dallas Metroplex in developing this procedure and it has their enthusiastic endorsement even though it will require a good deal of work on the church's part. This is not an attempt to spy on anyone or to become legalistic with our students. Instead, it is an effort to be good stewards of the resources of the seminary and to help our students realize the importance of commitment to the local church—not only later when they serve those churches, but also now while they're in Fort Worth.

Of course, nearly all of our students are faithfully involved in church life while they complete their academic work. For these, the requirement will not be a problem. If some have let this commitment slip, it will be a reminder that those preparing for ministry ought to be exemplary church members while they're in school. After all, when God gives them their first place of leadership, they'll be expecting that kind of faithfulness from others.

It's a new step for Southwestern. But we believe it's one that moves us closer to a responsible management of enrollment.

February 1986: Utilizing Trained Ministers

A special workgroup of the Inter-Agency Council of the SBC has just completed a study of the Utilization of Trained Ministers in our denomination. This week the Council heard the results of the study and will be reporting its findings to the Executive Committee who in turn will report to the convention.

Following a motion adopted by the 1982 convention, the six seminary presidents were asked to decide if such a study were needed, and how the number of trained ministers not serving in ministry could be determined. Agreeing that the information would be valuable, the presidents recommended the procedure, which has been followed. While an official report will be released soon, it would not be inappropriate to share some of the "good news" of the report.

There have been widespread concerns in recent years that a large percentage of those who graduate from our seminaries never serve in the ministry, and therefore Southern Baptists were training more seminarians than we could possible put to work. Contrary to these opinions, which until now had no convention-wide data on which to be founded, the situation is encouraging.

One encouraging projection from the study is that in the next five years there will be 97,094 ministry positions needed in the churches and in the programs of our convention, an increase of 25 percent over the present situation.

Another encouraging report shows that from 1950 to 1983 the six Southern Baptist seminaries graduated 46,741, and that this number can be maintained during the next five years. (The number of pastors with a seminary degree increased from 36.5 percent in 1973 to 43 percent in 1983. An even better report comes from the 1983 church letters which indicate 45.5 percent of the pastors in the convention have seminary degrees.)

The most encouraging part of the report has to do with the number of trained ministers who have never served in ministry. The study shows that only 12 out of 100 seminary graduates have never served in Southern Baptist ministry. Sixty-seven and six-tenths percent of all those who are seminary graduates are presently serving. Because of the definition given to "ministry" in the study, those who have never served or who are not now serving include: wives of ministers, international graduates who may be serving in their own countries, ministers serving in other denominations, ministers who are retired or disabled and other categories which would generally be considered "in ministry."

Acknowledging there are some seminary graduates who ought not to be in ministry for a number of reasons, we are still concerned when any one graduate with a seminary degree is willing to serve and cannot find a place of service. We are concerned when those who have served turn to non-ministry vocations through no fault of their own. But apparently that number is very small, and the situation is not serious, certainly not as serious as some have contended.

Nevertheless, we must continue to be selective in admitting students to be sure they understand the full implications of ministry and are certain of God's call. We must continue to match our curricula and enrollments to the emerging ministry needs of our convention. We must do more in helping graduates find the places where God would have them serve. Even though it is a small percentage, we must find ways to decrease the number of those graduates who never serve in ministry and find ways to re-engage those not now serving. We must continue to "call out the called" and challenge them especially to the urgent needs of home and foreign missions.

But on the basis of the preliminary reports, we can affirm again what we've been saying for these past eight years: "No. We are not graduating too many from the seminary. How can there be too many when God has called them and when there are so many lost people in our world who need to hear the gospel of Jesus Christ?"

March 1986: The Peace Committee Visit

Recently, the Southern Baptist Convention Peace Committee divided itself into subcommittees for the purpose of visiting the various convention agencies. Representing the total committee, these smaller groups were asked to discuss with the agency leaders all the concerns about that agency which have been raised during the recent convention debates.

Southwestern's subcommittee came to our campus January 28-29. To what shall we liken their visit?

In some respects, their visit was like an accreditation review. A few years ago, we hosted a visiting team from the Southern Association of Colleges and Schools and the Association of Theological Schools who carefully examined Southwestern's work with respect to academic quality. It happens every ten years, and as expected, the seminary passed this last review with "flying colors." Southwestern is once again fully accredited without notations. We welcome such an external appraisal because it objectively substantiates our own subjective impressions about the quality of our school.

In a similar manner, it seems just as appropriate for Southern Baptists to send a visiting team to our campus to examine Southwestern's work from the standpoint of doctrinal and denominational quality.

Jim Henry (the chairman), Robert Cutino, Bill Poe, and Jerry Vines are the subcommittee members assigned to us. I invited John Newport, vice president for academic affairs, and Jerry Gunnells, chairman of our board, to join the president as representatives of the seminary.

In a very cordial, frank, and positive meeting we discussed some of the crucial questions with which the peace committee is dealing. "How does your school apply the Baptist Faith and Message Statement?" "What do you and your faculty believe about the Bible as truth without mixture of error?" "Who have you invited over the years as guest lecturers and speakers?" "How are text books and curricula chosen?" "How do you respond to questions and criticisms sent to the seminary?" "What are the strengths and weaknesses of your school?"

Then, several specific questions about Southwestern, which had been received by the Peace Committee, were raised and answered to the satisfaction of the visiting team. Later, we, the representatives of the seminary, were given an opportunity to voice our concerns related to the recent denominational controversy.

It seemed to be the consensus of the subcommittee members that Southwestern had no serious deficiencies to be addressed. In fact, in a letter following the meeting, the chairman of the visiting team wrote: "I sense that our committee feels that Southwestern is solid in every area and at the heart of traditional Southern Baptist history."

Those of us who have known Southwestern through the years would not be surprised at these findings. This institution has always been known for its simultaneous commitment to academic excellence and conservative biblical theology. Now there seems to be a strong objective basis for that claim.

I'm glad the committee came. Our doctrinal discussions can be carried out so much more effectively through a prayerful, reasonable meeting of an "official" committee of brethren than through the emotional, strident harangues of a public rally or through the inaccurate words of an uninformed media.

So, in a sense, Southwestern has received from our visiting team an endorsement, a denominational "accreditation" without notations. If the larger discussions of the Peace Committee can be as open, forthright, fair and spiritually motivated as the one held on our campus, then I for one am optimistic about the prospects of their guiding us to a new level of understanding and harmony within the Southern Baptist Convention.

April 1986: Keeping the Main Thing, the Main Thing

Trustee Ron Lewis, church growth specialist from Tennessee, recently delivered a stirring message in chapel in which he shared a timely quotation: "The main thing is to keep the main thing, the main thing!"

"The main thing," according to Lewis, is obedience to the commission of our Lord Jesus Christ in sharing the gospel with the lost world, or to put it another way—evangelism, church growth and missions.

One of Southwestern's strengths has been its focus on "the main thing." We are not in the business of teaching the classic disciplines of theology in a theoretical manner detached and isolated from the main purpose of winning people to Christ, planting and growing churches, discipling believers, ministering to human needs and preaching the gospel around the world.

The purpose, for example, of teaching philosophy of religion is not simply to see that students know the world's great philosophical systems, but how philosophy of religion can give them apologetic tools for defending the faith and helping believers overcome intellectual problems on their way to faith. We want to teach ministers how to deal with the problem of evil and suffering as they counsel parents who have lost a young child.

We are not a trade school producing denominational functionaries armed with instruction manuals on how to do the job, but who have never learned to think critically or to engage in intelligent reflection on the truth of the gospel. On the other hand, neither do we want to graduate theoretical "eggheads" who don't know how to witness, start a church, or lead a congregation to grow.

We need graduates who can serve a great university church with a membership of PhDs but who could on the other hand, in the words of Ron Lewis, "parachute behind the lines with nothing more than a pocket knife and survive in the pioneer world of church growth."

To keep the main thing the main thing, Southwestern's World Mission/Evangelism Center focuses the attention of the whole seminary on evangelism, church growth and missions. Specialized courses of study are provided. Conferences are sponsored. Research is building a database on effective church growth strategies in different world settings. Interspersed throughout the curriculum of all three schools are courses dealing with church growth principles, urban evangelism, and mission strategies.

We are especially proud of new programs, internships, apprenticeships, evangelism and missions practica. Under the new direction of Dan Crawford, Operation Penetration has just sent out two hundred students in twenty-eight states and two Canadian provinces during spring break for revivals, personal witnessing, and discipleship training. Summer practica will engage hundreds of other students—literally around the world—in hands-on experience in church planting and church growth.

With trustees like Ron Lewis to encourage and reinforce these efforts, I predict we will realize our vision for Southwestern—to become America's leading center of evangelical conservative scholarship and practical training in missions and evangelism. We believe "the main thing is to keep the main thing, the main thing!"

May 1986: Theological Education and the Soviet Union

(This column reported on a trip Betty Dilday and I made with other SBC leaders behind the iron curtain to the Soviet Union. We were encouraged that in spite of difficult circumstances, Baptists were able to provide some limited theological education for their ministers. They were also exploring ways our six SBC seminaries could partner with them to strengthen their work.)

June 1986: Southern Baptists Need Biblical Leaders

When the secular world idolizes the glamorous stars of Washington and Hollywood, Southern Baptists need biblical leaders who humbly acknowledge that without Christ we are nothing, and that our convention must rely not on political power, or stardom, or even doctrinal uniformity, but on the power of the Holy Spirit for our effectiveness in fulfilling Christ's commission.

From Joshua in the Old Testament to Paul in the New Testament, biblical models of spiritual leadership reflect a balance between courageous forthrightness and servant-like humility. This leadership style finds its superlative personification, of course, in Jesus who "being in the form of God . . . made himself of no reputation, took upon himself the form of a servant . . . and humbled himself" (Phil 2:6-8).

Southern Baptists are hungry for that kind of leadership in these troublesome and crucial days in our convention. They want leaders who have biblical leadership styles—not the styles of corporate business, or secular politics, or dictatorial autocracy, or messianic self-righteousness.

When those who've been given the great responsibility of choosing directors for our agencies are persons who have never participated in our convention, and who, even though they have never been on our campuses, harshly condemn our teachers, Southern Baptists need biblical leaders who have proven records of experience in and unquestioned loyalty to our convention.

When some trustees seem more interested in the political agenda to control the convention than in the health and welfare of the agencies they were elected to direct, Southern Baptists need biblical leaders who know and love these institutions and who strive to make them better.

When in the midst of struggles over crucial denominational issues, some whose voices need to be heard remain silent, unwilling to risk involvement, Southern Baptists need biblical leaders who will put the future of the convention above personal security and speak out in courage and love.

When heavy-handed authoritarianism has replaced scriptural servanthood as the popular model of church leadership, Southern Baptists need biblical leaders who lead with a Christ-like balance of strength and humility.

When Baptist ideals of freedom, individualism, church autonomy, democratic congregational polity and the priesthood of the believer are being casually ignored or blatantly discarded, Southern Baptists need biblical leaders who know and value the heritage of our denomination.

When on the one hand, charges of liberalism are exaggerated and used to incite support for a certain party, or when, on the other hand, real theological weaknesses in an institution are flippantly excused or defensively covered up, Southern Baptists need biblical leaders who are truthful and who lead with integrity.

When concerns about whose party is going to win take precedence over concerns about our mission to a lost world, Southern Baptists need biblical leaders whose spiritual priorities are in order.

When suspicion and distrust continue to erode the spiritual brotherhood and fellowship which have been a great strength in the denomination we love, Southern Baptists need biblical leaders who practice forgiveness and who readily admit "There is none righteous, no not one . . . all have sinned and come short of the glory of God."

There is a yearning—a deep hunger—an urgent need—for biblical leaders. It begins "at the top"—in the churches. It is visible in the associations and states. It is stirring among the messengers preparing to attend the upcoming convention. It is deeply felt in our agencies and institutions.

So much is at stake. That's why so many here at Southwestern and across the nation are praying:

> God give us leaders! A time like this demands
> Strong minds, great hearts, true faith, and ready hands;
> Leaders whom the lust of office does not kill;
> Leaders whom the spoils of office cannot buy;

Leaders who possess opinions and a will
Leaders who have honor, leaders who will not lie.

("The Day's Demand" by Josiah G. Holland, paraphrased)

July/August 1986: What's Ahead for Southwestern?

Southern Baptists appear to be marking time in a forced intermission between acts until a new and clearer vision of our future comes into focus. This intermission is marked by political power struggles, divisiveness, controversy, diversion from missionary purposes, and an enormous leadership vacuum.

Some are predicting that the inevitable outcome is a convention doomed to the sidelines of God's ongoing purpose as a divided, weakened, denominational "has been." But I believe out of it all can emerge a new spirit that will propel Southern Baptists to new heights of accomplishment in our world mission task.

Meanwhile, the leadership vacuum may be filled, not so much by charismatic individuals as has been the case in most previous years, but by institutions like Southwestern. We can become, if the Lord wills, a leading source of intelligent, informed, positive, biblical conservatism, guiding the churches of this convention with an emphasis on scholarly evangelistic and missionary strategy and theological research with integrity.

The troubled doctrinal waters of these last years of the 20th century will carry the Southern Baptist Convention into deeper discussions of revelation, biblical interpretation, Christology, Baptist history and ecclesiology, and ministry. It will also be important to clarify the relationship between faith and reason. The future will call for the re-establishment of the historical position that man comes to God by faith alone. Intellectual argument and rational apologetics follow and undergird faith, demonstrating its reasonableness and helping us understand its implications. But faith is not dependent so completely upon airtight intellectual arguments that it will not function until all the questions are answered.

Southwestern is strategically positioned to lead Southern Baptists through these tricky theological waters and call the convention back to its ultimate purpose, which is not doctrinal uniformity, but bold missions and evangelism.

It is difficult to look at the future without some measure of anxiety. The new problems we face are immense and frightening, but they are not greater than the old ones, just different. Under God, they are all manageable. The big question is not "Can we do it?" but "Is God in it?" More promising than human cleverness in meeting an unknown future is the certainty of God's providence. If Southwestern continues to be His school on His mission in His world, then we can depend upon His unfailing support. While we can't anticipate the future, God, the Eternal One, has already lived the future and has promised to lead us through it.

Given the nature of academic routine, so much of the education process is cyclical. Another circle of events begins each academic year very similar to the events and activities of the last: registration, education, examination, graduation. Our hope and intention at Southwestern is that the circularity does not remain within a single plane, but follows a spiral pattern upward and onward toward a higher ground of spiritual excellence. That is not a bad way to diagram Southwestern's future as we pursue our essential purpose in changing times and circumstances, looking unto Jesus, the author and finisher of our faith.

God's promise through Joshua is one we can claim with confidence: "Sanctify yourselves, for tomorrow the Lord will do wonders among you!" (Joshua 3:5)

September 1986: Dream of Teaching a Reality

There were times during my student days at Southwestern when I had the strong impression God was calling me to be a teacher. That impression was heightened by a developing admiration for faculty members who became my spiritual heroes.

In fact, the impression was so profound I completed, with my wife's encouragement, a doctor's degree in Philosophy of Religion. We wanted to be prepared for what we thought might be an academic career.

However, after only a brief period of college and seminary teaching, the will of God pointed us instead to local pastorates until 1977 when I was elected president of the seminary. No one could have had a more gratifying ministry than we had during those twenty-five years in the pastorate. But upon returning to Southwestern, the urge to teach was reignited, and I hoped as president it might be possible occasionally to teach a course in my discipline of Philosophy of Religion.

That hope has finally become a reality. This fall Dr. John Newport and I are coteaching Philosophy 771-435, Religious Authority and Biblical Interpretation. The catalogue description of the course is: A study of religious authority and methods of biblical interpretation. Such related issues as the nature of language, the canon, inspiration, inner witness of the Spirit, accommodation, analogy of faith, typology, prophetic and apocalyptic exegesis, and the literary nature of the Bible will be considered. Two hours.

Already the experience has given me a new appreciation for the demanding challenge our professors face in fulfilling their teaching responsibilities. It's a big job!

First, purposes and objectives for the course must be defined and stated. Reading assignments, grading procedures, exam schedules have to be developed. Textbooks have to be requested in time so the bookstore can have them in stock. A student grader must be enlisted and trained. Class outlines must be developed and a syllabus prepared for printing. A calendar of class meeting days has to be coordinated with the topics to be covered in each lecture. Of course, in addition to all this, time must be spent in reading, research, and preparation of content material.

Then when all the preliminaries are completed, the lectures begin—about thirty hours of them—in Fleming 111 from 2:00 to 4:00 p.m. each Thursday afternoon. Additional time must be given to counseling students, evaluating student assignments, keeping records, and turning in grade reports.

Admittedly, my teaching assignment this fall is limited; it involves only one two-hour class, and I share the responsibility with a team teacher. By contrast, our regular professors are required to teach the equivalent of five two-hour classes each semester! It's a demanding task, even for those who offer the same courses year after year.

As I "walk in their shoes" this semester, my appreciation for the men and women on our faculty is growing every day. In addition to a more accurate understanding of the demands of the job, I am also receiving a new understanding of the fulfillment seminary teaching gives. Helping to train God-called men and women for ministry is immensely gratifying.

I have only one anxiety as I look toward the end of the semester. Along with the rest of the faculty, I will have to submit to "Student Evaluation of Teaching" and a formal appraisal by the dean!

October 1986: Annual Request for Cooperative Program Funding

The following is the report I presented to the Southern Baptist Convention's Executive Committee in its meeting September 23, 1986, as a part of our annual request for Cooperative Program Funding.

Last week I accepted the invitation of the U.S. Eighth Air Force to accompany the crew of a KC-135 tanker on a Strategic Air Command refueling mission. Somewhere over Louisiana we rendezvoused with a giant B52 Stratofortress bomber.

At 33,000 feet, that huge plane pulled up within 12 feet of the tail of the KC-135. I stretched out prone beside the crew-member called "the boomer" and watched out the window as he, also in a prone position, guided the boom from the tail of our plane into an opening on the top of the B52.

He signaled a positive connection to the pilots of both aircraft who held their planes steady in that position while the boomer off-loaded thousands of pounds of jet fuel into the bomber. When his tanks were full, the refueling boom was disconnected and the B52 pilot waved to us through his windscreen and dropped back to continue his mission without interruption.

Would it be an inappropriate stretching of an analogy to suggest that the Southern Baptist Convention Executive Committee is like that skilled Eighth Air Force crew? It is their responsibility on behalf of Southern Baptists to "refuel" the various units of our convention. On behalf of the churches, you are to share with the agencies appropriate allotments of hi-octane CP—Cooperative Petrol.

Like the tanker crew, you don't manufacture the financial fuel for the mission agencies, you deliver it. You become the connecting boom through which those financial resources given by the churches are off-loaded into the empty tanks of agencies like Southwestern.

You see the listing of our major accomplishments during the current budget year and our program priorities for 1987–1988 along with our request for Cooperative Program funding for the new year. "Exciting" is too tame a word to describe the unprecedented evidences of God's work among the largest concentration of missionaries, evangelists, and ministers in training in the history of the Christian faith.

What we are asking you to fund is not just another denominational institution, but an essential ingredient in the convention's effort to fulfill our Lord's command to His churches. We believe both the record of accomplishments and the goals for the future justify our request for the 12 percent increase or a total of $8,438,000.

During the Strategic Air Command flight over Louisiana, the crews performed what they called an "emergency breakaway." It is a critical and dangerous maneuver in which they practice a sudden disconnection of the refueling boom and a rapid separation of the two giant aircraft flying a dozen feet apart.

The boomer shouts, "Breakaway! Breakaway! And the pilot of the tanker immediately pulls the plane into a sudden climb while the bomber pilot puts his plane into a steep dive. (I was glad each remembered which way he was to go!) They described the frightening possibilities of fire and mid-air collision, which might result from such a disconnection and cause their mission to fail.

I can think of a dozen destructive dangers to our mission should such a "break-away" occur in our essential connection through the convention's Cooperative Program. And I for one am grateful to the Lord for this providential and effective connecting we call the Cooperative Program. It is indeed our lifeline for continued operation.

While it would be inappropriate to thank the Executive Committee for the CP fuel, we do thank you for being a skilled flight crew in delivering that fuel. In so doing you are permitting Southwestern to continue its mission without interruption as we carry the education payload for Southern Baptists.

Now you can be sure that we have ample auxiliary tanks to hold and use any amount of financial fuel you would like to give us, but our main tanks for 1987–1988 are programmed to hold $8,438,000.

We respectfully request the Executive Committee flight crew to "Fill-er-up!"

November 1986: Peace Committee Meeting in Glorieta

The following statement was unanimously endorsed and presented by the six seminary presidents to the Southern Baptist Convention's Peace Committee meeting in Glorieta, NM, October 20. It has become the basis for resolving the committee's discussions related to theological concerns within the SB constituency. I believe it represents a significant breakthrough in the reconciliation process.

[*Note:* The "Glorieta Statement" is included in the Appendix at the end of the book.]

December 1986: "What Do You Want for Christmas?"

Preparing for a seasonal feature in the local paper, a reporter called to ask me that question the other day. From childhood Christmases long ago came back memories of mounting anticipation, waiting for that special gift under the tree.

It's that time again as we celebrate the coming of the Lord Jesus, God's greatest gift to mankind, and the reporter's question waited for an answer: "What do you want for Christmas?"

While the readers of the *Fort Worth Star-Telegram* might not understand it, my answer will be readily understood by Southern Baptists everywhere. To me the best gift this Christmas would be a healthy and positive resolution of our convention's long controversy. And there are reasons to believe it just might be possible!

Since the Glorieta meeting of the Southern Baptist Convention Peace Committee, so many different letters have come from all sides of our convention constituency. The letters are diverse, but they all carry one theme: "We are on our way now to reconciliation!"

For the first time in these past seven turbulent years, there are indications that we may be moving through the controversial storm into a new day of strength and opportunity. It isn't a matter of winning or losing, it's a matter of can we learn something positive from these confrontations and emerge a stronger denomination than ever? I think we can.

While we may differ on whether or not Southern Baptists were drifting from our conservative foundations, one thing is certain. If we ever were, we are certainly not now! The debate has focused our attention sharply on our distinctive theological ideals and we have been called back again to our conservative, biblical heritage with new appreciation and new commitment. That can only make us stronger.

Since our fellowship and unity have been dangerously threatened, there is emerging now a new appreciation for the God-given genius of cooperation that has made this convention uniquely effective through the years. That cooperative approach to missions and evangelism has built the largest and perhaps most effective mission force in the history of Christendom! As the dust settles on our debates, we are realizing anew how valuable our cooperative "Koinonia" is.

We agree there are theological parameters which define what a Southern Baptist is. There are some things a person cannot believe if he or she wants to be a Southern Baptist. We have also learned how difficult it is to define those parameters to the satisfaction of all Southern Baptists.

Our 1963 statement of faith is being rediscovered as a good statement with which nearly all of us can live. We are discovering that we can be Baptist brothers and sisters without being twins. And that there is room within the parameters of Baptist faith for differences of opinions.

Join me in prayer that the momentum toward reconciliation may continue to increase and that Southern Baptists will receive the blessed gift of peace this Christmas. While renewing our commitment to our Baptist beliefs we should also reaffirm our allegiance to the ideals of individualism, freedom of conscience, and the priesthood of the believer.

In our churches and conventions alike we Southern Baptists have always been able to disagree agreeably, express our convictions, come to resolutions and move on to the future stronger and more unified than ever. In the unforgettable words of Richard Jackson, "That's the Baptist way, and I like it!"

1987

We Are Not Divided; All One Body, We

The welcomed "lull" in the heat of controversy continued into 1987, the tenth anniversary of my election as president. The spring meeting of the board was positive with a commendation of the president for his work on the Glorieta Statement. The announcement that this was trustee Ralph Pulley's final meeting on the board was widely received as good news among the seminary family. He had been the leading voice of opposition, and we felt his leaving would advance the new spirit of reconciliation. (Little did we know that the Patterson/Pressler party would reappoint Pulley a short time later so that he would lead the successful effort to fire the president!)

With the assistance of the other five seminaries, Southwestern planned and carried out the very successful Conference on Biblical Inerrancy at Ridgecrest, NC. Leading evangelical scholars, many of them self-described inerrantists, helped clarify the widespread misconceptions about the concept and the word "inerrancy" itself. We also headlined key personalities from the SBC fundamentalist camp and employed our faculties to lead group discussions. As a result, criticism of Southwestern about the Bible died down to an insignificant trickle.

It had become clear that the issue was not the nature of scripture, but the interpretation of scripture.

One of the evangelical speakers, J. I. Packer, rode with me from the airport, and warned me that he would probably support the "conservative wing" of our denomination (meaning the fundamentalist leaders). I told him that was no problem, and his contribution would be helpful. Later on the ride back to the airport, after having listened to "our conservative wing," he told me he had changed his mind. They were not the kind of conservatives he supported. In fact, Packer publicly criticized Adrian Rogers's message on "The Word of God" as unscriptural, saying that most of the scriptures Rogers used did not refer to the Bible at all! He indicated that he now understood our division more accurately and was at home with our "moderate" wing.

One disappointing setback in the trend toward reconciliation was the resignation of our colleague at Southeastern Seminary, President Randall Lolley. I wrote about my reactions to his resignation in my November column.

Buoyed by a fragile hope that the controversy might be moving toward a positive resolution, we longed for the day when Southern Baptists could sing again truthfully, "We are not divided; all one body, we."

Key Events in 1987

January

12   • Meeting of Seminary Presidents with Atlanta Pastors at Stone Mountain, GA, on SBC Issues

28   • Annual enrollment for 1986–1987 reaches record high: Annual head-count of 5,247

February

1   • Preached at First Baptist Church Ft. Smith, AR, with trustee Ken Lilly

3   • Delivered Founders Day address on E. Y. Mullins at Southern Seminary

4-5   • Spoke at First Baptist Church, Amarillo, TX, on biblical authority

20   • Spoke at Pastor's Conference at Houston, First Baptist Church on SBC issues

March

1-2   • Spoke at Church Growth Conference at Prestonwood Baptist Church

5   • Miles Seaborn spoke in chapel

9   • Spring Trustees meeting

- This was to be Ralph Pulley's last meeting we thought, so he was recognized, but later, he was renamed to an unprecedented third term. This time his obvious mission was to replace the president.
- Announced the Inerrancy Conference in May
- Ken Lilly moved appreciation to the president for leadership in Glorieta Statement (They said in the last meeting that I shouldn't participate in such a statement.)
- Elected Jim Denison, of New Hope Baptist Church in Mansfield, TX, to faculty
- Leon McBeth gave founders day address on women in ministry. Trustees later criticized the address and me for allowing him to speak.

April

10
- Fundamentalist Larry Lewis elected to head Home Mission Board
- D. L. Lowrie, pastor of First Baptist Lubbock, preached in chapel

15
- Met with student Jim Tuell about his legal challenge for Southwestern's not awarding his degree. Later, because of the interference of Jimmy Draper, the Seminary faced a lawsuit which we won but which was very expensive.

25-26
- Spoke at First Baptist Church Enid, OK, and Pastor's Conference on Biblical Authority

May

1
- Spoke at First Baptist Church Montgomery and Pastor's Conference on SBC issues

4-7
- Participated in Conference on Biblical Inerrancy at Ridgecrest
- John Newport and I planned the conference and enlisted lecturers: J. I. Packer, Kenneth Kantzer, Clark Pinnock, Millard Erickson, Mark Noll, Robert Preus
- Our professors led small discussion groups, SBC preachers led worship

15
- Largest graduating class in history—503 (later, class of 1988 was larger—520)

17
- Taught Tim LeHaye's Bible Class at Prestonwood Baptist Church, Dallas, TX

June

14
- SBC met in St. Louis
- Adrian Rogers reelected over Richard Jackson with 59.97 percent -25, 607 messengers. Calmer, but not because the controversy had died out. Moderate political efforts were practically nonexistent, but Jackson carried 40 percent of the vote anyway.

July

3   • I made a formal response to the SBC Peace Committee on behalf of Southwestern. (The response is printed in the Appendix of this book.)

September

3   • Gave Convocation address at New Orleans Seminary
         • Joel Gregory preached in chapel
8   • Visited with Trustee Chairman Jerry Gunnells, AL, and new trustee Jimmy Draper all day at DFW Airport about ways to relieve tensions on the board. We felt Draper was less strident than others. Not much success.
9-18   • Visited with new trustees Lyle Seltman, Damon Shook, Roger Freeman, Don Taylor, and Pat Campbell
18   • Jimmy Draper preached in chapel

October

29   • John Sullivan preached for Seminary revival
7   • Visited new trustee, Grady Roan
15   • Spoke at First Baptist Church, Dallas, TX, on behalf of Huber Drumwright Chair
18   • New trustee, Don Taylor, NC, and wife Elizabeth came early to meet with our counseling faculty. It was their first time on campus, and he wanted his wife, a lay counselor, to check out our faculty.
19   • Fall trustee meeting
         • Fundamentalists elected without opposition their slate with Ken Lilly, chairman
         • They passed a resolution affirming faculty
         • Otherwise calm meeting
         • This meeting marks the tenth anniversary of my election as president. Nothing was said about this milestone.
22   • Randall Lolley resigned in protest of fundamentalist takeover
29   • Spoke at inauguration at Houston Baptist University for Doug Hodo

November

20   • Billy Weber preached in chapel

Note: In the fall meeting of 1987, the thirty-seven-member board of trustees had the following composition: 19 hard-core fundamentalists, 12 traditional mainstream Baptists, and 6 swing voters.

January 1987: Faculty—Old and New

A brand new year calls us to look, as did that mythical deity Janus, in two directions: past and future. In Southwestern's case, the view in both directions is encouraging. This was brought to my attention by two recent experiences at the seminary. One was the annual awards luncheon during which we recognize those faculty and staff who have served here the longest. Along with several staff members with long years of service, we honored a number of faculty who have invested enormous blocks of time in this one school. What a valuable asset to theological education in general and specifically to Southern Baptist Convention ministry training.

Retiring after thirty years was Leon Marsh, distinguished professor of foundations of education; and after thirty-two years Robert Douglass, distinguished professor of musicology and associate dean for doctor of musical arts studies. Recognition was also given to Robert L. Burton, professor of conducting and ensemble activities, for thirty years of service.

While their tenure of service did not fall on one of the five-year blocks which received recognition, there are others on our faculty who have taught at Southwestern for more than thirty years: William R. Estep, distinguished professor of church history, thirty-two years; Boyd Hunt, distinguished professor of theology, thirty-six years; J. W. MacGorman, distinguished professor of New Testament, thirty-eight years; James McKinney, dean and distinguished professor of voice, School of Church Music, thirty-six years; John P. Newport, vice president for academic affairs and provost and professor of philosophy of religion, thirty-two years; Ralph Lee Smith, professor of Old Testament, thirty-seven years; Curtis Vaughan, Professor of New Testament, thirty-six years; Charles Williamson, professor of voice, thirty-one years.

As president, I find myself wondering how we will ever find persons with credentials and potential to follow these "long-termers" who have made and are making such immeasurable contributions to Southwestern.

But my second recent experience helped me to look from the past to the future with new hope and encouragement. God is preparing and calling some very impressive young scholars into the ministry of teaching. Recently we have interviewed a number of them as possible candidates for faculty positions. They are splendid young men and women who have paid the price of authentic academic study. At the same time they are mature and serious followers of Jesus Christ and have proven their commitment to the local church and our Southern Baptist Convention. Ranging in age from twenty-eight to forty, in addition to degrees from Southwestern, they have studied at: Oxford University, Trinity Evangelical Divinity School, and Vanderbilt.

These young teachers are not typical "egghead" types whose narrow interests and specializations blind them to the larger world. Instead, they are balanced, multi-talented healthy personalities. In addition to their theological disciplines, their hobbies include music, drama, art, creative writing (including poetry and hymns), numismatics, and sports.

If God calls any one of them to serve on this faculty, Southwestern can rest assured that the future will be as bright as our past. They have the potential to become the kind of distinguished Christian Scholars who are now the senior faculty here. Isn't it reassuring that the Lord obviously has in mind an even greater day for the seminary than ever before! There must be a bright future ahead for this school and the convention of churches it serves.

So, 1987 begins with an impressive reason for optimism and gratitude: Faculty—old and new—God's gift from the past and hope for the days ahead.

February 1987: Affirmation, Registration, Cooperation

Affirmation . . . The Atlanta Baptist Pastor's Conference sponsored a special program a few days ago at the Smoke Rise Baptist Church, Truett Gannon, pastor. In years past, such a meeting would have been considered routine and would not have generated much excitement. But the "situation" in our convention gave this gathering a unique quality that drew several hundred participants. We stayed from 10:00 a.m. until 2:00 p.m. with one purpose in mind: "Affirming the Southern Baptist Convention Seminaries!" All six of the seminary presidents shared insights from their own spiritual pilgrimages and from developments on their campuses.

The uniqueness of the meeting was its positive purpose and spirit. It felt good. It also reminded us of how it used to be, how it ought to be, and how we hope it will be in the future as Southern Baptists join ranks, turn aside from distractions and invest our time on our main business.

Registration . . . More than 300 new students have completed the process of registration and orientation this week and beginning their first week of classes along with more than 3,500 others as the spring semester starts.

As a result of computerization, the matriculation ordeal at Southwestern has been streamlined and therefore requires far less time than it used to—thanks to Terry Bratton and his computer team and Dan McLallen and his admissions team. In addition, Lawrence Klempnauer and his student affairs team have enlarged and improved the orientation procedures to make the new students' first semester as manageable as possible. The mood on campus is "upbeat." It almost makes you want to begin seminary again! (Almost)

Cooperation . . . At the Texas Baptist Evangelism Conference a few days ago, John Bisagno brought a major message on evangelistic motivation. He stressed the importance of our cooperative plan for winning our world to Christ:

The last thing we need is another sending agency, another board, another plan. We have in our Home Mission Board, our Foreign Mission Board, and our Cooperative Program the most God-blessed, God-ordained, united plan to do together what we cannot do alone in the name of Christ this world has ever known!

Dr. Bisagno expressed his great appreciation for the cooperative method of world evangelism because of its total inclusivism of mission strategy and because it works in difficult economic times. "We're suffering economically in Houston, and our mission offerings will not be as generous this year, but churches in other parts of the country where the economy is flourishing will take up the slack, and our mission outreach will not decline." He mentioned how independent missionaries and evangelists have to be recalled when finances are depleted. "But in all history, not one Southern Baptist missionary has ever had to be called home for lack of funds."

The congregation applauded these timely remarks—as we all do.

March 1987: Southwestern Graduates in Leadership Roles

I've just returned from the February meeting of the Southern Baptist Convention's Executive Committee in "snowy" Nashville. Our seminary's presence was pervasive throughout the meeting.

First, the committee voted to recommend to the convention in June that Southwestern be given $7.86 million from cooperative funds for our 1987–1988 budget year. This is the third largest allocation from the Cooperative Program, exceeded only by the foreign and home mission boards. The committee also approved a slightly adjusted formula for distribution in the next three years.

Second, I was impressed by how many graduates of SW were involved in key positions of service and responsibility in the convention:

James Flamming (BD 59, Thd 63) was confirmed as a member of the Peace Committee.

Ernest Mosley (BD 55 [MDiv 73]) was elected as the executive vice president of the Executive Committee.

Al Shackleford (BD 57 [MDiv 73] was elected as the vice president for public relations.

Keith Parks (BD 51, ThD 55) reported on Nancy Wingo (MRE 63), one of two missionaries remaining in West Beirut.

After some modifications, the Baptist Joint Committee on Public Affairs was reaffirmed, with James Dunn (BD 57, ThD 66, PhD 79) as its leader.

We welcomed the new director of the Christian Life Commission, Larry Baker (BD 63, ThM 66, ThD 74).

We heard a report from the chairman of the Peace Committee, Charles Fuller (BD 57).

The committee received reports from the following agency executives:

Baptist Sunday School Board's Lloyd Elder (BD 61 [MDiv 73], ThD 66);
Radio and Television Commission's Jimmy Allen (BD 51, ThD 58);
Home Mission Board's Bob Banks (MRE 56);
Annuity Board's Darold Morgan (ThM 47, ThD 53, PhD 82);
Stewardship Commission's Rudy Fagan (BD 55 [MDiv 73]).

The presidents of all six SB seminaries met to complete plans for the Conference on Biblical Inerrancy:

William O. Crews (BD 64);
Milton Ferguson (BD 54, ThD 59);
Russell Dilday (BD 55, ThD 60, PhD 76);
Randall Lolley (ThD 64);
Roy Honeycutt and Landrum P. Leavell III.

(Well, four out of six is pretty good!)

It's easy to see why our popular motto is accurate: "The sun never sets on the Southwestern family."

April 1987: Important Stake in Southwestern

Southwestern is not a stock-issuing organization and therefore we have no stockholders. But we do have a lot at stake in this institution, and therefore we have numerous "stakeholders." Students, alumni, faculty, staff, and major donors obviously are in this category, but what about you?

As a contributing member of a Southern Baptist Convention church through the Cooperative Program, you will have a part in investing $7 million for seminary operations this year. Webster defines "stake" as "a share or interest, especially a financial one, in property, a person, or a business venture." Unless you are one of those rare persons who care nothing about what happens to your investments, you have an important stake in Southwestern.

Since about one third of our students are missions volunteers who are preparing to share the gospel with the world as Southern Baptist missionaries, if you have any concern for world evangelization, you have an important stake in Southwestern. About half of all our denominational home and foreign missionaries are trained here. That fact alone should make you an involved "stakeholder."

If you care about the quality of pastoral and ministerial leadership in the churches of the nineties and beyond, you must surely be concerned about the future of this seminary. What kind of preachers will your children hear? Who will direct the youth programs for your grandchildren? With what kind of music will they be led to worship the Lord? How well prepared will the denominational leaders of tomorrow be? Who will pass on not only our Christian ideals but our Baptist heritage as well? Even those of us who expect the imminent return of the Lord must be vitally concerned with such questions. That gives you a stake in Southwestern.

There is little doubt that the most effective way to influence the future of a denomination is through the training of its ministers. (Even those who have acknowledged their efforts to take control of the convention have centered their attention on the seminaries!) All Southern Baptists have an important stake in Southwestern.

What should informed and interested "stakeholders" do? First, you should pray. Prayer is the most important and effective strategy for insuring the future of Southwestern. Never have we been more conscious of convention-wide prayer support than we have these past few years.

Second, do what you can to insure the most capable and devoted trustee possible will be elected to represent the Baptists in your state. Trustees must be persons with a vital relationship to Christ who also have wisdom and understanding of the complexities of institutional management.

Third, continue to encourage and send God-called men and women from your church to the seminary. You should maintain that encouragement and support throughout their years of training, and let the Holy Spirit work through you to help them find their places of service when they graduate.

Fourth, stakeholders should continue to help the seminary carry out its purpose by your financial support through the Cooperative Program of your church and through your direct gifts.

Webster also defines "stake" as "something, especially money, risked or hazarded, as in a wager or a game: as they were playing for high stakes." The stakes are indeed high, but as a "stakeholder" in Southwestern, the risks are minimized. The returns on your investment are underwritten by the promises of the King Himself.

May 1987: First Baptist Church, Houston and Wichita Falls

About 15,000 senior adults from across the Southern Baptist Convention gathered for their convention here in Fort Worth this week. Without a doubt, 14,000 of them came out to see Southwestern. It was a delight to have them on our campus.

Anticipating the week, Betty thought it would be a good idea to extend a special invitation to a small group of them to come by our house for refreshments and fellowship. So we invited the senior adults from First Baptist Houston, where Betty grew up and from First Baptist Wichita Falls, TX, where I grew up to come to a reception at the president's home.

Over 150 from these two churches showed up at our door in huge buses! It was great. We saw people we hadn't seen in years who had made significant contributions to our lives. Longtime members of First Baptist Houston recalled working with Betty when she was in Sunday school, GAs, and Training Union. "I remember how cute you were in your long brown curls when you held the Bible between the two flags in Vacation Bible School," reminisced one church member.

With me it was a little different. The older members of First Baptist Wichita Falls could only recall embarrassing escapades of my mischievous days as a "junior" boy. What little dignity I might have acquired through the years was considerably diminished by the memory of our talkative guests! It's amazing how exaggerated those apocryphal childhood stories can become.

When the last guest had boarded the bus, Betty and I reflected on the importance of early church life in our pilgrimage of faith. How grateful we are that we were raised as Southern Baptists in these two strong churches.

We also remembered that the local church is the proper focus for kingdom work and the basic element in the purposes of Southwestern. We are an agency of the churches. We are supported by the churches. We are primarily training ministers for the churches. We are accountable to the churches. The Bible tells us that our Lord "loved the church and gave Himself for it." We are at our best when we serve with that same commitment.

June 1987: We Are Not Divided, All One Body We

"We Are Not Divided, All One Body We . . . ." With thousands of other Baptists gathered in the beautiful sanctuary of the Prestonwood Church in Dallas a few Sundays ago, Betty and I sang those familiar words of "Onward, Christian Soldiers."

A lump came up in my throat and I wept a little when it dawned on me that we Southern Baptists could no longer sing those words as sincerely as we once did. Local congregations can still sing them. Most associations and state conventions can still sing them. But unfortunately, division within our Southern Baptist Convention family grows deeper and wider every day.

To sing those words today in our annual meeting would be awkward, inappropriate, and perhaps even hypocritical. We are divided. We are not one body. And therefore no longer are we "like a mighty army marching as to war, with the cross of Jesus going on before."

A heartbroken mother confessed that she and her husband no longer talk about convention matters with their Baptist preacher son. She said the resentments and feelings are so hostile that they've learned to avoid the subject. One of our leading educators testified to a similar painful division within his own family.

Unfortunately, along with other traditional questions, church search committees are asking potential ministers, "For whom did you vote in the last convention presidential election?" Certain churches are casually labeled, and members of that church automatically classified on one side or the other in the convention controversy. Longtime faithful participants in SBC concerns are saying, "Convention politics have become so ugly and divisive we've lost all desire to attend the annual meetings. We don't plan to be there next year."

Most of the denominational family members with whom I talk say, "This fragmentation has gone far enough. Whatever the convictions and motives might have been that led to the discord, surely it is time now to rally behind the goal of reconciliation and pull our unraveling fellowship together again."

The recent Conference on Biblical Inerrancy has demonstrated that Southern Baptists are practically unanimous in our conviction that the Bible is the perfect Word of God. It demonstrated that while we disagree about the interpretation of certain biblical passages, about terminology, and about other non-essentials, we enjoy a remarkable theological unity in the great center of conservative evangelical belief.

We agree that any drift away from the centerline of these great truths calls for a course correction, but once that correction is made we must be careful not to drift off course again in the opposite direction. As the dust settles around our debates, it seems clear that we still agree on the great basic tenants of biblical faith expressed sufficiently in our Baptist Faith and Message.

Let's focus on these strong agreements and work to build again on our unity a rich fellowship of mutual trust and Christ-like charity. The future of this great denomination and the spiritual welfare of our children and grandchildren depend on it, to say nothing of the eternal salvation of a lost world.

My hope and prayer is that some day soon, we will hear thousands of Southern Baptist voices filling our convention hall singing sincerely and gratefully:

> We are not divided, all one body we,
>   One in hope and doctrine, one in charity.
>   Onward, then, ye people, join our happy throng,
> Blend with ours your voices, in the triumph song,
>   Glory, laud, and honor, unto Christ the King,
> This through countless ages, men and angels sing.

July/August 1987: It's a Matter of Perspective

(In this column I reprinted an interesting article written by Dr. Drew J. Gunnells, pastor of the Spring Hill Baptist Church in Mobile, Alabama, and chairman of our Southwestern board of trustees. In a day of TV preachers, he called for authenticity among Baptist pastors.)

September 1987: Climate Shock—
Spiritual Climate at Southwestern

One recent afternoon when the temperature was a sweltering 102 degrees, a couple from Virginia arrived for their first visit to the campus. As new students, they were experiencing not only "culture shock" but "climate shock" as they anticipated moving to Fort Worth.

Those of you who came to Southwestern from milder climates will remember the uninviting Texas heat which seemed to extend far too long into the autumn months and which made it so difficult to feel at home here. You can identify with the wilted young couple from the Southeast who were trying so hard to adjust.

This is my tenth fall semester as president of Southwestern, and I'm getting pretty good at identifying for new students some important features of seminary life which compensate for the heat. Of course, typical of this part of the country, all our facilities are air-conditioned. So, in spite of the temperature, we have no problem carrying out the day-by-day functions of theological education. That's an important compensation.

Furthermore, because of a recently installed automatic irrigation system, our landscaping staff (mostly students) is able to maintain a beautiful green campus—incidentally, at significant financial savings over the old manual irrigation methods. The grass, the trees, the shrubbery, and the flowers on Seminary Hill never looked more beautiful. Somehow the heat seems less severe when you walk across the attractive, shady campus. It's like a refreshing oasis surrounded by the dusty, dry, brown landscape of west Texas.

The most effective compensation for the heat, however, is the positive and supportive "spiritual climate" at Southwestern. Students comment on it frequently. They are welcomed and encouraged by fellow students, staff, and faculty who are friendly and helpful.

Nothing makes you forget the heat and feel at home more quickly than realizing that a busy teacher will take time to pray with you and advise you about your course of study, or that, in spite of the large enrollment, a staff member will help you find a place to live. New students soon discover that Southwesterners are interested in more than just the routine facets of education; they want to go the second mile to help students find and fulfill God's purpose for them during this stage of ministry.

Knowing this allows me to assure those anxious new students who are arriving every day that in a few weeks they'll be saying about the weather (not about the seminary), "It's not so hot here after all!"

October 1987: Revival, Requests, Renovation, and Reports

Revival . . .Preparation and anticipation for the annual seminary revival has been the most intense and carefully planned ever. Student body, faculty, and staff alike are caught up in the excitement of what the Holy Spirit will do on our campus during this special week.

Our evangelist Dr. John Sullivan, pastor of Broadmoor Baptist Church in Shreveport, LA, and Michael Wierick have been undergirded in our prayers for these many weeks. We are confident the Lord will use them as instruments to direct each of us in Southwestern family to a clear understanding of God's will, to a closer walk with the Lord himself and to renewed commitments in our service for him. You'll be hearing about this revival in days to come.

Request . . . One responsibility I have as president is making frequent requests for financial support of the seminary. Since the Cooperative Program provides only 44 percent of the annual cost of operating Southwestern (down from 56 percent a few years ago), we are under an obligation to raise an increasing amount from other sources. So I often go before foundations, corporations, groups and individuals to ask for money.

Among those many occasions, the one, which is most enjoyable and rewarding, is the meeting of the Southern Baptist Convention Executive Committee in Nashville each September. Along with nineteen other institutions and agencies of the convention, I stand before that committee to appeal for Southwestern share in the 1988–1989 budget. On the basis of a list of accomplishments during this past year and our goals for the upcoming year, I made a request for $8.8 million. That was the third largest request from the agencies, exceeded only by the request of the Foreign Mission Board and Home Mission Board.

Based on our average full-time annual enrollment, the amount I have requested calculates to $1,974 per student. By comparison our smallest seminary, Midwestern, requested $2.4 million which calculates to $4,700 per full-time student enrolled. That means Southwestern is requesting three and one-half times the amount of money Midwestern is requesting in order to train eight times as many students! It also means Southern Baptists are getting outstanding value for their investment in theological education at Southwestern.

Furthermore, it means Southwestern is under a heavier obligation to raise additional funds from direct contributions to the seminary. We need all the help we can get from alumni and friends to find and solicit those gifts. We have the worthiest of causes, so whether it's before the Executive Committee of our convention or an individual whom God has blessed with wealth, we never hesitate to make a bold request for the future health and operation of this great school.

Renovation . . . Be sure to walk through the first floor of the newly renovated Scarborough wing of the B. H. Carroll Memorial Building the next time you're on campus. This used to be the "infamous" basement of Scarborough Hall, but because of ingenious planning and intense work on the part of our building crew here at Southwestern, openings were drilled through the massive concrete foundations, dirt was removed, windows installed, and now the dark and dreary basement floor has become a bright and sunny first level!

The former Scarborough Chapel has been rebuilt to provide two beautifully appointed preaching laboratories with updated television control rooms. It gives an opportunity for double the number of students to preach in a "church-type setting" and be evaluated not only by their peers but their professors as well. Those who gave the money and those who did the work deserve our heartfelt thanks.

Reports . . . Our enrollment continues to remain stable. This past year the annual headcount at Southwestern was 5,066. This fall semester 4,001 are enrolled, down a few from last fall. The morale and spirit are high and we believe the best semester in the Seminary's history is now underway on "Seminary Hill."

November 1987: Dr. Randall Lolley's Resignation

The announced intention of Dr. Randall Lolley to resign as president of Southeastern Baptist Theological Seminary has been one of the most disturbing developments in the 10-year struggle in our Southern Baptist family.

Some have already announced that they are "elated" and are "rejoicing" at the news of the resignation. But the fact is that Southern Baptist Convention theological education has been robbed of one of its most committed and capable leaders.

During these past ten years at Southwestern, I have worked closely with the other seminary presidents and have come to appreciate Dr. Lolley, our graduate, as a man of integrity and intellect, a man with profound biblical faith, and a spirit-filled preacher of the gospel.

His resignation is understandable. Sensitive, peace-loving Christians have no heart for struggling in an environment of divisive confrontation, unethical manipulation, and that contentious spirit which seems always primed for a fight. It is almost impossible to work with those (according to Carl F. H. Henry's recent description) "whose battle cry is 'we've got the votes and we can take over.' They have elevated raw political power above the redemptive gospel as the main means of change."

This grievous development in the life of our sister seminary has serious implications for all six of our schools and for our divided convention. Surely all SW will join those of us here on Seminary Hill in praying for Randall and Lou Lolley. One of our students sent me this quote from Pilgrims Progress, which seems appropriate:

> Poor man! Where art thou now? Thy day is night.
> Good man! Be not cast down, thou yet art right.
> Thy way to heaven lies by the gates of hell.
> Cheer up! Hold out! With thee it shall be well.

We will also intercede for the faculty, staff, and students at Southeastern, and for the trustees of that institution as they grapple with the enormous decisions that lie before them. We will also lift again to the Lord in prayer our beloved denomination during its darkest days in many years.

Our own board meeting here at Southwestern was characterized by a positive and constructive spirit for which we are grateful. Many of you were praying about the meeting, and the Lord has graciously answered those prayers.

Our hope is that in spite of difficulties and disappointments, the future of Southwestern will continue to be as bright as the present is and the past has been.

December 1987: "Alumni"—A Definition

Alum'ni, alum'nae, n.; pl. [Lat., from *alere*, to nourish.]
Persons who have attended or been graduated from a school.

Just how a Latin word for "nourish" came to be used as the name for an ex-student of an educational institution is unclear, but there are a number of appealing possibilities. It may be that the name evolved because of the obvious fact that a school nourishes its students. As enriching as student years are at the seminary, it would certainly be appropriate to label Southwestern graduates as "nourished."

However, there is another possible explanation for the word, and I like it even better. Perhaps the early linguists wanted a term, which would acknowledge that graduates, indebted as they are for what their school has done for them, should express their gratitude by nourishing that institution.

That makes sense. Furthermore it matches the reality of what Southwestern alumni are doing to "nourish" their "alma mater." (Another Latin term meaning "fostering mother.")

Annually, each autumn, former seminary students gather at alumni meetings during the various Baptist state conventions. This year those meetings broke attendance records in nearly every state. In Texas, for example, 1,000 alumni packed the convention dining room in Fort Worth in the largest state meeting ever! Similar record turnouts across the Southern Baptist Convention sent out a timely signal of affirmation, cheering Southwestern faculty, administration and students, and nourishing the entire seminary family.

But it was not just the unprecedented attendance at these meetings that nourished the seminary. It was the positive mood, the upbeat spirit. I felt it in the ones I had the privilege of attending and discovered that the representatives we sent out to every state sensed the same tone in their gatherings, a heartening atmosphere of appreciation, support, encouragement.

Thank you, every one of you who participated in your state, for nourishing your school.

An encouraging number of alumni have given valuable assistance in finding and encouraging contributions to Southwestern development projects. The financial goals of Upward 90 cannot be reached without the help provided by our graduates. That nourishes your school.

Last, and most important, former students of the seminary have been praying for us regularly. All of us here on campus have been very conscious of that prayer support recently. Through your prayers the power and wisdom of the Lord are made available, and that nourishes your school.

To nourish means, "to supply with matter necessary to life and growth, to support, to maintain, to encourage, to promote." Whoever motivated linguists to name former students "alumni" after the Latin word for "nourish" made a wise choice.

1988

Southwestern–
A School for the Church

Weary of the long, wrenching strife in our convention, the Southwestern family along with Baptists everywhere were praying and hoping that the 1988 SBC meeting in San Antonio would finally see a breakthrough in the pattern of these past years and a return to normalcy.

That concern was expressed well by Dr. Herschel H. Hobbs, former president of the convention and member of the Peace Committee: "It is possible, but not probable, that by continuing this infighting we might hone down our faith to a razor's edge of agreement. But what a tragedy should we do so and go forth to proclaim it—only to find that no longer is anyone listening to us."

Pastor Richard Jackson, who like most of us was strongly conservative but not aligned with the Patterson/Pressler takeover party, was to be nominated as president. We believed that those who set about to "capture the convention" were ready to thank God for the fact that our denomination remained strongly committed to the Word of God and the conservative theology of our Statement of Faith, and that they would therefore give up their efforts to control. Then surely those who had organized to oppose the "takeover" would see no further need for political strategies, and we could all redirect our time and effort to the real tasks for which our convention existed: missions, evangelism, and education.

Even the two trustee meetings of 1988 gave us hope. Even though the twenty-one hard-core fundamentalists now held a strong majority on our board, they recognized the president's ten-year anniversary, affirmed my election as president of ATS (The accrediting agency for seminaries in North America), dedicated a new preaching center, named the new Music Library, and returned the Hispanic Seminary to the Baptist General Convention of Texas.

But our enthusiasm was dashed when Paul Pressler circulated false accusations about Richard Jackson, W. A. Criswell labeled moderates "skunks," a resolution was adopted at the San Antonio convention condemning the doctrine of the Priesthood of Believers because it "undermines the authority of the pastor," and Jerry Vines was elected over Richard Jackson by a narrow margin of 692 votes out of 32,727 ballots cast! Had 347 switched their votes to Jackson, he would have been elected. It was so close.

I found myself wishing some of our defenders who made caustic, unrestrained speeches against the fundamentalists had been more conciliatory. I'm convinced that some who had decided to vote for Jackson were driven to vote for Vines by some of the unnecessary "moderate" rhetoric. It also occurred to me that one other factor may have inadvertantly contributed to Jackson's defeat. The Woman's Missionary Union, whose members at the SBC usually voted for traditional mainstream Baptist issues and against the fundamentalist extremists, did not attend the San Antonio convention in their usual large numbers. This was the year of their centennial celebration, and they held their annual meeting in May in Birmingham instead of their usual practice of meeting in conjunction with the SBC. Had that group been there to vote, I'm convinced Jackson would have been elected.

I am also convinced that had the fundamentalists lost even one election, the momentum would have shifted and they would not have been able to continue their political domination of convention votes. Unfortunately, there were messengers—especially among pastors—who wanted to be on the winning side. Once the winning side shifted to those opposed to the takeover, this group would have quickly adjusted their votes to be with the majority.

Following this disappointing defeat, those opposed to the takeover, pretty well gave up the battle. Future conventions saw very little "moderate" involvement, and the fundamentalist domination continued.

Key Events in 1988

March

14 • Spring trustees meeting

• Recognized president's ten years, which should have been last November. Dedicated new preaching center in Scarborough Hall.

• Lewis Drummond elected president of Southeastern Seminary

April

25-28 • Conference on Biblical Interpretation at Ridgecrest. The third conference on "Application" cancelled for lack of interest

May

2-4 • Peace Committee met in Atlanta to hear seminary presidents' responses

4 • Professor T. B. Maston's funeral

13 • Southwestern Commencement

• Largest graduating class ever—520

14 • WMU Centennial Celebration in Richmond, VA

June

14 • SBC met in San Antonio

• Jerry Vines narrowly elected over Richard Jackson 50.53 percent, 692 votes out of 32,727 attended.

• W. A. Criswell labeled moderates "skunks"

• Resolution adopted condemning the Priesthood of the Believer because it undermines authority of the pastor!

• Joel Gregory preached convention sermon on "The Castle and the Wall"

• Paul Pressler circulated false accusation against Richard Jackson

17-23 • Elected president of the Association of Theological Schools for two years

September

6-7 • Met with SBC Agency heads in Washington, D.C., to discuss strategies for addressing the fundamentalist take over.

12 • Fundamentalist Richard Land elected head of Christian Life Commission

27-30 • Ed Young, Pastor Second Baptist, Houston, preached for Seminary revival

October

17　　• Fall trustee meeting
　　　• Affirmed my election as ATS president
　　　• Returned Hispanic Seminary to the Baptist General Convention of Texas
　　　• Named new music library in honor of donor Kathryn Bowld

November

18　　• Jerry Vines preached in chapel and had lunch with faculty as SBC president. "All indications to me are that Southwestern is a strong evangelical seminary on target with what Southern Baptists are all about and I believe people feel very good about Southwestern."

Note: In the fall meeting of 1988, the thirty-seven-member board of trustees had the following composition: 21 hard-core fundamentalists, 8 traditional mainstream Baptists, and 8 swing voters.

January 1988

The Seminary President
Largest Religious Seminary in the U.S.A.
Southern Baptist Seminary
Fort Worth, Texas

A Christmas card was delivered to my office from a supporter in New York, which had this unusual address. With only the above information, the U.S. Postal Service delivered the card with no trouble. Southwestern's reputation may be more widespread than any of us has realized!

We are known as a "Southern Baptist Seminary" (not to be confused with that other school in Louisville, Kentucky), and that is as it should be. While there are students enrolled at Southwestern from thirty-five different denominations, our student body is 98 percent Southern Baptist. Our faculty and staff are all active members of Southern Baptist churches. And we strive not only to educate and train, but also to "denominationalize" our students, helping them to adequately understand and appreciate the heritage and program of the Southern Baptist Convention.

We are also known as "religious." While much that we do here is similar to any other educational institution, Southwestern is distinctive in its spiritual purposes. Our task is not merely to foster intellectual growth but to assist our students in spiritual formation as well, to help them grow in the likeness of our Lord and Savior, Jesus Christ, and to be able to lead those with whom they will work some day in constructive discipleship.

We are known also as the "largest seminary." The 5,247 plus students enrolled here is unprecedented in the history of theological education, but we are working to be known as the best as well as the biggest seminary. Our search for quality is not to give glory to man but to give glory to the Lord who saved us and called us and Whose incarnation motivated the sending of that unusually addressed Christmas card in the first place. Our hope and prayer is that Southwestern will always reflect the song of the angels, "Glory to God in the highest."

February 1988: World-class Library

With instructions from a room full of expert librarians and with anxious volunteers peering over my shoulder, I affixed new classification data to the spine of a book from Roberts Library. It was a ceremonial act symbolizing the conclusion of the massive task of reclassification all 300,000 volumes in the seminary's collection of theological books.

Thirty-two months ago the decision was made to change our library system from the "Union" classification used for years to the more practical "Library of Congress" classification. Now with the invaluable assistance from lay volunteers from local churches, the huge job was finally completed. As the cameras recorded the symbolic reclassification of book number 303,561 I was reminded again that Southwestern has a "world class" library.

It is a large library, always in the top ten in the nation by every category of measurement. Its new facilities are beautiful and functional providing three floors of inviting, bright reading areas and twenty miles of bookshelves.

The library features the latest in high-tech services with its own "online" catalog, electronic data search and cataloging systems, a CD ROM edition of Books in Print, the latest in audio visual material and compact shelving. Now there is a newly installed computer lab for teaching classes in computer use for ministry.

Assisted by a special library committee of the faculty, librarian Carl Wrotenbery has expanded the comprehensive dimensions of the collection to a high level with notable strengths in biblical studies, religious education, Christian ethics, church history, philosophy of religion, preaching, and church music. Continued enhancement of the collection is insured as faculty recommend new books and as quality libraries of retired scholars around the world are identified and purchased. Recently the library acquired one of the largest collections of Third World missions periodicals in existence.

While Southwestern's ranks near the top in quality and size among the theological libraries in the United States, it ranks eleven from the top in the category of "dollars spent." This demonstrates a careful stewardship of the resources Southern Baptist make available for this important enterprise.

A recent article on theological libraries asked the question, "Is the library a servant or a partner?" While A. Webb Roberts Library serves all of the various functions of seminary life, we here at Southwestern consider this "world class" resource a valuable partner in the educational process.

March 1988: Southwestern—A School for the Church

Both of our distinguished guest lecturers this year effectively addressed timely issues, which are important to Southwestern and to Southern Baptists. In his Northcutt Lectures, R. T. Kendall, the distinguished minister of Westminster Chapel in London, argued for the importance of preaching expository sermons with the unction of the ungrieved Holy Spirit. Students (and all of us for that matter) needed to hear his reminder that preachers may grieve the Spirit:

(1) By wisdom of words (pride of eloquence)
(2) By perverting the true meaning of the text
(3) By not being ourselves and imitating others
(4) By not giving the obvious application of the text
(5) By not letting one's mind be mastered by the Spirit during sermon preparation
(6) By not letting the Spirit master the delivery
(7) By trying to preach "at" the people. (To preach "at" the people is cowardice. To preach "for" the people is performance. To preach "down to" the people is arrogance. To preach "up to" the people is fear. We should preach "to" the people, which is transaction. "The pulpit is no more the preacher's than the communion table.")

Kendall concluded his first lecture by warning us of the frightening possibility of "being perfectly orthodox and perfectly useless"

In the Day-Higginbotham Lectures, Gabriel Fackre, a courageous and clear evangelical voice at Andover Newton Theological School, called us to responsible hermeneutics based on a firm conviction of biblical authority.

Analyzing the differences in theological schools today, he drew an apt analogy. There are "church" seminaries, "school" seminaries and "school for the church" seminaries.

A "church" seminary is one, which, with little emphasis on academic scholarship, is content to be merely a "trade school" cranking out ecclesiastical functionaries. Students are given skills and competencies for ministry, but are not confronted with intellectual issues nor challenged to be critical thinkers.

A "school" seminary, on the other hand, is one, which places all the emphasis on critical learning and academic scholarship with little attention to spiritual formation and ministry skills.

A "school for the church" seminary is one, which harmonizes both the need for excellence in academic scholarship and the need for practical training in evangelism and ministry.

I agree with his perception that Southwestern fits better into this last category. Here, we use the term "practical scholarship" to describe our unapologetic commitment both to the scholarly study of biblical theology and to the practical training of men and women who will know how to do evangelism and ministry.

Southwestern is indeed a "school for the church," helping our convention to communicate a reasonable and thoughtful evangelical faith, and at the same time helping our students to become committed, thinking ministers who are able, in the power of the Holy Spirit, to persuasively challenge modern secular alternatives with the never-changing gospel.

April 1988: Exemplary Trustees

At a dinner gathering of trustees, faculty, and staff during the recent Southwestern board meeting. We honored four who were completing their ten-year terms of service on the board. They are especially significant to me, because they were the first to be elected to our board after I became president in 1978.

As our trustee chairman and I acknowledged their contributions to the seminary, it occurred to me that they were also significant because they so clearly personified those qualities of leadership Southern Baptists would expect from trustees of this institution.

James Coggin (Texas), Davis Cooper (Colorado), Stanley Hand (Florida), and Art Sherwood (Texas)—two pastors, two laymen—each with a strong faith in our Lord and a sacrificial commitment to their local churches.

James Coggin, pastor emeritus of the Travis Avenue Baptist Church in Fort Worth, brought to the board, along with other qualities, a forthright dedication to our convention. He pointed us time and again to the importance of being Southern Baptists. It's no wonder he served twice on this board and was twice its chairman. He has given a large part of his life to helping this institution become what God wants it to be.

Davis Cooper, pastor of the University Hills Baptist Church in Denver, brought to the board, among other things, a strong advocacy for missions. He was brought up on the mission field, speaks fluent Spanish, and kept our eyes focused on the Great Commission. As a chairman, his sense of humor and gracious spirit guided us through some tense sessions.

Stanley Hand, president of Hand Enterprises, Inc. in Winter Park, Florida. He is a hero of twenty-nine B17 missions over Europe in World War II and a former pilot with the Strategic Air Command. He is an enthusiastic witness for Christ who loves his local church, First Baptist, Orlando. Seldom was their a meeting of the board that Stanley didn't help us with organizational insights from his regimented military background, and never was their a meeting when he did not remind us that the seminary was to serve the churches.

Art Sherwood, a biomedical physicist who is director of the Research Institute for neurosciences at Baylor College of Medicine in Houston, is an active layman in Willow Meadows Baptist Church there. With his PhD degree and extensive experiences in the academic world, he brought to the board valuable insights for enhancing our education programs and lifting the level of scholarship at the seminary.

All four considered their trusteeship on the Southwestern board to be more than a place of honor. They understood their position to be a solemn responsibility for which they would be held accountable not only by fellow Southern Baptists, but by their Lord as well. Looking back over these past ten years, I can say without reservation that these four trustees fulfilled that responsibility with honor and distinction.

We gave them plaques and public applause, but someday they will receive a far greater acknowledgement, "Well done, good and faithful servants."

May 1988: Conference on Biblical Interpretation

The Conference on Biblical Interpretation at Ridgecrest was the second in a series of three sponsored by the six Southern Baptist Seminaries as a result of a commitment made in "The Glorieta Statement." The first conference on biblical inerrancy proved that while we prefer different terminology, given all the qualifications of inerrancy, Southern Baptists are not really divided over the nature and authority of the Bible. We are practically unanimous in our conviction that the Word of God is perfect, absolutely trustworthy, and our authority for faith and practice.

The second conference at Ridgecrest has demonstrated that the issues dividing us in these days of denominational struggle are primarily differences in how we interpret portions of the Bible. We saw that equally devout persons with the same high view of scripture and identical commitments to conservative theology could differ sharply about what God's Word teaches on such matters as eschatology, woman's role in the church, charismatic gifts, worship, church and state etc.

While Baptists have officially expressed their convictions about the fundamentals of our faith—those essential beliefs that make us Baptist—we have never established certain interpretations of last things, worship, etc., as test of orthodoxy. In humility, we have realized that none of us can claim to be an infallible interpreter of the Infallible Word. We must acknowledge the importance of relying on the illumination of the Holy Spirit while at the same time learning how to better interpret the Bible so we may apply its authority accurately.

That's why Southwestern recently added a required course in hermeneutics (biblical interpretation) to the first year curriculum of every Master of Divinity student.

Biblical authority is an important doctrine, but it is a useless doctrine unless the one who believes it learns how to "rightly divide the Word of Truth."

June 1988: The Convention, the Commencement, and the Campus

The Convention . . . Wherever I travel across our Southern Baptist realm preaching or attending meetings, the same longings are expressed. Weary of the long, wrenching strife in our convention, people are praying and hoping that San Antonio will be the place where we will finally see a breakthrough in the pattern of these past years and a return to normalcy. Nowhere is that longing more intense than among the students, faculty, and staff of the seminary.

Our concern was expressed well by Dr. Herschel H. Hobbs, former president of the convention and present member of the Peace Committee: "It is possible, but not probable, that by continuing this infighting we might hone down our faith to a razor's edge of agreement. But what a tragedy should we do so and go forth to proclaim it—only to find that no longer is anyone listening to us."

It is the heartfelt hope of so many that those who have set about to "capture the convention" will thank God for the fact that our denomination remains strongly committed to the Word of God and the conservative theology of our Statement of Faith and will give up their efforts to control. Then surely those who have organized to oppose the "takeover" will see no further need for political strategies and will redirect their time and effort to the real tasks for which our convention exists: missions, evangelism, and education.

Then the process of healing the deep scars of suspicion, accusation, hurt feelings, and broken fellowship could begin. Redemptively, we could start to focus on positive factors which may have emerged out of the controversy—factors which can make us a stronger convention—and get on with meeting the spiritual needs and challenges of the last decade of the twentieth century.

Many are cynical, resigned to the conclusion that nothing can save us now; we are too sharply divided. But those who follow the risen Lord must remember that there is always hope! Miraculous, divine intervention is still a possibility. "With God all things are possible!" Let's gather in San Antonio praying, participating, and expecting it to happen!

The Commencement . . . What an impressive sight! Five hundred twenty men and women in black caps and gowns adorned with colorful academic regalia who, along with their proud families and friends, filled every seat in the expansive Travis Avenue Auditorium for spring commencement. The challenging message from Dr. Jesse Fletcher, the music, the recognitions, the awarding of diplomas—it was a dramatic demonstration of what we're about here at Southwestern. and this was the largest number of graduates in the history of the seminary. Praise God from whom such blessings flow!

The Campus . . . Winter browns have turned to spring greens on Seminary Hill, and the trees, flowers, and grass have never been more beautiful. Two comments made recently are appropriate.

Evelyn Phillips, retiring after forty years on the faculty of the music school, reminisced about her arrival on this dusty campus from Tennessee so many years ago. "This was the 'tannest' place I'd ever seen. The buildings were tan. The trees were tan. The grass was tan. The dust-filled sky was tan. Everything was tan!"

The second comment was from an Asian student who upon her arrival at Southwestern years ago from her beautiful lush homeland looked around the bleak campus and said, "There is no place on Seminary Hill to rest your eyes."

No longer are comments like these heard on this beautiful campus. We wish you were here!

July/August 1988:
Looking Ahead to Decade Two—1988–1998

In 1978, the beginning of a new presidential administration provided the seminary a natural opportunity to examine itself and adopt new objectives for the future. Since we were also faced with a regular tenth year accreditation review which called for an extensive self-study before the visiting team from ATS and SACS arrived on campus, there was an additional reason for a serious assessment and revision of the total life and work of our school.

We pondered our weaknesses and strengths and tried to determine what God would have Southwestern be and do during the upcoming decade. Back then, 1988 seemed such a distant point to aim for, but the ambitious goals we adopted were demanding enough to require at least those ten years to accomplish. Now, looking back from that "distant point" in 1988, we are amazed at how God's providential blessings have enabled us (in spite of the convention controversy) to accomplish close to 100 percent of those dreams.

So, on the eve of my second decade as president, it's time for another new beginning. A new "distant point" is beckoning to us from 1998—the threshold of a new century. Southwestern's faculty/administration team is gearing up for another tenth year accreditation self-study, but we will go beyond the routine procedures to accreditation to "re-dream the dream" and fashion a new vision for the future.

Even before the work is done, I have a sense of what that new vision for the last decade of the century will look like. It will ensure that Southwestern's basic distinctions will continue:

(1) Unwavering commitment to our Southern Baptist biblical theology,
(2) Uncompromising commitment to academic excellence,
(3) Unapologetic commitment to a practical curriculum, which emphasizes missions and evangelism.

Necessarily, the new seminary strategic plan will include increased financial support, buildings, renovations, and landscaping, equipment—all necessary vehicles for moving the vision forward Certainly there will be plans for curriculum changes, new courses, programs and teachers. Of course there will be emphases of spiritual vitality and growth.

But beyond all these, and welding them together into a single vision, there must be a grand, unifying theme toward which the diverse elements of our large institution can be focused. Identifying and defining that unifying theme is the program for our faculty retreat in August. We hope to come back from those two days of prayer and discussion with an over-arching concept that will capture the enthusiasm of faculty and students in all three schools. It must be crucial enough and demanding enough to stretch our capacities and harness all out efforts to accomplish it.

And who knows, maybe that new vision can not only inspire Southwestern to new heights for the Lord, but it might be contagious enough to capture the energies of all Southern Baptists and lead us out of the quagmire of dissention. Could that be the solution to our denominational dilemma? That we get so busy again at the main task that we simply don't have time for pointless trivialities as we once again "press toward the mark of the high calling?"

We'll let you know how the retreat turns out. It would help if you would remember to intercede for us in your prayers.

September 1988: Endowed Chairs

Chair, n. [Gk. *kathedra*]

1. A piece of furniture for one person to sit on, having a back and, usually, four legs.

It's not that kind of chair we're trying to endow at Southwestern, although we can always use donations to buy new furniture. It's Webster's second definition with which my column deals:

2. An important or official position, as a professorship or chairmanship.

In the world of higher education the term "chair" refers to a certain position in a department of the faculty for which an endowment fund has been set up to pay the equivalent cost of providing a teacher, secretary, supplies etc. for that subject. The chair is usually named for the donor who gave the money, or for a person who exemplifies that particular field of study.

We have twelve endowed "chairs" at Southwestern Seminary which have been fully funded or for which sufficient funds in wills and trusts have been designated for future endowment. ($500,000 is required to endow a chair):

1924 Bottoms Chair of Missions, Justice Anderson, Professor of Missions

1957 L. R. Scarborough Chair of Evangelism ("Chair of Fire), Roy Fish, Professor of Evangelism

1965 Wesley Harrison Chair of New Testament, Lacoste Munn, Professor of New Testament

1976 George W. Truett Chair of Ministry , Dan Crawford, Assistant Professor of Evangelism/Missions

1982 Bessie M. Fleming Chair of Childhood Education, Jeroline Baker, Professor of Childhood Education

1983 Fred M. and Edith M. Hale Chair of Prayer and Spiritual Formation, Bruce Leafblad, Associate Professor of Church Music and Worship

1984 Thad Roberts Chair of Music Ministry, Fall (vacant); Spring, Charles Gatwood.

1986 Ralph M. and Bess Noble Smith Chair of Preaching, Harold Freeman, Professor of Preaching

Four chairs have been funded by annuity trusts and will be activated in the future:

1974 Earl L. and Vivian Gray Shoemake Chair of Personal Growth Ministry
1985 James C. McKinney Dean's Chair of Church Music
1985 Robert L. Burton Chair of Conducting
1985 Albert L. Travis Chair of Organ

Five additional chairs have been approved by our trustees, substantial initial gifts have been designated, and money is being raised to fully fund them:

1984 John Drakeford Chair of Counseling
1985 Huber L. Drumwright Chair of New Testament
1985 Paul M. Stevens Chair of Christian Communication
1986 R. Hooper Dilday Chair of Religious Education
1988 E. F. "Preacher" Hallock Chair of Student Ministry

We are encouraged by enthusiastic efforts on the part of alumni and friends to complete these endowments, enhancing Southwestern's efforts toward excellence. Ultimately, our goal is to have at least one endowed chair in every department of the curriculum so that regardless of financial emergencies, there will always be a teacher in that discipline at this seminary.

By designating your gifts to one of these developing chairs, you can invest in the future of Southwestern and in the future of quality Christian ministry.

October 1988: Cooperative Program Threatened

For the first time in my thirty-six years of ministry in the Southern Baptist Convention, the future of the Cooperative Program as a denominational funding vehicle is seriously threatened.

Most Southern Baptists are now aware that statistics in nearly every area of our convention work are trending downward, some measurements at their lowest level in many years. This bleak picture is made even worse by new evidences of decline addressed at the September meeting of the Southern Baptist Convention Executive Committee.

For one thing, Southern Baptist Convention Seminary enrollments, which have grown dramatically over the last two decades, are now decreasing. For example, Southwestern's annual head count is 5.57 percent below the year before, and our 1988 fall enrollment is down 5.12 percent.

However, there was even greater concern in the September meeting for the declining pattern in Cooperative Program gifts. For the first time in the ten years I have attended the meetings, the Committee was compelled to recommend a zero increase in the Cooperative Program operating budget for the next year (1989–1990).

This unprecedented step was taken because there is still concern for the 1987-88 budget, to say nothing of the dim prospects for 1988–1989. Furthermore, the Cooperative Program short fall has left a multi-year, accumulating deficit of over $26 million in capital funding.

While economic problems in some parts of the country have contributed to the decline, it is clear that the denominational strife of these past years is largely to blame. In Nashville, the question was, "Whose fault is it?" According to the Baptist Press report of the meeting, the factions in the Southern Baptist Convention controversy are blaming each other. But it seems to me there is enough blame to go around for everybody! More important than "Whose fault is it?" is the question, "What can be done about it?"

God led Southern Baptists to a unique and, up until now, effective concept for funding missions—all kinds of Baptist churches voluntarily cooperating to provide the money for a world evangelization. It is a fragile concept at best, and now it is struggling for survival.

Even in normal, peaceful times the concept of cooperation has to be promoted, encouraged, and reinforced in the churches. But these are not normal peaceful times, and the Cooperative Program is threatened. When prominent churches that ought to be models for the rest of us only give a pittance, when other churches having given generously and proportionately over the years decide to hold back their gifts as a political strategy, when still other churches simply loose their enthusiasm for increasing their mission giving—the future of the Cooperative Program is questionable.

Now is the time to move beyond our differences and reaffirm our commitment to cooperation as the proven way to fulfill Bold Mission Thrust. Each Baptist ought to help revitalize and increase his or her church's missionary giving through our convention. We must do everything we can to "rescue" the Cooperative Program. If we don't, this God-given concept of cooperation, which is indeed fragile, may be irretrievably impaired.

November 1988: Thanksgiving and Southwestern

(This column introduced the annual report for the 1987–1988 academic year. We thanked God for an outstanding year.)

December 1988: State Baptist Conventions

(Having spoken in three state Baptist conventions in November—Texas, New York, and Hawaii—I summed up those gatherings in this column and requested prayer for upcoming meetings of SBC committees who allocated funds for Southwestern. (Every six years it was my turn to represent all six of our Southern Baptist seminaries in Hawaii. It was a tough assignment, but somebody had to do it!) Acknowledging these were tough times in Baptist life, I quoted Paul's conclusion in 2 Corinthians 1:9 that God allows trouble so "that we should not trust in ourselves, but in God who raises the dead.")

1989

A Battle Born Spirit

During 1989, following the disappointing close vote in the San Antonio convention, Southwestern continued its work with lingering hopes that somehow the tide would turn. It was clear Southern Baptists were going in the wrong direction. Statistics were trending downward. Financial support was declining. Convention programs were being cut back. Enthusiasm and momentum grew sluggish. Surely Satan was rejoicing as the SBC goals under the "Bold Mission Thrust" theme sputtered along on a sidetrack, while the convention's attention was focused on lesser things.

This decade-long struggle of "takeover efforts" by some and "resistance" by others had sapped the spirit of our Baptist family. Young people considering God's call to the ministry were discouraged and often used the convention "situation" as a reason for delaying or saying "no" to a future in Southern Baptist ministry. Following a pattern in the other seminaries, enrollments at Southwestern began trending downward.

My discouragement increased when we read the report that Joel Gregory, Fort Worth Pastor and former Southwestern professor had announced his plan to join the takeover effort. Because of his rising popularity among the fundamentalists as an outstanding preacher, evidenced by his memorable sermon at the San

Antonio convention on "The Castle and the Wall," I believed he might be the person to bring our divided convention together.

Back in 1985, Gregory had found himself in an unusual position. Both parties in the SBC controversy had asked him to nominate their candidate for president, Charles Stanley the fundamentalist nominee, and Winfred Moore, the opposition candidate. Joel approached me with a novel and appealing idea. Maybe this indicated a providential intersection of trust. Maybe both candidates could step aside and Joel Gregory could be unanimously elected to a one-year term as "moderator" of the SBC to give the convention controversy an opportunity to cool down. By not using the term president, and by limiting the election to one year, there would be time to ratchet down the tensions and move toward reconciliation. I liked the idea.

The two of us contacted Winfred Moore who readily agreed. He'd be glad to step aside if it meant a compromise and healing. Gregory and I then went to see Paige Patterson in his Dallas office to present the idea, asking them to also withdraw their announced plans to nominate Charles Stanley. Patterson responded, "We'll have to pray about it." Gregory boldly corrected him. "You mean you'll have to talk to your cohorts about it!" Patterson acknowledged as much, and we left. Some weeks later, Patterson reported that their plans had gone too far and they couldn't change them. It was another occasion of hopes dashed. I continued to believe, however, that Joel Gregory was in a position to help heal the rift.

Now, in 1989, even that hope was gone. Joel Gregory publicly announced that he and a few other "unaligned pastors" (including Ken Hemphill and Charles Fuller of Virginia) were planning to support Jerry Vines over Dan Vestal for SBC president.

I met privately with Gregory at the Fort Worth Club for lunch and express my disappointment, reminding him of his unique popularity that would enable him to lead out in a healing process. His rationale for his shift to join the fundamentalists was that if Dan Vestal were elected, the fundamentalist leaders would call for a "bloodbath," firing all the SBC leaders who were not in their camp and immediately taking control of all the agencies, including Southwestern. (Ironically, that happened anyway, even though Vines was elected over Vestal.)

Looking back, I suspect Gregory was already positioning himself to be considered the Pastor of First Baptist Dallas. His book *So Great a Temptation* implies as much.

The fall meeting of Southwestern's board brought a new surprise. Under the leadership of new chairman, Ken Lilly, a physician from Arkansas, there was an unexpected and unsuccessful attempt to fire me as president. The details of this attempt are sketched in the following calendar of "Key Events in 1989."

It was in August 1989 that representatives of the FBI interviewed me in my office about the possible appointment of Paul Presler to head the U.S. Ethics Commission. We all knew this possible appointment was a reward for Pressler's role in helping garner SBC votes in the presidential election. See my comments about this meeting in the following "Key Events in 1989."

Key Events in 1989

February
9   • Jimmy Draper spoke at Southwestern

March
10   • O. S. Hawkins, pastor in FL, spoke in chapel
13   • Spring Trustees Meeting
           • Announced that for first time in my tenure, the Seminary will get less from SBC Cooperative Program

April
1   • Professor Russ Bush accepted position with Paige Patterson at Southeastern—School of Religious Education observed seventy-fifth anniversary
5   • Richard Land for lunch with Seminary faculty
10   • Jimmy Allen resigned from SBC Radio and Television Commission
23   • Preached at Prestonwood Baptist Church, Dallas, TX

May
12   • Met with trustee Jimmy Draper and graduate student Jim Tuell. Faculty rightfully denied his doctorate, and Draper inappropriately defended him, leading to expensive lawsuit.
22   • John Tietjen, former president of Lutheran Seminex told faculty about their experiences with fundamentalists. Many similarities

June
1   • Met with Joel Gregory about his announced plans to join the fundamentalists' effort. He indicated Ken Hemphill and Charles Fuller would also join. They would support Jerry Vines because "if moderates win, there will be a bloodbath of firings by the fundamentalists!" There was anyway.
11   • SBC met in Las Vegas—Jerry Vines reelected over Dan Vestal 56.58 percent, 20,411 messengers

August

21-25 • Visited with new trustees Lee Weaver, David Bruce, Ken Faught, Charles Lawson, and Gerald Dacus

31   • Sean Joyce and a colleague with the FBI met with me to discuss appointment of Judge Paul Pressler to the U.S. Ethics Commission. I told them that naming him as head of ethics commission would be like putting Pete Rose in charge of getting gambling out of baseball. They asked about specific accusations and rumors about his conduct and indicated most of their reports had been negative. Pressler later withdrew from consideration.

September

2   • Visited with new trustees Jack Robertson and Ward Walker

12-15 • Dan Vestal, Pastor Dunwoody Baptist, Atlanta, preached for Seminary revival. Curtis Vaughn called it "The best revival in my tenure." Freddie Gage offered to pay for sending tapes of his messages to all the students and to pastors.

17   • Preached Dauphin Way Baptist Church, Mobile, AL

October

16   • Fall trustees meeting

       • After Monday p.m. session, Chairman Ken Lilly told Betty and me that there would be an executive session the next morning. He felt he should tell us they had thirty charges against me and enough votes to fire me. We went home wondering what in the world they were talking about and laughed, predicting that Paige and Dorothy Patterson would be in our house after they elected him as president! Little did we know!

       • Tuesday morning session, Jimmy Draper asked that this session be an executive session. Don Taylor and John McKay made motion to postpone action on my recommendations until the executive session. But it failed. They were trying to delay the appointment of Dr. Scotty Gray as the Executive Vice President hoping I would be fired and they could name Vice President John Seelig. Later I learned Seelig had helped them with their plans to fire me after they had promised to promote him to operating officer of the seminary.

       • Executive Session began at 11:00 a.m. lasted till 6:00 p.m. Huge crowd. Chairman Lilly dismissed all but members of the board. All three TV stations were recording the meeting. One student remained and the chairman asked him to leave. He responded, "I respect your authority, but I've prayed about this and God told me to stay." With the TV cameras rolling, Chairman Lilly replied, "Son, this is a trustee meeting. God doesn't have anything to do with it." That statement ended up on the 10:00 news!

- In the executive session, I decided to hear all their "charges" before responding. Their "charges" were things like: "You hired a facultymember who endorses homosexuality." Another fundamentalist board member quickly interrupted: "I rebuke you in the name of the Lord. I talked to that man and it's not true. I warned you not to raise that." They dropped that "charge" and went to the next.
- Not a one of the thirty "charges" had any basis, and they then had to find a way to end what had become an awkward session without merit. Crowds of supporters had gathered outside the room, singing. They asked Jimmy Draper, Jerry Gunnells, John McNaughton and me to draft a conciliatory agreement. It was adopted and the crowd was invited back in with good news that a crisis had been avoided and all was well.

18   - Met Seminary officers, then with John Seelig alone. He wept and confessed his involvement and their promise to reward him. I told him he would have to leave, but he could have time to talk to his wife and retire instead of being dismissed. He could live in the seminary house for modest rent if he did not interfere with seminary matters again.

20   - Walter Kaiser, innerantist, gave lectures

November

9   - Spoke at Washington, D.C., and Virginia Baptist State Conventions

Note: In the fall meeting of 1989, the thirty-seven-member board of trustees had the following composition: 21 Hard-core fundamentalists, 11 traditional mainstream Baptists, and 5 swing voters.

January 1989: Remembrances, Recognitions, and Review

Remembrances . . . Mailboxes stuffed with beautiful Christmas cards, baskets of homemade "goodies" left at the door, fruitcakes delivered by UPS—all reminders from Southwesterners across the world that the Seminary is in their thoughts as the new year begins. It's encouraging to be remembered.

Christmas is always a distinctive holiday on Seminary Hill. Although book reports, research papers, and final exams due at the end of the fall semester tend to distract us, and while graduation activities capture our attention, still we are reminded of the joy of Nativity and the promise of new beginnings by meaning-ful worship services in chapel, festive decorations, and of course the annual presentation of Handel's *Messiah* in Truett Auditorium. We are still luxuriating in the afterglow of Christmas remembrances.

Recognitions . . . Year-end is also the time for our annual "Faculty/Staff Awards Luncheon." In five-year increments, thirty-three persons were recognized for service to the Seminary.

. . . I wish you could have heard the eloquent tribute Mrs. Ruth MacGorman paid her husband Jack as we established the "MacGorman Scholarship Fund" in recognition of his forty years at Southwestern. He repre-sents the sacrificial investment of a lifetime in our school. Thank God for that kind of abiding dedication.

Review . . . Year-end is also the time for appraisal reviews, and I've just completed evaluations on the work of the five Seminary vice-presidents. The Lord has brought together an exceptional team of gifted leaders with whom I am privileged to work.

Dr. John Newport, Vice President for Academic Affairs (since 1979)

Dr. Jeter Basden, Vice President for Planning and Research (since 1983)

Dr. Lawrence Klempnauer, Vice President for Student Affairs (since 1980)

Mr. Hubert Martin, Vice President for Business Affairs (since 1984)

Dr. John Seelig, Vice President for Public Affairs (since 1960)

Pray for us as we begin the new year with gratitude for 1988 and with Christ-centered hope for 1989.

February 1989: "The Lord Gave and the Lord Has Taken Away, May the Name of the Lord Be Praised" (Job 1:21)

The Lord has taken away . . . The seminary family was shocked and saddened by the sudden death of Dr. Virtus Gideon, who taught New Testament here for thirty-one years. Poignant letters from his former students remind us again that teachers at Southwestern are more than just academicians in a graduate school, more than technical scholars in a large seminary. They become role models, mentors, spiritual coaches, ministers who encourage and inspire the men and women in their classrooms. Some of the complimentary comments from these letters have appeared in Baptist papers across the convention, pointing to the widespread, immeasurable influence teachers like Dr. Gideon exert for our Lord. We miss him.

The Lord gave . . . Providentially, Dr. Curtis Vaughan, who had taken early retirement, and moved to North Carolina, felt impressed by God some months ago to "unretire" and return to his teaching ministry. We were in the process of welcoming him and his wife Frances back to the campus when Dr. Gideon died. This semester, Dr. Vaughan is picking up the classes Dr. Gideon would have taught. As one of our most popular teachers, Dr. Vaughan is also more than a scholarly professor; he is a servant-minister of Christ for whom we are grateful. (Incidentally, he was one of my teachers when I was here in the fifties!) We are grateful to have him back.

As Job said, "The Lord gave and the Lord has taken away, may the name of the Lord be praised."

March 1989: Finding a Place of Service

One of the pressing needs at the Seminary over the years has been an effective "placement" service. With an increasing number of graduates each year, it is important that we do all we can to help current students and those who are graduating find where God wants them serve.

Past efforts have been mostly informal, and even when assigned to a staff position, placement efforts were usually added to existing responsibilities and therefore received only part time attention at best.

With the coming of Ed Seale seven years ago, that changed. Under his leadership, a full time "placement" office was organized and is now functioning effectively. Of course, Southern Baptists don't really "place" their ministers. (Missionary appointments are the closest we come to assigning positions.) Nevertheless, our Office of Church/Minister Relations (the name we give to our "placement" office) has been most effective in bringing needs and prepared ministers together.

The office sponsors seminars such as "Bivocational Ministry," "How to Find a Fulfilling Ministry," "Beginning Your Ministry," "Vocational Enrichment for Women," "How to Write a Resume," "How to Work with Search Committees."

Lists of available students and graduates are mailed to associational and convention offices. Internships, apprenticeships, and other forms of supervised ministry are arranged with churches and denominational agencies to allow students to have practical experience while they study.

The office makes arrangements for state convention leaders, pastors, and search committees from across the nation to interview students and recent graduates about positions. Resumes, some of them in the form of videotapes, are mailed. (A total of 6,657 were sent the first five months of this semester!) In addition to church related positions, Ed Seale's office now serves as the referral center for all off-campus secular employment.

On the last day of January, a letter came from the chairman of a search committee from a church in a distant state where resumes had been sent. It expresses the appreciation we all feel for this important service. Here are some excerpts:

"Our Search Committee reviewed the resumes carefully and invited four of these individuals to submit additional information. We considered two of them as top candidates and invited them to visit us. One of them accepted a call to another church. The other candidate . . . . visited us and has, subsequently, accepted the call to serve here . . . . Again let me thank you for the fine service you have rendered. The resumes were right on target, and the 'Methods That Work' pamphlet was extremely helpful. The material we received from you was far superior to that received from any other source . . . ."

April 1989: Where Is the Money Coming From?

On March 14, the Southwestern board of trustees approved the seminary operating budget for 1989–1990. Of the twelve budgets recommended to the board since 1978 when I became president, this is the first one based on a decrease in revenue over the previous year. The 1989–1990 budget will be 1.2 percent smaller than the 1988–1989 budget.

It is also the first time (in more than 30 years!) that our Cooperative Program allocation will be less than the previous year. Because of these factors, this is the first budget in my tenure as president with no salary increases.

Basically, Southwestern has four sources of income. While those sources have been the same for twelve years, the percentage ratios between them have shifted somewhat:

Source	1978	1989
Cooperative Program	51 percent	43 percent
Student Fees	15 percent	20 percent
Endowment & Gifts	15 percent	19 percent
Auxiliary Enterprises, etc.	19 percent	18 percent

Notice how student fees and income from endowment are bearing increasing percentages of the cost of operation, while the Cooperative Program percentage has declined significantly.

Three decisions were made in the Southern Baptist Convention Executive Committee meeting last month which negatively affected Southwestern's share of the Cooperative Program:

(1) A decision not to increase the total CP budget for 1989–1990 (the first time in more than 30 years)

(2) A decision to pay from CP funds the remaining $2.5 million indebtedness on the new Executive Committee Building in Nashville.

(3) A decision to allocate an additional one-time $200,000 beyond the formula allocation from the CP for Golden Gate Seminary.

The SBC building decision (2 above) cost Southwestern about $212,000 and the Golden Gate decision (3 above) cost us about $17,000, giving the seminary $229,000 less from the 1989–1990 CP budget.

Mirroring this shortfall in CP income are decreases in other sources as well. While our 1989–1990 income from endowment and gifts will be about level, income from auxiliary enterprises and miscellaneous sources will be down about $160,000, and revenues from student fees will decline $152,000.

After reaching an all time high in 1986–1987 of 5,274 students, the annual enrollment has been about level for three years. This past year, however, enrollment dropped 9 percent below the highest to 4,784 students, the most significant decrease in over 20 years. It appears the present year's enrollment will show a similar decline.

In order to balance next year's budget we have had to exclude any salary increases for faculty and staff; we have been forced to trim program expenditures, and all capital projects are on hold. "Biting the bullet" is no easy task for a "personnel intensive" institution like ours, but we are doing it while maintaining our commitment to educational excellence.

What hope is there for increased revenues in the future?

(1) Hopefully, our churches will return to higher levels of Cooperative Program giving, and our state conventions will pass on a larger portion of those gifts to Southern Baptist Convention causes. This is our primary support base at Southwestern. We must reverse the CP shortfall of recent years and return to the point where 50 percent of our support comes from Southern Baptist Churches through the Cooperative Program.

(2) Hopefully, the economy will continue its recovery and earnings from our investment portfolio will begin to climb again.

(3) Hopefully, there will be an increase in students from among those God is calling into ministry. The recent decline is largely caused by the denominational conflict. In spite of the turmoil these past twelve years, the convention still offers the best avenue for ministry; and Southwestern offers the best preparation.

(4) Hopefully, more individual stewards will contribute to Southwestern. Already, our intensified fund-raising efforts are showing encouraging results.

Southwestern needs the help of every one of its friends and alumni, and every Southern Baptist who cares about the quality of future ministers. This is God's school. As He has faithfully done in other difficult days, we believe He will see Southwestern through.

May 1989: "A Battle Born Spirit"

As we approach the 1989 meeting of the Southern Baptist Convention, it is obvious that our denomination is seriously divided, and it is equally obvious that this division has profoundly diminished our effectiveness.

We are going in the wrong direction. Statistics are trending downward. Financial support is declining. Programs are being cut back. Enthusiasm and momentum have grown sluggish. Surely Satan is rejoicing as Bold Mission Thrust sputters along on a sidetrack, while our convention's attention is focused on lesser things.

This decade-long struggle of "takeover efforts" by some and "resistance" by others has sapped the spirit of our Baptist family. Young people considering God's call to the ministry are discouraged and often use the convention "situation" as a reason for delaying or saying "no" to a future in Southern Baptist ministry.

We are very much aware of the negative repercussions here at Southwestern. Enrollments are declining. For the first time in over thirty years, cooperative program support is diminishing; resulting in lower budgets, no salary adjustments, reduced programs, etc.

In spite of it all, Southwestern is still finding ways to move forward with its purpose—even if short of its full potential. With strong faith in God's providence, our faculty and students are going about their tasks courageously, but there hangs over all our work a melancholy cloud of despondency. Suspicion has displaced trust. Our credibility before the lost world is lower than ever, robbing us of evangelistic effectiveness. Southern Baptists are not what we used to be or ought to be.

But this is no time to give up on the Southern Baptist Convention. More than ever, we need Southern Baptists who will remain Southern Baptists, attending the meetings, and doing their best to restore the convention.

New leaders must emerge who will challenge us to nobler agendas, inspire us to put the past behind us, encourage us to stop fixing blame for what has happened, and lead us to get on with God's business.

Messengers must vote for leaders not because they are on the "right side," but because they are more likely to pull us out of the morass. Messengers must express their honest convictions on issues rather than voting the "party line." They must refuse to be intimidated or cajoled by others around them and be willing to take a stand in spite of ridicule or pressure.

Even when restoration begins in the Southern Baptist Convention, it will take a long time for scars to heal, fellowship to be restored, and trust to return, but the sooner we start, the sooner our effectiveness for our Lord will return.

Nevada became a state in 1864, during the middle of the Civil War, and was therefore nicknamed "The Battle Born State." Let's pray that in Las Vegas, Nevada in the middle of our Baptist civil war, a new spirit will emerge—"a battle born spirit"—of peace, trust, cooperation, and renewed effectiveness.

June 1989: We've Had a Lot of Help

In his commencement address to the graduates of the Texas College of Osteopathic Medicine here in Fort Worth the other day, television medical personality, Dr. James "Red" Duke (one of our Southwestern graduates) offered this bit of wisdom: "If you ever see a turtle on a fence post, you know it had to have a lot of help!"

That statement could apply to institutions. When you see a school as strong and effective as Southwestern Seminary you know it had to have a lot of help. [Note: In this column, I listed some evidences of the assistance Southwestern has received.]

July/August 1989:
Report to the Southern Baptist Convention

(This column featured a summary of my report to the SBC meeting in Las Vegas.)

September/October 1989: Southwestern at Oxford

Sixty-five students, faculty, alumni, and friends of Southwestern participated in this year's summer session at Regent's Park College, Oxford. Credit courses from all three schools were offered, including the course in biblical hermeneutics Dr. Newport and I taught. It was a memorable experience, convincing me that this activity is important, and that we owe a debt of gratitude to director Cecil Roper and his team who planned the 1989 program.

Lectures from Oxford evangelicals enhanced those of our own professors and introduced us to the distinctive educational environment of one of the world's oldest universities. Surrounded by the beautiful old spires and quads of the thirty-five colleges, the libraries, museums, and monuments one is gripped by an irresistible desire to read and learn.

There was spiritual inspiration too. A painted cross on the pavement in downtown Oxford marks the place where three sixteenth-century preachers: Cranmer, Ridley, and Lattimer were burned at the stake for their convictions. I was reminded of the priceless Baptist principle of liberty of conscience that can be so casually ignored in our day.

We also traced the steps of our early Baptist forebears. Walking down a narrow alley in Tewksbury where one of the oldest Baptist churches still stands, we felt the intimidation those members must have felt when they emerged from their insignificant alley into the High Street. There the shadows of the massive cathedral with its brooding spires and stained glass windows overwhelmed their tiny little back-street chapel. We remembered that it never dawned on these early Baptists to believe that worldly success, power, and numbers were evidences of God's blessings. They expected persecution, not wealth as the reward for obedience and faithfulness.

We visited William Carey's church in Kettering and his nearby home with its leather shop. On the wall was a copy of the hand drawn map of the world that challenged him to missions as he worked. We realized we were standing where the modern mission movement was born.

All this has significance for us as we begin another semester at Southwestern. We want to be an effective center of piety and learning where twentieth-century disciples can prepare to serve the same Lord these early British believers served.

Hopefully our graduates will exhibit similar characteristics: scholarly yet committed to the Lord Jesus no matter what the costs, faithful even if it means persecution, burdened by the lostness of the whole world.

November/December 1989:
"All Four Lanes Narrow to One at Seminary"

Following the traditional annual cycle, I presented Southwestern's request for 1990–1991 Cooperative Program funds to the Southern Baptist Convention Executive Committee in Nashville last month. After briefly presenting the statistical data, I turned toward a facet of Southwestern's life that can't be so easily reduced to facts and figures—the Seminary Revival.

It started at the faculty retreat this fall, when our professors redirected their attention to "Spiritual Formation." They came away committed to making every class and lecture an occasion for calling students to a closer walk with the Lord, to a more vital, dynamic Christian experience.

Revival Preparation Week followed, and it was clear something spontaneous, something "over and beyond" the planned meetings was emerging. Prayer groups came together across the campus. Classes spent time in prayer. Lectures were stopped as students and teachers prayed. Churches were caught up in the mounting anticipation.

The Revival Week itself exceeded any other revivals in remembered history. Under the theme "Coming Home," evangelist Dan Vestal and singer Dave Briley spoke and sang to capacity crowds in Truett Auditorium and overflow participants in classrooms across the campus. Public decisions were made. Some were saved; others confessed their sins to the Lord and were forgiven and renewed. Broken relationships were restored. People got right with God. Couples were on their knees together recommitting their lives to God and to each other.

As the week progressed, students dropped by the President's Office to say, "Something's happening!" "Something's different." Dr. Curtis Vaughan said it was the most effective revival on campus in his long tenure as a teacher. Even yet, the revival continues, reminding us that the Seminary's task is not just academic preparation, but to develop in the lives of future ministers a profound personal faith, Christ-like character, authenticity, morality, a daily walk with God, and a life overflowing with the fruits of the Holy Spirit.

You remember when driving south on I-35 in Fort Worth that the freeway exit to the campus is called "Seminary Drive." The freeway is under construction and they've put up a "state-of-the-art" electronic traffic sign across all four southbound lanes. The other day I was amazed at the message on the flashing sign: "ALL FOUR LANES NARROW TO ONE AT SEMINARY."

It seemed to be reminding us that all the worthy purposes of a Seminary education actually narrow down to one basic task: to produce graduates who:

- not only understand the faith, but experience it.
- not only reflect on Christology, but live like Christ.
- not only study the theology of prayer, but pray.
- not only recite the attributes of God, but become godly.

"All lanes narrow to this one at Southwestern!"

1990

These Are the Times that Try Men's Souls

Since the last board meeting in 1989 closed with a failed attempt by the fundamentalists trustees to fire the president, it is understandable that events in 1990 were overshadowed by anxiety that "they might try it again." When the trustees gathered on campus for the spring meeting, rumors abounded. But the good seminary reports seemed to avert any negative action. In January, *Christianity Today* reported on their survey that ranked Southwestern "the best seminary in the United States."

The goals of our five-year plan called Upward 90 had all been met, including the completion of Scarborough Hall remodeling, the adding of new parking areas, the acquisition of major library collections, the funding of twelve academic chairs, the opening of the new Preaching Center, and the raising of $36.3 million.

So even though the fundamentalist elected their slate of officers (Jimmy Draper, Chair; Damon Shook, Vice Chair; T. Bob Davis, Secretary), the meeting was fairly routine. They did pass a resolution honoring John Seelig who had helped them with their failed plan to fire me. Reversing my arrangement with him, they gave him the use of the seminary home rent-free and named the banquet room after him—all as a reward for his help. While they claimed this was done to celebrate his retirement, the fact is I had forced him to either retire or be dismissed.

Two weeks after the meeting, I had quadruple heart bypass surgery at Harris Methodist Hospital in Fort Worth. The likelihood of closed arteries had been discovered during a treadmill stress test at the Cooper Clinic in December of 1989, and confirmed by an ensuing angiogram a few days before the surgery on March 28. Since there was no heart attack or damage to the heart, recovery was routine and quick. I came home from the hospital in five days and returned to the office in less than a month.

Echoing the peaceful spring meeting, the fall session of the trustees took the form of a retreat, and ended quietly with the election of Bruce Corley as Dean of the School of Theology.

Patterson and Pressler persevered in their assault on Southwestern by continuing to name hardliners to our board. For example, Olin Collins, a fundamentalist Fort Worth pastor, was among those elected in the June SBC meeting in New Orleans. When his name was released before the convention met, a woman called to warn me he had been accused of having affairs with women in her church. I called Collins who denied the accusations and suggested I talk to his mentor, Richard Jackson, who would vouch for him. Jackson felt there was no problem, and since there was not much I could have done anyway, Collins was elected. Later, after he took a leading role in my firing, he became chairman of the board and then was dismissed as pastor of his church because of accusations of misconduct with several women in the church. The headline-making scandal led to his resignation from the board.

Somehow the "Victory Celebration" in December held by Patterson and Pressler at the Café Dumond in New Orleans where their takeover campaign was hatched seemed like an empty charade.

Key Events in 1990

January

1	• Upward 90 goals achieved
17	• Jack Graham, pastor or Prestonwood Baptist, Dallas, preached in chapel
19	• Jimmy Draper preached in chapel
20	• *Christianity Today* survey ranked Southwestern best Seminary in U.S.

March

12
- Spring trustees meeting
- Bill Tolar elected Vice President
- Fundamentalist slate of officers elected—Jimmy Draper, chair; Damon Shook, vice chair; T. Bob Davis, secretary
- Jim Bolton offered resignation because of conflict of interest
- Resolution passed honoring John Seelig upon his "retirement"
- Passed a resolution honoring John Newport at his retirement

28
- Dr. Nazarian performed my triple bypass heart surgery at Harris Hospital in Fort Worth
- Richard Land preached in chapel

April

3
- Came home from hospital after five days

23
- Returned to office
- Celebrated seventy-fifth anniversary of the School of Church Music

June

10-14
- SBC met in New Orleans
- Morris Chapman elected over Dan Vestal with 57.68 percent
- 38,403 messengers
- Olin Collins among new trustees elected
- Answered question from floor about my remarks that the worldly use of crass political power to take over the convention was wrong, evil, satanic. The Convention gave a standing ovation.

July

17
- At Paul Pressler's insistence, Southern Baptist Convention staff members Dan Martin and Al Shackleford fired behind closed doors, armed guards, etc.
- Associated Baptist Press started as an alternative to controlled SBC press

27
- Met in Jimmy Draper's office to talk about my intention to recommend Bruce Corley as Dean of the School of Theology

August

13
- Baptist Sunday School Board voted to destroy Professor Leon McBeth's history of the board because it did not take fundamentalist slant

16-29
- Visited new trustees: Richard Mason, Byron Ramsey, Larry Brown, Paul Balducci, Everett Powell, Charles Lawson, and Richard Barrett

30   • Met with Jimmy Draper about the lawsuit being brought by student,
            Jim Tuell. He acknowledged he shouldn't have defended him, but too
            late now.

September
4   • Henry Blakaby preached in chapel
13   • Met with denominational relations committee, First Baptist Church,
            Plano, TX
20   • Spoke at Houston's Union Association Pastor's Conference on SBC
            issues
21   • Baylor University Board votes to amend its charter to remove itself
            from Baptist General Convention of Texas control because of funda-
            mentalist threat
26   • BWA president Denton Lotz preached in chapel
            • Jimmy Draper preached in chapel

October
3   • Visited with new trustee Olin Collins
15   • Fall trustees meeting
            • Met in a retreat at DFW Hilton Hotel to try to rebuild unity. Rumors
            that president would be fired. T. Bob Davis led worship.
            • Reported return to full schedule after surgery
            • Reported on Baylor's intention to start Truett Theological Seminary
            • Recommended Bruce Corley as Dean of School of Theology. After
            much discussion in which he answered their questions well, he was
            elected.
            • Passed a resolution affirming the faculty
24   • Trustee Olin Collins preached in chapel
25   • Broke ground for Bowld Music Library Building
30   • Spoke at state Baptist conventions in Colorado, Ohio, and New
            England

November
20   • Met Bishop K. H. Ting in Dallas with missionary Britt Towery

December
            • "Victory in Jesus Celebration" by Paige Patterson and Paul Pressler at
            Café du Monde in New Orleans to mark their success in taking over
            the SBC (same place where they launched their political campaign.)

Note: In the fall meeting of 1990, the thirty-eight-member board of trustees had the following composition: 27 hard-core fundamentalists, 7 traditional mainstream Baptists, and 4 swing voters.

January/February 1990: Staying on Top

I've just had breakfast with the Seminary's last graduating class of the '80s. 283 in number, these diverse men and women will be the church leaders of the nineties and into the 21st century!

Some completed their work here in two years, for others it was as long as seven. A significant number studied in one of our remote campuses: Houston, Shawnee, San Antonio, or in off-campus centers at Dallas and Lubbock. They came from all sections of the USA and from other nations. Most already have places of service. Most of the others will be placed within a year. About a third of them are mission volunteers.

Remembering that I completed the master's degree at Southwestern thirty-five years ago, I tried to imagine where these graduates would be thirty-five years from now on December 13, 2025, and what challenges and opportunities they would face? I thanked God for them and their immeasurable potential for good.

Obviously, they could have taken some shortcut to an easier "seminary degree," so I congratulated them for choosing a demanding, legitimate, quality theological education. The Bible makes it clear that God-called ministers should be educated and trained. They should develop and sharpen their gifts in order to place in God's hands the best possible instrument for His use (cf. 1 Tim 4:6-16). These Southwestern graduates have obeyed that biblical admonition.

And they did it in what we believe is the BEST seminary in the world! Of course, all Southwesterners hold that somewhat "biased" opinion of our school, but notice in this issue of the Southwestern News that Southwestern Seminary was ranked No. 1 in the USA by an objective *Christianity Today* survey. You can be sure that with appropriate humility I shared that news with these 283 new alumni!

March/April 1990: Lessons from a Lecturer

Fellow Baptist Millard Erickson, vice-president of Bethel Seminary and this year's Day-Higginbotham lecturer, spoke to us on the theme "Where is Theology Going." As one of America's foremost evangelical scholars, Dr. Erickson not only traced future doctrinal trends, but he also spoke objectively about our Southern Baptist situation. His insights were timely and helpful.

He reminded us that trends in theology usually move in one direction until they go beyond the parameters of normative biblical concepts, and then, almost inevitably, a reaction to and reversal of that trend begins. The danger is that usually the reaction becomes a trend in the opposite direction and returns, not back to the middle, but to the opposite extreme and in turn has to be reversed. The task for responsible believers is to maintain a steady course in the midst of these "undulations," guided by the authority of Holy Scripture.

In this process of maintaining a steady course, Dr. Erickson reminded us that we must not become ecclesiastical highway patrolmen spending our time setting radar traps to catch our brothers and sisters in what we consider to be violations, and writing them theological citations.

He warned us not to make the mistake of assuming the worst about persons whose views differ from ours. Rather than questioning their motives, we should try to understand their positions and judge those positions on the basis of biblical verification, all the while respecting their right as fellow believers to differ.

To the denomination, his advice was to give theological education high priority in funding and support. Since the work of the seminary does not appear to many to be as exciting as missions or evangelism or church planting, it sometimes receives inadequate support. A "bases empty" home run is more exciting than two walks, a bunt, and a sacrifice fly; but both have the same result—one run. He reminded us that ministry preparation and scholarly reflection in the seminaries are vitally important to the future of a denomination's theological understanding, and hence its effectiveness in missions and evangelism.

Timely words—especially as we go to Nashville this month to discuss what portion of the Cooperative Program gifts from Southern Baptist churches should be allocated to the Seminaries.

May/June 1990: Heartfelt Thanks

Note: On March 18, the president underwent successful bypass surgery in Harris Hospital in Fort Worth. Heartfelt thanks go out to:

BETTY, who for the first time in our thirty-eight years of marriage is discovering what it really means to promise: "in sickness and in health." Of course, I couldn't get by without her.

ROBERT, NANCY, AND ELLEN, our three children, and their families who came across the country to stand by us and help in a thousand ways.

THE METHODISTS for providing their excellent hospital here in Fort Worth. We Baptists are proud of the Baylor Medical Center in Dallas, but Harris Hospital is one of Fort Worth's own world-class medical facilities.

SKILLED PHYSICIANS. Christians sometimes disparage scientific technology as "secular," but thank God for medical scientists who pay the price of disciplined training and "hands-on" practice in order to fulfill their essential calling with such competence. (Sounds like my speech on the importance of theological education for ministers). My "heartfelt" thanks to:

1. Dr. Kenneth Cooper, who spotted my problem from his stress test cardiograms. I had no visible symptom, but he showed me the tiny "aberration" on the squiggly chart indicating I had a problem. I never could see the distinction his experienced eyes could see. What's more, he cared enough to keep up with the tests year after year and to insist on the angiogram, which eventually led to surgery.

2. Dr. Jack Schwade, who with his expertise in cardiac catheterization, actually let me see for myself the blocked arteries on the TV screen while the angiogram was going on.

3. Dr. Manucher Nazarian, whose reputation as a heart surgeon has brought national attention to Fort Worth. He has even learned how to stitch the incision from the inside so the scar hardly shows! His fifteen-hours-a-day schedule is extraordinary. (Don't make the mistake of believing a preacher's calendar is the only one that is demanding.)

PRAYER AND ENCOURAGEMENT. In the past, I've called, visited, sent cards and flowers to others, but this is the first time I've been on the receiving end of so many prayers and contacts from family and Christian friends. While too many visits can be tiring, the prayers, calls, letters, flowers, balloons, fruit, books etc. have been most encouraging. (I even received a live Venus's Fly Trap!)

THE COMFORTER. I have a new appreciation for the personal presence of the Lord who not only heals, but cheers, calms, and sustains. One quote among many that touched me was, "You can rest because He is awake." It's been just fifteen days since the surgery, and I'm already walking a couple of miles a day and doing a little paper work at the office at home (just across the street). I'll be phasing back into a regular schedule in the next few weeks. Even though things are going extremely well, don't forget to keep praying.

July/August 1990: A Letter to You . . .

Frequently letters come from students or recent graduates who express their appreciation for their experiences here at Southwestern. These are an encouragement to the entire seminary family—especially our faculty. Listen to a portion of one of these recent letters to one of our faculty members:

> I was a student of yours in January of 1979. In fact, you were my first professor in my first class at Southwestern. I want to relate a story that I have told many times to many people when speaking about my seminary days.
>
> I'm sure in your many years of teaching that this particular first day of class was like many other opening days for you. For me, however, it was a day I will never forget. My wife and two small children moved to Fort Worth just before one of the area's worst ice storms.
>
> . . . We were iced in, everyone got the flu, our money ran out, we couldn't find jobs and I was scared to death that I couldn't keep pace on the graduate level. Things looked bleak to say the least. My wife and I knew the Lord had led us to Southwestern from a happy and prosperous ministry. During this time we had our doubts—perhaps we had made a mistake.
>
> The first day of classes in my very first class I was sitting in the back of the room bewildered and scared. I just knew that my first professor was going to try his best to "weed me out."
>
> As you walked in, you put your notes down, exchanged some pleasantries with the class and than said, "Some of you are new students. You are apprehensive, perhaps your financial resources have been drained, your families have been sick, you can't find jobs and you are wondering what you are doing here." As you can imagine, I began to sit up and take notice. Your next words were, "Now, we are going to pray about these things." I don't know what you said in your prayer, but I do know that the Lord spoke to me and reconfirmed His leadership—everything I had faced you named. Peace flooded my heart. Confidence in God and myself began to grow again and I knew that the Lord had His hand on me and my family.
>
> Chapel was next. I went not expecting anything else from God, but what a continuance of the confirmation He had begun! As we sang "Amazing Grace," emotion and tears overflowed as I realized that the Lord knew exactly what I needed and where I was. Our days at Southwestern continued to be ones of struggle—but how we grew in trust in God.
>
> My family considers our days at Southwestern to be the best days of our lives. We found teachers to be caring and encouraging men and women who taught and believed God's word. Thank you for giving us the tools and the inspiration to go out and make a difference.

September/October 1990:
"Ready for Any Good Work" (2 Tim 2:21)

It's always an impressive sight—Truett Auditorium packed with brand new entering students for the opening session of orientation. Remember your first days at Southwestern? The excitement, anticipation, anxiety are still the same as students begin what will be the busiest but most significant years of their ministry.

Here's a portion of the president's welcome message to this fresh crop of Southwesterners:

First, let me congratulate you for choosing what we around here humbly believe is the best Seminary in the country. It didn't increase our humility any to have Christianity Today acknowledge this fact in a recent poll of its readers, identifying Southwestern as the number one seminary in America.

You could have taken a shortcut, sending your check to one of the many "degree mill" mail-order seminaries and receiving your credentials by return mail. But you took God's call to ministry seriously and have chosen to pay the price of a legitimate, accredited, quality preparation.

1. This will be a challenging, strenuous educational experience. Southwestern is a graduate school with demanding requirements, and it will call for your highest performance as you balance study, family life, and church involvement.

You are students. That word comes from the Latin root studere, which means to apply the mind in order to acquire knowledge. But the basic meaning of that Latin word is "to be eager, to be zealous." If you meet this upcoming educational challenge with enthusiasm, you will leave here with informed convictions, able to give a reason for the hope that is within you.

2. This will be a spiritually fulfilling experience also. Our purpose here is not only to help you gain knowledge, but to help you grow spiritually.

Our purpose is "formation." You will be encouraged to employ the devotional disciplines of prayer, Bible study, and worship to become more like the Master. We want you to have a clearer understanding of God's will for your life.

You will soon be aware of a unique mood here at Southwestern, a special mystique, which we call S.O.S.—the Spirit of Southwestern. It is indefinable, a complex of distinctive attitudes and feelings surrounding this place. We believe that mystique is an evidence of the presence of God's Spirit here.

So take full advantage of these years. If you do, you will be taking a giant step toward becoming a "vessel for noble use, consecrated and useful to the Master of the house, ready for any good work" (2 Tim 2:21).

November/December 1990: Unity and Thanks

"These are the times that try men's souls." This quote from American revolutionary writer Thomas Paine calls us to rise above selfish interests for the good of the whole. He was suggesting that tough times bring out the best and the worst in human character, revealing who we really are. At our fall trustee meeting, historian Dr. Robert Baker reflected on difficult times in Southwestern's past that "tried men's souls." In those days, faculty and administration of the Seminary demonstrated by heroic sacrifices their commitment to the Lord and to this school.

In order to keep the vision alive, they "stayed with it" when they could have accepted easier positions. God honored their courage, and the Seminary not only survived its crises, but prospered. As a result, they passed the Southwestern heritage on to us. Now it's our turn. These days in Southern Baptist life are "the times that try men's souls." If the Southern Baptist Convention, so blessed of God in the past, survives as a viable force for missions and evangelism in the future, leaders with courage, statesmanship, and personal integrity must rise above self-interest for the good of the denomination.

It's time to "forget those things that are behind and reach forward to those things that are ahead." We must not dwell on the past twelve years, blaming one another for what has happened to our denomination. History will tell that story soon enough. Now is the time to put aside self interests and personal hurts and pull together to salvage our Southern Baptist ship before it sinks.

I commend the chairman of our board, Dr. Jimmy Draper, for his bold step in calling together last month an unofficial group to discuss what we can do to restore trust. He led us to search for a cure for what he accurately diagnosed as a "sick" denomination. Furthermore, during the recent trustee meeting, Dr. Draper led our board to a time of renewed focus on the vision of Southwestern. Amid rumors and anxieties of likely confrontation, the trustees constructively worked through some of our differences. In spite of tensions, they affirmed the administration and the faculty, and unanimously approved all the president's recommendations.

Even though they knew their actions would not be popularly received by all their constituents, some of whom expected harsher action, the board acted courageously to restore an atmosphere of trust and cooperation at Southwestern. . . . Could it be that this unexpected outcome is the harbinger of new steps toward reconciliation in the larger convention family? I have great hope that it is.

"These are the times that try men's souls," bringing out the best and worst in us and determining who we really are. These are also the times to "renew the vision" of the spiritual ministry to which we are called.

1991

Hope Springs Eternal, but Disappointment Reigns

Any lingering hope that the fundamentalists on the board were relenting in their drive to control Southwestern disappeared at the meetings in the spring and fall. Perhaps any sympathy they may have had for a president recovering from heart surgery was now over, and it was back to the business of completing the Patterson/Pressler agenda for Southwestern.

In their spring meeting, individual trustees raised a variety of complaints. T. Bob Davis, Dallas trustee, was unhappy about the room arrangement. He wanted the chairs in a circle so they "look each other in the eye." (I interpreted this to mean, "so they could intimidate and influence the votes.")

They objected to a resolution our faculty had passed supporting their colleague, History Professor Leon McBeth, in his conflict with the Baptist Sunday School Board when they ordered his history of their board shredded. They objected to the new five-year plan, Vision for Excellence, because they suspected it was designed to encourage the recruiting of female faculty members. It wasn't.

Bud Funk, New Mexico trustee, expressed his opposition to electing females to the faculty by saying, "I think the Bible teaches that women should not teach men anything. I guess that's just the way I was raised."

Any lingering hope that the SBC was returning to normalcy disappeared when the convention met in Atlanta. The Patterson/Pressler party was now attempting to justify their takeover by offering a variety of "reasons" for their strategy. One of those was that for years, "conservatives" had been left out of leadership in the SBC. Now it was their turn to be on boards and committees and hold convention offices.

Robert Dilday, Associate Editor of the *Religious Herald* in Virginia, did research and responded with a report showing well-known fundamentalists who served in significant SBC positions in the years preceding the takeover, 1967–1978:

WIDELY KNOWN FUNDAMENTALISTS WHO SERVED IN SIGNIFICANT SPOTS IN THE YEARS 1967–1978

W. A. Criswell: SBC President, 1968–70. Annuity Board, 1965–73.

Jaroy Weber: SBC President, 1974–76. Foreign Mission Board, 1967–75. Committee Boards, 1969, 1973. Committee on Committees, 1967.

W. O. Vaught: Committee on Committees, 1969. Foreign Mission Board, 1967–75.

Hugo Lindquist: Committee on Boards, 1969.

Homer G. Lindsay Jr.: Southwestern Seminary, 1963–68. Chairman, Committee on Committees, 1969.

Homer G. Lindsay Sr.: Midwestern Seminary, 1975–80.

Charles Fuller: Committee on Boards, 1967. Committee on Committees, 1969, 1971. Committee on Resolutions, 1973. Radio & TV Commission, 1970–78.

James Draper: Committee on Credentials, 1970. Annuity Board, 1974–82.

Tommy Hinson: Committee on Committees, 1971.

James Bryant: Committee on Tellers, 1971.

Ralph Smith: Southwestern Seminary, 1964–74. Foreign Mission Board, 1978–82.

Paige Patterson: Credentials Committee, 1972.

Tom Eliff: Committee on Boards, 1975.

Coy Privette: Committee on Committees, 1975.

Bailey Smith: Committee on Committees, 1975.

Adrian Rogers: Committee on Committees, 1975.

Ed Young: Committee on Resolutions, 1976. Southeastern Seminary, 1975–80.

Clark Hutchinson: Credentials Committee, 1976.

Jerry Vines: Committee on Boards, 1976.

Nelson Price: Credentials Committee, 1978. New Orleans Seminary, 1969–79.

Johnny Jackson: Credentials Committee, 1978.

Morris Chapman: Committee on Boards, 1978. Foreign Mission Board, 1978–82.

Jim Henry: Sunday School Board, 1968–76.

Scott Humphrey: Foreign Mission Board, 1971–79.

Bill Bennett: Sunday School Board, 1973–81.

Bill G. Grubbs: Golden Gate Seminary, 1973–78.

Fred Wolfe: Home Mission Board, 1977–81.

Billy Weber: Home Mission Board, 1977–81.

Ralph Pulley: Southwestern Seminary, 1977–82.

The complaints continued from individual trustees in their October meeting. While the board took no actions on the complaints, the tone of the meeting was one of negative grumbling. Finally, we encouraged the board to name a committee to plan a forum for the trustees on "Women in Ministry." They agreed and eventually this forum was held. It was well-done with lectures by John Newport, Bruce Corley and others. However, it made little difference in the attitudes of most of the hardliners.

There was also a committee named to find ways to improve relationships between the board and the administration. We eventually received a grant to finance this program of trustee education. It was effective, but carried the embarrasing connotation of a remedial program for unprepared board members.

They also approved my plan to expand faculty and staff appraisals to include the trustees themselves. It would be a self-appraisal of their work, but it would nevertheless be a step in the right direction. I also recommended an enhancement in the board's appraisal of the president which involved formal written criteria. They approved it, but after using it to give me a good appraisal in 1994, they fired me!

Key Events in 1991

January

17   • Lloyd Elder forced to retire from SBC Sunday School Board

27   • Preached at Travis Avenue Baptist Church, Ft. Worth, TX

31   • Met with trustees T. Bob Davis, dentist from TX and John Mckay, evangelist from TX and the School of Music faculty about their complaints

February
16   • Article in *Richmond Dispatch* that Paige Patterson's board at Criswell College asked him to stop traveling around leading the SBC controversy. He should stay home and raise money, etc. Patterson denied that he is about to be fired, that new pastor Joel Gregory wants him out, etc. He promised to take a low profile as a power broker. "The turn in the convention has been accomplished and is secure. A lower profile for me will be a healthy development for the convention as a whole."
24   • Preached First Baptist Church Norfolk, VA, for Ken Hemphill
26   • Special meeting of trustees and music faculty to discuss differences

March
11   • Spring trustees meeting.
          • Objected to our faculty's resolution to the Baptist Sunday School Board for Leon McBeth after they shredded his history manuscript
          • Announced ten-year accreditation from ATS and SACS and warned about fundamentalists' plan to create their own accreditation association
          • Trustees objected to new five-year plan Vision of Excellence, but eventually adopted it.
12   • Jimmy Draper preached in chapel

April
18   • Morris Chapman preached in chapel as SBC president

May
17   • Spoke at commencement at Dallas Baptist University
25   • Spoke at commencement at Palm Beach Atlantic College in Florida

June
4-6   • SBC met in Atlanta
          • Morris Chapman reelected unopposed. 23,465 messengers
          • Oliver North and President George Bush spoke at pastor's conference

August
20   • Attended Draper's "inauguration" at Baptist Sunday School Board

September

10   • Baptist Theological Seminary of Richmond launched

11   • Visited new trustees Dr. William Cutrer, and Lu Walker

27   • Ken Hemphill preached for Seminary revival. Then pastor of First Baptist Church, Norfolk VA (no idea he would be president of Southwestern)

October

1-4   • Visited new trustees Danny Williams, Ron Coppock, and Lynn Cooper

15   • Mike Dean, pastor of Travis Ave. Baptist, Ft. Worth, preached in chapel

21-23   • Fall trustees meeting

• Don Taylor, NC, wanted more trustee discussion time on agenda and wanted a committee appointed to discuss women in ministry

• Charles Lawson, MD, complained about faculty serving on Baptist Center for Ethics

• Jim Bolton, TX, elected as trustee chairman in place of Jimmy Draper

• I reported SBC Executive Committee studying withdrawing the six SBC seminaries from accreditation with ATS and SACS and forming "our own accrediting agency"—thus accrediting ourselves

• Reported completion of renovated Counseling Center, and new entrance to Southwestern Campus, Classes by Satellite through ACTS network

• Presented new strategic plan, Vision for Excellence 1991–1995, in part thinking it would encourage them to forget about firing the president and plan ahead at least to 1995

9   • Ruschlikon Seminary defunded by SBC Executive Committee

30   • Evangelist Bailey Smith preached in chapel

November

13   • Spoke at Kentucky Baptist State Convention

18   • Spoke at Jerry Baucom inauguration at Mary Hardin Baylor University

19   • Spoke at Arkansas Baptist State Convention

December

9   • I recommended plan for trustees to provide formal annual appraisal of the president on written criteria. The trustees would also appraise their own effectiveness

Note: In the fall meeting of 1991, the thirty-eight-member board of trustees had the following composition: 25 hard-core fundamentalists, 8 traditional, mainstream Baptists, and 5 swing voters.

January/February 1991: Sabbatical Study— A Southwestern Investment in Excellence

(Southwestern had a very generous sabbatical leave program. While still receiving full compensation, a professor was relieved of all regular responsibilities for up to a full calendar year. In this column, I described the guidelines of the program and listed ten teachers who had been granted leaves for the coming year.)

March/April: Credit Where Credit Is Due

ACCREDITATION . . . The verb accredit comes from Latin roots and means "to esteem or have a high opinion of, to give credentials to, to believe in, put credit in." Although it is a demanding discipline, every serious educational institution values the process of academic accreditation, which gives it legitimacy.

Last week, following a two-year self-study of all components of Seminary life, we completed our decennial accreditation review by SACS and ATS. A thirteen-member team of educators from across America spent several days on campus examining, interviewing, questioning, and probing in order to objectively evaluate the overall institutional effectiveness of our school. The team affirmed the quality of our faculty and staff. They had good words to say about the administrative team, and of course the excellent work of the self-study committee chaired by Dr. Scotty Gray.

By itself, apart from the visit of the impressive accrediting team, the discipline of self-evaluation has been extremely valuable. Our findings have become the basis for our next strategic plan which we are calling Vision for Excellence— 1991–1995. Nevertheless, we must quickly add that the objective evaluation by "outsiders" was indispensable, providing us with essential data for future planning. The team assured us that Southwestern would be accredited for the next ten years. Then, with a series of suggestions, recommendations and notations, they pointed out areas needing attention and improvement. Our own self-study had already surfaced most of these needs, and we are already addressing them in the objectives, goals, and actions of our new strategic plan. After the plan is approved by our board of trustees at their next meeting, you'll hear more—much more—about Vision for Excellence—1991–95.

OUR PROFESSOR IN SAUDI ARABIA . . . Listen to excerpts of a recent letter from Dr. James Spivey, (Major Spivey) Assistant Professor of Church History who is serving as a military chaplain in Operation Desert Storm:

> My role, as you can imagine comprehends several functions—preaching, counseling, advising the commander, morale, welfare, etc. But, of course, I must focus my attention on the truly vital mission in the cure of souls. Anything less than a virile Gospel proclamation is unacceptable. And the people are receptive to this. We are seeing significant response. Our units cover such a wide area that I feel more like a Methodist circuit rider than anything else right now . . .
>
> Seeing God's mighty work through the ministries of Methodists, Baptists, Presbyterians, etc. side by side with Pentecostals, Lutherans, and Episcopalians—this reminds me that He can still work a miracle of healing within our own denomination in order to refocus the great middling majority on the call to evangelism and missions . . . . Thank you for your prayers . . . you all have a genuine investment in the souls of these young men and women who come to the Lord and who are nourished by his providential care.

Thank you, Dr. Spivey. We're praying for your safe and imminent return to the classroom.

May/June: The Sun Never Sets on the Southwestern Family

World Missions. It always has been and is today a unique distinctive of Southwestern. The seminary's global perspective is pervasive, noticeable in every facet of its life; but sometimes it is seen in impressive concentrated events. From Leningrad, USSR, Sergei Nikolaev, a Baptist pastor and Director of Missions, was on campus for DMin studies. As a rising star in the constellation of future evangelical leaders in the Soviet Union, Nikolaev helped us see more clearly the current situation in his country.

From Poland, Marek Izdebski and Chris Benedyktowicz, pastors/teachers from Warsaw, visited the campus to explore possible relationships in theological training in a nation heretofore closed to missionary involvement.

Some of our faculty have just returned from Romania, South America and other countries while others are planning mission involvements overseas this summer. Each overseas experience updates our awareness of current needs.

Chapel a few weeks ago featured Southwesterners who are being appointed by the Foreign Mission Board to Israel, Brazil, Kenya, Guinea, Indonesia, and Pakistan. We also heard from 31 students who will be involved in Home Mission work this summer in Florida, Georgia, Maryland, Minnesota, New Jersey, New York, North Carolina, Oklahoma, Virginia, Wisconsin, and Canada. Home Mission Board Evangelism Director Darrell Robinson brought the closing message. The missions beat goes on in the heart of our school!

AN APPEAL TO ALUMNI FOR HELP
As most of you know by now, the SBC Executive Committee's Institutions Workgroup is studying a request to withdraw our convention seminaries from traditional accreditation. I hope many of you will join us in expressing to the committee how important you believe it is for Southwestern to maintain its peer accreditation through ATS and SACS. To give up this objective affirmation of the credibility of our institution would have serious consequences. Accreditation not only encourages the highest academic standards in our work, but has other important implications as well:

(1) Bivocational ministers rely on our accredited degrees for employment in public schools and other institutions to supplement their church employment.

(2) Prospective students are attracted to the seminary because the work here is accredited.

(3) Transferring academic credit from/to Southwestern from/to other institutions depends on accreditation.

(4) Appointment to many positions such as chaplains, professors, counselors, missionaries etc. depends on accredited degrees.

(5) Fund-raising, particularly from foundations, depends on accreditation to measure the legitimacy of the institution. Accreditation causes no compromise of our doctrinal beliefs or denominational polity.

July/August 1991: Sights
and Insights Atop Seminary Hill

INSIGHTS FROM THE CLASSROOM . . . Occasionally during my tenure as president, I have assumed the role of professor and taught classes here at Southwestern. This last semester, it was a section of Biblical Hermeneutics 051-332, one of three required courses added to the MDiv curriculum in the last few years. Of course, to take on a weekly classroom assignment for five months along with ongoing duties in administration required some "creative" scheduling, but with team teacher John Newport sharing the lectures, I was able to do it.

When I was completing the doctor's degree here at Southwestern, I felt God's call to be both a preacher and a teacher. As it worked out, most of my ministry was in the pastorate, but from time to time along the way, I was able to follow that teaching call as an adjunct professor at Baylor and Southwestern. Now, as president, I find it very fulfilling to return occasionally to the classroom.

However, in addition to the personal fulfillment, becoming a professor for a while also provides some valuable insights for the president. For one thing, this first hand experience gives me a more accurate understanding of the challenge and excitement our faculty members face. Furthermore, working directly with a group of students gives me a better feel for their unique situations and needs.

The class was a microcosm of the entire student body. They are so diverse—men and women, young and old, coming from every part of the nation and from several foreign countries. Some were religion majors, graduates of Baptist colleges. Others from state universities had never had a course in Bible. A few had already earned masters degrees in religion, while a few others were older students with no college degree. They came from fundamentalist, conservative, moderate, and liberal churches. Some are children of well-known Southern Baptist leaders. Their understanding of God's will for their lives covers the entire spectrum of professional ministry.

In their diversity, they represent the future of the Southern Baptist Convention, and on the basis of my firsthand acquaintance with their Christian commitment, their attitudes, and their God-given abilities, I have to believe that in spite of our current problems, the future of our denomination is positive and hopeful. Our children and grandchildren will have capable leaders for their churches, missions, and convention agencies.

SIGHTS FROM THE CAMPUS . . . (1) Construction has begun on the new Bowld Music Library southeast of Cowden Hall. It will be a beautiful and useful addition to our campus master plan, providing much needed space for the School of Music.

(2) The newly renovated Walsh Counseling Center (formerly the Walsh Medical Center) was occupied by the faculty and staff of the Department of Psychology and Counseling in the School of Religious Education. The building not only houses a counseling ministry for persons in the community, but a laboratory for students working under the supervision of the faculty on counseling degrees.

(3) Beautification of the main entrance on Seminary Drive, the west entrance on Gambrell Street and east entrance along James Avenue is nearing completion. Our capable staff is doing a commendable job maintaining and upgrading the campus.

Come see for yourself.

September/October 1991:
A New Beginning for an Old Task

(As a new academic year got under way, I focused on the cyclical characteristics of an educational institution that brings recurring newness to the task. A new academic year at Southwestern meant new students [747], new faculty [4], new staff [60], and new trustees [5]. A new music library building was under construction while several renovation programs were renewing existing buildings. New academic programs were under way to enable us to fulfill with excellence God's purpose for the Seminary.)

November/December 1991: A Positive Trustee
Meetings Points to a Positive Future

Everyone is aware of the political tensions surfacing occasionally during past meetings of our board of trustees. Even our reaccrediting team noted these strained relationships and recommended steps be taken to improve them.

So it was heartening to see evidences of a new spirit of cooperation and understanding in the recent annual meeting. While the meeting couldn't be described as "docile," (and no important meeting should be) it was positive and constructive. After thorough, spirited discussions, all the recommendations of the president were unanimously approved, including the election to our faculty of well-known Southern Baptist pastor and author Calvin Miller.

First we were encouraged by the five newly elected board members who were welcomed to their first meeting. Two are pastors, one is a homemaker with impressive Southern Baptist Convention leadership experience, one is a physician, and another is a bank president. Along with those who joined the board last year, they bring urgently needed competencies and cooperative spirits, which will serve the institution well in the days ahead as the membership of the board changes significantly.

Furthermore, two sensitive concerns were addressed by the board resulting in the appointment of two ad hoc committees to study and bring recommendations. The issue of women in ministry, which has divided Southern Baptists in recent years, has also been a controversial topic in our meetings. Sometimes emotions and political concerns have prevented objective considerations. So it is encouraging to work with a capable committee who will carefully examine the scriptures to help the board answer crucial questions in a fair and open forum.

The other committee will address ways to improve relationships between the board and the administration and to provide the board with training in educational trusteeship. Both these studies promise to enhance the new spirit of togetherness we see emerging. But perhaps the most hopeful sign of the future is the affirmative statement made to the board by newly elected chairman, Jim Bolton:

"I pledge to you not perfect service, but what I do as I work with President Dilday will be done in perfect love. He and I have a love for one another that goes back more than forty-five years. I have promised him that in the confines of his office we may disagree, . . . but when we come out you will not hear me criticizing the president of this institution. We will work together."

So, heartened by this positive meeting, my intention is to leave the tragic difficulties of the denominational political struggles behind, to relinquish the question of blame to the judgment of God and human history, and to move forward in the crucial task of training ministers for the gospel of Jesus Christ. Our prayer is that a strong Southwestern with cooperative trustees may be an instrument to bring Southern Baptists together again as a great missionary force for the next century.

1992

Reinventing the Southern Baptist Convention

With elections and decision-making in the SBC firmly in the hands of the Patterson/Pressler party, the convention began to take on a radically different nature and appearance. By 1992, several traditional Baptist leaders had resigned or were forced out of office including Keith Parks, head of the Foreign Mission Board, Randall Lolley and Roy Honeycutt, seminary presidents, and Harold Bennett, President of the SBC Executive Committee. Fundamentalist replacements would soon occupy the chief executive positions across the convention.

That was to be expected as the takeover plan moved toward total victory. But what was most unseemly, was the way the two leaders of the takeover positioned themselves in these vacated positions of influence and power. They had controlled the appointment of trustees, and now those trustees in turn named them to key positions! I saw first hand how Paul Pressler manipulated his election as chair of the SBC Executive Committee and was not surprised when he arranged for his appointment to the SBC Foreign Mission Board. Patterson, his colleague in arms was elevated as the new president of Southeastern Seminary and now serves as president of Southwestern, which was at one time the largest seminary in the world.

While I was still president of Southwestern, I attended the inauguration of Patterson on the campus of Southeastern in Wake Forest, NC. The inaugural addresss was delivered by the newly elected president of the SBC, Ed Young. He spoke to the gathered students, faculty, denominational leaders, community representatives and the traditional coterie of scholarly representatives from various educational institutions across the nation. Hailing the election of Paige Patterson as the event that would "return the seminary to its biblical heritage and conservative theology," Young tried to justified Patterson's leading role in the convention takeover. He quoted from a catalogue of Wake Forest College on whose former campus the seminary was now housed. Here was the proof that there really was rampant "theological liberalism" in our Baptist Educational institutions, and that Patterson and Pressler were foreced to launch their campaign to correct it.

The passage he quoted described the purpose statement of Wake Forest College in which, Young said, the school openly admitted their theological liberalism. "It says here in black and white, 'This School is committed to liberal learning.'" He seemed unaware that this reference to "liberal" described the college's academic studies in literature, philosophy, languages, history the "liberal arts," courses in humanities that make up a typical Bachelor of Arts degree. It had nothing to do with theological liberalism. There were embarrassed glances exchanged by the faculty and the scholarly representatives at the uninformed and naïve remarks by the one elected to lead the denomination.

But as bad as things had become in the SBC under the fundamentalists, I still held out a hope that it could recover its effectiveness and greatness even if in a new form. So I wrote a series of articles suggesting ways in which the SBC could be reinvented, move beyond the struggle, and become even better than the "good ole days" before the Patterson/Pressler attack. Those articles begin with my November/December column.

As you will see in the following pages, Southwestern made notable progress during 1992, adding impressive new faculty members, new degrees, new members of our Advisory Council, new Music Library, and a new ten-year accreditation without notation. We even won the "Fort Worth Beautiful Award," a prestigious community recognition of our campus improvements.

All this in spite of the addition of another group of hard-line trustees, including the re-election of Ralph Pulley from First Baptist Dallas, one of the most contentious. Tensions continued in the meetings with particular complaints being raised about my column on "Carnal Conservatism" (October) and "Reinventing the SBC" (November/December).

Key Events in 1992

January

3   • Spoke for Alabama Baptist Convention

19   • Preached at Prestonwood Baptist Church, Dallas

24   • Drayton McClane, Houston, spoke in chapel. Advisory Council now has Drayton McClane, Dr. Ken Cooper, Tom Landry, et al.—the quality of people who should have been on our board of trustees.

30   • Held seminar on Women in Ministry for Ad Hoc Committee of Trustees

February

17   • Morris Chapman elected president of SBC Executive Committee

20   • Met with Trustee Bolton and his partner, Frank Hess about his new venture in oil and mineral rights in Oklahoma. He wanted Southwestern to invest our endowment with him. We refused. Conflict of interest.

March

9   • Spring trustees meeting

         • Announced Millard Erickson's appointment as Research Professor of Theology

         • Jim Bolton announced resignation so he could pursue his proposal for Southwestern to invest endowment in his new oil drilling company. We didn't discourage his resignation!

         • Damon Shook elected as chair, Pat Campbell vice chair. Campbell told me it would help me if he were chairman, so he would "go along with them" to get elected. He then might move up to chairman.

20   • Keith Parks announced retirement from Foreign Mission Board, October 31

23   • Spoke at Castle Hills Baptist Church, San Antonio Pastors Conference

April

13   • Miles Seaborn spoke in chapel

16   • Spoke at Samford University Christian Emphasis Week

May

5-6   • Preached at Falls Creek Assembly Bible Conference in Oklahoma

14   • Paige Patterson elected President Southeastern Seminary

16   • Spoke at Mary Hardin Baylor College Baccalaureate

18-19   • Cooperative Program dialogue with SBC leaders at DFW Airport

June

8-12
- SBC met in Indianapolis
- Ed Young elected over Nelson Price (Price angered the fundamentalists by running without their blessing)
- Paul Pressler manipulated his election to Foreign Mission Board

August

22
- Ray and Jester Summers Funerals in Waco. I gave eulogies.

25-31
- Visited with new trustees: Laura Cogswell, David Allen, Ralph Pulley (Pulley reelected by Patterson/Pressler party after rotating off)

September

1-10
- Visited new trustees: Charles Lord, Sid West, Jack Price, Robert Anderson

18
- Met trustee T. Bob Davis again about his complaints about music school

30
- Bill Pinson, Executive Director of BGCT preached for Seminary revival

October

1
- Met with Bill Ramsey, pastor First Baptist Church, Fort Worth (Frank Norris's old church) about their coming back into the SBC. With the fundamentalist takeover, this independent, fundamentalist church now feels at home. The Tarrant Baptist Association required him to meet with me before they were admitted

13
- Paige Patterson inaugurated at Southeastern Seminary

19
- Fall Trustee Meeting
- Dedicated new Bowld Music Library
- Announced new MA and THM degrees, first new degrees since 1954
- They held a forum at the Holiday Inn so they could carry out objectionable matters without the press or other observers
- I reported focus visit from ATS SACS and our full accreditation without notation.
- Committee appointed to study worship and music
- Don Taylor complained about my article in Southwestern News about J. I. Packer's Power Religion which denounced "carnal conservatism"

21
- Larry Lewis, President of Home Mission Board, spoke in chapel

26
- Spoke at Shelby County Pastors Conference in Tennessee

29
- Southwestern received the "Fort Worth Beautiful Award" for our campus
- Roy Honeycutt announced retirement for December 1993

November

4   • Trustee Chair Damon Shook and I attended Lilly Endowment conference at Purdue University in Indianapolis on trustee development—how to train trustees

6   • Claude Thomas, pastor of First Baptist Euless, TX, preached in chapel

11   • Spoke at Oregon State Baptist Convention in Eugene

19   • Funeral for Professor Robert Baker

December

• Adrian Rogers hosted meeting of fundamentalist leaders at his church to plan takeover of forty State Baptist Conventions using same tactics used in SBC

Note: In the fall meeting of 1992, the thirty-nine-member board of trustees had the following composition: 25 hard-core fundamentalists, 7 traditional mainstream Baptists, and 7 swing voters.

January/February 1992: "Mr. Southwesterner"—1909–1991

For nearly forty years, Mr. J. T. Luther was a valuable friend to Southwestern Baptist Theological Seminary, serving as chairman of its board, directing its foundation, promoting the school in the Fort Worth community, and generously giving his own financial resources to its operation. He did it out of a profound love for the Lord and his awareness of the eternal significance of this school in the kingdom.

In addition to his monumental institutional contributions, he was also an encourager, advisor, and friend to Southwestern's president.

Having heard about his good work with Texas Baptists, I was surprised and impressed to hear from him in 1977 when he and other members of the Southwestern search committee made the initial contacts that eventually led to my coming to the seminary as president. I quickly learned to trust his judgment and common sense, and his uncanny ability to get right to the point of any consideration quickly and suggest reasonable solutions.

The Attorney General of the United States, Judge Griffin Bell, was a deacon in our church in Atlanta where I served before coming to Fort Worth. J. T. Luther called Judge Bell at the Justice Department in Washington, D.C. With typical Luther persistence, he finally got past all the associates and secretaries and talked directly to the attorney general to get his personal appraisal of his pastor. When Judge Bell expressed reluctance to allow their pastor to leave Atlanta for the new assignment in Texas, J. T. Luther reminded him that presidency of Southwestern was like the papacy in the Roman Catholic Church. It was the highest office in the convention! Therefore Mr. Bell ought to be willing to give up his pastor to become the Southern Baptist Pope!

That was the kind of boldness tempered with appealing good sense that endeared this great man of God to all of us who knew him.

Only a few weeks before his death, J. T. and I were on Lake Texhoma fishing for stripers. It was one of those memorable days when the two of us had all day (beginning at 4:00 a.m. at J. T.'s office!) to discuss the work of the seminary and the challenges of the denominational situation. I will never forget that day or this man.

I encourage all the Southwestern seminary family to join me in thanking the Heavenly Father for "Mr. Southwestern" and in praying for his wife Zelma and their family during these days of sadness. May God raise up many more like him in the future.

March/April 1992: The Call to Missions

(Global Missions Week on Southwestern's campus featured forty staff members from the Foreign Mission Board in Richmond, Virginia, including Keith Parks, in classroom lectures, conferences, chapel programs, and feature presentations. The highlight of the week, of course, was the message from Dr. Parks on February 27 to a packed Truett Auditorium. When the invitation was given more than sixty-six came forward to make public commitments for foreign mission service. It was a stirring spiritual experience.

In this column, I described the event and included a testimony from Steve Booth, a PhD graduate who with his wife was being appointed to serve in Hungary.)

May/June 1992: Good Words from G.A.'s

I have always had a profound appreciation for Woman's Missionary Union and the mission auxiliaries they sponsor. It started when I was a boy and personally benefited from Royal Ambassador training which was under their sponsorship. Later, as a pastor, I found this organization was irreplaceable as an ally in helping the church understand and support world missions. My wife Betty continues to take an active part in our local church WMU, associational, state, and convention-wide activities, so my appreciation has been reinforced through the years.

That's why I'm glad that we have here at Southwestern mission education courses that remind our students about the important role WMU plays in our denominational response to the Great commission. I wish all our Southern Baptist Convention leadership shared this life-long experience with WMU and felt that same esteem for their worthwhile contribution.

Recently, I received some encouraging mail from Girl's Auxiliary, girls across the Southern Baptist Convention who were obviously learning about denominational mission agencies. These letters added to my already strong regard for WMU.

FROM OKLAHOMA:
"I'm 10 years old, in the 5th grade. I feel small for my age, and I weigh 63 pds . . . I'm very proud to be able to write you, the president of Southwestern Seminary. I need to know your name because we don't have the book that tells us your name. Well, I've probably taken up too much of your time already and I've gotta go. Bye."

FROM SOUTH CAROLINA:
"Dear Dr. Dildway,
I just wanted to tell you that I'm praying for you and your ministry. . . . I don't expect you to write back, but if you have time it would be nice."

FROM GEORGIA:
"Hi! In my GA class we are learning about your job. I am praying for you!"
(Valentine stickers all over the page)

FROM LOUISIANA:
"Dear Mr. Russell,
I am in the fourth grade. I have blond hair and blue eyes. My favorite colors are pink and purple. How are you doing? I'm doing fine. I have to go now. Bye. P.S. You don't have to write back."

FROM ARKANSAS:
"I think you seminary is nice. I will be praying for you as you help prepare leaders for ministry throughout the world. P.S. Write back. PLEASE!!!"

FROM TEXAS:
"I am writing you because it is a step in my GA book. I am supposed to pray for you, I will. P.S. My pastor went to Southwestern."

FROM ALABAMA:

"Hi. I hope your theogical Seminary is going good. I hope they get taught real good . . . ."

So do I, Amy! And thank all of you for your prayers.

July/August 1992: The Indianapolis Report

Reporting for Southwestern to messengers at the Southern Baptist Convention each year is a responsibility I take seriously even though the time allotted is frustratingly short (seven minutes with three minutes for questions). By contrast, I must admit it is more enjoyable to bring the report each year to alumni gathered for our annual luncheon. This year's Southwestern meeting at Indianapolis was no exception.

I reminded the 500 assembled alumni that while the seminary still occasionally receives baseless criticism from the right accusing Southwestern of liberalism, we are now having to defend our school from misinformed critics on the left. They say that since our board is appointed by the party now in control of the convention and is therefore dominated by fundamentalists, then quality, authentic graduate education is no longer available at Southwestern. They say we have capitulated to the political leaders of the convention and that our professors are no longer free to teach the truth. Some have said publicly that the seminary is "paralyzed" because of this.

It is true that the unfortunate denominational developments of these past years have created a difficult climate for theological education. But the fact is that in spite of this, Southwestern is not just surviving, it is managing to move forward. Evidence of this continuing quality are the new degrees (now twelve compared to six a few years ago), new specializations, a new correlation program with Baptist colleges, expanded summer school and night programs, and exciting new faculty (i.e. Millard Erickson and Calvin Miller). Southwestern's quality work was recently affirmed when SACS and ATS announced their reaccreditation of our school until the year 2001.

Furthermore, with the help of a generous grant from the Lilly Endowment, we are working on a program of trustee education and development that will strengthen relationships between the board and the seminary administration.

In spite of the serious economic limitations challenging higher education in general, we are also managing to maintain a strong financial position for Southwestern. Even with its $2.6 billion endowment, Yale University has a $15 million operating deficit that will grow to a devastating $50 million over the next few years. Most of Yale's current record-breaking $1.5 billion fund-raising goal must be used to patch up a neglected and seriously decaying plant. As a result Yale is doing what has become typical in higher education this year: abolishing academic programs, reducing faculty, and merging departments. Schools are euphemistically describing these actions as "rightsizing."

Southwestern is not only having to grapple with the same financial woes other schools like Yale are facing, but we also face additional problems brought on by the convention controversy. The cooperative program shortage (now $3.2 million) continues to grow. If it remains at this level it will mean a serious $250,000 revenue decline for Southwestern. Donors, reluctant to invest in the seminary during these tense days, are changing their wills, placing revocable clauses in their trusts, shifting donations to non-convention institutions, etc. But in spite of these obstacles, we are operating with a balanced budget, we have no debt, and we have been successful in recent fund-raising campaigns in Dallas and Fort Worth. The Bowld Church Music Library building is nearing completion, seven academic chairs are being funded, and our current endowment has grown to $65 million.

So the annual report to both the Southern Baptist Convention and the alumni is one of positive accomplishments under difficult circumstances. For this we give glory to God. In the words of Robert Shuller's new book, "Life's not fair, but God is good!"

September/October 1992:
Carnal Conservatism vs. Constructive Conservatism

J. I. Packer in *Power Religion*, a book just released by Moody Press, joins fourteen other conservative evangelical leaders in a timely warning against what they call "carnal conservatism." The book critiques and offers better alternatives to such excesses as:

• triumphalistic church growth strategies.
• authoritarian styles of pastoral leadership.
• the use of secular political methodology in spite of prohibitions in 2 Corinthians 6:7; 10:3-4.
• the fanning of emotional fears by supposed conspiracy theories.
• government entanglements that reduce the church to little more than another special interest group.
• the use of peer pressure to enforce conformity, ostracizing, withholding rewards from those who refuse to go along—called "ganging up."

• the total defeat of those who disagree—called an ugly denominational version of ethnic cleansing.

The authors argue that these excesses have created a distorted evangelicalism which Packer and others label "Carnal Conservatism." It is unbiblical and dangerous, they claim.

In the light of this evangelical study, it is good to remember that through the years, Southwestern Seminary has tried to promote what John Newport has called, "Constructive Conservatism." Echoing a popular country-western song, Southwestern was conservative when conservative wasn't cool! However, our brand of conservatism has avoided the rigid, legalistic, argumentative characteristics so often found in fundamentalism. We have tried (successfully I believe) to avoid the pitfalls of "Carnal Conservatism" which to some extent has infected our convention as it has the evangelical world.

For that reason (and a number of other reasons also) I believe Southwestern is in a providential position to give direction to our Southern Baptist Convention as it struggles to find its shape and form for the future. To be sure, there will be a future shape to the Southern Baptist Convention, but who will be the architects of that future, and what will be the contours of the new shape? Those questions nudge us to consider Southwestern's role in helping to plant and nurture a "neo-Baptist" movement, a re-formed (not Reformed) Baptist denomination.

Of course, any restated edition of the Southern Baptist Convention should closely resemble the old, bringing forward and maintaining the best of our distinctive character, heritage, and identity, but in a vigorous new form enlivened by the Holy Spirit.

Now I must admit that some of us who once truly believed that the SBC was the best, maybe the ultimate expression of the New Testament pattern of cooperating church life, find it difficult to concede that out of the turmoil of these past dozen years an even better denomination could arise. But the intriguing possibility is there, and it offers hope and challenge in the midst of the vacuum.

November/December 1992:
Reinventing the Southern Baptist Convention

It can be done. It demands the cooperation of Baptists of good will across the vast mainstream of our denominational life, but the task of re-inventing the SBC is not an impossible one.

The SBC, after all, is an "invention"—created by cooperating Baptists in another century. Stirred by profound biblical faith, they decided their churches should voluntarily cooperate in order to obey their Lord's commission. So they put together a convention of cooperating churches to do missions and education around the world in the name of Christ. This concept was distinctive and bold, and over the past century, it has put the convention in the vanguard of evangelistic, missionary denominations.

But the denominational problems of these last dozen years have diminished the SBC dream for some. A faltering uncertainty has replaced the surefootedness of earlier years, and our convention seems stalled in a denominational vacuum.

So it's time to reinvent the SBC. Southern Baptists should not give up on the convention. Today's problems, although real and large, are not immutable. As I wrote in the last issue of the News, the possibility of a reshaped, New Southern Baptist Convention (NSBC) is intriguing and hopeful.

A few years ago the home of one of our faculty families burned. Almost immediately, on the very same foundation, in the identical historical, geographical location, with the same architectural roots, they built a new and better house. While similar to the original, the new one has an improved floor plan, takes advantage of new technology not available when the first one was built, and is more beautiful than the previous one. Despite all the newness, the family is still surrounded by the familiar aura of the former dwelling. So a rebuilt Baptist house should also be a blending of the old and the new.

It seems to me, the NSBC (New Southern Baptist Convention) should be crafted by persons from within the tradition, from the authentic mainstream, not by those who have given up neither on the convention nor by those on the periphery whose understanding of the SBC may be distorted and inaccurate.

What would be the shape of this reinvented convention? Let me suggest some features of the NSBC:

I. THE NSBC SHOULD PRESERVE THE DENOMINATIONAL SOLIDARITY OF THE PAST, BUT SHOULD BE LESS AFRAID OF RESPONSIBLE TRANS-DENOMINATIONAL NETWORKS AND COALITIONS.

Traditionally, Southern Baptists have shied away from any involvement with other denominations—even evangelical denominations to which we generally acknowledge some kinship.

Now the time is right for Southern Baptists to broaden the cooperancy that is so characteristic of our internal relationships and include in our cooperation a larger segment of like-minded believers in other groups, particularly in the evangelical world without diluting our denominational distinctives, or leaping carelessly into ecumenical alliances, we can find ways to work together and draw strength from our evangelical "cousins."

The traditional complaint non-denominationalists raise against groups like the SBC is that denominational bureaucracies inevitably become corrupt and stifle spirituality and initiative. But Southern Baptists have proved this is not necessarily the case. Our experience shows that even in a large and complex denomination, missions and evangelism can be very effective. In fact, we have found in our denominational solidarity numerous and significant advantages which we treasure.

So the NSBC should jealously maintain its denominational solidarity while it turns away from un-Christlike pride, smug exclusivism, and the unlovely triumphalism so prevalent in the past.

II. THE NSBC SHOULD REFUSE TO USE POLITICS, POWER, AND PRESSURE TACTICS AND ADOPT INSTEAD SPIRITUAL WEAPONS SUCH AS PERSUASION AND PROCLAMATION IN ITS SERVICE FOR CHRIST.

The book *Power Religion* warns evangelical conservatives of the dangers of political entanglements that tend to reduce the church of the Lord Jesus Christ to little more than another political special interest group. The book's message is timely for Southern Baptists as they consider a reshaped convention for the next century.

In 1984 the SBC annual sermon called Higher Ground warned Southern Baptists to turn from "the muddy swamps of political coercion to the higher ground of spiritual persuasion." Jesus made it unmistakably clear by His commands and example that the power we are to employ in our work for Him is not political or conscriptive power, but spiritual power. Our Savior wept over Jerusalem, but He never besieged it, never rallied its legislature or courts to favor His cause, never formed a political coalition to advance His kingdom. He preached, prayed, served, loved, and, even at the sacrificial cost of His life, stead-fastly rejected worldly force.

Baptists in the future need to imitate their Lord who even though He could wither a fig tree at fifty paces with a spoken rebuke, and with one word de-fang a howling windstorm into a whimpering breeze, refused to force His will on others. The NSBC should adopt the biblical model and be content with spiritual weapons.

1993

Fixing Our Broken Convention Family

The year 1993 was distinguished as the year of the two most contentious trustee meetings to date. Ralph Pulley was now back on the board and leading the charge. (Later, his pastor, W. A. Criswell, publicly acknowledged him as the man who "single-handedly saved Southwestern from liberalism!) It began with the spring meeting in March, as the board assembled at the Holiday Inn for their pre-meeting "forum." This preliminary, unofficial session from which outsiders were barred, allowed the hardliners to vent their anger and engage in tactics hidden from public view. Then when the official meetings began, they could appear docile and cooperative.

Before the forum, David Allen, trustee from Dallas who later chaired the presidential search committee that brought Paige Patterson to Southwestern, asked to meet with Bruce Corley and me. He claimed Richard Land, the fundamentalist head of the SBC Christian Life Commission, had been "banned" from the campus by our ethics department. Allen finally admitted he had a copy of my letter to Paige Patterson denying this same accusation and declaring that Land had not been banned. He also had a copy of Professor Tillman's letter to Land

and was apparently trying to catch us in a lie. Corley and I confirmed our position that Land had not been banned from Southwestern's campus.

Trustees Paul Balducci and Laura Cogswell mounted a vitriolic tirade about what they called the lack of pro-life sympathy on campus. They had a letter from a troublemaker named Ginn who claimed he was not welcome on campus because he was pro-life. (Actually, he had threatened Richard Land's and Professor Ray Higgins's lives and the faculty called in local police. Ginn was escorted off campus.)

The trustees continued their accusation that Southwestern had forbidden students from organizing a pro-life club. (Not true) "Your professors talk out of both sides of their mouths. The trustees have voted, (not true) but the seminary hasn't listened. We will not tolerate a pro-choice spirit at Southwestern. It is unacceptable that the largest seminary in the world doesn't have a pro-life organization." etc. (This issue was later debated in the Student Services committee and a recommendation was passed that we create an environment that would allow such a club. We did, but no students wanted to form such a club.)

Complaints were raised that the music school with its recommendation of two new faculty members was not following the wishes and music tastes of the board. (That is, some of the board.) We found out later that Dallas trustee T. Bob Davis had called trustees asking them to vote against the new candidates. He told some of them that Jimmy Draper had suggested this tactic as a way "to get Dilday's attention and move the music school in the right direction." I confronted Davis after the forum and told him this kind of strategy was out of line. The debate later led to a narrow vote in the Academic Affairs committee, with the chair forced to break a tie defeating the election of the new teachers. We then asked T. Bob Davis and fellow trustee Olin Collins to visit with the two music candidates. They came back bragging on them, and they were finally elected unanimously.

Lyle Seltman from Michigan went ballistic over some of my articles in the *Southwestern News*. He said they broke my promise not to be involved in denominational politics, and that I had no integrity. It was brutal. Even some of the other fundamentalist board members called him out of line and suggested he should resign from the board. He didn't.

Pulley brought up an incident about John Seelig's house. When I called for Seelig's resignation following the 1989 attempt to fire me, I offered him the opportunity to continue to live in the seminary house he had occupied for several years. I gave him two options: live in the house without rent, but be responsible for repairs and maintenance or pay $500 a month rent, and the seminary would take care of repairs and maintenance. He chose to live there without rent and take care of repairs himself.

When the air conditioning unit went out at the house, Seelig came to ask if the seminary would pay the $6,000 bill. I reminded him that he could have chosen to pay rent and have the maintenance and repairs paid, but he had turned down that option. Even though we had no responsibility for the bill, I agreed to share the expense. Instead, he went to Pulley, and in this 1993 spring meeting, Pulley announced that he wanted Seelig to live in the house not only without rent, but without other expenses as well. (As a reward for his help in trying to fire me, they not only expanded my housing arrangement with him, but they also named the dining room for him!) Rather than have the board vote on this issue, I agreed we would pay Seelig's bill.

Following the board meeting, the trustee officers met with me to plan next fall's meeting. During the discussion, T. Bob Davis asked me to keep them informed about any retirement plans I might have. (This was the first time this had been mentioned!) I told them I had no immediate plans to retire, but that in 1998, I would be sixty-eight, the seminary would celebrate its ninetieth birthday, I would have served twenty years, and we would be completing a five-year strategic plan. I told them that would be a logical time to aim for, but that I was not ready to announce these plans, and I asked them to keep this discussion confidential

The rest of the spring meeting was routine, except that Damon Shook, the new chair, reported on the Executive Committee's annual appraisal of the president. He indicated that they had given me the highest ranking on all ten categories of the appraisal. They also made the following suggestions:

(1) Continue to lead seminary on the cutting edge of change.

(2) While faculty recommendations in the past have been conservative biblically and theologically, efforts should be made to recommend faculty who are also "conservative politically" (meaning faculty who support the Patterson/Pressler takeover of the SBC).

(3) Administration should continue to hear trustee concerns and implement policies of the board. (We always followed this practice. However, when individual trustee raised concerns, we listened, but individual suggestions are not official policies of the board, only those policies voted by board are official.)

(4) President will send monthly fact sheet to board with brief report of what's going on. (This was my suggestion.)

Then Shook summarized the appraisal, "The Trustees remain confident in the president's administrative and organizational skills and his effectiveness in leading the faculty."

After all was said, and done, all my recommendations were approved, the reports were accepted and we got through another trustee meeting. The faculty and staff expressed their appreciation, acknowledging publicly that the only way Southwestern had gotten through all the controversy better than any other seminary was "the president's courageous and wise leadership"

The Fall meeting was no better. During the forum, individual complaints continued. They questioned David Music, our nominee for dean for the school of music, claiming we had not followed proper procedure or informing them soon enough. We defended the procedure as correct and no action was taken.

Ralph Pulley rebuked me for speaking at the Southwestern Alumni breakfast during the CBF meeting in Fort Worth, saying Southwestern doesn't belong to CBF and no Southwesterner should participate. He also suspected we had accepted other gifts with "hidden conditions" like the Hultgren chair. (This academic chair given in honor of pastor Warren Hultgren, had the condition that the person appointed to the chair was to be approved by the president of Baylor University in addition to the Southwestern administration. The donor wanted to ensure that the chair would never be occupied by a fundamentalist. It was not a hidden condition) Later, Pulley did a massive search of all gift documents and found nothing.

Don Taylor said I opposed the godly leaders of the Southern Baptist Convention. Laura Cogswell said I shouldn't have written the columns about the convention, that I was the most political person in room, and that I should never have had James Dunn on campus.

In the regular meeting that followed the forum, routine matters were approved, and the meeting concluded without undue contention.

But it was clear that our hopes for some kind of reconciliation in the SBC was growing fainter. I did continue my series of articles on "Re-inventing the Southern Baptist Convention," but it was clear these suggestions were not likely to be taken seriously by the new fundamentalist leadership.

Key Events in 1993

January

1   • My anniversary: fifteen years at Southwestern

February

12-13 • Trustee Study Committee on Governance met as a requirement for accreditation

        • Fundamentalists accuse SBC Woman's Missionary Union of committing adultery for offering to accept support from Cooperative Baptist Fellowship

March

8-19   • Spring trustees meeting

        • Forum before the meeting was another occasion for individual trustees to offer their complaints.

        • The annual appraisal of the president was held by the Executive Committee and the chair reported that the president had been given the highest marks in all ten categorties of the appraisal.

        • After all was said, and done, all my recommendations were approved, the reports were accepted and we got through another trustee meeting.

March

9   • Damon Shook, pastor of Champion Forest Baptist, Houston, spoke in chapel

10   • Ed Young spoke in chapel as SBC president. He said, "I have so much confidence in this institution, in the faculty, in what's being taught here. I had two boys go through here and they had a blue-chip experience. Both of them came out with great images of the school and a great love and appreciation for the faculty and what happened here."

April

1   • Southwestern received study grant from Lilly for a board study of theology. This was part of a "remedial" program to improve our board.

11   • Preached Bell Shoals Baptist Church in Brandon FL for Bob Reccord. He had gone to First Baptist Church, Norfolk, VA, then SBC Home Mission Board president.

25   • Preached First Baptist Church, Pt. Neches, TX—where I was baptized in 1939

28   • Evangelist Rodney Gage spoke in chapel

29   • Preached at Tennessee Baptists Pastors Conference

May

8   • Preached at South Main Baptist Church and spoke on SBC issues

12   • Spoke in chapel—Founders Day—"A Narrative Inquiry: Finding
         Southwestern's Uniqueness in Stories"

June

13   • Spoke at SBC Music Conference, Champion Forest Church, Houston

14   • SBC met in Houston

         • Ed Young elected unopposed.

         • Paige Patterson's paper at Southeastern Seminary booth named the
         following as Neo-orthodox (liberals) Dilday, Honeycutt, Sherman,
         Lolley, Ferguson, and "most Baptist state paper editors

         • He also named the following as Neo Orthodox schools, Baylor,
         Gardner-Webb, Cumberland, Carson-Newman, and Midwestern. He
         later "apologized" saying his paper should not have been distributed.

16   • Dinner with Judge and Mrs. Paul Pressler with six seminary presidents,
         a polite gathering without confrontation.

21   • Met with Professor Earl Ellis to plan Biblical Research Library at
         Southwestern

July

18   • Preached First Baptist Church, Norfolk, VA

23   • Visited new trustee Craig Atherton

August

9-30   • Visited new trustees Richard McClure, Ted Russell, Ed Litton,
         Michael Marshall, Willie Brumfield, William Wyrick, Miles Seaborn,
         and James Leftwich

September

14   • Jack Graham preached for Seminary revival

28   • Jimmy Draper preached in chapel

October

1   • Met with trustees Jack Price, T. Bob Davis, and Olin Collins about my
         recommendation of David Music to be new dean of Music School

11   • Fall trustee meeting

         • Forum before the meeting continued the pattern of individual
         complaints.

         • Regular sessions of the board meeting

         • Reported our new Lay Theological Studies Program leading to a two-
         year master's degree

- Reported new computer system in place for $1.5 million. This was the fulfillment of my book on computers and our plan to get the seminary up to speed on technology
- C. J. and Ophelia Humphreys approved for B. H. Carol Award. (This was fiercely debated because of her involvement with CBF, motion to withdraw failed. It finally did pass, but I had to call Ophelia because their opposition was in press release. She understood and accepted.)
- In response to SBC resolution, board discussed whether we should have Southwestern booth at CBF meetings. I proposed we relate to all our alumni around the world. They rejected this. Don Taylor said, "The CBF exists for the purpose of maliciously creating a chilling and adversarial relationship within the SBC for the purpose of depriving the SBC of the needed funds to finance the Cooperative Program missionary endeavors." (Obviously language provided to him by others.)
- Charles Lawson complained there were no copies of Salt & Light, Richard Land's fundamentalist publication on tables in Library. Librarian Wrotenbery explained we do subscribed, but they do not send enough copies for free disribution
- The rest of the meeting was routine.

15	• Attended Al Mohler's inauguration at Southern Seminary
19	• Evangelist Luis Pulau spoke in chapel
25	• Spoke at annual Baptist General Convention of Texas annual meeting. "Family of Faith—Faith of the Family"
28	• Jerry Rankin, President of the SBC Foreign Mission Board, spoke in chapel

November

8	• Attended Richard Mauw's inauguration as President of Fuller Seminary in California.
9	• O. S. Hawkins preached in chapel and had discussion with faculty at lunch
15	• Spoke at Church Music Conference Alabama Convention, Huntsville AL
16	• Spoke at the Kentucky Baptist State Convention.

Note: In the fall meeting of 1993, the thirty-nine-member board of trustees had the following composition: 15 hard-core fundamentalists, 6 traditional mainstream Baptists, and 8 swing voters.

January/February 1993: The "NSBC"—
Additional Features

Recently, with a suddenness that caught even political experts unaware, the structures of Eastern Europe and the Soviet Union were radically altered, reminding us that in His providence, God can surprise us all with sudden, unpredictable changes in His world. That's one reason we must not give up on the Southern Baptist Convention. Whatever interpretation you give to the recent struggle for denominational control, we must remember that the Lord of history is able to intervene in our situation with changes beyond our boldest imagination.

So, as I wrote in the first article in this series, I believe there will emerge from the dust of the controversy a reshaped and hopefully stronger denomination, a New Southern Baptist Convention (NSBC). And because of the possibility of God's unpredictable intervention, the new form could surface sooner than we think. Many of you have written indicating that, like me, you want to turn your attention away from the past strife and focus your efforts toward shaping the NSBC of the twenty-first century.

In the last article, I suggested two essential aspects of a renewed convention:

I. THE NSBC SHOULD PRESERVE THE DENOMINATIONAL SOLIDARITY OF THE PAST, BUT SHOULD BE LESS AFRAID OF RESPONSIBLE TRANS-DENOMINATIONAL NETWORKS AND COALITIONS.

II. THE NSBC SHOULD REFUSE TO USE POLITICS, POWER, AND PRESSURE TACTICS AND ADOPT INSTEAD SPIRITUAL WEAPONS SUCH AS PERSUASION AND PROCLAMATION IN ITS SERVICE FOR CHRIST.

Here are some others:

III. THE NSBC SHOULD WELCOME AND ENCOURAGE BELIEVING INTELLECTUALISM AND REVERENT SCHOLARSHIP.

It should champion a scholarly, thoughtful, conservative, biblical theology that aggressively engages secular modernity without obscurantism. Southwestern is in a good position to take the lead in this effort to put faith and reason in proper perspective.

The secular philosophy which dominates so much of society today may have grown up not so much from a conspiracy of atheistic educators and political leaders as from the negligence of conservatives who surrendered the scholarly turf to liberalism.

Unfortunately, some evangelicals are afraid of education and suspicious of intellectual reflection. This fear appears to motivate much of the criticism our seminaries have received these last dozen years. Remembering that Jesus commanded us to love God with "all our mind" (Matt 22:37), future Baptists must counteract this widespread fear by a firm commitment to study and learning.

IV. THE NSBC SHOULD BE NON-CREEDAL, BUT AT THE SAME TIME IT SHOULD BE WILLING TO ARTICULATE BIBLICAL DOCTRINES WITH GREATER PRECISION, TAKING MORE PAINS TO THINK OUT CONVICTIONS AND TO EXPRESS THEM CLEARLY.

In contrast to the scholastic approach of some other evangelicals with their intricate doctrinal nuances and detailed qualifications. (e.g., the Chicago Statement on Inerrancy), Southern Baptists have been described as "simple biblicists." The New Southern Baptist Convention should still maintain its aversion to man-made creeds, its mistrust of fallen human reason, and its unashamed allegiance to the authority of scripture. However, we should give more attention as "constructive conservatives" to careful theological reflection and formulation.

V. THE NSBC SHOULD SEEK A HEALTHIER BALANCE BETWEEN THE PERSONAL AND SOCIAL IMPLICATIONS OF THE GOSPEL OF JESUS CHRIST, IMPROVING ON THE STEPS WE HAVE ALREADY TAKEN TO COORDINATE EVANGELISM AND SOCIAL MINISTRY.

The neo-evangelical model that emerged after World War II helped the old evangelicalism realize that conservative theology with its call to aggressive evangelism does not exclude equally aggressive efforts to meet humanity's social needs.

The NSBC of tomorrow should understand that legitimate concerns for the eternal salvation of the lost need not conflict with, but should actually complement and inform, equally legitimate concerns for human suffering and injustice in the here and now.

VI. THE NSBC SHOULD CONTINUE TO RELY ON "COOPERANCY" AS THE RELATIONAL GLUE THAT HOLDS THE CONVENTION TOGETHER IN ITS PRIMARY TASK OF OBEYING THE GREAT COMMISSION.

It may be expressed in new organizational patterns, but cooperation should remain as the distinctive method of convention work. We must be willing to include all like-minded Baptists in cooperative efforts to accomplish the over-whelming tasks our Lord has given us, realizing that within the boundaries of our common theological convictions, "Baptist diversity" is not only possible, but also desirable.

How do we go about shaping a New Southern Baptist Convention? That's the topic of the next article.

March/April 1993: Actualizing a New Southern Baptist Convention (NSBC)

How do we go about shaping a New Southern Baptist Convention? That was the question raised at the end of the last article about the NSBC. Some would conclude that any essay purporting to answer that question is, to use Farley's terms, "inescapably a contribution to utopian literature."

It is relatively easy to describe what a new SBC should look like (as I've tried to do in the previous articles). It is quite another thing, however, to explain how we can get from here to there—how to actualize the new form. And I must admit, given human nature and the state of the convention, such an effort might be considered unrealistic, or "utopian." Nevertheless, even utopian ideas can provoke significant discussion, and if that should be one modest result of these essays, the effort has been worthwhile. So, here are some ways we can help bring the dream into reality:

(1) We can encourage and inform Ed Young, the Southern Baptist Convention President, in his declared efforts to leave the past behind and bring Southern Baptists together again under the banner of missions and evangelism. He has appointed a cluster of committees to study various components of denomina-tional life, and this has potential for renewal.

Clearly, any substantive changes in the near future can only be initiated by those who, by virtue of political victories, now hold elected denominational posi-tions. They are the only ones who can make key appointments, set goals and objectives, and even mandate certain actions. Since their denominational influ-ence is no longer threatened by opposing parties, these leaders can afford the risk of broader, more inclusive participation. They can once again make appoint-ments based on appropriate criteria other than party loyalty.

On the other hand, those who have disagreed with the ones who are now in power can suspend their disagreements and cooperate with them in reshaping the convention. We should all be big enough to rally behind any bona fide effort (even if initiated by "the other side") to unite the family and chart our course into the next millennium.

(2) Another way forward is education. (You would expect me to list that one.) In the initial article of this series, I stated that Southwestern Seminary seems providentially positioned to help our convention find its shape for the future. That conviction was reinforced when, at a recent reception, I welcomed another group of new students. I was reminded again that over 40 percent of all masters and doctoral students in SBC seminaries are enrolled at Southwestern!

What an enormous opportunity the seminary has to influence the pastors, church vocational staff, missionaries, and denominational leaders who will eventually shape Southern Baptist life in AD 2001 and beyond. By enriching the curriculum to include required courses in Baptist heritage, ministerial leadership, church development, and future trends, we will be able, so to speak, to shape the shapers.

But the seminary has a broader task beyond the training of students. By means of scholarly research, critical thinking, and thoughtful conversation about doctrinal matters, we also lead the convention in doing theology. That is, we are to help our Baptist people understand God truly, help them discern His word for the church today, and help them articulate and defend their distinctive beliefs.

So, in addition to regular classes, Southwestern is also hosting colloquiums and calling together "think-tanks" to deal with subjects such as the future of the Southern Baptist Convention. Lectures and publications by our faculty and staff will address this topic, and we are already lending some of our distinguished "experts" to Ed Young's special committees.

(3) However, the most effective mechanism for shaping the NSBC may not be seminary education or intentional organizational efforts by committees, as important as these are. The NSBC may emerge more naturally from informal, simultaneous involvement by individuals across the convention who "unofficially" contributes to shaping the future. That's how each one of us can have a part in shaping the NSBC.

Who can forget the dramatic political changes that recently erupted in the Soviet Union and Eastern Europe, bringing down communism and walls of oppression which experts thought were immovable? These sudden transformations were not brought about by military assault or international negotiation, but by an irrepressible shared vision that spontaneously arose among thousands of individuals. In His omnipotent providence, God often surprises even the experts.

When we Baptists begin to dream again about new beginnings, when we start talking to each other about possibilities, and, more importantly, when we ask the Lord to bless our quest, a shared vision begins to emerge among our people. That's the Baptist way, and we can be sure that such a vision empowered by the Holy Spirit is irrepressible and will eventually prevail.

The latest management theory, called TQM (Total Quality Management), suggests that instead of focusing on an organization's financial bottom line, managers should focus on involving each employee in shaping the organization. "Quality teams" are named from across divisional lines, and each team is asked to solve certain problems and implement improvements. According to TQM, when the people who make up the organization begin to share the vision for quality, the bottom line will take care of itself.

Perhaps the goal of actualizing the NSBC can be achieved the same way— through a common vision so exciting in its possibilities that it challenges all of us to cooperate toward its ultimate fulfillment.

For still the vision awaits its time . . . . If it seem slow, wait for it; it will surely come, it will not delay. (Habakkuk 2:3)

May/June 1993: "XL" Indicators at Southwestern

Without specific definition and without some objective standards for measuring it, "excellence" is little more than a slogan. That's why we have worked hard to craft a seminary measuring stick—a list of "Quality Indicators." Holding this measure of standards alongside our work at Southwestern tells us how we are doing in our quest for excellence.

However, there are other indicators of excellence at Southwestern that are not so easily measured by scales on an instrument. Sometimes, we speak of these as "XL INDICATORS." (Get it? XL = excel) For example:

I. WE HAVE A FACULTY THAT "XLs." There are abundant examples of this excellence in all three schools, but a typical illustration is the performance this week of a new oratorio composed and conducted by Music Professor Michael Cox. His musical setting of Luke 1:40-55, The Magnificat, not only added to the church's repertoire of praise and worship, but it brought enthusiastic community recognition to Southwestern as well. After a full page feature story on Dr. Cox the day before the premier, the *Star Telegram* gave Professor Cox high praise with the headline: "Composer's 'Magnificat' Was Just That."

II. WE HAVE A STAFF THAT "XLs." Following a regular meeting this week with the vice presidents of the seminary, I reflected with gratitude to the Lord, on the high quality of leadership He has given Southwestern. Each of these five officers skillfully guides his component of this complex organization with commendable skill and commitment. Functioning as a team, they help the president guide the seminary toward its goals.

Later, after the meeting, I walked across the campus—manicured and blooming with spring colors—and I thanked the Lord for the dedicated talents of our graduate, Kevin Walker, supervisor of landscaping. Kevin believes God called him to use his gifts here to create on this hill an appealing environment for learning. He is only one of more than 100 career employees who, having invested their lives here, serve Southwestern with distinction.

III. WE HAVE A STABILITY THAT "XLs." Someone recently said that Southwestern is "like an oasis of stability" in the midst of the unrest and turmoil in our convention. This stability is seen in the following: Our current board of trustees is supporting the administration and faculty in our quest for institutional quality. While resignations are depleting the ranks of other agencies, Southwestern's faculty and staff are "staying with the stuff." Even though new seminaries are proliferating all around us, and even though we are "competing" from a diminishing pool of students; Southwestern's enrollment is edging upward. There is a positive, up-beat spirit among our students.

In spite of declining revenues from the cooperative program, from endowment, and from other sources, Southwestern's financial situation is stable—a result of our commitment to prudent fiscal management. Salaries, while embarrassingly low compared to those outside education, are at the top when compared to other seminaries. Even though they are going up, student fees are still a fraction of the costs at non-SBC seminaries.

Admittedly, no one can predict how long this uncommon stability can last, so we do not want to presume. Neither do we want to gloat while our sister institutions endure hard times. But we would be most insensitive if we did not express our humble gratitude to the Lord for these clear indications of progress in the midst of difficulty. Southwestern has been and still is a seminary that "XLs." Praise be to God.

July/August 1993: Revisiting the Past

"You can't go home again," was the conclusion of Thomas Wolfe. Generally, that's true, but sometimes you can come close! This summer, as a result of intersecting circumstances, Betty and I have retraced some spiritual steps.

The first of those intersecting circumstances was the death of Betty's ninety-four-year-old aunt, Bess Smith. Aunt Bess and Betty's mother, Jewel Doyen, were longtime members of First Baptist, Houston, so the memorial service was held there. Betty grew up in that church; E. D. Head (later president of Southwestern) baptized her; and we were married there by Boyd Hunt (later professor at

Southwestern). So the trip back to Houston, seeing some of the same faithful saints of the church still serving the Lord there and thanking God for Baptist roots and the godly influences of early church life, was an opportunity to go "home again."

Another circumstance was the retirement of Dr. Robert Marsh, my successor fifteen years ago in the pastorate of Second–Ponce de Leon Baptist Church in Atlanta, Georgia. The church's pulpit supply committee invited Betty and me, as former pastor and wife, to return to Atlanta to preach.

Once more, we were "home again," in what turned out to be a moving reunion of fellow church members and friends cherished from nine years in that great church. That exercise in home going re-focused our attention on the mysterious providence of God in bringing pastor and church together, and the "blessed ties that bind our hearts in Christian love." We soaked up the affection, affirmation, and prayers of that congregation like blotters, and thanked God for those years.

The third circumstance of the summer was the location of the Southern Baptist Convention in Houston, where Betty and I served as the first pastor and wife of Tallowood Baptist Church for ten years—a decade of unprecedented church growth. In fact, during that time, Tallowood was the fastest-growing church in the Southern Baptist Convention, leading to pioneering innovations such as three morning worship services, three Sunday Schools, rented school buildings, and repeated building programs. But, more importantly, our experience at Tallowood taught us how the Holy Spirit can blend together an uncommon fellowship of talented, sacrificial, visionary, and committed people who were willing to risk much to build a great church.

During the convention, we had a chance to visit Tallowood, and found ourselves "home again" with friends in Christ from the past. It was encouraging to see the same aggressive spirit—alive and well—among a people who beginning as a mission in 1959, are still serious about carrying out our Lord's purpose for a church.

All three experiences from the past confirmed the importance of the Seminary's task in equipping leaders for the churches for the future.

So, with apologies to Thomas Wolfe, you really can go home again. We proved it this summer and it was heartening.

September/October 1993:
The Color This Fall at Southwestern Is Green

Green, adj. *1. Of the color that is characteristic of growing grass. 2. Overspread with or characterized by green plants and foliage (a green field) 3. Flourishing, active (to keep someone's memory green) 4. Not mature, unripe, not trained, inexperienced. 5. Fresh, new.*
Each of these definitions applies in one way or another to the beginning of our new academic year. Southwestern is "GREEN" in the following ways:

"FRESH AND NEW" . . . Southwestern is "green" with newness. There are new faculty: Steve Lyon, Jill Sprenger, and Lyndel Vaught. There are eleven new trustees.

Major buildings have new facades, a result of cleaning and tuck-pointing. There is a new music library, a new office suite in the Cowden building, new chimes, and an impressive new entrance to the campus.

"NOT MATURE, UNRIPE, NOT TRAINED, INEXPERIENCED" . . . Southwestern is "green" with incoming students. There are 698 new students at Southwestern. These "green" students are the reason for our existence.

A Lutheran church in Iowa mistakenly printed a line from a hymn, "You are the door; through you we pass to gain the pastors green." We have a wonderful group of "pastors green" on Seminary Hill this year! Several of these new Southwesterners commented on why they came to Fort Worth:

"My dad was not all that pleased that I wanted to pursue a seminary education until I told him I was interested in Southwestern. Then he really got excited and encouraged me."

"The entire staff at my church are Southwestern graduates; they led me to believe that there was no other choice."

"FLOURISHING, ACTIVE" . . . Southwestern is "green" with a flourishing, active morale and spirit. It is this positive spirit, an awareness of the presence of God, that sets this campus apart as sacred. Like a green oasis flourishing in a barren land, Southwestern maintains its historic identity and effectiveness even in the midst of uncertain times.

A number of new students remarked that they had intended to attend some other school, closer to home; but decided to enroll here because "Southwestern seemed to be a place where learning could be carried out in a stable environment."

"GREEN GRASS AND FOLIAGE" . . . Southwestern's campus is literally "green." In spite of the drought of '93, the grass, trees, and foliage on campus are green and verdant, providing a friendly environment for learning and spiritual growth.

One new single student told Betty and me, "When my parents drove me to Fort Forth, they admitted they had been reluctant to let their 'little girl' go to Texas, but when they saw the beautiful green landscaping they breathed a sigh of relief. They felt good about saying goodbye."

Psalm 23 describes the "green pastures" of God's grace and care. We are grateful the blessings that come in "green" at Southwestern this year.

November/December 1993: The Family of Faith

(Excerpts from address to Baptist General Convention of Texas, October 15, 1993)

The Bible often uses the term "family" for believers in Christ, giving us a biblical precedent for using "family" as a paradigm for the Southern Baptist Convention. Just like your own family, we in the Baptist family have our crazy cousins, eccentric aunts, and black sheep; but we're still family. We've had our share of squabbles in the past, but we were always still family; we stayed together.

But today, like the American family, our Baptist family is divided. It is broken and needs fixing. Out there, in the eyes of the skeptical, unbelieving world our credibility is at an all-time low. Our denominational witness for Jesus is blemished by our bickering. We've become a target for ridicule and sarcasm.

In Howell Raines' bestseller about fly-fishing, he speaks about the history of the fish as a religious symbol, particularly during the first Christian century. With undisguised irony he writes: "As a fly-fisherman, I begin to wonder if having fish shapes around me is a way to stay in touch with the ideas of Jesus without having to go near the people who do business in his name."

That's us he's talking about. We're the people who do business in His name, and our family divisiveness exposes us to ridicule. How can we repair our fractured family?

I. Christian Commitment Can Fix our Broken Convention Family.

Let's get our attention focused on the Lord again—on a renewed commitment to Christ—not on political devices. "Both the one who makes men holy and those who are made holy are of the same family. So Jesus is not ashamed to call them brothers."

By refocusing our attention on the one who makes us all holy, we can begin to call each other brother again.

II. Christian Love Can Fix our Broken Convention Family.

Our Baptist family of faith is in the grip of a famine of love. Let's restore AGAPE as the prevailing, supreme theme in our convention. "Therefore as you have opportunity, do good to all people, especially to those who belong to the family of believers." "Be ye kind, one to another, tender-hearted, forgiving one another." "Above all these things put on love which binds everything together in perfect harmony."

III. Christ-like Simplicity Can Fix our Broken Convention Family.

Let's give up some of our grandiose schemes and repent of our unlovely denominational triumphalism and get back to a plain and simple concentration on missions and evangelism. Let's get back to basics, saying with Paul, "This one thing I do." Then our critics will have no ammunition with which to ridicule us except to say, "They are one-sided in their desire to win the world to Christ."

IV. Christian Conscience Can Fix our Broken Convention Family.

Let's get our conscience back. Let's return to the moral principles of truth, and integrity, of openness and fairness. "It is time for judgment to begin with the family of God." "He who brings trouble on his family will inherit the wind."

V. Conclusion:

Maybe we could begin to put into practice the song we love to sing so often:

I'm so glad I'm a part of the family of God,
I've been washed in the fountain, cleansed by his blood.
Joint heirs with Jesus as I travel this sod,
For, I'm part of the family, the family of God.

1994

Fired

v.; To hurl with force or suddenness, to dismiss from a position, to discharge

I wrote only two columns in 1994—January and February—unaware that they would be my last after sixteen years as president. We began the new year still anticipating some breakthrough that would defuse the conflict and lead to resolution. In fact, an article appeared in the January 13 Fort Worth Star Telegram with the tantalizing headline, "Southern Baptist Groups Seek Truce: Leaders at convention conference report signs of healing."

So my January column expressed again the unique nature of Southwestern as a scholarly institution that had remained true to its biblical heritage and its Baptist convictions. It was a reminder that in the light of the "leftward" drift of other denominational schools, Baptists should be grateful for the strength and orthodoxy of Southwestern and should turn from inner strife to a renewed commitment to our main purpose.

The February column presented another facet of the seminary's uniqueness, that is, its emphasis on hands-on practical experience along with classroom instruction in the training of young ministers. What a potential we had in these enthusiastic new leaders for the fulfillment of the Great Commission. Looking back, I'm glad my last two columns focused on the positive qualities that had made Southwestern so outstanding.

In February, as recommended by the board, there was a called meeting of the trustee executive committee. In its 1993 fall meeting, the board had asked the committee to study issues related to the CBF and its impact on Southwestern. When the committee met, I saw it as a chance to take a constructive stance and thereby reinforce the small steps of reconciliation being taken. After a long and frank discussion, the executive committee decided to present positive recommendation that re-affirmed the seminary's commitment to the SBC Cooperative Program giving plan. The resolution did not condemn the CBF. Instead, it reflected an uncommon spirit of restraint and wisdom. I was encouraged.

I also asked the executive committee to give me their reactions to the Administrative Realignment Plan which I planned to present at the spring meeting as a way of streamlining our administrative structure and save over $300,000 annually in operating costs. I was surprised that the committee seemed unimpressed, even suspicious about the plan, and the members were unusually hesitant about endorsing it. The same cool response continued in the sessions of the spring meeting, and eventually, they voted to postpone action on the plan. Now, looking back, it seems apparent that they were already plotting the dismissal of the president and wanted to delay any such reorganization.

Chapter 18 is a detailed narrative of the events surrounding the firing, and will put this chapter and its final two columns in perspective.

Key Events in 1994

January

11   • Preached for Baptists General Convention of Texas Evangelism
          Conference, "None Other Name"
23   • Preached First Baptist Church, Lubbock, TX
26   • Richard Land spoke in chapel and lunch with faculty
30   • Article in Southwestern News about Betty Dilday's role in Metochai
          (Southwestern's student wives organization). Jan 94. She is described as
          Metochai's "PERMANENT" Sponsor." We were fired two months
          later!

February

4   • Called meeting of the Trustee Executive Committee to consider issues
          related to the CBF which were referred to the Committee from last

board meeting and to consider what actions might be taken at upcoming meeting.

- They decided to present a resolution opposing Cooperative Baptist Fellowship and reaffirming Southwestern's positive support for SBC.
- I presented my "realignment plan" as an organizational simplification, reduction in adminstrative staff, and financial saving: Scotty Gray— Vice President and Dean, Jack Terry—Vice President and Dean, and Bruce Corley—Vice President and Dean. They were not impressed. Looking back, it is apparent they knew about next month's plan to fire the president, and wanted to put their own choices in these positions. In the Spring Meeting, the realignment plan was tabled and never revived.

6   • Preached at First Baptist Church, Midland TX

March

7-9   • Spring trustee meeting, amid rumors that the president would be dismissed

7   • Monday, 9 a.m. Informal forum at Holiday Inn preceding main session (see chapter 18 for details of the forum and regular trustee meetings)
- 12n–4 p.m. Lunch and Business and Advancement Committees
- 6:45. Dinner for trustees
- 8 p.m. Student Services Committee met

8   • Tuesday, 7:30 a.m. Academic Affairs Committee met
- 10 a.m. Trustee Robert Anderson preached in chapel
- 11 a.m. First General Sesson of Board (see chapter 18 for details)
- 12n Lunch for Trustees
- 2 p.m. Second General Session of Board (see chapter 18 for details)
- 6 p.m. Dinner for Trustees
- 8 p.m. Executive Committee met to give annual Presidential Appraisal (See Chapter 18 for details and copy of Appraisal in Addenda)

9   • 7:30 a.m. Breakfast for Trustees
- 8 a.m. Third General Session of Board (see chapter 18 for details)
- 10 a.m. Olin Collins preached in Chapel
- 10:30 a.m. Ralph Pulley asked me to meet in my office with him and T. Bob Davis, Damon Shook, Lee Weaver, and Gerald Dacus to offer ultimatum: Resign effective immediately or be fired. (see chapter 18 for details)

- 11 a.m. Fourth General Session of Board. They declared executive session, and voted to fire me, having changed the locks on my office door during meeting. (see chapter 18 for details)
- I left for the house while the board concluded its meetings.

May

1   • *Southwestern News* features Tolar's appointment on cover. Small story on page 3, "Seminary Trustees Relieve Dilday of Presidency." Open Letter from board explaining reasons for firing.

June

6   • Moved from Presidents home to our newly-purchased home on East Park Drive

11   • Appreciation dinner in Dallas

October

25   • Spoke in the Kansas/Nebraska Convention

November

2   • Spoke in New Mexico Convention

Note: In the spring meeting of 1994, the forty-member board of trustees had the following composition: 32 hard-core fundamentalists, 8 traditional mainstream Baptists, and 0 swing voters.

January/February 1994:
The Demise of Seminary Education?

In a Methodist periodical, Thomas C. Oden, professor at Drew University Theological School, speaks broken-heartedly of the "demise of the seminary" brought on in his opinion by "a surrender to modernity." In a companion article, Riley Case, a Methodist pastor, writes:

(1) The School of Theology at Claremont: Chung Hyung-Kyung, an Asian theologian who integrates Buddhism, Shamanism, Taoism, and Confucianism into a new Asian understanding of Christianity, receives a creative ministry award.

(2) Drew University Theological School: Communion is offered in the name of Sophia, Goddess of wisdom.

(3) Garrett-Evangelical Theological Seminary: Professor Rosemary Radford Ruether writes liturgies for women that celebrate the cycles of the moon.

(4) Perkins School of Theology, SMU: A seminar on witchcraft is held during Women's Week.

Welcome to United Methodist seminaries, where what has historically been called paganism is now celebrated as diversity and multi-culturalism.

Since 1908, Southwestern Seminary has been blessed with faculty who bring to their task first rank scholarship wedded to an unashamed commitment to the Scriptures and to our Southern Baptist theological tradition. Long before our convention political conflicts called attention to the importance of doctrinal orthodoxy, Southwestern's faculty members had positioned themselves firmly as constructive biblical conservatives, Each teacher has given an unreserved commitment to carry out his or her vocation "in accordance with and not contrary to" the Baptist Faith and Message. And the administration, equally committed to that tradition, has kept the institution on course across these eighty-five years.

Although we face other threats equally as dangerous as those described in the Methodist monthly, Southwestern Seminary is not adrift, orphaned from its theological roots, or as Dante put it: "Midway upon the journey of our life I found myself within a forrest dark, for the straightforward pathway had been lost."

One evidence of Southwestern's strong theological mooring is found in recent publications by our faculty, There have been numerous books and articles published by our teachers in 1993, but I call your attention to a few that have been released in the past few weeks:

Boyd Hunt, *Redeemed! Eschatological Redemption & the Kingdom of God*, Broadman.
Ralph L. Smith, *Old Testament Theology*, Broadman.
E. Earl Ellis, *Prophecy and Hermeneutic in Early Christianity*, Baker Book House.
Millard J. Erickson, *Evangelical Interpretation,*Baker Book House. *Evangelical Mind and Heart*, Baker Book House.

Thank God for committed professors who demonstrate the fact that faith and reason can live together.

March/April 1994: Experience that Counts

Students who participated in the Spring Evangelism Practicum through the years have written some of their experiences which I wanted you to see. They demonstrate again how important personal experience is in balancing classroom studies here at Southwestern.

FROM SOUTH CAROLINA:

"My assignment was to the Pine Street Baptist Church in Berwick, Pennsylvania, about three hours drive from where I grew up. The congregation of about thirty was discouraged; their pastor had recently resigned due to terminal cancer. After a thirty-hour bus ride without sleep, I learned this sad fact upon arrival about 2:00 a.m. Sunday morning. So, instead of getting some much-needed sleep, I stayed up all night writing another sernmn, the theme of which was hope. They needed it and so did I; the first service was a wonderful experience. It was my first sermon ever in a church.

The week we spent in Berwick remains one of the highlights of my Christian life. . . . There were a few decisions, but the main work of God's Spirit in that church was to bring restoration to a broken community. I'll never forget one night late in the week, an hour after the service, I watched that entire congregation gathered around the piano, singing praises to God. They simply would not leave! They were in love with God and with each other again, and I thanked God for letting me be a part of it."

FROM OKLAHOMA:

"All week long I've wore out shoe leather and knuckles only to preach to the same group of faithful Christians. Late Saturday afternoon before the final day we had worked our way to the outskirts of town. One house remained, isolated. Discouraged from lack of results and our tired feet protesting the Prospect of another two blocks of walking, we almost quit. God impelled us to go on, and gave us the reason for our whole trip. In that last house we found a young mother of two, recently widowed, and without Christ. Having had no church background at all, she nevertheless had concern for her little sons' spiritual welfare. She was considering taking them to a priest to be baptized, thinking that would save them. What a joy to present God's plan of salvation and witness her new birth! I have no idea the cost of these many years of Pioneer Evangelism, but that one soul was worth it all."

FROM TEXAS:

"I am from Arizona. . . . So you can imagine what it was like to be sent to Tucson. Whoopee! Some excitement there! Not! "With some sadness I accepted that assignment and worked hard to prepare. In the meantime I told my parents that I would be in Tucson for a week participating in a revival. They asked if they could come. I said, 'No way. I will be too embarrassed.' (I had never preached before!) They showed up anyway. The Wednesday of the revival my mother accepted the Lord Jesus Christ as her personal savior. The angels rejoiced . . . and so did I. I do not think I would have ever had the nerve to ask my mom, the most wonderfully loving, caring, giving person I know, if she knew Jesus. It was always assumed. But God knew better than my little nose."

FROM WASHINGTON:

"In 1976 we were sent to Las Vegas to hold revival at Desert Hills Baptist Church. My partner was the preacher and I was the personal worker. We had a young singer with us. That week we saw over 65 people give their lives to the Lord Jesus in a revival effort that can only be described as Heaven sent. . . . Five weeks later the Pastor called us and said he was still baptizing as a result of our meetings. My partner had never preached a 'real' sermon before in his life and he was so nervous he got sick. The second night we began the meeting by asking for testimonies. One man stood up in the back and after he said a few words I asked him if he would receive Christ right now. He said he would and came to the altar. In front of the entire group he received Christ. When we finished praying, we looked up and there were ten others waiting to do the same thing. My partner was so scared he began to sweat. He never did preach that night and almost three dozen people came to Christ without a sermon. I learned after eighteen years that my partner is now a full time evangelist."

The Dismissal

Introduction

Since my dismissal by the fundamentalists on the board of trustees at Southwestern on March 9, 1994, I've been amused by various attempts to soften the reality of what happened when others talk about it—especially when a host pastor or moderator of a meeting where I'm to speak or preach tries to introduce me. Some will overlook the firing incident altogether. Others will choose euphemistic expressions that seem less harsh: "He was unfairly terminated, "His work was abruptly interrupted," "He ended his career," "He was forced to leave," "He was relieved," etc. But I will never forget the introduction one outspoken west Texas pastor gave me. No beating around the bush for him. He bluntly said, "He was 'fawred,' that's what happened to him, they 'fawred' him!"

In the light of these experiences, I began to collect synonyms—some familiar, others unusual—for being "fawred." Here are a few: ax, banish, boot, bounce, can, cashier, dethrone, discharge, disemploy, dismiss, displace, drop, eject, expel, fire, force out, get rid of, give notice, give the gate, give walking papers, kick out, lay off, let go, manumit, oust, push out, release, relieve, remove, sack, send packing, suspend, terminate, unseat, and shut out. One of the synonyms was one I'd never encountered: To send to Coventry. According to the dictionary, this idiom originated from events during the English civil wars of the 1640s between forces loyal to the king and those loyal to Parliament. It seems royalist troops who were captured were taken to the city of Coventry, a parliamentary stronghold. Understandably, the citizens of Coventry considered them enemies and made their stay there miserable. "To send to Coventry" became a metaphor for getting rid of someone in the worst possible manner.

This chapter is an attempt to revisit the events of March 9, and the weeks following in 1994 when I was "sent to Coventry" or "fawred!"

Spring Trustee Meeting, March 7-9, 1994

For weeks before the spring meeting of Southwestern's board of trustees, March 7-9, 1994, rumors were circulating around campus and across the Southern Baptist Convention that the hyper-conservative hardliners on the board would attempt to dismiss the president when they gathered in Fort Worth. This was not all that unusual. Since 1985, when radical hardliners appointed to our board by Patterson/Pressler ringleaders became a majority, similar rumors typically surfaced as the date for board meetings approached.

The rumor intensity was ratcheted up considerably in 1992 when Dallas lawyer Ralph Pulley was reappointed to Southwestern's board by the Patterson/Pressler political bloc. A deacon in First Baptist Church, Dallas and close ally of Pastor W.A. Criswell and then Associate Pastor Paige Patterson, Pulley had already served an unprecedented twelve years on the board, during each of which he was a source of contention at nearly every meeting.

Even though he had been a star on the Baylor University varsity basketball team, Pulley had long since lost his athletic physique. With puffy cheeks and deep-set eyes, he always had that serious, intense visage of a man on a mission. In what appeared to me to be an indication of a deep-set insecurity, he tended to overpower some of his naïve fellow board members with subtle reminders that he was an attorney. It was a great relief to me and to the seminary family when he completed his long term as a trustee in March 1987.

Who would have guessed that the fundamentalist political regime would put him back on the Southwestern board in 1992. Surely there were other qualified churches in Texas other than First Baptist, Dallas from which to draw trustees. Pulley would make five members or former members of that church who were serving on the seminary's board in 1991–1992. And surely, even from that church, there were other qualified persons than Ralph Pulley! It became obvious from his first meeting in 1992 that this time his objective was to remove the president and elect someone else—anyone else—who would salute the fundamentalist agenda.

Pulley's resentment goes back to 1977 and his failed attempt to block my election and substitute his brother-in-law instead. Huber Drumwright, who married his sister, was dean of the School of Theology at Southwestern. When the search committee reached its decision to recommend me to the trustees as the next president, Pulley launched an unsuccessful campaign to nominate Drumwright instead. He was able to muster only eight votes.

Our relationship became sourer a year later when I refused his strong plea to name his brother-in-law as the academic vice president of Southwestern, opting to recommend John Newport instead. Pulley again campaigned behind the scenes to elect Huber Drumwright, and he became very angry when Newport was elected. In 1985, "sourer" became "vitriolic" when he was defeated in his campaign to be elected chairman of the board.

He could become so angry at times, and his anger was always visible—red face, shaking jowls, intense eyes glaring over half glasses, bitter sarcasm in his speech. A series of personal tragedies and professional setbacks no doubt lay behind much of his unhappiness and bitter spirit.

So we had become accustomed to foreboding rumors before trustee meetings. This time however, the rumors were unusually strong and came from surprising sources: friends on the staff of the SBC Executive Committee in Nashville, Texas Baptist Convention personnel, Cooperative Baptist Fellowship leaders, and pastors.

We also suspected something was up when one after another, most of the local trustees (including Pulley), who normally did not require hotel accommodations while attending the meetings, asked us to make reservations for them too at the Holiday Inn. Various reasons were given: "I need to have more fellowship with other trustees," "It's too difficult to get ready for the board meeting while staying at home tending to local church duties," "The traffic from Dallas is too heavy." It seemed curious too that trustees who had reserved space in convenient on-campus guest rooms also asked to be transferred to the Holiday Inn so as "not to be isolated from the rest of the board."

Later, a clerk at the hotel called to get approval for a change in T. Bob Davis's reservation. A dentist by profession, Davis, a contentious trustee from First Baptist Church, Dallas, was an outspoken critic of the seminary and a cohort in Ralph Pulley's drive to fire the president. He wanted the clerk to change his accommodations to have a two-room suite equipped with a video tape player. We later learned Davis wanted extra space for a secret Sunday night caucus of like-minded trustees who were planning the firing, and the VCR was used to review part of Professor Boo Heflin's formal convocation address on "Women in

Ministry." They would include Heflin's speech in a list of allegations about "problem" professors.

Out of this caucus, to which trustees who supported the president and new and uninitiated trustees were not invited, there appeared a printed document titled "Concerns RE: Southwestern Seminary (Revised March 3, 1994)." This document, prepared by Davis, instructed trustees how they should handle the various recommendations to be presented during the business sessions in the light of their plans to dismiss the president. (Weeks before the meeting, we always mailed each trustee a packet of reports and data supporting items on the agenda, i.e. faculty tenure, faculty elections, annual budget, administrative realignment plan, etc.) Basically, Davis coached them to defer, postpone, or delay most recommentations until the October meeting when I'm sure they hoped their own administration would be in place. Sure enough, those were exactly the actions they took during the plenary sessions of the board.

Informal Trustee Forum, March 7, 1994

For several years, the fundamentalist majority had inserted a "forum" before the regular meetings of the board. Attendance was restricted to trustees, the president, and selected officers of the seminary and was held off-campus at the hotel. At times, only the president was allowed to attend. It was a clever device implemented to let the hardliners voice their gripes with no reporters or other non-members present. In this way, most of the shameful, strident actions of the narrow-minded trustees could be carried out behind closed doors so their public behavior in the regular sessions would appear benign and even honorable.

Just before the meeting began at 9:00, Herb Hollinger from Baptist Press, Toby Druin from the *Baptist Standard*, and the Ledbetters from the fundamentalist Indiana Baptist paper showed up at the hotel to cover the meeting. We often had reporters at our meetings, but this group was not typical. They had obviously been tipped off about what was going to happen, and looking back, all these developments should have signaled the seriousness of things to come. As usual, the chairman of the board asked them along with faculty and other spectators to leave the room when the forum was about to begin.

In spite of all the signals, that now looking back seem so obvious, I didn't really believe the "hardliners" on the board would actually attempt to fire the president. I assumed that if they were planning such action, their complaints would first be brought up at this forum on Monday morning or would surely be raised during the regular appraisal of the president's performance scheduled for Tuesday night, March 8.

In keeping with a grant for trustee development we received from the Lilly Endowment, and with the approval of Chairman Damon Shook, I had enlisted three faculty members to give testimonies at the beginning of the Forum and had invited ATS representative Dr. Robert Cooley to bring a concluding address on seminary governance. Dr. Cooley, the president of Gordon-Conwell Seminary, was also the president of our accrediting agency, the Association of Theological Schools. He was to speak on "Trends in Theological Education." This still allowed about two hours between the opening testimonies and the concluding address for their unstructured discussions.

Professors Lyndle Vaught, Rick Yount, and Tommy Lea gave testimonies. Then Vice Chairman Pat Campbell presided over the discussions which included concerns about such items as: a student who complained he was embarrassed in Professor Keith Putt's class, Boo Heflin's convocation address on "Women in Ministry," and criticism of my recommended administrative realignment plan.

In the light of budget restraints, and in an effort to reduce administrative personnel costs, I had put together, with the help of the seminary vice presidents, a streamlined reorganization that would save the seminary about $304,000 a year. The vice presidents would also serve as deans of the three schools, eliminating an entire layer of administration and bringing academic decisions into the forefront.

In the case of the music school, the plan called for Dr. Scotty Gray to continue as executive vice president, but also accept the responsibility of dean of the School of Church Music following James McKinney's retirement. The rationale I sent the trustees argued that having been directly involved and intimately aware of concerns raised by some of the trustees about the School of Church Music, and having years of experience in strategic planning as a means of shaping the future of the seminary, Dr. Gray was a logical choice. In this proposed position, working closely with the board and the president, he would be able to keep the school in touch with local churches and provide them balanced and qualified music ministers.

The realignment plan was a worthy proposal that should have met with enthusiastic board approval, but in the forum, before it was to be officially presented the next day, they vigorously trashed it. In retrospect, this too was another piece of their strategy related to their plan for dismissal.

As the 11:00 hour approached, Chairman Damon Shook interrupted the discussion to remind the presider, Pat Campbell, that Dr. Robert Cooley was waiting outside to make his presentation. Trustee Olin Collins became testy, "Who authorized this? Who invited him anyway? We're not through talking yet." Others joined in the tirade, some accusing me of improperly assuming the authority to plan the program, which they wanted to use for unstructured discus-

sion. Chairman Shook reminded them that Cooley's visit was one of the provisions of the Lilly grant for "Trustee Development and Communication with
Administration" which they had approved. He also sheepishly admitted he had
given me permission to extend the invitation on behalf of the board.

They grudgingly took a break and then welcomed Cooley as though they
had been eagerly waiting to hear him. His comments were cogent and relevant,
including a testimony about how well his board at Gordon Conwell treated him
as president with annual study leaves and generous vacation, and how they
protected him from overwork and stress and from inappropriate outside influence from special interests. (I was envious and silently cheering him on!) But the
board didn't seem to apply his counsel to their situation. They politely applauded
and complimented him, and he later joined us for lunch with the trustee officers,
committee chairs, and seminary vice-presidents. There was not a hint of what
was to come. (The next day, after the news of the firing broke, Cooley called me,
"Russell! What in the world happened? I can't believe it! Did I do something
wrong?")

Trustee Committee Meetings, March 7, 1994

After lunch, the four committees of the board met, with most other board
members participating in each committee meeting. The fundamentalists on the
board didn't trust the committee process, so for the last few years, each committee became in practice another plenary session of the entire board, with
non-committee members participating fully in the other deliberations. At times,
non-committee members actually voted in the committee meetings.

I should have picked up on the pattern that began to emerge. One after
another of my recommendations was opposed. The committees recommended
that the board defer each one until October, saying: "We're not quite ready to
recommend this." "Let's wait until we see what the financial situation is in the
fall." "We haven't had time to let this sink in," etc. It was not typical procedure,
but still, it didn't seem to forewarn us of the impending plan for dismissal.

The Business Affairs Committee had a long discussion of the revenues
projected in the proposed budget. They voted to remove a proposed increase in
student fees and asked us to bring a revision making up for the resulting
$600,000 decrease. Financial Vice President, Hubert Martin, and I quickly
worked out an increase by adding more revenue from endowment earnings. It
was not a prudent solution, but with some more cuts, it did provide a balanced
budget.

Chairman Lee Weaver surprised us by his unilateral decision to invite investment managers from Nationsbank to make a presentation to the committee

about how they would manage our endowment should the board choose to move it from the Texas Baptist Foundation. Failure to inform the administration before proceeding was a serious breach in proper operating procedures. It was obvious that something was different about Lee. He was cold and unfriendly. Usually he operated with common sense and congenial good judgment, even bravely arguing and voting against his opinionated pastor, Miles Seaborn, on occasion. But this time he was noticeably distant.

The institutional advancement committee had an uneventful meeting under Lynn Cooper's leadership. Cooper, from Kentucky, had also been a very supportive trustee. He was grateful that I had helped him with some issues in his church, and his comments were always levelheaded and positive. At times he too opposed some of the fundamentalist's actions. But this time, he found a reason to leave after the committee meeting and before the session where the firing was to be presented. Later he told the Kentucky Baptist newspaper that he did not disagreed with the decision to dismiss the president and was looking forward to working on the search committee. I was disappointed.

The Monday night dinner was routine, recognizing outgoing trustees. Following the dinner, the Student Services Committee had a positive meeting with various staff persons reporting on their work.

Academic Affairs Committee and First Two Plenary Sessions of the Board, Tuesday, March 8, 1994

The next morning, the Academic Affairs Committee met with almost all the rest of the board present and participating fully. They passed T. Bob Davis's resolution of appreciation for retiring Dean James McKinney after years of his sharp criticism of the dean and the school of music. Later, McKinney thanked him for the commendation, but said he wished someone else had presented it!

After a long discussion about faculty promotions, they eventually voted to approve them, but faculty tenure was another matter. They were threatened by tenure and rejected our recommendations. Later, I discovered that the caucus handout from T. Bob Davis told them faculty tenure should not be granted because it strained the budget and having so many tenured professors would make it harder to downsize in the event of financial restraints. (The fact is we could have "downsized" eighty adjunctive and non-tenured teachers before touching a tenured professor.) The handout also warned that 70 percent of the faculty was the limit for tenure and my recommendation would put it over the limit. (The fact is that the figures he quoted were from the previous year. The current recommendations were within the 70 percent limit. Furthermore, the 70 percent was our own self-imposed guideline, not a requirement.) They voted to recommend to the board that tenure recommendations be deferred.

They also recommended that the election of Stephen Stookey and Karen Bullock be deferred to the fall meeting, but discussed the election of C. Mack Roark separately. Lee Weaver and other non-committee members in the gallery complained that Roark should not be elected because he was a member of a "CBF church" (First Baptist Church, Shawnee, OK). So Lyle Seltman made a motion that he not be recommended because he was affiliated with a church that supports the Cooperative Baptist Fellowship. The motion was seconded and was being debated when, at the coaching of his colleagues, Seltman replaced his motion with a substitute that left out the reason for their opposition. It passed and the committee adjourned.

Dean Corley quickly contacted the finance secretary at First Baptist Church Shawnee who explained that they are not a CBF church. While some members do give directly to CBF causes, the Cooperative Baptist Fellowship is not a line item in their budget. The church gives 10 percent of its receipts through the SBC Cooperative Program. (This was greater than the Cooperative Program percentages of most if not all the fundamentalist churches represented on our board!). We brought this correction to the attention of the chairman who decided to reconsider their vote in a special called meeting.

In this meeting, attorney Ralph Pulley, the fundamentalist trustee from First Baptist, Dallas, attempted to rewrite the minutes of the first meeting that had already been recorded and circulated by Norma Haynes, secretary to Vice President John Newport. They wanted to conceal the fact that Roark had first been denied because of the false accusation of his CBF affiliation. Pulley and Davis rudely accused Norma Haynes of "inaccurately recording Seltman's first motion in the minutes," claiming Seltman hadn't included the reason in his first motion. He accused her of adding the CBF accusation herself. She cried. Seltman finally admitted he had indeed put that wording in his motion. Not satisfied, they insisted that the tape recording of the meeting be replayed, and of course Norma was right.

I told Pulley the minutes belonged to the committee, and they could change them if they wanted to, but not because they were inaccurate. Besides that, the minutes of the current meeting would have to reflect their attempt to change the minutes showing that in truth, they were attempting to conceal what had actually happened. With reluctant anger, they finally let the first minutes stand as recorded. This was not the only time the radical members of the board tried to "sanitize" the minutes of their meetings.

The first and second plenary sessions of the board meeting were routine. In my regular report to the board, I mentioned that Keith Parks was to be our May commencement speaker. The faculty program committee had extended our invitation three years earlier in 1991 while he was still president of the SBC Foreign Mission Board. Charles Lawson interrupted with a motion to withdraw the invitation because of Parks' sympathy with the CBF. After angry discussion, they voted to rescind the invitation. One trustee suggested that in order to be "gentlemanly and fair," they should send him the honorarium he would have received. (Unbelievable!) I later conveyed the decision of the board to the Parks, and Helen Jean Parks laughingly suggested they send the honorarium to the CBF mission fund as a gift from Southwestern's board!

Next, I presented the administrative realignment plan which would have streamlined the vice-presidential structure and provided a substantial financial saving. Claiming it was too complicated, and that they needed more time to consider it, they voted to defer to the fall meeting. Looking back, this pattern of deferring important decisions was a planned effort to delay matters until they had fired the president and had their own candidate in place.

During the afternoon session, the board quickly elected by acclamation, their new officers for the next year: Ralph Pulley, chairman, Lee Weaver, vice chairman, and T. Bob Davis, secretary. It is important to note that, according to the bylaws, they would not take office until the end of the meeting.

President's Annual Performance Appraisal, Tuesday Evening, March 8, 1994

Following the usual schedule, after dinner, the Executive Committee met for the annual appraisal of the president's performance. (Chairman Damon Shook, Pat Campbell, T. Bob Davis, William Cutrer, Lee Weaver, Charles Lawson, Ralph Pulley, David Allen, and Danny Williams—all fundamentalists except for Pat Campbell who often went along with them. Lynn Cooper had left the meeting.)

Years earlier, I had initiated this appraisal procedure as part of a total personnel policy that provided for written performance reviews and goal-setting by all faculty and staff each year. The plan included the president as well as a formal self-appraisal of the performance of trustees. Although they never took their self-appraisal seriously, they adopted the plan. This annual appraisal had become a constructive tool for recording accomplishments, considering any shortcomings, setting goals for the next year, and considering any salary adjustment for the president. Over the years, the appraisals had been consistently complimentary of my performance.

As usual, I handed out the printed appraisal form and began to review with them the ten criteria measuring my performance during the past academic year. (A copy of the form I distributed is included in the addendum at the end of the chapter) At the conclusion of my report on criterion number one, "In his advisory capacity, the president has provided administrative support to the board and its committees," they offered no complaints. Then T. Bob Davis quickly covered the remaining nine criteria of the appraisal by saying "Russell, you're doing a marvelous job in all these areas." There was not a single negative criticism of any phase of my performance as the chief executive officer of Southwestern.

In fact, in every formal performance review during my sixteen years as president, including this one and the one completed just twelve months before the firing, my work was appraised as commendable in every category and never once was any of the reasons later given for the firing brought up in these reviews.

According to the seminary bylaws, this meeting would have been the appropriate legal time to bring up the surprising list of failures that were concocted and released during the month after the firing. The unjustified and inconsistent list was revised and enlarged week by week indicating the ringleaders were frantically scratching around to make up reasons to explain their actions. In fact, recently dismissed seminary vice president, John Seelig, whom Pulley had quickly rehired, actually solicited the trustees by mail. They were asked to send him reasons they believed "justified Dr. Dilday's firing!"

A compilation of these "reasons" (which I will answer later) includes:

- mismanagement
- poor administration
- insubordination
- stonewalling
- failure to live up to agreements
- frequent attacks on trustees
- arrogance
- isolationism
- disdain for authority
- discouraging of dissent
- lack of openness
- lack of vision
- lack of strategic planning
- unscriptural doctrinal beliefs
- writing *The Doctrine of Biblical Authority*, which denies biblical inerrancy
- berating, misrepresenting, and assailing those who hold the Bible to be the inerrant, infallible, authoritative Word of God

Were any one of these true, it would certainly be reason for grave concern. Put them all together, and the accusations are staggering. But they're all, without exception, blatantly false. Not one of them—much less the entire collection— was mentioned in the appraisal on March 8, 2004, or the preceding one in March, 2003, or any of the appraisals going back to 1978!

From time to time, trustees would voice individual complaints about the seminary, and those complaints would be handled in a timely and serious fashion by the board or the administration. For example, a complaint was raised during the failed attempt to fire the president in the October 1989. One trustee accused me of "hiring a professor who endorses Homosexuality." But without my having to respond, another fundamentalist trustee corrected the false accusation, and it was dismissed as unfounded. Another complaint raised occasionally by individual trustees was that I opposed the Patterson/Pressler takeover. I did not deny this charge, but made it clear that my opposition was not against conservative theology, which I endorsed, but against the shameful, worldly political methods the takeover group employed. But none of these individual allegations was ever raised in official presidential preformance reviews.

After Davis's blanket commendation of my performance, the Executive Committee quickly shifted the discussion to replay tired complaints about what they called "liberal professors" at Southwestern. Leon McBeth was singled out because he "always speaks adversarially about the SBC." His recently completed History of the Baptist Sunday School Board "did not reflect positively on the conservative resurgence," and he would not allow students to record his lectures, etc. We always tried to take their concerns seriously, would follow up with the professors, but there was seldom if ever any basis for their accusations.

I brought up my concerns about board structure, including their practice of having all the trustees participating in committee meetings, transforming them into nothing more than plenary sessions. They needed to trust their committees and abide by the committee plan of organization outlined in the bylaws. Davis insisted "We believe it's best to let all the board hear all the discussions." "That may be advisable," I answered, "But the non-members are not just listening; they're participating in discussion and even voting. Why not then just have plenary sessions the entire meeting?" There was no response.

It was also a good time to mention the inappropriate distribution of T. Bob Davis' packet of material from their "secret" caucus guiding a selected number of trustees how to vote. Even though by then I had a copy, he flatly denied having anything to do with it. "It was just some thoughts from some of the trustees, etc." Lee Weaver's surprise invitation to local bank officials to bring an investment proposal to the Finance Committee was also a concern, but it was also casually dismissed as harmless.

They complained about the location of their upcoming meeting. In 1978 when I led the board to hold open meetings, we relocated the meeting place from the conference room adjacent to the president's office to the larger Williamsburg Room in the Student Center Building. This allowed room for faculty, staff, press, and others who wanted to attend. The location had worked well for fifteen years, but a few days before the meeting, while I was out of town, T. Bob Davis had asked the staff to move the meeting to the smaller Truett Conference Room. The staff appropriately waited for my decision before making the change. Since this was only one trustee's request and not the action of the board, I decided to leave the meeting in the Williamsburg Room where we had already set up the tables and chairs. When he arrived for the meeting, Davis chewed out Administrative Assistant Barbara Walker because the location had not been changed as he had requested. Now, at the appraisal meeting, he was still complaining about it

The next morning, the board voted at Davis's request to move to Truett. Although it was not obvious at the time, his purpose was to limit the number of faculty, staff, and press who could sit in on the meeting when they planned to fire me. However, our staff still managed to squeeze in 100 chairs for spectators, all of which were filled the next day for the opening session and for the 11:00 executive session before all the spectators were asked to leave.

There were more grievances. They wanted more unstructured time in the forum, again grousing about having Dr. Cooley as a speaker, hinting again that it was my plan to intentionally limit their discussion time. I reminded them that the board had voted, even amending the bylaws, to have such programs at the forum and that the chairman had approved the agenda and the invitation to Dr. Cooley.

They alleged that Professor Kirkpatrick said in class, "It's actually a heresy to ascribe male characteristics to God" and asked if I used feminine names for God or changed male references for God in the Bible. I told them I didn't and knew of no faculty who did.

Although he had no specific evidences, David Allen, one of Paige Patterson's close allies, suspected there had been "many concerns" over the years about liberal Southwestern professors: George Kelm (ret.), Ralph Smith (ret.), the entire ethics department, and Keith Putt for example. Allen, a Dallas pastor, was one of those elected to the trustees as a result of the Patterson/Pressler takeover and had become a direct channel for passing on information about trustee meetings to Paige Patterson. (Ironically, David Allen led the campaign to elect Paige Patterson as Southwestern Seminary president in 2003. In 2004 Paige Patterson, in a quid pro quo fashion, recommended David Allen as the new dean of the school of theology at Southwestern. He was elected by the board.)

They grumbled again about Boo Heflin's address on "Women in Ministry" which they believed "opened the door" for women pastors, and the fact that Public Relations Director Scott Collins offered to print the address in The Southwestern News so alumni could read it. The address, which did not champion the promotion of female pastors as they claimed, had been warmly received as a balanced, biblical treatment of the subject from a conservative, Baptist perspective. Miles Seaborn would later try to justify their concern about the speech by pointing to some of Heflin's bibliographic references!

T. Bob Davis fussed that the seminary wasn't listening to his suggestions that an outsider be recommended as dean of the music school. "When a trustee expresses a desire, the administration ought to fulfill that desire." I answered that the board governs by its official actions taken when the entire board is in regular session, not by the wishes of individual trustees however sincere they may be. I explained that we respect the opinions of individual trustees, but their personal desires are not the policies of the board.

Charles Lawson, a layman from Maryland, accused Southwestern of having a "disdain for conservatives." I reminded them of Southwestern's long reputation as a conservative school and that our teachers are careful not to ridicule or "put down" other positions. We always receive any complaints about liberalism—authentic or imagined—in good faith and examine them according to the bylaws. If he had any evidence of liberalism or any so-called "disdain for conservatives" we would take quick and appropriate action as we had in the past. He offered no evidences.

As the discussion wound down, I decided to bring up the rumors that the trustees were displeased with my performance and were planning to fire the president at this meeting. They glibly dismissed the rumors as unfounded. "There are always rumors at these meetings; we can't control that."

They joked about the crowd of concerned students and faculty who, because of the rumors that the president might be fired, were gathered outside the room praying and singing. Even though the appraisal had ended positively, they wondered how they could "escape through the mob." I told them it would be no problem and led them to a balcony area in the Student Center Building overlooking the gathering of more than 200. Getting their attention, I introduced the members of the executive committee, telling the students that we had just completed a frank but positive appraisal, that the committee had commended my performance, and that, in spite of rumors, I was still president! The students cheered, asked if they could lead a prayer of gratitude, and then greeted the committee with handshakes and embraces of appreciation.

Walking across the street to our house, I was relieved. I told Betty that they hadn't brought up performance failures, or reasons for dismissal, or even suggestions about retirement. In fact, they had commended my work, and we had survived another meeting. I even called our three children, thanking them for their prayers for us and assuring them everything was all right. Little did I know that the very ones who had blatantly denied any plans to fire me, already had the printed news releases in two versions ready to distribute: one if I accepted their offer for immediate resignation and another in case I refused and they had to fire me! Several faculty members told me later that they had mistakenly received the wrong release!

Later, one student reported that he had asked T. Bob Davis in the hallway of Scarborough Hall about the rumors. "Are you trustees planning to fire Dr. Dilday?" he inquired. Davis reassured him, "Not in a million years!" The next day, after the firing, the same student sought out Davis and confronted him. "You told me this was not going to happen!" he pled. "Why did you lie to me?" Davis smiled, "Didn't you see me wink when I told you that?"

Third Plenary Session of the Board, Wednesday Morning, March 9, 1994

Following breakfast, the regular third general session of the board took up where Tuesday afternoon's session left off. The student services committee gave their report followed by reports and recommendations from the academic affairs committee. The resolution honoring Dr. James McKinney upon his retirement as dean of the School of Music was approved, as were regular promotions for eight faculty members.

The approval of tenure for Professors Ellis, Cox, and Music should have been routine, but like other key issues at this meeting, was postponed until the fall meeting. However, the recommendation to elect new faculty members was split. They agreed to elect Mack Roark whom the committee had accused of being from a "CBF church," but voted to defer the election of Karen Bullock and Stephen Stookey. (Roark later declined the invitation, and now Bullock and Stookey, who were eventually elected, have both been forced out.)

Everybody seemed to be in good spirits as we then adjourned for chapel where fundamentalist trustee Ollin Collins preached a sermon ironically calling on us to focus on the main tasks and to avoid detours of divisiveness! Collins was a trustee from the Fort Worth area who was later elected chairman of the board and while serving in that office, had to resign his pastorate because of a scandal involving women in his church. In the light of the sordid headlines, he also resigned as chairman of Southwestern's trustees.

Meeting in the President's Office,
Wednesday Morning, March 9, 1994

At 10:30, after chapel on March 9, Ralph Pulley, accompanied by T. Bob Davis, Damon Shook, Lee Weaver, and Gerald Dacus waited at the front of the auditorium and asked to meet with me in my office to discuss a matter. We gathered around my small conference table and spent a few minutes in polite small talk. Damon Shook was still the board chairman, but Ralph Pulley, even though he as yet had no official position, assumed the role of spokesman. (Pulley, Davis, Shook, and Weaver were all fundamentalists, but Gerald Dacus, a supportive pastor from California, had reluctantly agreed to come along as a friendly member. He later explained that at first he had refused to join them saying, " I'm not like you, I don't believe like you do, I don't act like you, etc." But when he discovered there were not enough votes to head off the firing, he agreed to join the group so I would have at least one friendly voice in the room.)

Pulley came right to the point. "We've come to ask for your immediate resignation. We have here an offer for early retirement with generous financial provisions." He made it clear that my resignation would be announced at the upcoming session and would be effective immediately. If I did not accept the offer, I would be fired at once with no financial provisions. Either way—resign or be fired, I would be relieved of all responsibility and would vacate my office at the conclusion of the board's vote.

I indicated that my understanding of God's plan for my life did not include immediate retirement, but that I would be glad to discuss retirement again with them in this meeting. I reminded them that last year, in the forum before the spring meeting of the board, someone had asked about my plans for retirement. My answer was that I had not settled on a date, but had been looking ahead to 1998. That year had a natural appeal since I would be sixty-eight years old, I would have served twenty years, the seminary would be ninety years old, the 1993–1998 strategic plan would be completed. Also I would have accumulated sufficient SBC Annuity Board retirement savings. That would be a logical time, and I was open to putting these plans again on the agenda for discussion.

Then I asked, "For what reason would you fire the president?" Pulley answered, "We're the board, we don't have to have a reason. We have the votes to do it and we will." My response was, "In that case, I have to follow my conscience, and do what I think is right. You'll just have to do what you've obviously already planned to do." I stood; they all stood; and without further comment, they left for the meeting in the Truett Conference Room adjacent to Truett Auditorium. I gathered my materials and as I made my way to the meeting, it was obvious that the word was out. Crowds of students, faculty, reporters, and spectators lined the hallways leading from my office to the conference room. Professional security guards—not our seminary security officers—armed and in uniform—were stationed at strategic points.

Inside, the room was packed to capacity, with the trustees in place around the table surrounded by faculty, staff, press representatives, and other spectators. I stopped by the place where Betty was seated and said to her, "Honey, they're going to fire me!" She caught her breath, and I took my regular seat next to the chairman at the head of the table as whispers of what was about to happen quickly circulated around the gallery of spectators.

Fourth Plenary Session of the Board:
The Meeting to Fire the President, March 9, 1994

Chairman Damon Shook called the meeting to order at about 11:15 and recognized trustee Lyle Seltman to lead in prayer. At the "amen," Ralph Pulley stood and moved that the Board go into executive session, with only members of the board and the president attending. Don Taylor seconded the motion. It carried by voice vote and Chairman Shook asked everyone in the gallery to leave, including Betty and the vice presidents. It was a solemn departure, and I felt suddenly alone. Only the trustees and I remained. There was also that empty feeling that I may have put Betty and my family at risk financially—out of work and salary at the age of sixty-three and forced to vacate our home. But I experienced an indescribable sense of peace, a deep feeling of having done the right thing, and a growing conviction that I was not really alone after all. When the room was emptied of all spectators, Pulley then made a motion that voting be by written ballot. Ollin Collins seconded the motion. It passed by voice vote.

Suddenly, Miles Seaborn interrupted, angrily warning that a crowd had gathered behind the door at the rear of the head table and were eavesdropping. They could hear because the public address system was on. He demanded that the microphone be turned off. It was. This also meant however that no recordings of the proceedings were made as they usually were to confirm the accuracy of the minutes.

Then Pulley calmly reported on the meeting in my office indicating that I had refused their exit plan. So he read the following motion: "I move that Dr. Dilday be relieved of the duties and from the office of president of the seminary effective immediately, and that the severance pay and terms outlined in the 'severance agreement' be adopted by the Board of Trustees." The motion was seconded by Ron Coppock and Charles Lawson.

The severance agreement referenced in Pulley's motion, which I did not get to see until later, was very limited, in contrast to the more generous offer they had brought to my office with the ultimatum. I subsequently learned that Pulley originally planned for no financial provisions in his motion, but trustees like Robert Anderson insisted before the meeting that he at least add the restrictive ones listed below:

- Basic salary for sixty days—March and April
- No contributions to annuity plan
- Medical insurance for sixty days—March and April
- At the end of sixty days, a lump sum of $48,000—$3,000 for each of my sixteen years
- No office provision
- Access to present office restricted (They were changing the locks as we met!)
- Move out of our house in sixty days
- The deferred compensation for housing would be immediately cancelled.
- Acceptance of another position would terminate all benefits.
- Conferences, interviews, speeches, lectures, actions, or activities not deemed by the Executive Committee to be in the best interest of Southwestern would immediately cancel these provisions.

There was a place for the chairman to sign and a place for me to sign agreeing to the conditions.

Originally the first paragraph read, "upon the immediate resignation or termination of Russell H. Dilday." At some point, Pulley scratched out "resignation" leaving only "termination." He also scratched "within sixty days" from the paragraph about accepting another position. This seemed to say that if I accepted another position after the sixty days, they could reclaim the lump sum of $48,000.

Pulley then explained that the seminary needed a new direction which he believed only new leadership could provide and that the seminary was bigger than one individual. He believed it was time to make a change and move on.

Chairman Shook opened the floor for discussion, and various trustees responded. Several who were supportive raised strong objections, asking for an explanation for the grounds for the action, but Pulley indicated his comments were self-explanatory.

Others expressed concerns about the effect this action would have on students, faculty, and the public in general, since it was contrary to the spirit and name of Jesus. There were questions raised about the appropriateness of the procedure, lack of warning, and secret caucuses that were held. Warnings were raised about the negative impact such action would have on Baptist work in general and the Baptist General Convention of Texas in particular.

When one trustee objected that the firing was a personal vendetta by Ralph Pulley, others who later voted against the motion responded with "amens."

None of the objections was answered, and after two trustees complained that I should have accepted the offer to resign, questions were raised about financial provisions. Since Pulley's motion included a "severance agreement" with limited provisions, a substitute motion was made by a supportive trustee to provide the more generous agreement that had been offered in my office. This original severance agreement provided for:

- Base salary to age sixty-five (September 30, 1995—eighteen months)
- Continued contributions to annuity plan to age sixty-five
- Medical insurance coverage to age sixty-five
- Immediate access to the deferred compensation for housing of $150,000 (Even though this was deferred compensation reported on my W2 salary report each year as compensation, Pulley did not want to release it. Even when this motion to release it was passed, Pulley as the new chairman, refused to do it, and I had to secure a lawyer to write letters and make calls to eventually retrieve it. Finally Pulley gave the seminary office permission to pay it, but in the wrong manner. I then was asked to give the money back so they could release it again in extended payments.)
- Office allowance of $3,000 a month until age sixty-five (Although after the first month when I purchased supplies, etc. within the monthly allotment, Pulley was angry and after that would approve only a fraction of the allowance.)
- Move from the house by June 7—three months instead of two
- If he accepts another provision, no salary, no annuity, and no office expense
- Same restrictions: that conferences, interviews, speeches, lectures, actions, or activities not deemed by the executive committee to be in the best interest of Southwestern would immediately cancel these provisions. (Sometime later in an interview I made what I thought was a constructive remark, "The first challenge Southwestern faces is to restore credibility with the donors and other constituents." But Pulley quickly wrote me a threatening note, condemning this quote as an example of the kind of statement that would cancel all future provisions!)

The severance agreement also had a place for the chairman to sign and for me to sign agreeing to the conditions and limitations, but I was not given an official copy nor asked to endorse it. Pulley would later say that my comment in the meeting, "I accept," was tantamount to my agreeing to the conditions and limitations of the severance. I explained that my comment "I accept" meant only that I accepted the board's decision to fire me. A few weeks later, Pulley sent me a copy of the agreement in the mail.

I eventually received a portion of these benefits for four months until I accepted a position at Baylor University in August:

Salary	$8,075 x 4 = $32,300
Annuity	$807 x 4 = $3,230
Medical	$400 x 4 = $1,600
Office expense total	$7,500 (Out of a $12,000 allowance)
TOTAL	**$44,630**

Someone called for the question, and they ended debate and voted on printed ballots that T. Bob Davis had already prepared. There was then what seemed like an interminable period of silence in the room as they distributed the ballots, collected them, and then tabulated the results. I found it very awkward to look up at the group as they voted. I kept my eyes lowered, and had only a vague impression of what the vote might be. Finally Davis announced it: twenty-seven for dismissal; seven against.

At the time, the Board had forty members with one vacancy (Jack Price had resigned) leaving thirty-nine possible votes. Three were absent: Charles Lord, Dick McClure, and John Patterson. Bill Hightower walked out of the meeting before the vote. That left a possible thirty-four votes: 27-7. So 67.5 percent of the trustee board voted to dismiss the president. The seven who voted for me came to be known among supporters as "The Magnificent Seven!"

As soon as T. Bob Davis announced the vote, I gathered up my notebook and papers, stood, and said, "I accept your decision [to fire me]. Thank you for adopting the more generous severance." Then I turned and walked out the back door of the Truett Conference Room and into the adjacent entry hallway west of the Truett Auditorium stage. A large crowd of faculty, staff, students, and reporters had gathered there, spilling out into the parking lot. Some of our staff had escorted Betty to that area and our son-in-law had brought up our car so we could leave without fanfare. I told the crowd, "You no longer have a president." There was a stunned hush. Then somebody said, "Dr. Dilday, they're changing the lock on your office door." I was shocked, but said nothing. We drove home.

I have copies of several versions of the official minutes of the executive session. One is a brief one-page list of motions: (1) to vote by written ballot, (2) to dismiss the president, (3) To name a search committee, (4) to authorize the appointment of an interim president. It omits the motion to declare an executive session and ends with an abbreviated rendition of my brief closing comment.

Each of the other versions is longer and includes three variations of the severance agreement, (1) "Severance Agreement," the one with limited provisions presented by Pulley with his motion to fire me, (2) "Retirement Plan," which I assume was the one offered to me in my study, and (3) "Severance Agreement," the one supposedly approved by the trustees.

However, this third one, which purports to be the final agreement, differed in several instances from the second. The board voted that the second agreement called "Retirement Plan" be the final one. So apparently, as they tried to do on other occasions, Pulley and Davis slightly altered the one the board had voted on and then included it in the minutes. One of their alterations was the omission of a place for my signature agreeing to the conditions.

In view of the fact that I didn't receive their final copy until weeks after the meeting, I never gave my approval nor signed any agreement to abide by its conditions. Pulley would later explain that my signature was not essential since to him, my comments upon leaving the meeting, "I accept," was in essence an official endorsement. I reminded him that in the meeting I never saw a copy and that my comments meant only that I accepted the board's decision to fire me. So, in fact, there never was an official agreement between the board and me.

The minutes also inaccurately show that I remained in the room while they considered motions to appoint a presidential search committee and authorized the appointment of an interim president. The fact is, I left the meeting immediately after the vote was announced.

Pulley's Called Meeting in Truett Auditorium to Explain the Firing to Students and Faculty

In the afternoon following the firing, Ralph Pulley called a meeting of students, faculty, and alumni in Truett Auditorium and read a letter of "explanation" to a standing-room-only crowd. The Dallas Morning News and *Fort Worth Star Telegram* reported what happened. Standing behind the pulpit on the stage of Truett Auditorium, Pulley explained that the trustees were only trying to keep the school's religious spark alive. The crowd stood and shouted, "Puppets! Pharisees! You were the ones who just put the fire out! How do you get rid of trustees?"

When he declared, "Students are the most important element in our school, the room erupted in laughter! Students shouted, "It's the trustees who ought to be fired, not the president." "Why? Why?"

Unperturbed, Pulley ignored the question and then claimed the trustees would welcome names from them to consider as a new president. Students began chanting, "Dilday!" "Dilday!"

Pulley and Weaver finally gave up and left the room escorted by armed guards as students shouted angrily, "Way to go, you Pharisees!" It was ugly.

After the meeting, Don Taylor, fundamentalist trustee from North Carolina, was asked to explain the firing. He responded, "You could say it's politics. He's liberal. We're conservative. Water and oil don't mix. He traveled across the country politicking against Southern Baptist conservative candidates. Dr. Dilday is an excellent administrator with many good qualities, but if you can't work with somebody, you have to make a decision."

Ed Young, pastor of Second Baptist Church Houston and president of the Southern Baptist Convention, responded to a reporter, "The firing will have little impact. I know Dr. Dilday and his board had some disagreements, but I really don't know the issues that were involved. There hasn't been some Machiavellian plan to do anything at Southwestern that I know of. Dr. Dilday's firing was largely in internal issue. It's not an SBC matter."

Many of the media quotes were supportive and complimentary. One pastor summed it up, "What they did was merciless. The most ruthless firing of a secular CEO would not be handled as cynically as this." Another stated, "Dr. Dilday was a peacemaker. He preached peace and reconciliation to a largely hostile audience with deaf ears and bloody swords." One student reported, "Dr. Dilday was always in the halls, not cloistered. The trustees contrasted this open spirit with their secrecy shrouding the dismissal." Another staff person said, "The trustees have no honor, no integrity. Dr. Dilday knows nothing but honor and integrity."

Buckner Fanning, Pastor of Trinity Baptist Church in San Antonio, responded to an interviewer, "Russell has leaned over backward, farther than any moderate institutional leader, to try to work with fundamentalist trustees and keep the seminary in a position of strength."

An editorial in the *Houston Post* titled "Amazing Graceless" concluded, "To Dilday's credit, he has not urged any boycott or inflammatory activities. This stand in itself underscores Dilday's reputation—established long ago when he was a Houston pastor—for peace and understanding . . . . What a sad day for the nation's largest protestant denomination."

From my perspective, most media reports got it right. For example, Daniel Cattau wrote in the *Dallas Morning News*, "Dr. Dilday is considered a moderate, but not even his critics say that he is anything but a Bible-believing theological conservative. His problem, say those close to the situation, was his criticism of the 'conservative resurgence' in the SBC. Southwestern was considered a conser-

vative seminary—but still remained free from the absolute control of the fundamentalist power leaders."

The Southwestern Faculty's Quick Response

On Wednesday afternoon following that morning's dismissal, a large group of
professors, representing what they said was the entire Southwestern faculty,
crowded into our living room to encourage and pray with Betty and me. They
asked what they should do. They were willing to explore all the options: strike,
demonstrate, shut the school down, even resign en masse and start a new seminary like the Lutheran Seminex professors had done. I was deeply moved, but
indicated their first concern should be for the students who had made sacrifices
to pursue their preparation for ministry at Southwestern. They were the real
victims. As teachers, they should do their best under the circumstances to
continue ministering to those students whom God had sent there. That was their
calling as teachers.

So the faculty stayed by their posts, but first they made a bold formal appeal
to the trustees, urging them to call an emergency meeting of the board to reverse
their action. There was no response from the board. Without wavering, the
Southwestern faculty and staff continued their overwhelming support and
encouragement throughout the ordeal, publishing open letters of defense, giving
interviews condemning the action, and counseling confused students.

Southwesterm Students' Spontaneous Gathering

Thursday, the day after the trustee meeting, over 1,000 students—some estimated 2,000—gathered in the front yard of the house for Betty and me to come
out and talk with them. Spring break was to begin the next day, Friday, and most
of them would be scattering across the country. They wanted to hear some word
from us, and they wanted to show their support and encouragement. They were
confused. Should they call a strike? Walk out of the classrooms? March on the
administration building? Boycot the school? The tension was volatile; emotions
were soaring. The staff quickly set up a temporary platform on the front steps of
our house where Betty and I could stand. What should we say?

It was one of those unforgettable moments when the Lord seemed to give us
the words: something to the effect that the work of the kingdom is bigger than
any of us—bigger than trustees or presidents or even students, that their noblest
response would be to get back into class and continue their studies, to apply
themselves more dilegently than ever to the work God had called them to do.

But in addition to the words, the Lord also gave us a song. And spontaneously, after our comments and after a prayer, without having planned it, through our tears, Betty and I led them to sing, "Open our eyes, Lord: we want to see Jesus."

I will always remember that moment—it was a moment that said to them and to us; "God is at work in all things for good. God can bring good out of evil. God's way is to leave the past behind and focus on Jesus."

Pulley-Weaver Press Conference, Thursday, March 10, 1994

The day after the firing, under pressure from the seminary family, Baptists worldwide, and the public media, newly-elected chairman, Ralph Pulley and vice chairman Lee Weaver held a press conference in the Justin Conference Room on campus. This conference was videotaped and reported on local television newscasts. (A transcript of the press conference is included in the Appendix at the end of the book.)

"Pro-Dilday Rally," Friday, March 11, 1994

The next day, March 11, about 600 alumni, faculty, pastors, and others gathered for a news conference and what was called a "Pro-Dilday Rally" at the Gambrell Street Baptist Church across the street from the campus. Their stated purpose was to oppose the firing and call on the trustees to reinstate the president. The group included Clyde Glazener, pastor of the church, Jerold McBride, president of the Baptist General Convention of Texas, Leroy Fenton, chairman of the BGCT executive committee, and other Baptist notables from across the state such as Phil Lineberger, First Baptist Church, Tyler, George Gaston of Abilene, Rick Davis, First Baptist Midlothian, Dennis Wiles, now pastor of the First Baptist Church, Arlington, and a host of others. Their published comments included:

"The firing was an injustice made behind closed doors." "We're tired of being led by the lowest level in our denomination." "The fundamentalists on the board are fearful of education and paranoid about the things they can't control." "Dr. Dilday's undoing was that he refused to go along with the fundamentalist takeover." "This group, if they cannot control you, then you cannot work with them. Russell Dilday refused to be controlled by them." "This is a sad day for the SBC. A lot of people hoped things were getting better and that reconciliation would come, but now their hopes are shattered."

Days Following the Firing, March 11-31, 1994

The days after the firing were a blur of activity. It was like the bustling commotion and mixed emotions a family experiences at the loss of a loved one. Family members and friends came to the house from far and near to answer the telephone, meet the door, and sort the mail. Supporters brought food and flowers. Telegrams, phone calls, and letters poured in every day from long-time friends, leading Baptists, professional colleagues, community leaders, and in many cases perfect strangers. Former president Jimmy Carter called to offer his outrage and support. My friend, Dr. Kenneth Cooper called me every day for 30 straight days—even when he was out of town—to offer encouragement and help. An article in the *Fort Worth Star Telegram* quoted Billy Graham's response. He was "heartbroken" and said, "Russell Dilday, who was fired, is a good friend of mine, I have great respect for him."

Betty was unbelievably heroic in her steadfast support. In some ways she bore more of the pain than I did. But her positive attitude in spite of the hurt would not allow either of us to sink into self-pity or depression. She maintained sanity in our home under impossible circumstances and kept the entire family and our friends on a steady course.

There were times, in the midst of the bedlam, when our sense of humor helped us through. For example, as the months past, several of the fundamentalist trustees encountered a variety of difficulties. One pastor was the victim of a scandal in his church, others had to leave pastorates because of conflicts, others had business setbacks, illnesses, a couple of them died, some, considered less important by the ringleaders, were cast off and shunned by their fellow-fundamentalists as no longer useful to their cause. While we both were working through the resentment and trying hard to forgive, we sometimes humorously would look at each other and make an imaginary mark on the wall as if we were "keeping score." It was all done in private, and as a joke between the two of us, we would say, "Well, another one bit the dust!

I once joked in a small gathering that Betty was not as far along the road to forgiveness as I was, and that at times she was still keeping score. Everybody laughed, but a report of that event reached the ears of the fundamentalist operatives. Soon after, during a Sunday morning televised worship service at the First Baptist Church, Dallas, the pastor reported that "the wife of a recently-dismissed SBC leader" had publicly "rejoiced at the death of one of the trustees who had voted to fire her husband!"

We didn't hear the telecast, but several heard the comments, concluded he was obviously referring to Betty, and told us about it. I called the pastor and expressed my shock and disappointment. Surely he knew my comments about Betty had been told in jest, and he knew she was not guilty of such insensitive behavior. He regretted making the statement from the pulpit, but the personal hurt and embarrassment aimed at my wife could not be recalled.

Reporters from across the nation came to our home on campus or called. Television cameras and photographers were all over the house, even leaning out upstairs windows to capture gatherings on the lawn and at the front door. Some reference to the firing, often in bold headlines, accompanied by large colored photographs, appeared on the front pages of the *Star Telegram* and the *Dallas Morning News* for about a month, with additional coverage following that. National periodicals such as *New York Times, Wall Street Journal, Time, Newsweek, U.S. News and World Report,* and most city newspapers and religious journals printed major articles. Of course, the Baptist press had recurring articles and editorials. Television and radio newscasts included the story along with interviews for several weeks. Pastors dedicated their regular columns in their weekly church periodicals to voice their discontent or, in the case of some fundamentalist pastors, their agreement with the firing.

In the midst of this widespread media coverage, Betty and I found some comfort in trying to diffuse the embarrassing headlines with a positive Christian witness. Sometimes it came through. For example, one young seminary student told me that her father, who was not a believer, sarcastically ridiculed organized religion every chance he got. He took delight in reminding her of embarrassing church scandals and in mocking notable Christian leaders who had failed. These incidents became his cumulative excuse for rejecting the Christian faith.

She told Betty and me that when the news of the firing hit the front pages and became the lead stories on the ten o'clock television news, she dreaded the worst. Her father would surely call to say this was one more reason he wanted nothing to do with the church or religion. "Well," she said as tears began to form, "It happened. He called me last night after seeing you interviewed on television. I grimaced, knowing he was about to lash out at the self-righteous behavior of the fundamentalist trustees." "But was I surprised," she went on, "Instead, my father uncharacteristically said, 'I just want to say that I finally saw a Christian leader I like. That president they fired is real.' I want to thank you, for the way you and your wife have handled all this," she added, "It might be the answer to our prayers that something would help him be more responsive to the Christian faith." I realize this sounds terribly self-serving, but in the middle of all the disappointments, it was a positive note of affirmation for which Betty and I were both grateful.

Tragically, one question I had to answer frequently had to do with the changing of the locks on my office door. While we were in the meeting where the vote was taken to fire me, Pulley and others had arranged for a locksmith to change the locks on my office door so my key wouldn't work. They also had the computer technicians cancel my coded access to the seminary database. Reporters from the secular media assumed this meant I was under suspicion for embezzlement, stealing money, fraudulent mishandling of seminary business, or even having an immoral affair. It was demeaning and slanderous.

Later, under pressure, the fundamentalists tried to rationalize their action, explaining in one interview that they were trying to protect me! "We changed the locks because we were afraid angry students would go into Dr. Dilday's office and steal mementos!" (or as they pronounced it—"momentos.") Of course, this illogical explanation angered students who responded, "Do they think we're a mob of hoodlums? Do they think we all have keys to the president's office and now we can't go in because they changed the lock? They obviously think we would act like they've acted!" One of the fundamentalist ringleaders disclosed another "reason," "Dr. Dilday is a computer whiz. There's no telling what he might have done to the computer data!"

When this rationalization for their action was ridiculed, they tried another explanation, "It's no big deal. We were simply following standard operating procedures in the business world. This is the usual course of action when a CEO is fired." But corporate executives quickly countered that this did not happen in the business world unless there was suspicion of financial malfeasance or criminal offenses.

When these explanations did not ease public criticism, Pulley finally offered a lame apology to the board and to the public (not to me) for what he called "an overabundance of caution."

The fundamentalist trustees were barraged by outraged supporters clamoring for explanations. They demanded reasons for the firing. Under siege, Ralph Pulley quickly rehired former seminary staff member, John Seelig, to serve as their public relations consultant. They needed immediate help to manage the unexpected negative publicity. Seelig, a former Southwestern vice president who resigned under pressure in 1989 after siding with the fundamentalists and inciting the indignation of his staff and the rest of the seminary family, wrote the trustees who had now scattered back to their home states, asking them to send him "reasons" the trustees could use to explain the firing! He collected them, and from time to time he would pull out "the best ones" to use in press releases and to provide the trustees with ammunition for their interviews.

Several of the trustees were called before groups of outraged Southwestern alumni in their home states to answer for their actions. In Alabama, for example, Southwestern graduates responded with indignation. Some of their comments recorded in The Alabama Baptist illustrate the widespread support the seminary had and how infuriated the Southwestern family was.

Pastor Neal Hughes, president of the Alabama Alumni Association: "I'm surprised and extremely disappointed. Dr. and Mrs. Dilday are tremendous individuals, and I had a great deal of esteem for him as president. It's almost like a death in the family."

Pastor Drew Gunnells (former chair of Southwestern's Trustees): "It's a sad, sad day in Baptist life. If anyone represented the integrity of traditional Southern Baptist theological education, it was Russell Dilday, a man who is conservative theologically. He has forgotten more about the Bible than his critics know about it. But this is not about the Bible, nor about theology; this is about power and control. The alumni know the seminary was conservative. Every evaluation, including the SBC peace committee's evaluation, proved it. Dilday is a super person. I've never seen him act outside his Christian character. He will tell you what he thinks, but he is a person of impeccable integrity. When I reported the firing to the Spring Hill congregation, there was an audible gasp. He preaches here at least once a year, and he's one of their favorites."

Samford Professor Dennis Sansom: "I think the fact and the manner in which the trustees fired Dr. Dilday bring shame on not only the SBC, but on the Kingdom of God. It is disgusting to see another Southern Baptist institution become traumatized by this mean-spirited ideology."

Education Minister Dennis Anderson: "I think it's terrible. When they look at what happened at the seminary during his tenure—the way it's grown, the quality of faculty developed, the capital improvements—it would look to me like what the seminary is doing is exactly what we want a seminary to do. He's one of the most supportive, encouraging, and nurturing individuals in my life, and our pulpit is open if he ever needs a place to preach."

Alabama seminary student Scott McGinnis: "I see the firing in its stark, political aspect rather than as a theological issue, which has not been mentioned. What the students here found as ironic was the lack of reasons as to why he was dismissed. Even if we had heard a reason, we suspected that it was really a political move and an assertion of power, and not about theology. There really is a lot to the Texas motto, 'Don't Mess with Texas.' In this case, Dr. Dilday was an extremely, extremely popular person, and I think a lot of people feel messed with."

The Alabama trustee, a fundamentalist, explained to the alumni group that the seminary office had asked them to send in reasons they felt could be used to explain their actions. He mentioned some of the "reasons" that had been submitted, but took exception to one of them: the accusation that my book, *The Doctrine of Biblical Authority*, was liberal. Inaccurate claims that the book denied the inerrancy of the Scriptures were often repeated as a "reason" for dismissal. But the Alabama trustee disagreed. He said, "I've read that book, and there's nothing wrong with it. It's a good conservative book."

The Trustees' Failed Attempt
to Redress Excesses in the Firing

A few days after the firing, I got a call from Louisiana trustee Robert Anderson who was one of the "Magnificent Seven" who voted against the motion to dismiss the president. Anderson was the congenial pastor of the Parkview Baptist Church in Baton Rouge, and he told me that a growing number of trustees were having second thoughts about the way they had handled the whole affair. They hoped I would join them in a called meeting of the board to explore ways to repair the damage done to the Kingdom of God and to Baptist work in particular. When Anderson and I agreed it would not be an effort to reinstate the president, an action I would not consider even if they had the votes to do it, I consented to participate in such a discussion. He said he would get back with me about a date and place for the meeting. Later he called to say that a group of about twenty trustees was ready to arrange a called meeting of the board. I would attend, and together we would address some of the mistakes they had made.

With my willingness to participate confirmed and with his list of agreeable trustees in hand, Anderson telephoned Ralph Pulley with a request that as chairman he call a meeting of the Southwestern board. Pulley stubbornly refused, warning that to revisit their decision would open the dooor for all kinds of "dangerous legal consequences." As a lawyer, he advised them to leave well enough alone.

Not to be dissuaded, Anderson discovered a provision in the seminary bylaws: "The Chairman shall call a meeting of the board upon the request of a majority of the members of the board." Armed with this mandate, and knowing it would only require twenty-one of the forty trustees, he set out to enlist another one or two to force a meeting in spite of Pulley's refusal.

Over the course of the next few days, Anderson would call me to indicate it they had the necessary number. We would agree on a date, and then, disappointed, he would call again to tell me the meeting was off. Ralph Pulley had contacted some of those on the list and badgered them to withdraw. Some of them reported that Pulley implied that calling a meeting might risk financial losses not only to the seminary, but maybe to them as well. He also warned them that Anderson's secret agenda for the called meeting was to reinstate the president. He hinted to some that if they supported such action, their loyalty to the SBC "conservative resurgence" would be questioned.

Anderson eventually gave up on his plan and it never materialized. It did show, however, that a substantial number of the board felt they had not done the right thing, or at least not done it in the right way.

Sunday, March 13, John Baab, a new trustee from Ely, Nevada who had just attended his first meeting, called to ask how we were doing. Baab was a bivocational pastor who worked on a cattle ranch to supplement his salary at the small church he was serving. In the meeting on March 9, he had objected courageously and voted against the motion to fire me. He still detested the "underhanded, unkind way" I was treated. He decided the reason they planned it secretly was that it couldn't stand the light of day.

He wanted me to know that "The gang" had pressured him to go along their plan. "They threatened me. They warned me, 'You'd better be concerned about your future. If you don't support this, your ministry will be hurt.' I answered them, 'Are you saying that if I don't go along with you guys, I might end up in some remote little church nobody knows about, so small that it can't afford a pastor, and that I might have to work at a rough secular job to pay my salary?'"

He continued, "I laughed. 'That's my calling! I've been serving like that for several years!'" I congratulated him, and we agreed it was not only sad, but arrogant that the fundamentalists consider his kind of ministry a dishonorable punishment! He said he didn't have any power, but he had a voice and a backbone, and he would continue to speak his convictions.

Trustee Bill Hightower, a director of missions from Charleston, South Carolina called. He was shocked by the developments at the board meeting. He was incensed and angry. He knew I had done a good job as president, and he didn't know how I had endured their badgering so long. He couldn't sit by and let it happen without speaking out, but he also couldn't stay for the final outcome. He wished us the best. Had he been able to stay, he would have been the eighth vote against the firing.

On March 17, 1994, the Association of Theological Schools in Pittsburgh, PA, the primary accrediting agency for the seminary issued a warning to Southwestern trustees that their action "placed in jeopardy the vitality and integrity of the institution." There were serious follow up warnings and a request for explanations and corrections. Eventually, the board responded in such a way that ATS discontinued further accreditation actions.

As the students returned from spring break, more than 1,000 of them rallied on campus to condemn the firing and ask trustees to "repent of their unchristian behavior and reverse the action." They organized committees "to gather facts, make media and churches aware, and minister to the Dildays." They also circulated lapel buttons and coffee mugs with my picture around the campus. It was a disruptive and difficult semester for students and faculty alike. Students were confused, wondering if they would encounter this kind of behavior when they moved into full-time church ministry. No wonder this event, along with all the other fall out from the fundamentalist takeover of the convention, has discouraged young people from responding to the call to ministry and has resulted in precipitous enrollment declines in all six of the SBC seminaries.

Jack Graham's Nomination of Jim Henry

On March 23, in a surprise move, Dallas pastor Jack Graham publicly condemned the firing. It was an extraordinary step because Graham had been an avowed supporter of the so-called "conservative resurgence." It was the first threat of possible division from inside the monolithic structure of Patterson/Pressler party. Newspaper articles carried his criticism that the firing showed "little if any compassion, fuels the belief that conservatives are unloving, and mean-spirited, and could be harmful to the SBC's conservative movement." He announced his plan to call together younger "conservative" pastors to develop fresh approaches in the Southern Baptist Convention and correct the excesses of its current leadership. As a step in this reformation, he intended to nominate Florida pastor Jim Henry as the next SBC president directly opposing the announced plan of the Patterson/Pressler party to promote Fred Wolf of Alabama as their candidate.

It created an understandable stir in the fundamentalist political camp, and high-level notables in the ruling bloc tried unsuccessfully to discourage him and whip everybody back into line. They needed to continue their unbroken chain of convention presidential elections, and if Henry were elected it would be their first defeat since the takeover began. But Graham didn't budge, and he followed through with his plans to the dismay of the fundamentalists.

Earlier, before the firing, and before Jack Graham's decision to nominate him, I had called Jim Henry and asked him to consider being nominated for president as a "constructive conservative" and as a healer. He promised to give the idea prayerful consideration. Later, he accepted Jack Graham's offer, and on June 14, 1994, Graham presented him to the convention in what some described as "one of the greatest nominating speeches ever made for a candidate for president of the SBC." Well-known fundamentalist pastor Charles Stanley nominated Fred Wolf, the candidate promoted by the Patterson/Pressler party, and based on their unbroken string of victories, conventional wisdom predicted he would be elected by a landslide. But when the votes were tabulated, Jim Henry won easily with 55 percent of the votes.

For the first time in their long political domination, the Patterson/Pressler candidate was defeated. This incensed the takeover leaders, and Graham was thoroughly chastised. One of Graham's church members, trustee T. Bob Davis, publicly chided his pastor, "I'm disappointed in his taking a political stance when the board has acted with such good judgment."

Jim Henry, like most Baptists, was clearly conservative, but he did not exhibit a hard-line absolutist mentality. His term in office, while a welcomed break in the fundamentalist domination, did little to reverse the takeover momentum, and two years later, the string of Patterson/Pressler nominees continued—even to the present day. It did, however, mark a historical "blip" in the hyper-conservative dominion in the convention. Graham, a formidable rising star among mega church pastors, was later forgiven, welcomed back as a member in good standing by the takeover party, and in 2002 was himself elected president of the SBC as the official Patterson/Pressler candidate.

National Association of Baptist Professors of Religion

In their 1994 meeting in Dallas, the National Association of Baptist Professors of Religion, Southwest Region, unanimously approved a resolution deploring "the unprovoked and unjustified termination of president Dilday." They credited the president's leadership for creating a "flourishing center of theological education of the highest quality," and warned that the firing "gravely imperils the future of theological education at the seminary and other Baptist institutions of higher learning."

Seminary Advisory Council Resignations

In the days following the firing, two dozen members of the seminary advisory council abruptly resigned, expressing their outrage, and canceling what the chair of the council estimated to be $15 million in gifts and pledges. Other resignations came during the following months.

"Horse Collar Award," April 1, 1994

Since 1947, the Fort Worth Chapter of the Society of Professional Journalists have sponsored an annual Texas Gridiron Club dinner. Local politicians and media celebrities perform in the show as well as attend it. While governor of Texas, Ann Richards participated in the annual show, as has the Honorable Jim Wright. At each annual affair, the journalists single out the one personality who is "demonstrably deserving of disclaim," and grant that person the "Horse Collar Award." For example, the award was given to Dallas Cowboys owner Jerry Jones when he fired beloved coach Tom Landry.

At their 1994 dinner on April 1, the journalists presented their annual "Horse Collar Award" to the fundamentalist trustees of Southwestern Seminary! They adorned an empty chair on the stage with their famous Horse Collar, and a voice off-stage gave a withering critique. The proclamation reads:

> Long before savaging people in power became a national media obsession, it was a cherished tradition of the Texas Gridiron Club. The practice of singling out someone demonstrably deserving of disclaim finds no lower expression than on these occasions. And tonight, the tradition continues.
>
> What Cleopatra did for chastity, the trustees of Southwestern Baptist Theological Seminary did for education. This group of fundamentalists has succeeded in doing what even the late Fort Worth preacher J. Frank Norris couldn't do—they have managed to take the "mental" out of fundamentalist.
>
> The reason for giving the 1994 Horse Collar Award to this group, to quote the chairman of the trustees Ralph Pulley, are "not pertinent." We don't have to have a reason. We have the votes, and we can do it."
>
> With that attitude, the trustees at Southwestern kicked out students, faculty, staff, and media on March 9 and within 60 minutes summarily fired Russell H. Dilday, the school's president for 16 years. They gave no reasons for the firing, and what's more, the coup seems to have been planned for days prior to the meeting.
>
> When the public refused to accept their "not pertinent" response to questions about why Dilday was fired, they decided to find pertinent reasons, none of which seemed very reasonable.
>
> For plunging religion to new depths, and for elevating stupidity to new heights, the Gridiron's Horse Collar Award for 1994 goes to the 27 trustees of Southwestern Baptist Theological Seminary who voted to can Russell Dilday.

It would be hilarious if it were not for the fact that Southwestern's positive reputation in the community had been slowly built up across many years. In spite of our embarrassing denominational failures, most citizens of the Dallas-Fort Worth Metroplex had come to appreciate Southwestern Baptist Theological Seminary as a valuable asset to the community—spiritually, educationally, economically, and culturally. Fort Worth, especially, was proud of having the largest and "the best" seminary in the world in their town. Now, as the wording above suggests, Southwestern's reputation was "plunged to new depths," and our beloved school became a public laughing stock worthy of the Horse Collar Award.

President of the SBC? April 13, 1994

During a personal phone call followed by an open letter to state Baptist papers around the convention, John Reid, a director of missions for a Baptist association in North Carolina asked me to consider being nominated as president of the Southern Baptist Convention during its June meeting in Orlando. He felt it was time to invite fundamentalists to share leadership with other Baptists in the family, and that I would be the best one to get this process started. Reid's suggestion was picked up by a modest groundswell of Baptists throughout the convention who encouraged me to accept his proposal. I was moved by Reid's proposal and the broad support it won, especially with the hope it raised that some reconciliation might result. But after serious consideration, I declined the invitation and decided to back the election of Jim Henry as the best candidate to break the fundamentalist domination of the past 16 years. As it turned out, it did break the domination, but made little difference in the continuing fundamentalist control of the convention.

Trustee Ollin Collins's Letter to SBC Leaders, May 9, 1994

In a letter to fundamentalist bellwethers Bailey Smith, Adrian Rogers, Ed Young, James Merritt, Charles Stanley, Jerry Vines, and Homer Lindsey, Southwestern trustee Ollin Collins expressed his dismay at the reaction following the firing of the president. The uncanny epistle speaks for itself:

> I have to ask, why has there been such a strange silence from you men who have been in leadership over the Southern Baptist Convention concerning the action taken by our board in terminating Dr. Dilday on March 9? I say strange silence because it just seems strange that when we finally did what you men had been leading us to do, and saying needed to be done for some ten years now, and yet once it was done it was as though we had leprosy and nobody wanted to touch us or be associated with us.
>
> We really feel like we have been hung out and left by our self…we received over 450 letters, are bombarded from every news media, Baptist included, telling us what reprobates we are, calling us ecclesiastical bigots and told that there are special places in hell reserved just for us.

"For What Reason Would You Fire the President?"

Immediately upon adjourning their notorious trustee meeting on March 9, 1994, newly-elected officers Ralph Pulley, Lee Weaver, and T. Bob Davis found themselves bombarded by the question "Why?" Just as I had done in the meeting around the table in my office before the firing, the public was asking, "For what reason would you fire the president?" They demanded some explanation of their motives.

So these newly-elected officers, having obviously overlooked the need for a carefully crafted rationale before taking such drastic measures, launched a frantic, clumsy attempt to justify their actions after the fact. Every few weeks, they would release another list of concocted "reasons." Bizarre, inaccurate, and often contra-dictory, these explanations were at best ill-disguised rationalizations. They begin with the first explanation in my office, "We're the board; we don't have to have a reason. We have the votes to do it and we will," to the letter mailed on April Fools Day to every SBC church and association giving their final list of mythic "justifications." It was this mailing that incited friends of Southwestern to finance an equally expensive mail-out to the same churches and associations to correct the exaggerations and mistruths in the trustee letter.

Here is a chronological log of their various attempts to explain:

I. March 9, 1994. The first explanation given in my office by Ralph Pulley when I asked, "For what reason would you fire the president?" He answered, "We're the board; we don't have to have a reason. We have the votes to do it, and we will!"

RESPONSE: The board does indeed have this authority, but as David Hubbard, then president of Fuller Seminary, warned in one of our trustee training sessions, this absolute governing power should be wielded with guarded restraint. Only in dire circumstances when fully justified, as a last resort, should this authority be employed, and never in a "ham fisted" fashion, according to Dr. Hubbard.

Even though admittedly it was their prerogative, there was then and is now no justifiable excuse for their action other than their desire to have a president who would endorse and openly advance the Patterson/Pressler agenda to control the Southern Baptist Convention and its agencies.

II. March 9, 1994. Board meeting in which Ralph Pulley made the motion to fire the president. He said, "The seminary needs a new direction and a breath of fresh air which only new leadership can provide."

RESPONSE: His "new direction" was actually a sharp detour down a road that would lead the seminary to become nothing more than a legalistic fundamentalist training camp, replacing authentic education with narrow indoctrination. They had been placed on the board for that purpose and now they finally had their hands on the steering wheel and could drive the seminary in that direction. Unfortunately, this radical redirection has now been accomplished, and the Southwestern Seminary we traditional Baptists treasured for years no longer exists. Jerry Falwell recently put the last nail in the coffin when he bragged that Southwestern and the other SBC seminaries "are now fundamentalist schools." I doubt Pulley's "new direction" could be accurately described as "fresh air."

III. March 9, 1994. Meeting of students, faculty, and staff called by Pulley and Weaver in Truett Auditorium. When the students chanted, "Why? Why? Why?" Pulley answered, "We are trying to keep the school's religious spark alive."

RESPONSE: The response of the students is adequate. They shouted, "Puppets! Pharisees! You were the ones who just put the fire out! How do you get rid of trustees?"

IV. March 10, 1994. First press conference called by Pulley and Weaver in the Justin Conference Room. A full transcript of this press conference is included in the Appendix at the end of the book. Here is a summary of the reporter's questions and their responses:

> "What were the reasons for the firing?"
> "We really don't want to comment on the reasons . . . ."
> "We have no criticism of Dr. Dilday that we want to make."
> "Was it his disdain for the conservative movement, or because the institution needs to move in a conservative direction?
> "That was not really a factor of it, not really."
> "Not even a little bit?
> "In my opinion it was not a factor."
> "Not at all?"
> "Not as far as the board was concerned."
> "Why can't you comment on the reasons?"
> "I just don't think it is pertinent."
> "How do you see Dr. Dilday as an administrator, personally?"
> "Dr. Dilday is a good administrator."
> "What do you think, Mr. Weaver?"
> "Dr. Dilday is a fine administrator."

RESPONSE: These answers contradict later accusations that the president's theology was liberal and that he was a faulty administrator who mismanaged the institution. The fact is that my theological convictions expressed publicly in preaching, teaching, writing, and institutional decisions, have been affirmed by faculty and colleagues in ministry as biblical, orthodox, and "unimpeachably conservative." What's more, objective accreditation and professional audits ranked the management and administration of the seminary during my tenure as exemplary. Even in this press conference, Pulley and Weaver acknowledged, "Dr. Dilday is a good, a fine administrator.

IV. Mar. 11, 1994. Press release composed by former seminary vice president John Seelig, recently re-employed by the trustees as their public relations consultant. Here is a summary:

"Irreconcilable differences between trustees and Dilday. Difficulty in working with Dr. Dilday philosophically had reached a stalemate, however, he had earned high marks for his personal skills and relationships."

RESPONSE: The "philosophical" differences are not identified, but as the board changed under the Patterson/Pressler appointments, there were growing differences between seminary personnel and the new breed of trustees. During the first decade of my tenure, most of the trustees were traditional, mainstream Baptists, representing what I still believe is the majority of our denomination. But by the mid-1980s most of the trustees were hard-line fundamentalists or at least sympathetic with their absolutist agenda for the SBC. There had always been a few hyper-conservatives on the board, and in open discussions, their viewpoints were heard and respected, but they remained a loyal minority. Now that minority fringe had become dominant.

However, the growing differences did not result in "stalemate." With one or two exceptions, the trustees accepted all the recommendations I brought to the board during the sixteen years I served—even when the fundamentalists had become a majority.

During a trip to the Soviet Union, I was inspired by the creativity of Baptists who found ways to continue their work under adverse circumstances. So after a lot of soul-searching prayer, I accepted this changing situation with hostile trustees as the "playing field" we'd been given, and decided with God's help, we too could find creative ways to adapt. We learned how to listen to the criticism, navigate around the differences, and shield the work of the seminary from the harshest assaults. We learned how to move forward with a high level of efficiency in spite of underlying disagreements.

"His reluctance to move in concert with policies established by the board."

RESPONSE: The minutes of the board of trustes show that the president and the administration carried out every policy adopted by the board—precisely and without exception. Never in the sixteen years did the board accuse the president of disobedience or failing to carry out an official board directive. This is a false allegation concocted to justify the firing

"He has continued to speak out on political issues fostered by others, in contradiction to his earlier agreement with the trustees not to do so."

RESPONSE: I vigorously opposed the political takeover efforts of the Patterson/Patterson party from 1979 to 1989. However, after a covenant agreement with the board in 1989 that "neither board members nor the president would be involved in the politics of the SBC controversy," I kept my word and did not at any time violate this covenant agreement. Some members of the board, however, continued their involvement visibly and aggressively in spite of the agreement.

"Dilday was confrontational and critical and the conflict seemed to accelerate in recent years with frequent attacks on trustees for lack of cooperation."

RESPONSE: I was never reluctant to speak to individual board members one on one about issues, including what I considered to be inappropriate conduct, but I never did so in anger or in an "attack" mode. As a matter of fact, in the mid-eighties, frustrated by the poor quality of those being nominated, all six SBC seminary presidents met with convention president Adrian Rogers, who named the committee that nominated our trustees. We told him our objection was not that they were theologically conservative. "Give us the most conservative board members you want to, but please give us people who know and appreciate theological education, who have qualifications and expertise that can help us." He admitted that recent appointments were often "people I wouldn't let serve on committees in my church." He promised to do what he could to help, but we never saw any indication that he did. To claim there were frequent attacks on trustees is unjustified.

"There are no implications of moral wrongdoing on Dilday's part."

RESPONSE: Thanks for the compliment!

V. March 21, 1994. Called meeting of Tarrant Association pastors at Travis Avenue Baptist Church, at which trustees Lee Weaver, Miles Seaborn, and Ollin Collins gave another set of reasons. A full transcript of this meeting is included in the addendum at the end of the chapter. Here is a summary:

"Gridlock between the office of the president and the board of trustees."

RESPONSE: See responses above. While there were philosophical differences, they did not result in "stalemate" or "gridlock." Until this last meeting at which I was fired, and with one or two other exceptions, the trustees accepted all the recommendations I brought to the board during the sixteen years I served. The seminary moved forward with a high level of efficiency in spite of underlying differences.

"The president has repeatedly criticized the SBC and its elected officials and other leaders."

RESPONSE: See response above. I did not criticize the SBC, only the new leadership that were taking over its control. I did vigorously oppose the political takeover efforts of the Patterson/Pressler team from 1979 to 1989. However, after a covenant agreement with the board in 1989 that "neither board members nor the president would be involved in the SBC controversy," I gave up efforts. I kept my word and did not at any time violate the covenant agreement.

"The president has repeatedly been cited for insubordination. The president regularly refused to take direction given to him by those appointed to do so. The president's style of management was one of arrogance, isolationism, and disdained for authority."

RESPONSE: During my sixteen years, I was never cited by the board or anyone else for insubordination, disdain for authority, or failure to obey the directives of the trustees—until such accusations were listed by Pulley's group after I was fired. The minutes will show that as president, I carried out every one of the board's directives or policies. Rather than arrogance and isolationism, I persuaded the board to have open meetings, provided more than expected communication with trustees, even traveling across the nation to visit with newly-elected trustees in their home towns. On campus I practiced an "open door" policy in the president's office, and called for that same style of openness from seminary personnel. My management approach has always been relational, collegial, open, and aimed at consensus-building.

"Failure to strengthen and advance the growth of the school from 1985 to 1993. The annual enrollment of students declined 20 percent while the staff rose by a number of 20 percent."

RESPONSE: Southwestern reached its highest enrollments ever during my administration. Following the pattern of all six of our SBC seminaries, Southwestern enrollments did decline from their high in the mid 1980's—largely because of the negative impact of the denominational controversy. However, Southwestern increased its percentage of that declining pool of Baptist seminary students and still remained the largest seminary in the world. Furthermore, the enrollment decreases cited above do not take into consideration the transfer of our Hispanic Baptist Theological Seminary in San Antonio to the Baptist General Convention of Texas in 1988, resulting as expected, in a significant drop in enrollment figures. They also failed to mention that enrollment had increased the last six semesters, reversing the trend. It is also interesting to note that since the firing, under new fundamentalist leadership, Southwestern's enrollments not only declined precipitously, but its ranking among the other seminaries has also dropped. Each of the six schools, intended to offer graduate degrees, has started undergraduate, college programs which inflate the traditional calculation of enrollments. Additions to the faculty and staff were always justified and were made with the approval of the board of trustees. In fact one of the board-approved objectives in all of our five-year strategic plans was to reduce the student-teacher ratio by adding faculty. Furthermore had this staff/faculty student ration been their genuine concern, the fundamentalist trustees would have looked with favor on the significant staff reductions in the administrative realignment plan I recommended at the March 1994 meeting. Instead, they criticized it and refused to approve it.

"The president discouraged dissent and debate of the current issues important to students, faculty, trustees, and our society in general. These include biblical reliability, abortion, ordination of women, and the even the right of the SBC to revise its overall direction."

RESPONSE: On the contrary, under the president's direction, Southwestern sponsored three national conferences on biblical inerrancy, biblical Interpretation, and biblical application. We secured a grant to provide symposia where trustees and faculty would explore together various positions on current issues in the light of Scripture, including such controversial topics as "women in ministry." Southwestern professors were encouraged to present the strengths and weaknesses of a range of positions on current issues fairly so students could develop their own convictions from a biblical perspective. They were instructed not to ridicule alternative viewpoints with which they disagreed. This accusation is totally without merit. Ironically, "discouraging dissent and debate" is a well-known trait of the fundamentalist mentality.

"Lack of significant information and communications to the board."

RESPONSE: Our administrative staff prided itself in keeping the board fully informed about every facet of the institution's life. The president led in sending more than ample information about every recommendation to be presented at upcoming meetings. We encouraged questions, keeping everything above board with no surprises or hidden agenda. An examination of the trustee notebooks prepared before each meeting will show the extent of this open and detailed communication. Upon their election, I visited every new trustee in his or her hometown to get better acquainted, help them know Southwestern better, and be prepared for the upcoming meetings.

"Lack of professional management ability."

RESPONSE: Contradicting their own accusation, both Pulley and Weaver in their interview following the dismissal said, "Dr. Dilday is a fine, a good administrator."

"The president failed to receive favorable performance reviews."

RESPONSE: Absolutely not true. The minutes of the March 1993 meeting of the board report the official results of the Annual Review of the President's Performance measured by ten criteria: "The executive committee agreed unanimously to commend President Dilday on his performance in all the categories of the formal appraisal." Similarly, the March 1994 annual review of the president's performance measured by the same ten criteria was 100 percent favorable. The executive committee's response was summed up by the secretary of the board who said, "Russell, you're doing a marvelous job in all these areas." While from time to time in other meetings informal complaints might be raised, and while individual trustees at times would express their grievances to me, not once in my sixteen years was there a negative performance appraisal nor even a mixed review.

At the March 1994 appraisal, the night before I was fired, I even brought up the rumors that the board was unhappy with my performance and would attempt to fire the president. The executive committee flatly denied the rumors. Upon dismissal, the committee and I met with a large group of students who had gathered outside the meeting room, and I reported that we had just completed a frank and positive appraisal review and that the rumors were false. I was still president! They cheered and greeted the committee with appreciation.

"He was urged to retire, even offered a generous 'golden parachute.' He failed to even consider that or discuss it."

RESPONSE: Not true. While I did refuse their demand for immediate resignation, I did not "fail to even consider that or discuss it." Instead, I offered to discuss again with the board as I had a year earlier, future retirement possibilities. But in spite of my offer to discuss and consider retirement options with the board, they were adamant. It was "quit now or be fired."

Later, they exaggerated the amount of their "generous golden parachute," claiming it was worth $400,000. They did not explain that this inflated figure included $150,000 of deferred compensation approved by trustees in 1986. To accumulate this amount, a portion of my salary had been set aside each year in a special fund for housing at retirement. It was neither a provision from this current board, nor a legitimate piece of the severance. Furthermore, the other elements in the "parachute" were conditional. If I said or did anything Ralph Pulley considered not in the best interest of the seminary, all the severance provisions would stop. It would have been fatal to jump in a parachute with that kind of built-in unpredictability! I finally received my deferred salary plus a total of $40,600 in severance provisions.

When they boasted of their generosity, I could not help but wonder. If I had been guilty of that appalling list of offenses, would the trustees have likely offered their "generous golden parachute" as a reward? It would seem more logical that such a guilty person would be terminated without a parachute.

"Lack of vision and strategic planning aimed at solidifying the school's future."

RESPONSE: Unfounded. Long-range planning and strategic planning were a hallmark of my sixteen years as president. From the beginning, a sequence of five-year plans carefully crafted with input from faculty, staff, trustees, students, and various publics was presented to the board. The objectives and goals of each plan were monitored, updated, and reported annually. Management decisions and budget allocations at Southwestern were guided by these plans. They were named, "Eight by Eighty," "Vision 85," "Upward 90," and "Vision of Excellence." Already in 1994, we were projecting incipient goals and strategies for the next three-year strategic plan pointing toward the celebration of Southwestern's ninetieth birthday in 1998.

Vice President Lloyd Elder followed by Vice President Scotty Gray were assigned the specific responsibility to monitor, report, and update these plans, and Southwestern's efforts in this area were often cited as an example for other schools.

"Doctrinal beliefs that contradicted basic scriptures."

RESPONSE: In sixteen years, the board never raised one concern about the president's theology nor accused him of beliefs that "contradict basic Scriptures." In their interview immediately after the dismissal, the officers were asked if the president was fired because his theology was not conservative. They answered, "This was not a factor at all in the dismissal."

In response to this unfounded allegation of theological "heresy," the Southwestern faculty defended the president in an open letter: "We are dismayed and offended by these misrepresentations and distortion . . . . The charges are false." They further stated that the president "strongly affirms traditional, conservative, Southern Baptist views . . . ."

My book *The Doctrine of Biblical Authority* clearly presents my high view of the inerrancy, infallibility, sufficiency, and authority of the Bible as the perfect Word of God.

VI. March 24, 1994. Pastor Jack Graham (currently the president of the SBC) asked trustee T. Bob Davis about the reasons they fired the president and why they had not released them. He answered, "Oh we have lots of reasons, but we are afraid to release them because they might be libelous."Davis was also quoted as saying, "Dilday wasn't actually fired by trustees, but he fired himself. His ego and pride prevented him from retiring quietly, causing the public spectacle of his dismissal. We didn't want to fire him, or what you say is firing him. We made it as sweet as we could, but he terminated himself. Whether that's a martyr syndrome or what, I don't know. I can't read the man's mind."

RESPONSE: I rejected the demand for early retirement as a matter of principle. It was not pride or martyrdom that caused me to decline. It was an effort to take God's calling seriously and not to allow financial reward to tempt me away from what I believed to be God's direction in my life. I refused it because it isn't right to be "bought out." I'm sure the rest of the board is relieved that their secretary exonerated them from any involvement in the firing. It was really a "do-it-yourself" dismissal!

VII. April 1, 1994. Letter from the officers of the board to pastors giving their final "reasons" for firing. Here is a summary:

A. Irreconcilable philosophical differences: illustrated by (1) Keith Parks, an executive with the Cooperative Baptist Fellowship, was invited to speak at commencement. (2) Disagreement on programs of the music school. (3) His administration realignment plan.

RESPONSE: See responses above. (1) Keith Parks was president of the SBC Foreign Mission Board when a faculty committee extended our invitation three years earlier to speak at the 1994 fall commencement. This could not have been a reason for firing, because their decision to fire the president was made before Keith Park's invitation was reported to the board.

(2) The music school faculty were sensitively responding to the counsel of the board with special study committees, church surveys, and the creation of an advisory council of Baptist ministers of music to work with the faculty. In an

effort to work with the board, Dean McKinney and I met regularly with T. Bob Davis and John McKay, the two trustees who raised most of the complaints.

The fundamentalists' conception of the music school was that it should primarily train the future ministers of music to lead the contemporary praise choruses so popular with the churches today. To them, the use of classical "high-church" music was a waste of time and contrary to "conservative" principles. One trustee explained his philosophy very simply: "A church that begins its worship service singing, "The Lord Is in His Holy Temple" is a liberal church, and it will not grow. But a church that begins its service singing, "Because He Lives" is a conservative church, and it will grow." I agree that cold, formal, lifeless, predictable, worship services are unacceptable. On the other hand, contemporary worship can be shallow, repetitive, trite, empty, and therefore unacceptable as well.

Because of their simplistic conceptions, some of the critics never understood that to earn a masters or doctors degree in church music, students had to take courses like "Shenkerian Analysis," "Ethnomusicology," and had to study such topics as "Appoggiaturas" and "Acciaccaturas" in their theory classes. Students learned how to handle the most demanding musical scores they might encounter in their work. Once equipped, a minister of music could then employ other, less demanding genres of music. Of course they should be sensitive to the kind of music suited for each church, and help that church use the best in its worship of God.

(3) The realignment plan was an effort to streamline the administrative structure by combining the work of the vice presidents and the deans. It would have reduced staff significantly without diminishing efficiency, and would have provided a $304,000 savings in the annual budget. But in their secret caucus before the March 1994 meeting, the instruction to the trustees was to reject or defer the plan. Pulley and his group knew they were planning to dismiss the president, and did not want to make changes—even if those changes were justified and desirable.

B. Continued criticism of denominational leaders.

RESPONSE: Not true. See response above.

C. Failure to adhere to directives not to be involved in SBC controversy.

RESPONSE: Not true. See response above.

D. His book on biblical authority is liberal, committed to higher criticism. He berated, misrepresented, and assailed those who hold Bible to be inerrant, infallible, authoritative Word of God.

RESPONSE: Not true. See response above.

E. The report that he received a positive review the night before is a misstatement.

RESPONSE: Not true. See response above.

Southwestern Faculty Responds to False Charges Against the President

Immediately after the mailing of Pulley's letter of explanation to pastors, the faculty of Southwestern responded by releasing the following open letter in defense of the president:

An Open Letter to Southern Baptists

In their letter to pastors, Southwestern Baptist Theological Seminary trustee officers implied that president Russell Dilday holds liberal views of Scripture and uses "higher criticism" in destructive ways. Both charges are false. We respond not just to defend Dr. Dilday, but also to affirm valid methods of Bible study among Southern Baptists.

In *The Doctrine of Biblical Authority*, published by Convention Press in 1982 and widely used for doctrinal study in Southern Baptist churches, Dilday strongly affirms traditional, conservative Southern Baptist views of the Scriptures. No careful reader should miss his repeated statements about his firm confidence in the fundamental truth, inspiration, and authority of the Bible. The book opens with Dilday's saying, "My own conviction is an unapologetic and unconditional commitment to biblical authority" (p. 10) and closes with an appeal to obey the teachings of the Bible (pp. 129-90). Nothing in this book raises any question about the author's conservative views of the Scriptures. It is not true that Dr. Dilday is "dedicated to berate, misrepresent, and assail those who hold the Bible to be God's inerrant, infallible and authoritative word. " In fact, he has repeatedly urged us to avoid such practices. We are dismayed and offended by misrepresentations, distortions, and the use of guilt by association in the letter from the trustee officers.

We believe fully that "the Holy Bible was written by men divinely inspired and is the record of God's revelation of Himself to man" (SBC, Statement of Baptist Faith and Message, 1963). Because the Bible is the inspired record of God's self-revelation, we affirm its authority. Inspired by God, the Bible was written by men and is a historical and literary document. Christians must remain free to use in a reverent way literary and historical tools of Bible study to understand what God is saying to us through the biblical authors.

The Faculty of Southwestern Baptist Theological Seminary
(Paid for by the SWBTS faculty)

"Friends of Southwestern" Respond to Trustee Letter

The Pulley letter with its false accusations also incensed a growing number of Southwestern supporters and personal friends. It was the last straw in the continuing publication of false allegations from the trustees. Dr. Kenneth Cooper of Dallas led a group who raised $20,000 to mail a letter to the same SBC churches and associations to which Pulley sent his letter. It would give me and others a chance to "set the record straight."

[*Note:* A copy of the four-page letter is included in the Appendix at the close of the book.]

President's Letter to the Editor
of the *Fort Worth Star Telegram*

On October 7, 1998 while he was serving as chairman of the Southwestern board of trustees, Ollin Collins resigned from the board, and was suspended as pastor of his church, Harvest Baptist of Watauga, a suburb of Fort Worth amid accusations of sexual misconduct with women in the congregation. When this scandal hit the headlines, it was pointed out that Collins was a leader in the effort to fire me. The articles also referenced some of the unfounded "reasons" for the dismissal. I felt obligated to write the following letter to the editors of the *Fort Worth Star Telegram:*

From: Russell H. Dilday

Your story about the resignation of the Chairman of Southwestern Seminary's board of trustees referred to my termination as president, March 9, 1994, by the fundamentalist majority on the board.

The story rightly reported that, at the time, no reasons were given for their action. You indicated that weeks later, after widespread outcries, and after scattered contradictory explanations from individual trustees, board representatives released three "reasons:"

1. Insubordination
2. Mismanagement of the seminary
3. Doctrinal and policy disagreements with the board.

Seeing these "reasons" in print gives them a legitimacy they do not deserve, and prompts me to write this correction.

None of these "reasons" was mentioned on March 9 when the trustee officers confronted me with the ultimatum: "Accept our immediate early retirement buyout or be fired." When I asked the chairman why they would dismiss the president, he answered, "We don't have to have reasons. We are the board, and we have the votes to do it." Later, in the closed session where the vote was taken to dismiss me, none of the above three "reasons" was raised.

After the meeting, when the trustees had scattered back to their home states, the fundamentalist leaders wrote letters asking them to submit reasons they believed justified their action. These were collected, evaluated, and the "best" ones then released to the press.

As to the first charge of insubordination, while I did not always follow suggestions from individual trustees, the record shows that I carefully obeyed every trustee mandate, and carried out in a timely fashion every official decision the board made. There is no basis for any accusation of insubordination.

The second charge of mismanagement is curious in light of the fact that I received only high ratings from the trustees at every one of my 16 annual performance appraisals. In fact, the night before the firing, during the annual appraisal of the president's performance, members of the Administrative Committee praised my work as "marvelous." Furthermore, during a televised press conference after the firing, the chair and the secretary of the board were asked specifically, "Did you fire Dr. Dilday because of administrative mismanagement?" Both men answered, "No. Dr. Dilday is a good, a fine administrator."

The false accusation of mismanagement is an unfair slap at the capable professional administrative team that worked with me. Southwestern acquired an enviable record of institutional excellence commended by accreditation teams and auditors. In fact, in a 1990 reader survey, *Christianity Today* named Southwestern the "Best Seminary in America."

It is true, as your article pointed out, that beginning in 1985, our enrollments declined. Actually, enrollments in all six Southern Baptist Seminaries declined from that date (Ironically, in part because of the fundamentalist control of those institutions.) However, a majority of this decline was a result of our transferring the Hispanic Baptist Theological Seminary to the Baptist Convention of Texas in 1988. Those students were no longer included in our enrollment figures. Southwestern actually increased its percentage share of the available pool of Baptist theology students in our denomination.

The complaint that staff and faculty had "inappropriately increased" sounds strange. In light of the fact that the board's own adopted goal was to lower the student-teacher ratio, any such increases should have been a commendation! Furthermore, the board approved all additions to the administrative staff.

The third charge, that I disagreed with the board's fundamentalist positions, is closer to the truth. Indeed, I did disagree with the fundamentalist crass political strategy to control the appointment process of the Southern Baptist Convention. This resulted in the naming of trustees on the basis of their loyalty to the takeover party and with little consideration for competence or character.

I disagreed also with the narrow outlook and authoritarian methods of the fundamentalist trustees who were named during the late 1980s and early 1990s. Most of them had little appreciation for authentic theological education from a historic Baptist perspective nor did they have the competencies to govern a graduate school.

My disagreement on the above issues was not totally a doctrinal disagreement. My own theological convictions and those of the faculty of Southwestern have always been considered theologically conservative.

Then why was I dismissed? I believe there was only one reason. I had vigorously opposed the fundamentalist takeover and domination of the Southern Baptist Convention. I was therefore—even though a theological conservative—on the "wrong" side of the denominational controversy. The fundamentalist majority on the board wanted a president who favored the winning side and who would be unquestionably loyal to the new hyper-conservative leaders of the SBC.

The "reasons" the board later announced are unfounded, lame, after-the-fact rationalizations of an inappropriate action that unfortunately is still reaping damaging results.

Conclusion

As I reflect back on the dismissal and the ill-disguised attempts to legitimize it, some salient conclusions are worth noting.

(1) The sudden dismissal was the climactic step in a long-standing plan to remove the president and replace him with someone who would support the Patterson/Pressler takeover party. The contentious ringleaders who ardently championed the fundamentalist agenda were aggravated with me because I opposed their use of crass, secular political strategies to take control of the SBC and its agencies. They chaffed under the realization that Southwestern Baptist Theological Seminary was the last major institution not under their command, and they wanted very much to finally complete their coup.

But there was a another, more personal motivation. As reported earlier, Ralph Pulley, who took the lead in the dismissal, opposed my presidency from the beginning. In 1977, when I was elected, he led an unsuccessful campaign to have his brother-in-law nominated in my place. Later, when I did not name his brother-in-law to a vice presidential post, his bitterness intensified, and he became an avowed challenger of most presidential initiatives. After feeling a sense of relief when his term on the board finally expired, the seminary family was dismayed that the fundamentalist-controlled committee, renamed him to another ten-year term as trustee. His long-standing personal resentment made him the ideal point man to carry out their intentions.

(2) For the last dozen years before the firing, the Patterson/Pressler faction put their people on the Southwestern board with little or no regard for competence in governing a graduate theological school. With few exceptions, trustees were chosen only because they agreed to carry out the takeover agenda, including replacing the president. That produced a single-minded governing board woefully short on experience and know-how for the job.

(3) Even after they achieved a majority representation on the board, their plan at Southwestern was delayed because they could find no theological liberalism there to justify their actions. They actually seemed disappointed that my personal theology was not suspect and had been labeled "unimpeachably conservative." If the Patterson/Pressler goal truly was to keep the denomination biblically conservative, it seems logical they would have complemented Southwestern for its conservative reputation and lauded the seminary administration as examples of what they were trying to accomplish. But obviously, there were other motives behind their political grasp for power.

This helps explain why the chairman of our board would say, "Russell, you have recommended professors who are theologically conservative, but they are not 'politically' conservative"—meaning they are not in lock-step with the Patterson/Pressler political party. Or as Paige Patterson put it, "Russell, you're a conservative all right, but you're not a 'courageous' conservative,"—meaning you haven't supported our campaign.

(4) The growing group of fundamentalist trustees tried in 1989 to fire the president, but they had absolutely no valid reasons, their members began to argue with one another, and the effort failed. At that meeting a public covenant, which I helped to compose, was adopted between the board and the president calling on both trustees and president to refrain from political involvement in the convention controversy. I kept the covenant; most fundamentalists on the board disregarded it. This "covenant" bought them time until a majority of single-minded hardliners could be appointed to carry out the dismissal.

(5) As more assertive fundamentalist trustees were added, they finally had not only a majority, but a majority who were bold enough to take arbitrary action without justification, and with Ralph Pulley being appointed to the board again, they now had a leader with the persistence to carry it through. As Pulley acknowledged, "We had the votes, so we did it!"

(6) Some of their hardliners, like T. Bob Davis, were about to rotate off the board, so they were pushed to take action before their terms ended.

(7) I believe they thought I would accept their "golden parachute," which demanded my immediate resignation. I could not in good conscience accept the bribe and refused it. Instead, I offered to discuss retirement with the board. I had already hinted to individual trustees that a date in 1997 or 1998 seemed reasonable. It was a time frame that met my need to build up retirement assets, and would allow us to complete the objectives in our strategic plan. Symbolically it had appeal because the seminary would celebrate its ninetieth birthday, and I would have served twenty years. However in the office on March 9, 1994, they refused my offer to discuss retirement further, and called for my immediate decision.

(8) The manner in which the dismissal took place was appalling. It not only contradicted biblical standards of Christian behavior, but also violated the seminary's governing documents in its bylaws and procedures manuals. The seminary bylaws had been revised at my suggestion to provide for a formal appraisal of the

president's performance by the executive committee each year at the spring meeting. This annual evaluation meeting would have been the standard time and place to bring up mismanagement, poor administration, insubordination or any of the other charges given later as "reasons." But none of these complaints was raised when they reviewed the ten criteria for measuring the president's performance. Nor were such charges mentioned in earlier performance reviews. Their failure to even mention these charges until after the firing or to warn the president that disciplinary action might be taken because of shortcomings, violated the legal, legitimate, and ethical process for such action. This is one of several failures that led the accreditation association to send its warning and to promise further action.

(9) Other irregularities in the dismissal:

(a) It was secretly pre-planned by a coterie of fundamentalists who had garnered enough votes to force their plan on the board. I have a memo dated March 7, 1994, two days before the firing on March 9, announcing John Seelig's re-appointment by the board. The memo was signed by Ralph Pulley, "Chairman of the Board." This was before the board met to consider Seelig's employment, and even more significantly, before Pulley was nominated and elected as chairman! Pulley was furtively engineering the entire fiasco behind the scenes while pretending the trustee meeting was routine.

(b) Dishonesty. In the Tuesday night appraisal meeting, the executive ommittee members blatantly denied that the rumors of dismissal were true. T. Bob Davis told a student who asked if they planned to fire the president, "Not in a million years." Later, when the student asked for an explanation, he said, "Didn't you see me wink?"

(c) Ralph Pulley's original plan to dismiss the president had no provision for salary, benefits, or severance. These provisions were added by the insistence of other trustees and as amendments to his motion.. The copy of the amended agreement voted on by the board had a place for my signature of acceptance. Pulley did not send me the final draft of the agreement until two weeks after the firing, and he omitted the section that called for my signature of approval.

(d) The changing of locks on my office door and the blocking of computer access were repulsive and led to rumors that the president was guilty of embezzlement or other serious violations. It was not only scandalous, but an enormous inconvenience. (When I left the office to attend the last session of the trustee meeting that Wednesday morning, the desk was covered with unfinished business and correspondence in process. I never went back. Later, the trustee officers told the press that access to the office would have been provided with their permission, but they never told me that. Thankfully, Administrative Assistant

Barbara Walker arranged to have everything packed up, and the staff unloaded a truck full of boxes in our garage!)

(e) Each press conference, news release, and explanation of their action gave different and in many cases contradictory "reasons." For example, they said I was fired for "mismanagement and poor administration," after saying in the earlier press conference, "Dr. Dilday was a good, a fine administrator." It is obvious they had acted precipitously and were scrambling around to find excuses to cover their tracks. The letter to 40,000 pastors and churches a month after the firing concocted even more of these rationalizations.

(10) There was almost unanimous support for the president from faculty, staff, students, graduates, donors, pastors, lay leaders, and the general public. Even some who favored the fundamentalist takeover of the SBC expressed disapproval of the action. As one pastor put it, "This is the first time in the controversy that bi-partisan agreement has been expressed concerning an action."

(11) Their appointment of Vice President Bill Tolar as interim president a month after the firing was ironically an endorsement of the same philosophy, theology, and direction I had taken as president. Over the years, as dean and vice president, Tolar supported, shared, and in many cases initiated every faculty recommendation, and most of the other academic proposals to the board. His enthusiastic endorsement of the direction Southwestern was taking under my leadership was evident. He even sought my approval before he accepted the trustees' invitation to serve as interim. Now, under his term as interim president, it basically became business as usual, and the same trustees who complained that the seminary needed a "new direction" made no significant changes in the operation of Southwestern for years after the firing. This seems to me to be an admission on their part that their accusations against the president had no merit, but were excuses for an arbitrary decision.

(12) At the heart of the fundamentalist mindset is an anomalous self-contradiction. It is a glaring inconsistency, bordering on the oxymoronic, to raise the banner of faithfulness to the Bible on the one hand, while on the other hand employing methods that are glaringly unbiblical. That anomaly is evident in their assault and debasing of Southwestern Seminary in the name of reforming it and in the ugly political seizure of the Southern Baptist Convention.

Of course, none of us is blameless when it comes to inconsistent behavior, and there is room for repentance on all sides of the controversy. But this double standard is most conspicuous when practiced by those who claim to have a corner on truth, who force their standards on others, who use crass unethical strategies to get their way, and who do it all under the banner of "faithfulness to the Word of God."

A cynical newspaper reporter described one well-known Baptist pastor, a luminary in the Patterson/Pressler party, with these words: "That man knows the Bible by heart, but his heart doesn't know the Bible!" It's one thing to believe the Bible is the perfect Word of God, but it's another thing to live under the authority of the Bible and put its commands and precepts into practice. But at times in the midst of our Baptist battles, the rationale seemed to be "the ends justify the means." Even if the fundamentalists sincerely believed their goals were righteous, they often employed unrighteous methods including:

• cunning, dishonesty, slander, control, threat, gossip, ridicule, innuendo, hypocrisy
• partiality, self-promotion, subtle coercion, shrewd twisting of the truth
• secret caucuses to plot the destruction of others, guilt by association
• majoritarian silencing of dissent and contrary opinions,
• arousing false suspicions to enlist followers (McCarthyism)
• threatening and punishing those who disagree
• saying "I love you, brother," then secretly plotting to hurt you
• squelching free and objective press reports
• crass celebrations of "victories" in defeating fellow believers

The book *Power Religion*, edited by J. I. Packer, warns evangelical Christians about "Carnal Conservatism," a distorted version of orthodoxy characterized by a similar list of questionable tactics:

• government entanglements reducing the church to a special interest group
• ostracizing, withholding rewards from those who don't fall in line (ganging up)
• fanning emotional fears by supposed conspiracy theories
• authoritarian styles of pastoral leadership
• using secular political strategies to have your way
• using peer pressure to enforce conformity
• total defeat of those who disagree (an ugly denominational version of ethnic cleansing)

The Bible clearly denounces such tactics as evil. 1 Tim 5:21, 1 Tim 6:3-4, 2 Tim 2:14, 2:23, 3:2, 4:3, Acts 13:10, 1 John 3:10 are just some of the scriptural prohibitions. Jesus was unambiguous in his denunciation of self-righteous pharisaicalism. Surely anyone who truly believes the Bible is the authoritative, inerrant, Word of God could not ignore these admonitions.

Once, during the heat of the controversy, I was quoted as saying "the use of crass secular political strategies in the work of the Lord is satanic." A storm of indignant outrage erupted from the ultra brethren who accused me of calling the leaders of the takeover "Satan-worshippers." The dogmatic zealots on the Southwestern board demanded my apology. I denied labeling anybody a Satan-worshipper, reiterated my concerns about the use of worldly methods, and made my claim again that Satan was rejoicing because our internal strife had detoured us from our God-given tasks. I acknowledged the hazards of using inflammatory rhetoric and apologized for any misunderstanding my words may have caused.

However, as I review these past years, I continue to believe what the fundamentalists have done to the Baptist denomination is wrong. If the words "satanic" and "evil" are too harsh, then substitute the words "sinful," "unbiblical," "unchristian," "bad," "ungodly," "immoral," "unethical." The fact remains that the end, no matter how noble its supporters believe that goal to be, does not justify the means.

Our Baptist family needs to rediscover the clear biblical admonition to exhibit in all our actions, the fruit, the harvest of the Spirit: love, joy, peace, patience, kindness, goodness, faithfulness, gentleness, self-control (Gal 5:22-23). Even Almighty God, the Omnipotent Creator, is described in the Bible as "kind."

God's Word tells us that the wisdom from above is pure, peaceable, gentle, reasonable, and full of mercy (James 3:17). In 2 Cor 6:6-7 Paul plainly warns followers of the Lord Jesus not to use worldly weapons. We are to employ "weapons of righteousness for the right hand and for the left." These weapons of righteousness are listed: purity, knowledge, forbearance, kindness, genuine love, truthful speech, the power of God and the Holy Spirit. The glaring omission of these simple and clear Christ-like qualities among Baptists during these past two decades should shame us all, especially those who claim to be defending a high view of the Bible.

Last, Betty and I have been encouraged, and our sixteen years of ministry at Southwestern have been validated by several developments since the firing. For one thing, we were blown away by a spectacular banquet given in our honor at Loews Anatole Hotel in Dallas on June 6, 1994. Ken and Millie Cooper, Bruce and Lawanna McIver, and a host of other supporters organized the gathering. Paul Powell moderated the program, which highlighted achievements during our tenure at Southwestern and featured tributes from friends and colleagues. Our children and grandchildren were there along with more than 1,200 participants from around the country. On behalf of the group, Dr. Bruce McIver, the pastor of the Wilshire Baptist Church, presented us with a bronze sculpture of Hercules, saying, "This represents the Herculean way you two have upheld your convictions and your integrity." The statue hangs on my study wall as a constant reminder of that memorable event.

Beginning the day after the firing became public, we were overwhelmed by offers of employment and ministry. Pulpit search committees contacted us. Other Baptist educational institutions offered us immediate positions. I was even invited to meet with a group of Disciples of Christ leaders who offered to accept us in their denomination and give me a position in one of their seminaries or churches! I was deeply moved.

Then came the call from Baylor president Herbert Reynolds. Our entire family was at the house and stood around the phone to hear the news that Dr. Reynolds had offered me a position at our alma mater, Baylor University, as Special Assistant to the President and Distinguished Professor at George W. Truett Theological Seminary. I eventually accepted that position and Betty and I served there with great joy from 1994 to 2000, helping a brand new seminary get underway and serving as interim dean at Truett from 1995 to 1996. I was also recognized as outstanding Baylor University professor for the academic year, 1999–2000.

Later we were honored when *Texas Monthly* magazine named me as one of the 1994 "Texas Twenty" persons across the state who "have proved to be pivotal forces in their respective fields—and, by extension, in Texas." (Others included that year were Ross Perot, Jr., Bo Pilgrim, Hakeem Olajuwon, and Selena—not bad for someone whom Paul Powell described as "homeless and unemployed!")

Other recognitions followed. I was:

- Named by the *Baptist Standard* as one of the "ten most influential Texas Baptists in the twentieth century."
- Named as Texas Baptist Elder Statesman, June 4, 2000.
- Inducted into the Hall of Fame, Mainstream Baptist National Convocation, February 15, 2002.
- Awarded the Judson-Rice award by *Baptists Today*, Dallas, Texas, April 25, 2003.
- Awarded the George W. Truett Award for Church Service, Baylor University, May commencement 2004.

Invitations came to serve as interim pastor at three great churches: Park Cities Baptist Church in Dallas, First Baptist Church in Arlington, and First Baptist Church in Plano. Each of these lasted about a year, and the gratifying opportunities each one afforded and the new friends we made in each congregation are gifts for which we will always be grateful.

In 2002, Howard Payne University trustees invited me to serve as their interim president. Since over the years HPU had sent Southwestern some of our best prepared students, I had a high regard for that institution. For about a year, we shared in the life of another superb Baptist family and experienced another fulfilling and gratifying ministry.

More recently, in 2003, I had the privilege of helping launch the B. H. Carroll Theological Institute, a twenty-first-century seminary that carries forward the DNA of Southwestern in an exciting innovative form. I continue to serve as Chancelor of the Institute.

In addition to all these affirmations, we enjoy good health, preaching and teaching opportunities, an abundance of writing projects, a meaningful church relationship, a supportive family all of whom are serving the Lord in vocational ministries, interesting travel, and best of all, a life-long companionship begun when Baylor classmate Betty Doyen and I were married in 1952.

In fact, the ten years since I was "fawred" or "sent to Coventry" (see introduction to this chapter) have turned out to be meaningful and enjoyable. That leads me to share this important personal testimony:

I acknowledge that the Lord Jesus Christ—to whom I publicly surrendered my life in 1939, who forgave me and saved me for all eternity, who protected me through every youthful stage leading to adulthood, who called me in spite of my limitations to serve in the most exciting and fulfilling vocation imaginable, who led me to Betty Doyen, the beautiful and capable love of my life, who gave us three wonderful children all of whom are serving in church-related vocations, who directed us to a series of fulfilling ministry positions and enabled us for the tasks with His sufficiency, who sustained us through every disappointment and crisis—including the dark days of 1994, and who enriches every day of these later years with his forgiving presence. I acknowledge that time and time again He has demonstrated His faithfulness and has kept His promises, including the one when He said, "I will never fail you nor forsake you." Because of that promise, I join the writer of Hebrews in saying: "Hence we can confidently say, 'The Lord is my helper, I will not be afraid; what can man do to me? Jesus Christ is the same yesterday and today and tomorrow!'" (Hebrews 13:5-8).

Conclusion:
The Power to See It Through—
2 Corinthians 4:1-18

The collapse of Southwestern Seminary at the hands of its fundamentalist trustees in 1994 has to be the most disappointing chapter in my ministerial pilgrimage. Across fifty-two years, from the time I accepted God's calling to be the pastor of the Antelope Baptist Church in Jack County Texas to my present involvement with the B. H. Carroll Theological Institute, I cannot think of a more heart-breaking letdown. As with anybody's life story, my personal graph has its zeniths and nadirs, most of which become less dramatic as time goes by, but this one episode stands out as a paramount catastrophe. It was a great setback to our denomination, the full impact of which can only be measured by history, but the Southwestern calamity left personal grief and pain in its wake as well.

How do you cope with this kind of personal setback? How does one find the strength to keep going in spite of crushing disappointments? How can you resist the temptation to give up and instead, against great odds, muster the power to see it through?

In my Baylor University scrapbook, there is a newspaper article and picture from the sports section of the *Waco Herald Tribune*. It's a picture of a boxer in the boxing ring snapped just as he was struck by a right cross that knocked him out cold. His face is distorted, eyes closed, teeth gritted, sweat flying; he's on his way down. You can almost feel the pain and anguish. The caption under the picture is an understatement: "All is not well!"

I know about that pain and anguish because I'm the one who's falling to the canvas in that picture. Thinking it would be funny, my "sadistic" college roommates signed me up in the Golden Gloves tournament in Waco. Then they dared me to follow through and actually enter the tournament as a member of the Baylor boxing team. I had never been in a boxing ring, but I had to save face. So with a little "training" offered by the other Baylor boxers and with a momentary collapse of common sense, I began my very short career as a prizefighter. That's when I discovered that the opponents we Baylor boxers had to face were the street fighters from the reformatory prison at Gatesville, Texas! But it was too late to back out. Somehow I survived the first few bouts.

The news picture with its caption, "All Is Not Well," described the semifinal welterweight match toward the end of the tournament. Here is what the accompanying article says, "This fight in the semifinals was the best one to date. Dilday was floored in the first round, but he staged a comeback in the second and third round and won the judge's decision."

I remember waking up after that smashing right cross from the Gatesville inmate. I was flat on my face on the canvas. The referee was counting, "Three! Four! Five!" So I carried on a brief argument with myself, "Wouldn't it be better just to stay down here for a few more seconds and let this be over?" But to my surprise, I discovered that being unconscious, even for a few seconds, is like taking a nap. I felt totally relaxed and invigorated with a new reserve of energy. My opponent from the reformatory was already tiring. He had won every fight by expending all his energy and knocking out his opponents in the first round, and he wasn't used to going the distance. So I got up, outlasted him, eventually won the judge's decision, and went on to lose a close bout in the finals. (After that experience, I had no desire to continue a pugilistic career, although at times being a seminary president during the denominational controversy had similarities!)

But that brings us back to the question, "When you're down and out, flat on your face because of some tragic blow, when you hear the count and you're tempted to give up, what does it take to get up and see it through?

The Bible has a lot to say about the dangers of losing heart, fainting, despairing, or as Paul described it, "becoming a castaway." We read about Elijah the prophet who fell victim to self-pity and complained to God, "I'm the only faithful one left, you might as well take my life too. I quit." There have been times when we've felt like that. Then there is David, who in spite of composing all those uplifting poems, encountered debilitating despair. He repeats one forlorn phrase so often in the Psalms that it begins to sound like his trademark, "My soul is cast down. My soul is cast down." Most of us can identify with that. We've had that feeling of a cast down soul.

But the Bible also tells about people who somehow found the strength to keep going—women and men with the inner capacity, the faith, and some secret reserve that allowed them to see it through in spite of disappointments and discouragement. They're like that indomitable bunny who advertises batteries. They just keep on going and going and going.

The apostle Paul was one of those. He courageously endured unimaginable obstacles, and toward the end of his life summarized it by saying, "I fought a good fight, I kept the faith and I finished my race." His advice to us was, "Be steadfast, unmovable, always abound in the work of the Lord." Good advice, Paul, but how do we do that? His answer is in 2 Corinthians 4, and those verses from God's Word became a source of enormous encouragement to me during the dark days of 1994. Here are some of the verses from which I discovered three insights that helped me see it through:

Therefore, having this ministry by the mercy of God, we do not lose heart.

We have renounced disgraceful, underhanded ways; we refuse to practice cunning or to tamper with God's word, but by the open statement of the truth we would commend ourselves to every man's conscience in the sight of God. . .

For what we preach is not ourselves, but Jesus Christ as Lord, with ourselves as your servants for Jesus' sake.

For it is the God who said, "Let light shine out of darkness," who has shone in our hearts to give the light of the knowledge of the glory of God in the face of Christ.

But we have this treasure in earthen vessels, to show that the transcendent power belongs to God and not to us.

We are afflicted in every way, but not crushed; perplexed, but not driven to despair; persecuted, but not forsaken; struck down, but not destroyed . . . .

So we do not lose heart. Though our outer nature is wasting away, our inner nature is being renewed every day . . . because we look not to the things that are seen but to the things that are unseen; for the things that are seen are transient, but the things that are unseen are eternal.

I. Power to See It Through Comes from Involvement in a Significant Cause

Therefore, having this ministry by the mercy of God, we do not lose heart (2 Cor 4:1). The Apostle did not lose heart because he was involved in a significant ministry. There is a compelling motivation associated with being caught up in a crucial enterprise, an endeavor of ultimate value. Paul couldn't quit because he had been recruited by the Lord Jesus and given a vital role in the eternal work of His kingdom. The dimensions of that work were enormous, the tasks so challenging, and the stakes so high that it captured him, and pulled him along by its magnetic gravity.

Leadership guru Max De Pree quipped, "Once you teach a bear to dance, you have to dance as long as the bear wants to!" Once you give yourself to a gigantic cause that's bigger than you are, it has a way of capturing you, invigorating you, and you can't quit. That's the explanation Paul gives in 2 Corinthians 4, "I have this ministry, so I don't lose heart! That's how I keep on witnessing, I keep on traveling, I keep on preaching in spite of persecution and calamities. What I'm called to do is so compelling I can't quit."

"Trivial Pursuit" is not just the name of a popular table game, it also describes the empty existence a lot of Americans endure today. Their lives are trivial. They get up every morning and go through the same dull routine, never engaged in anything crucial or worthy of their best. But that's not you or me. Having given our hearts to the Lord, we've been transformed by His power and given responsibilities that stretch our capacities. Our work is not trivial. To share the good news of Jesus Christ, to reach out to people in His name, to build up His church so His word can be proclaimed, so men, women, youth and children can learn about Jesus and be transformed to serve him too—this is not a game. It is eternally important and therefore it calls out the best from us, giving us supernatural energy so that in spite of the hard times, we keep on witnessing and giving and worshiping and serving. We can't quit. This is too crucial. "Therefore having this ministry we do not lose heart!"

They say that when Handel wrote his incomparable oratorio *The Messiah*, he completed the entire composition in twenty-two days. He hardly ate and slept. The task was so engaging, so compelling that it gave him energy and endurance. He couldn't quit until he finished it.

It's that engaging motivation that encouraged Paul to write, "Be steadfast unmovable, always abounding in the work of the Lord in as much as you know your work is not in vain in the Lord."

In the dark depressions of those days in 1994, Betty and I both found hope and joy in rediscovering that we were not just employees of an institution. We were not ultimately working for a board of trustees. We were and are fulfilling a calling from the Lord Jesus in a ministry of eternal significance, and that work is not in vain. We tried to follow His command to "forget those things that are behind and press on toward those things that are before, looking unto Jesus the Author and Finisher of our faith." The one who issued that command has promised to be with us to the end of the age, so, God being our helper, we can do no other.

II. Power to See It Through Comes from Genuine Compassion for Others

One cannot fully understand the persistence of the apostle Paul without recognizing his intense compassion for other people. He had a broken-hearted concern for the lostness of the multitudes who inhabited his Mediterranean world. From the time he heard and responded to the call from Macedonia, "Come over and help us," Paul was driven by a compassionate regard for others.

In this fourth chapter of 2 Corinthians, he speaks of the unevangelized as "perishing," they are "blinded by Satan." Remember his impressive testimony in Romans 9 and 10? "My heart's desire and prayer to God for them (Israel) is that they may be saved." "For I could wish myself accursed and cut off from Christ for the sake of my brethren, my kinsmen by race." He cared about people, and that compassion kept him going, gave him the power to endure. He couldn't quit. He couldn't turn back. He kept on traveling and preaching and witnessing in spite jails and beatings and stonings and shipwreck, driven by their cry for help.

Following a serious automobile accident on a Dallas freeway recently, one car ended up on its side, burning with the driver partially trapped underneath. Another motorist pulled over, got out and rushed to the overturned car. With uncanny strength for a man of only modest stature, he lifted one side of the heavy car enough that the woman inside could free herself and escape. Later, when he was interviewed by television reporters at the scene, they asked, "How did you have the muscle to lift that big car?" He answered, "I don't know! I don't think I could do it again, but when I saw the fire spreading and heard that woman screaming for help, I just reached down and did it! Adrenalin, I guess!"

So when you truly care about others, you can't quit or turn back. There's something about a frantic cry for help that generates unexplainable spiritual "adrenalin" to see you through.

When the Southwestern faculty came to our house after I was dismissed by the hardliners on the seminary board, they sympathetically offered to strike, to demonstrate, to quit and shut down the school. It was a tempting offer, but together we agreed the students were the important ones. They were the true victims. Having been called by God, and convinced it was important to prepare, they had made great sacrifices to come to Southwestern. Now their training had been rudely interrupted. That's when it happened. When we turned our attention away from our own personal hurt to the greater needs of the students, Betty and I—and the faculty—experienced a new attitude, a new resolve, and a new reserve of strength. Like the unlikely rescuer on the freeway, hearing the cry of help gave us the power to see it through.

What we preach is not ourselves, but Jesus Christ as Lord, with ourselves as your servants for Jesus' sake (2 Cor 4:5).

III. Power to See It Through Comes from Faith in God's Transcendant Power Within Us

While the other two insights are helpful, Paul's ultimate secret source of power is supernatural. We are able to overcome adversity and discouragement because the Holy Spirit who inhabits the lives of believers offers us God's omnipotent power. Listen again to Paul's amazing declaration of that secret:

> But we have this treasure in earthen vessels, to show that the transcendent power belongs to God and not to us. We are afflicted in every way, but not crushed; perplexed, but not driven to despair; persecuted, but not forsaken; struck down, but not destroyed . . . . So we do not lose heart. Though our outer nature is wasting away, our inner nature is being renewed every day . . . . Because we look not to the things that are seen but to the things that are unseen; for the things that are seen are transient, but the things that are unseen are eternal.

The absolute power to see it through "belongs to God and not to us." When we have a personal relationship with the omnipotent God through faith in His Son, we have access to His unlimited power. Through our faith in Him we become "more than conquerors" and "all things are possible." Paul is amazed and humbled that this "transcendent power" abides in ordinary people, "earthen vessels," like us. (Literally, "terra cotta jars.") Without that power, we are weak, empty, and vulnerable to debilitating discouragement and headed to inevitable defeat.

If you're the kind of person who has to have accommodating circumstances to keep going, then when the circumstances turn sour, so will you, and you'll quit. If you have to hear applause to keep going, then on those many days when nobody notices, you're going to be discouraged, and you won't stay with it. If you have to see positive statistics, measurable evidence of progress in your work to keep going, then when the statistics are zero as they often are, you'll be disheartened and you'll turn back.

But if you know the Lord Jesus personally like Paul did, and if God's invisible presence lives within you, and if your relationship is so close that you hear him say, "Don't be dismayed; don't be discouraged; I'll be with you; I'll never forsake you," then that makes everything okay. It doesn't matter what the circumstances are. It doesn't matter whether anybody notices or not. It doesn't matter what the statistics say. Your sufficiency is not found in things that are seen, but in things that are unseen. His invisible presence provides all the staying power you need.

You see, your personal relationship with God gives you enormous advantages other people don't have. For one thing, you don't waste your energy worrying about the universe, crippled by grave cosmic apprehensions. That's off your hands. You trust the one who created it and who's got the whole world in His hands. You don't worry about eternity or the end of the world. Complicated eschatological charts listing the seven seals or dispensational predictions about being left behind may be helpful to some, but your faith is in the One who promised to "keep what I've committed to Him against that day."

But most of all when you know God through Jesus Christ, you have the advantage of unlimited, supernatural, reserves of sufficient strength. David, the same poet who said so often, "My soul is cast down," also said over a hundred times in his poems, "The Lord is my strength." He said it so often, he practically exhausts the Hebrew thesaurus, using eleven different synonyms for strength. Over and over again, in every possible verbal form, he repeats it, "The Lord is my strength." That's the lesson we need to remember. We're not alone. We don't have to depend on accommodating circumstances, or applause, or statistics, or human grit, or determination, or cleverness. We have an invisible source of power to see us through. That means, like Paul, we can be:

Afflicted in every way, but not crushed; perplexed, but not driven to despair; persecuted, but not forsaken; struck down, but not destroyed . . . . So we do not lose heart. Though our outer nature is wasting away, our inner nature is being renewed every day . . . because we look not to the things that are seen but to the things that are unseen; for the things that are seen are transient, but the things that are unseen are eternal.

I saw a dramatic illustration of that invisible power in New Mexico a few years ago. While at Glorieta, our Baptist assembly near Santa Fe, we drove into Albuquerque one afternoon to do what a lot of tourists do. We rode the famous tramway to the top of Sandia Peak just north of the city. It's the longest tramway in America. One of the passengers who boarded the tram with us at the base of the mountain was a young man with a huge canvas bag. We had to help him drag it on board, and when we arrived at the top of Sandia Peak, we again had to help him get it off.

He tugged that canvas bag over to the edge of the mountain where a sharp precipice dropped off straight down to the valley floor, and as we watched him, he unzipped that bag and pulled out pieces aluminum tubing and nylon cloth. It was a hang glider, and when he finished putting it together, he walked over to the edge of the mountain and tied a ribbon to a bush to check the wind direction. Then, putting on a helmet, he slowly walked around his glider twice carefully checking every connection and every guy wire. (If that had been me, I'd still up there walking around checking the connections!) When he was satisfied everything was okay, he strapped that thing on, and while we literally caught our breath, he ran and jumped off the mountain.

He fell a few feet as the air caught the sails of his hang glider, and then he began to glide so gracefully, effortlessly, silently across the Sandia valley until he encountered what aeronautical experts call a "thermal." It's an invisible column of warm air that circulates upward and provides lift. He circled over the warm air like the birds do, and it began to lift him higher and higher until he was at our eye level again, and then above us several hundred feet. He circled at ten thousand feet effortlessly, gracefully, silently suspended by that invisible thermal lift.

We were distracted by an echo from the airport on the other side of Albuquerque. It was the sound of a big commercial jetliner taking off. Burning hundreds of pounds of jet fuel, it lumbered down the runway, shuddering as it slowly lifted its load off the concrete and climbed over the mountains.

While all the time, there was our hang glider friend at ten thousand feet flying effortlessly, silently, gracefully suspended by that invisible column of air. And this passage came to mind. You don't have to depend on your own ability, drive, determination, and grit. You don't have to burn all that energy. You have an invisible lift, an unseen source of power enabling you. That unseen presence gives you the supernatural ability to overcome and see it through.

Because we look not to the things that are seen but to the things that are unseen; for the things that are seen are transient, but the things that are unseen are eternal.

Sometimes in the heat of controversy or the depths of despair you begin to suspect that your troubles are worse than the troubles other people are facing. Then you come across a heart-rending story or you hear about someone else's unimaginable tragedy, and your own plight seems almost petty. What Betty and I went through during the worst of the seminary saga was painful. It also hurt our family, the extended Southwestern family, and to some degree the entire Body of Christ. The extent of that damage should not be diminished, but listening to stories of how others have overcome enormous suffering puts our own in proper perspective and teaches us how to endure in spite of pain.

Jane Merchant's story is an example. She was a writer whose inspiring poetry was often printed in the *Saturday Evening Post* and *Good Housekeeping* a generation ago. Jane Merchant's hardships would make most of ours seem trivial by comparison. She endured a combination of physical distresses any one of which would have defeated most people. In a wheelchair as a little child, and then bedfast after the age of twelve, she eventually lost her eyesight and her hearing. But she had an indomitable faith in the Lord and experienced that invisible power Paul wrote about in II Corinthians. Here is how she expressed it:

For half a hundred times I've sobbed, I can't go on; I can't go on, And ye,t full half a hundred times I've hushed my sobs and gone. The reason, if you ask me how, may seem presumptuously odd, But I know that what kept keeping on when I could not, was God.

Appendix

101 Suggestions for the Future of Southwestern Seminary

Received primarily during early 1978, listed here in no particular order, and all addressed or accomplished by 1994!

1. Build a new library building with first rate facilities.
2. Enhance the quality of the library collection.
3. Revise the curriculum based on survey of constituents.
4. Build, stock, and manage a first rate book store.
5. Improve the cafeteria, too bare, dull, have varied menus.
6. Improve faculty offices, soundproof, better furniture etc.
7. Provide full time secretaries for teams of faculty.
8. Return "hooding" to graduating ceremonies.
9. Increase class schedules for evenings and Mondays.
10. Explore non-language option for certain MDIV degrees.
11. Rotate faculty department chairs, have conveners not rulers.

12. Reorganize scholarship and student aid division.
13. Provide full time counselor for students and staff.
14. Expand and improve field work.
15. Provide more academic advisement for students.
16. Provide college assistance for faculty children.
17. Encourage faculty spouses to take Seminary courses.
18. Provide more privileges for emeritus faculty.
19. Make computers available to faculty.
20. Find way to honor senior faculty i.e. Distinguished rank.
21. Establish a School of Missions or Mission center.
22. Provide better teaching equipment, TV, A.V., chalkboards.
23. Print graduate dossiers for students.
24. Increase faculty and staff salary and benefits.
25. Increase student fees, students should pay more for education.
26. Increase endowment and fund raising.
27. Offer more management courses for all students.
28. Develop intern and apprenticeship programs for students.
29. Streamline registration procedures.
30. Recruit best academic students from universities.
31. Build a "theater" classroom.
32. Provide study carrels for all doctoral students.
33. Affirm the accomplishments of faculty.
34. Have administration takeover some faculty committee responsibilities.
35. Free faculty from "leg work," "busy work."
36. Re-organize student evaluation of teaching.
37. Abolish, abandon, discontinue, terminate, end M.B.O!
38. Don't be so "stingy" on expense accounts.
39. Upgrade preaching lab facilities and TV taping equipment.
40. Sound proof and otherwise refurbish class rooms.
41. Separate faculty and staff pictures in the handbook.
42. Clarify and improve articulation with universities.
43. Develop a policy for hanging portraits of faculty.
44. Provide more continuing education conferences.
45. Improve faculty development program.
46. Reorganize and improve Journal of Theology.
47. President should teach a class occasionally.
48. Coordinate spring break with public schools.
49. Improve Post Office hours and service.
50. Install a HAM radio station.
51. Provide museums on campus: archeology, missions, heritage.

52. Help students deal with search committees, interviews.
53. Change personality test (MMPI) used at registration.
54. Provide 24-hour security on campus.
55. Improve maintenance of grounds and buildings.
56. Start a placement service for students and graduates.
57. Maintain a telephone switchboard at night and on weekends.
58. Reorganize the student council.
59. Reorganize student organizations.
60. Change the student work scholarship plan to cash basis.
61. Emphasize bi-vocational training.
62. Bring three schools closer together.
63. Decide if there should be a school policy for curving grades.
64. Put life, worthwhileness into faculty meetings, new location.
65. Encourage more concern for students throughout seminary.
66. Avoid mediocrity and inbreeding in faculty accession.
67. Change MRE terminology to MA.
68. Administration and staff should have annual appraisals too.
69. Write Seminary history on the 75th anniversary.
70. Create archeological program and an on site dig.
71. Build additional student housing.
72. Study feasibility of faculty housing.
73. Renovate Fort Worth Hall for male students.
74. Renovate Barnard Hall for female students.
75. Upgrade guest rooms on campus.
76. Enlarge children's center playground.
77. Install traffic light at Seminary Drive entrance.
78. Provide more parking.
79. Open trustee meetings so faculty, et.al. might attend.
80. Study and improve chapel program.
81. Provide majors and minors between the three schools.
82. Develop a "fast track" salary plan to aid younger faculty.
83. Reorganize the student affairs division.
84. Improve student orientation.
85. Build a physical plant building.
86. Change seminary hymn.
87. Make Mexican Bible Institute a part of Southwestern.
88. Develop a faculty manual.
89. Don't require faculty to sit on stage for chapel.
90. Upgrade the diploma program.
91. Add gerontology emphasis.

92. Improve and expand Pioneer Penetration and other practica.

93. Name "something" on campus for B. H. Carroll!

94. Provide space in Houston for our off-campus center.

95. Initiate a sabbatic leave program for administration.

96. Use video tape resumes and sermons for search committees.

97. Add programs for counselling, gerontology, social work, drama.

98. Provide programs for furloughing missionaries and candidates.

99. Upgrade the faculty retreat.

100. Improve method of finding and recruiting new faculty.

101. Begin classes for lay leaders.

Seminary Annual Reports 1978–1995

	1978	1979	1980	1981	1982
Assets	31,700,714	41,323,476	47,400,000	52,542,019	63,223,662
Budget	6,396,434	7,255,991	8,440,148	11,190,097	11,867,360
Endowment	12,500,544	16,638,958	19,375,421	21,645,682	27,346,073
Enrollment	4,136	4,154	4,336	4,412	4,605
Graduates	799	772	866	880	872

	1983	1984	1985	1986	1987
Assets	68,124,750	75,031,270	80,603,032	88,906,631	94,802,889
Budget	14,026,081	15,265,994	16,275,862	16,977,499	18,328,857
Endowment	28,772,890	33,339,893	36,675,632	41,318,113	43,654,281
Enrollment	4,865	5,120	5,086	5,070	5,096
Graduates	881	954	986	854	1,038

	1988	1989	1990	1991	1992
Assets	99,832,604	98,593,752	104,042,760	108,095,169	116,025,569
Budget	18,788,820	18,822,819	19,060,000	19,058,262	21,850,576
Endowment	46,139,449	47,874,767	48,250,555	52,283,346	56,396,232
Enrollment	4,784	4,569	4,477	4,034	4,014
Graduates	989	899	890	852	841

	1993	1994	1995
Assets	120,493,493	124,845,942	130,759,243
Budget	22,717,578	23,401,843	22,904,304
Endowment	59,340,558	61,374,634	62,838,429
Enrollment	4,022	4,157	3,751
Graduates	770	673	789

The Glorieta Statement

We, the presidents of the six SBC seminaries, through prayerful and careful reflection and dialogue, have unanimously agreed to declare these commitments regarding our lives and our work with Southern Baptists.

We believe that Christianity is supernatural in its origin and history. We repudiate every theory of religion which denies the supernatural elements in our faith. The miracles of the Old and New Testaments are historical evidences of God's judgment, love, and redemption.

We believe that the Bible is fully inspired; it is "God breathed" (2 Tim 3:16), utterly unique. No other book or collection of books can justify that claim. The sixty-six books of the Bible are not errant in any area of reality. We hold to their infallible power and binding authority.

We believe that our six seminaries are fulfilling the purposes assigned to them by the Southern Baptist Convention. Nevertheless, we acknowledge that they are not perfect institutions. We recognize that there are legitimate concerns regarding them which we are addressing.

We commit ourselves therefore to the resolution of problems which beset our beloved denomination. We are ready and eager to be partners in the peace process. Specifically:

(1) We reaffirm our seminary confessional statements, and we will enforce compliance by the persons signing them.
(2) We will foster in our classrooms a balanced, scholarly frame of reference for presenting fairly the entire spectrum of scriptural interpretations represented by our constituency. We perceive this to be both good education and good cooperation.
(3) We respect the convictions of all Southern Baptists and we repudiate the caricature and intimidation of persons for their theological beliefs.
(4) We commit ourselves to fairness in selecting faculty, lecturers, and chapel speakers across the theological spectrum of our Baptist constituency.
(5) We will lead our seminary communities in spiritual revival, personal discipleship, Christian life style, and active churchmanship.
(6) We will deepen and strengthen the spirit of evangelism and missions on our campuses while emphasizing afresh the distinctive doctrines of our Baptist heritage.
(7) We have scheduled for Southern Baptists three national conferences:
>A Conference on Biblical Inerrancy—1987
>A Conference on Biblical Interpretation—1988
>A Conference on Biblical Imperatives—1989

The first conference, focusing on biblical inerrancy, is scheduled for Ridgecrest Baptist Assembly, May 2-4, 1987.

We share these commitments with the hope that all Southern Baptists will join us in seeking "the wisdom from above" in our efforts toward reconciliation: "The wisdom from above is first pure, then peaceable, gentle, open to reason, full of mercy and good fruits, without uncertainty or insincerity" (James 3:17).

Southwestern's Official Response to SBC Peace Committee, July 3, 1987

Introduction

The committee which has worked for about two years was basically made up of 7 fundamentalist/conservatives, 7 moderate/conservatives, and 7 non-aligned persons. Appointing active participants in the denominational debate on the committee was a mistake, I believe, because it meant from the beginning there would be confrontational, intransigent discussions. Members said the meetings were constantly like a battlefield, with the discussions going over the same issues time after time with little progress.

The fundamentalists on the committee are younger men with less experience in SBC life; the moderates are older, with long records of convention participation. The fundamentalists are very strong personalities, dominating and in some cases manipulating the debate, while the moderates are for the most part "moderate" in leadership style as well, and therefore more conciliatory. All the major votes on the committee were won by the fundamentalists.

Moderates were only able to soften the report in places and effect some compromises so that the report was not as extreme as it might otherwise have been. A reader can almost tell which paragraphs were submitted by fundamentalists and which by moderates, one could almost "cut and paste" a version of the report which would group paragraphs which obviously came from each perspective. Therefore it is not so much a consensus document as an awkward compilation of both perspectives, with the fundamentalist position prevailing.

Concerns:

1. I disagree that the primary source of the controversy is a difference over theology (i.e. basic theological precepts.) The authority of the Bible has been the focus of our discussions, but our denomination is practically unanimous in our belief in the total trustworthiness of scripture. Given the qualifications and denials of

the Chicago Statement on Inerrancy, few among us would differ on a high view of biblical authority.

Our differences seem to be centered in (1) the nature and extent of denominational relationships (i.e. cooperative vs. independent), (2) interpretation of certain biblical passages, and (3) establishment/bureaucracy concerns (i.e. the "ins" vs. the "outs")

2. I disagree with the diversity statement of the report. The impression given by the examples is that about half of our faculties hold one view while another half holds the other. In most cases a very small minority, sometimes no more than 6-8 persons among the 500 SBC seminary teachers hold the extreme positions listed. (Bill Poe said the committee never surfaced more than 24 names of "problem teachers," including a large number who were later disregarded by the committee as no problems)

The diversity among us has been greatly exaggerated giving the misleading impression that our seminaries are split down the middle between "liberals" and "conservatives." There is diversity, but it is expressed within the overall framework of conservative theology.

3. The report does not come down hard enough on the shameful political manipulation of these past 8-9 years. It tends to legitimate the secular politics and leaves too much latitude for such activities to continue in the future. There is nothing in the report to greatly discourage, much less prevent, some group with narrow agendas to take over the control of the convention's processes.

No proper distinction was made between the political party which has admitted its desire to control the convention and the party which organized only to say to the other group, "please stop what you're doing," but had no desire to control. The report implies that the political organizations set up to stop the takeover are equally to blame for "intensifying" the controversy.

4. The report comes dangerously close to codifying or canonizing a list of scriptural and textual interpretations as addenda to the Baptist Faith and Message. While these examples represent the interpretations generally held by most of us as simple Biblicists, the danger is that we have never lifted certain interpretations to the level of criteria of orthodoxy. What will the next list include? Eschatology? Ordination of women? National political issues?

5. The report tends to legitimize the takeover successes of the militant party in the convention, indicating that the convention will have to accept the "changes" which have been put in place by the party now in control.

6. The warning about labels does not take into consideration the fact that the term "conservative" must not be claimed by only one group in the convention. The militants would like to be known as conservatives leading a "conservative resurgence," while designating their opponents as "liberals" or "moderates." Most of us want to be known as conservatives, not moderates, but we are not sympathetic with the takeover effort nor do we accept the idea that the convention has been drifting into liberalism.

7. It is a dangerous precedent to avoid discussing divisive or controversial subjects in order to maintain peace. It might be appropriate to refrain from such discussions for a short time while reconciliation is facilitated, but this practice should not become enshrined as a long range policy.

8. The continuation of the peace committee as an "oversight committee" is unwise. Those of us who endorsed the idea of a peace committee and voted for it in 1985 did so with the stipulation that its existence could only be extended one additional year, no later than 1987. However, if an oversight committee is needed, it is better to let the peace committee perform that responsibility than to give such a task to the SBC Executive Committee or to try to name a balanced committee that would be acceptable in these divisive days of convention life.

Considering Our Legacy

Speech given by Mrs. Russell H. Dilday, president's wife, to Seminary Woman's Club—September 1988

In preparing this presentation I have become aware again of the providential pattern of God's leadership in my early life which intertwined my pilgrimage with Southwestern Seminary.

I was born during the depression in St. Joseph Hospital in Houston, Texas, the second of two children of parents whose own parents had migrated to Texas from Waltham, Massachusetts, and Ruston, Louisiana. My parents were Baptists, having met in the BYPU of the First Baptist Church of Houston. When they took me to the nursery of that church at three weeks of age, I never knew that my heritage would include Southwestern Seminary.

It was in this church in 1940 that I accepted Christ as my Savior and was baptized by the pastor, E. D. Head, who would three years later become the third president of Southwestern Seminary. My uncle who had audited the books of the church during Dr. Head's pastorate made annual trips to Southwestern for several years to audit the books of the seminary. My mother and aunt loved Dr. and Mrs. Head and kept their friendship until their deaths in Comfort, Texas.

During these recent years my aunt, who is 87 years old and who has visited us in the beautiful present president's home on many occasions, has told me of an experience when Dr. and Mrs. Head moved into the president's two story brown brick home across from the Memorial building. Upon seeing that the carpet in the home was threadbare and worn, she proceeded to go carpet shopping. But when she attempted to buy such an item she was told by the business office of the seminary that there was no money for such an expenditure.

After coming to the seminary in 1978 as president, Russell was reading some old Southwestern News printed during Dr. Head's administration. As we looked at the pictures and read the account of Dr. Head's early days, we learned that First Baptist had furnished his office at the seminary. We recognized two of the small leather chairs from a back storage area. The leather was worn and faded. Now they are recovered and are in the study of the president's home, furnishing a tangible reminder of my heritage with First Baptist, Houston, and Southwestern.

Dr. Head wrote in his will that should he precede his son in death, the son's funeral would be led by the president of Southwestern Seminary. When Douglas, Jr., mentally and physically handicapped for 58 years, died on April 13, 1983, in a nursing home in San Angelo, his body was brought to Fort Worth where he was buried in Laurel Land Cemetery. Russell H. Dilday, the president of Southwestern, led the graveside services. Amazing, that in the course of events, my husband was able to carry out the request of Dr. Head, my pastor, who had baptized me and personified in my early years the spirit of gentleness and love.

My heritage with Southwestern extended on through my high school years. I went to Palacios, Texas every summer on the Gulf coast for the annual church-wide encampment of First Baptist. When I was in high school, the pulpit committee of First Baptist, Houston, heard a young Southwestern Seminary professor preach at the evening service at Palacios. His name was Boyd Hunt. He was 30 years old and pastoring the Baptist church at Charlie, Texas. He was the special choice to become pastor of the First Baptist Church in Houston. In 1952 Boyd Hunt, as my pastor, married Russell and me; and in 1953 he returned to Southwestern Seminary as a professor.

When Russell and I came to the seminary in the fall of 1952, we sensed, as you did and as the students do today, an anticipation of an exciting future within God's will. Psalm 16:9 says, "My heart is glad and my glory rejoiceth; my flesh also shall rest in hope." We were motivated by enthusiasm and the hope of a happy life in ministry. During those days of study, teaching and pastoring the Antelope Baptist Church (80 miles northwest of Fort Worth), we read and believed John 14:12, "Verily, I say unto you, He that believeth on me, the works that I do shall he do also and greater works than these shall he do, because I go to my Father."

The Search Committee to find a president for Southwestern first contacted Russell in late 1976 and the winter of 1977. By summer and early fall of 1977, after talking and visiting with Russell, they were anxious for both of us to come to Texas to meet with the committee. I was reluctant to come for my fall school term had begun and I did not want to miss a day. In 1975 I had returned to public school teaching after 23 years so that I might help with the expenses of three children in Baylor University. When Russell assured me that, after the meeting with the committee, we would go on to Waco to see the three children, I quickly accepted.

On October 5, 1977, Russell met with the trustees and faculty which made up the Search Committee to nominate the seminary president. They met at D/FW airport and told him he was the one they would present as the sixth president of Southwestern to the entire board of trustees at their annual meeting on campus the next week.

It had been 17 years since I had been on the campus of Southwestern. Russell had been here for pastors' conferences, as a national alumni representative, for faculty retreat and revival. So there was much for me to learn about the campus and many people to meet.

When we moved to Fort Worth in January of 1978, we lived for six months in a patio house in Ridglea. We moved into the president's home in June of that year. January to August of 1978 was a period during which Russell met with every faculty member in that person's office, hearing their ideas and dreams. At Russell's inauguration in October of 1978, as Baker James Cauthen preached, our feelings were that we had become a part of a larger picture—a global ministry.

Joshua 1:9 became a part of the inaugural anthem, "Be strong and courageous. Do not tremble or be dismayed for the Lord thy God is with you." More than ever before I felt a part of a "cloud of witnesses." There were these times during which Southwestern had intersected with my life; now, both my life and Southwestern were brought together as one.

Heritage is predetermined for someone. She has nothing to do with it. She is unable to do anything about it. It is the status resulting from being born in a certain time, place and culture. It is something handed down by circumstances.

A legacy is something handed down by intention—a bequest. It can be property or money; but whatever it is, it is given by an intentional act.

Last month the program presenters did a excellent job in "recalling our heritage" of Southwestern in the vignettes of seminary faculty wives who distinguished themselves and pleased God by their ministry. Tonight we "consider our legacy"—what we want to pass on to the following generation in an intentional manner. Perhaps we have some fears of the future as all generations do. Perhaps we haven't even thought about our influence in the years ahead. We do know that we have warm feelings for our Southwestern heritage, and we have the desire for Southwestern to always be a strong institution for God.

Everyone doesn't view the seminary as we do. I was over in Dillards several months ago during the remodeling of Seminary South Shopping Center. As my ticket was being written up, the salesperson commented on the problems of remodeling and we began to discuss the name change to Town Center. I commented that I felt the new name was a little ambiguous, not really giving a location. The salesperson responded that she liked the name Town Center. Looking up at me, she said, "Seminary South! Ugh! Do you know what seminary means?" I assured her I did and let the discussion end there.

Many view a seminary as otherworldly, monastic, unappealing. In March 1988 Southwestern Seminary will be an octogenarian institution—80 years old! If the Lord tarries and the years continue to pass, Southwestern may become twice that in age. So what do we want to consider as our legacy—something that we intentionally pass on to generations following?

Well, let me name a few that I think would be worthy of all of us:

First, Southwestern was given 200 acres of land by citizens of the city of Fort Worth in 1910. Many of these acres had to be sold during the '20s and '30s for survival; but in the '60s, '70s and '80s, most have been repurchased. To see the continued caring for this legacy of property in the beautification of the campus with the irrigation system and the tree and shrub plantings has been a source of pride for all Southwesterners.

The buildings on campus bearing the names of past presidents and outstanding Christian donors are legacies which by their maintenance and refurbishing we continue to hand down to others who will follow us. There certainly is a legacy in properties being maintained and passed on.

Secondly, we want to pass on a legacy of a close connection between Southwestern and the local church. Faithfulness as church members has been foremost in the lifestyle of you as seminary wives and in those who preceded you. You wives are the ones who have taken, and are taking, your children to church; seen that they have participated in church activities (most of the time when professor husbands were preaching or ministering elsewhere); taught Sunday School; sang in choir; played the piano; and led out in mission education. This is a legacy which we must always continue—a close connection between Southwestern and our local churches.

Thirdly, I would like for us to always have a spirit of anticipation and excitement for the future. A legacy of hope in the days ahead is a worthy and intentional attitude for us before today's students. We do not want to be absorbed in the "good old days of yesteryear." As my friend, Carolyn Rhea phrases it: "Hope is a vase in which I arrange the flowers of health, happiness, prosperity, contentment. In reality the flowers are not always blooming; but, nevertheless, the vase is there in anticipation of some lovely arrangement."

Fourthly, I would like to see us retain and enlarge the legacy of a global perspective—a worldwide vision of need and ministry. As seminary wives I would like for us to see ourselves as part of a larger picture than just Fort Worth or even Texas. The generous sabbatical leave, the many missionaries, both former and now serving, that are on campus each year; the large number of international students—these opportunities and people help us continue to see ourselves in a large participation of faith with a global perspective.

Fifth, I would like for our legacy to continue to be one of a "Personal Touch" to students and faculty—a touch that has always distinguished the world's largest seminary. "People Count" has been a motto on Russell's desk for ten years. I hope all of us will continue the inviting of special student groups into our home. I hope projects of Seminary Woman's Club such as the buying of campus benches and car seats for added convenience to students will be a priority for us. I am happy to see the entertaining of faculty in our home, especially the crossing over into the three schools for fellowship. I like the February progressive dinner function. I hope occasions such as this which strengthen understanding of each other will be a legacy.

As I read the vignettes of the seminary wives who preceded us, I was impressed not only by their personal touch to students, but I was also impressed by their own desire to be educated and trained. In recent years a stipulation which allows faculty wives to attend seminary classes, matriculation free, has resulted in many of us enlarging our education. Many have taken advantage of other education facilities in the area and have completed undergraduate degrees after their husbands were on the seminary faculty. I hope that the sixth legacy of seminary wives might be to pass on the desire to always be learning—studying to show ourselves "approved unto God, a workman that needeth not to be ashamed, rightly dividing the word of truth."

In noticing again the lives of our predecessors, I see that they were good and helpful wives toward their husbands. They were described as "devoted to one another." I would encourage you to pray for your husbands. They have a tremendous job—possibly, teaching now in the seminary classroom is a greater challenge than ever before in the history of theological education. Be supportive of your husbands; loyal encouragers; partners. This is a legacy worth continuing.

In 1979 when the EEOC lawsuit was pending against Southwestern, a federal judge wrote some pertinent statements about the purpose of Southwestern. They are:

1. The seminary views a pervasively religious environment as essential to the cultivation of distinct attitudes of Baptist ministers.

2. This view affects all employment practices.

3. Employees are hired for a task but also are willing members of the faith.

4. All employees are expected to contribute to a unified religious endeavor and maintain a commitment to spiritual life.

5. Dedication to Baptist ideals and faithful participation in the activities of the church carry equal or greater weight than academic qualifications or scholarship.

6. The preserving of any faith lies in the institution that schools its ministers in transmitting doctrine in a pure form in the academic sense and endeavors to translate sterile doctrine into communicable faith.

This is the purpose of Southwestern Seminary as viewed from the creative view of a secular judge. I pray that our seventh legacy as seminary wives will be such that as we strive to be Christ-like in spirit, we will display kindness, humility, gentleness, and patience to students, faculty and administration and thus we will enhance a pervasively religious environment that will cultivate Baptist ministers and their wives and that we will translate any "sterile doctrine into communicable faith."

Matthew 5:15, 16 says it best, "Ye are the light of the world . . . . Let your light so shine before men that they may see your good works and glorify your father which is in heaven."

Transcript of Press Conference with Ralph Pulley and Lee Weaver After Firing of Russell Dilday

March 10, 1994
Seminary, Justin Conference Room

Ralph Pulley: Trustees of SWBTS relieved Russell H. Dilday of his duties and from the office of the President of the seminary effective immediately. The board adopted a severance agreement that provides a severance allowance: salary, benefits, and medical insurance. The President Search Committee will begin the process of nominating a new president for election by the board of Trustees. Members of the committee are Miles Seaborn, chairman, Paul Balducci, Robert Burch, Pat Campbell, Olin Collins, Lynn Cooper, T. Bob Davis, Edward Litton, and Damon Shook.

Dr. John Earl Seelig has been asked by the board of trustees to serve in an interim capacity in public relations and he will assume that assignment immediately.

The severance plan adopted for Dr. Dilday is, in our opinion, very gracious; and I have the meat of that plan here to distribute to you. Number one, if I can read it, Dr. Dilday will continue his base salary until 65 including the Annuity Board. Number two, he will continue medical insurance coverage for Dr. and Mrs. Dilday to age 65, consistent with plans concurrently provided to other seminary staff. Three, it provides for immediate access to the housing allowance adopted by the board of trustees March 11, 1986. Four, it provides allowance for up to $3000.00 per month until the age 65 for actual cost of off campus office and secretarial assistance. That basically gives you the plan and the adjustments that have been made since the actual statement by the board.

Question: Mr. Pulley, that is a very generous plan, obviously, but what do you say to the students' questions to why was Dr. Dilday dismissed?

Pulley: The board took action decisively. As far as the basic thinking of the board, we really don't want to comment on the reasons involved.

Question: Was he not doing a good job?

Pulley: We felt like that the institution needed new direction to move us into the 21st century. We have no criticism that we desire to make of Dr. Dilday.

Question: What is your reaction to the reaction you got in making that announcement? Obviously, the students aren't very happy about that.

Pulley: Well, of course, the students are the lifeblood the seminary. We don't like for the student body to be unhappy at all. I think it is a natural reaction for them, and we certainly are sensitive to their needs and requirements because they are the heartbeat of the institution. The stability of the institution will be maintained. There will be no problem with that. We hope they will go right ahead with their preparation.

Question: To what degree did Dr. Dilday perhaps showed disdain for the conservative movement and why do you feel that the institution needs to move in a conservative direction?

Pulley: That was not really a factor of it—not really.

Question: Not really?

Pulley: No.

Question: Wasn't it a little bit?

Pulley: In my opinion, it was not a factor.

Question: Not at all?

Pulley: Not as far as the board was concerned.

Question: Ralph, I understand that the executive committee of the board had a review with him last night and none of these things; no question was raised about his leadership. Why did this not come up then?

Pulley: That was an ordinary and regular review that the board makes each spring. The executive committee has the responsibility.

Question: I understand he got very, very positive marks, is that correct?

Pulley: We had a very thorough discussion with him in that. I really would rather not comment on it.

Question: Ralph, these rumors about this action have been rampant in the SBC especially in the last few days. Had you planned to do this before you came this week?

Pulley: We can't control what people, of course—what the rumors are or anything like that.

Question: All right, but you planned to do this though prior to this meeting—ask for his dismissal?

Pulley: There were certainly some discussions of the trustees.

Question: Prior to this board meeting?

Pulley: I don't know about prior to this week but their certain were some during the week.

Question: What direction does the institution need to move in? You said you need to move in a new direction. Please help us to understand what direction you want to move in the future.

Pulley: I think—uh—that, that will be established as the—as the—time will move ahead with our current officers.

Question: Just tell us, philosophically, what direction would you like to see?

Pulley: I really don't have any; don't want to philosophize about—uh—the—uh—direction personally.

Question: What about the students' complaints that this action was done in secret. That you've done everything you can to keep the students and faculty, who you say are the heartbeat of the institution, out of the process?

Pulley: Actions like this, of course, are never palatable. They are very difficult. Certainly, the board felt that difficulty.

Question: What was the vote?

Pulley: I'd rather not comment.

Question: Was it unanimous?

Pulley: I just don't have a comment about it.

Question: Don't you feel you owe the students some explanation and the Baptist community at large to understand to some degree, if not specifically why Dr. Dilday was dismissed? What are some reasons why new direction is needed? I can't understand why you won't give us some sense of the thinking behind this.

Pulley: We have the letters, of course—I read one that will go to the students. We have letters going out to the Advisory Council and others in due course.

Question: That's not answering the question.Do you have any idea yourself what this new direction is?

Pulley: No.

Question: Shall we report then that you had no direction in mind?

Pulley: I have no comment about that personally.

Question: Some of the students raised questions about being a good Christian and about honesty and they're challenging your honesty and integrity. How do you respond to this?

Pulley: I have no comment on that—on what some students may say.

Question: Was this a power struggle?

Pulley: (shakes head no)

Question: Mr. Pulley, when you were a trustee here before I covered these meetings, there was this tension between Dr. Dilday and some of the people who were going in a more conservation direction in the denomination, and I know back before when you were here, there was a lot of talk that you were hoping that Dr. Dilday would stop speaking out on these subjects about the denominational struggle. But he was not silenced and some people have gone so far as to say once you were back on the board you were just like a political vendetta, to get rid of Dr. Dilday. What do say to those charges?

Pulley: That's not correct.

Question: Have you felt that he's not quite as supportive of—you know, there's another group called the Fellowship—has he been too supportive of that group do you think?

Pulley: I have no comment about that at this point in time, what happened when I was first on the board—his position, that sort of thing—it's past history.

Question: Why can't you comment on the basic reason for the firing?

Pulley: I just don't think it is pertinent at this time.

Question: Don't you think it is pertinent to the future of the institution?

Pulley: What's pertinent to the future of the institution is for the search committee to move ahead and find us a new president. The action has been taken, and there's no reason for us to continue to talk about the past. We need to look to the future.

Question: What sort of president would you like to see as far as their theology, their style, would you like to see somebody who is more aligned with the conservative style?

Pulley: I'm sure our search committee will develop a profile as you normally do when you have a search committee of a church or institution like this. Let them set parameters for....

Question: One question: you said the base salary. What is the base salary?

Pulley: I—you know—I cannot tell you exactly. I just don't know.

Question: About what do you think?

Pulley: I just don't know.

Question: About $100,000?

Pulley: I'm not able to comment accurately.

Question: How long have you been on the board now?

Pulley: I've been on the board two years this time. The first time, twelve and one-half years.

Question: How long have you been chairman?

Pulley: Since yesterday.

Question: Just elected yesterday?

Pulley: Yes, yesterday.

Question: Mr. Weaver, are you comfortable with this position of not letting the students know why your board has taken this action? Do you think this is the right way to approach it? Are you really comfortable with that? Don't you think the students deserve an explanation? Don't you think Baptists deserve an explanation?

Lee Weaver: I think the action of the board speaks for itself and as Mr. Pulley: has eluded to, we are looking forward to a new vision in the future.

Question: What is that vision?

Weaver: I think that vision will be developed as we look at new presidential material and we are looking at the 21st century coming up and we are simply looking forward to that.

Question: Can you expound on that new future you are talking about?

Weaver: No, I really can't. That wouldn't be appropriate to go into that much detail.

Question: Is there any reason you saw it necessary to change the locks on the president's door immediately after this action? We were told that the knob was off the door and he is only allowed to go back with the trustee's permission or something like that.

Pulley: I don't have any comment about that.

Question: Are there hard feelings between some of the trustees and Dr. Dilday?

Pulley: I—uh—no. I don't anticipate . . . .

Question: How do you see Dr. Dilday as an administrator, personally?

Pulley: Dr. Dilday is a good administrator.

Question: Uh huh. What do you think, Mr. Weaver?

Weaver: I think Dr. Dilday was a fine administrator.

Question: Over all, is the Southern Baptist Church too moderate or too conservative? Tell us—I'm not a Southern Baptist—please tell me where the church is. To someone who is not a member of the church—please help me to understand where it's at today and perhaps what direction it is moving towards based on recent conventions.

Pulley: I don't have any comments on that, except to say that the SBC owns the institution. The convention has owned the institution since 1945. (Sic) It's set out in its charter and at least twice in the by-laws. The SBC contributes—I believe at this time it's about $8,000,000 to the institution. So, they care for this institution—and—uh—we are—the institution is devoted to the SBC.

Question: Who are the trustees accountable to?

Pulley: To the convention. To the SBC. We have a fiduciary capacity to the convention. Under the charter and by-laws, we are accountable to the convention.

Question: What sort of effect do you think this sudden firing will have on the seminary and its foundations and support—of the students coming here?

Pulley: The people are very devoted to the seminary. They give to the seminary. They are concerned about the seminary. They are interested in the seminary, and we do not expect that to change. We are dealing here with an institution that's been here since the early 1900's and it will continue in the future.

Question: Do you think this controversy that has come up is just temporary and that the students will get over it soon?

Pulley: I think we are having a normal reaction. I think certainly in due course, it will subside.

Question: This is what you believe the people who attend the annual meeting of the SBC would want the trustees to have done?

Pulley: Mrs. Ledbetter, I don't have any comment on that. That's just too broad a question.

Question: In the sense that you're accountable to them, do you feel you're representing what you believe you should do?

Pulley: We certainly are responsible for representing the convention.

Press Conference ended

Letter from Trustees to SBC Churches and Associations: April 1, 1994

Dear Pastor:

We are happy to announce to you the appointment of William B. Tolar as the Acting President of Southwestern Baptist Theological Seminary effective immediately.

Dr. Tolar is deeply devoted to our Lord Jesus Christ and has a great love for the seminary where he has invested his life in the teaching ministry for almost 30 years. He is greatly loved by those who have worked with him on the seminary campus, by the students who have sat in the classroom and by the thousands of Southern Baptists who have heard him preach in the pulpits of their churches over the years. We are most grateful that under the leadership of God's Spirit he has accepted this key position in such an important time in the life of the seminary. Due to the inordinate amount of publicity which the recent action by the trustees has generated, we feel it important to speak directly to our Southern Baptist family. Hence, this letter is being sent to the pastors in our Convention with the hope that the information contained herein will be shared with members of the congregation. Because directors of missions in each association are vital to our Southern Baptist witness, we also felt it important to send a copy of this letter to them. As you know, the Southern Baptist Convention elects members of the boards of trustees for SBC seminaries and has committed to them "the responsibility to operate the Seminary for the Convention with full authority in all matters of its operation...and is answerable only to the Convention for its acts in operating the Seminary."

Trustees of Southwestern come from 30 different states. We understand this trust and do not take lightly the responsibility of governing the Seminary as instructed by the Constitution and Bylaws of the Southern Baptist Convention. The board sets operating policies and the president is required to carry out these policies. We want you to know and hopefully understand that we had no choice but to require a change in executive leadership.

To effect this change an offer was made that Dr. Dilday elect early retirement. The offer was so generous that it has been referred to as a "golden parachute." It included continuation of full salary and benefits until he was 65 in September, 1995. Furthermore it provided secretarial assistance. Finally and importantly to his financial security, he has been given immediate access to a fund established in 1986 to provide a home at the time of retirement. The total package amounted to almost $400,000, an amount which many Southern

Baptists will consider extravagant. However, we felt this to be fair and equitable as well as a gesture of Christian compassion and grace.

The president was encouraged by the trustee officers to work with them on a retirement proposal which could be achieved in an orderly manner. The president rejected the proposal out of hand with an unwillingness to read the provisions. Subsequently, the trustees felt they had no choice but to dismiss the president. The vote was 80 percent affirmative for the dismissal. Although a strong attempt had been made during the last five years to work in concert with the president, it was increasingly impossible and an impasse had been reached.

Inevitably, a review of an event of this critical nature suggests that a few things could have been done differently. In retrospect we realize that an over-abundance of caution was exercised in limiting access to the presidents office, but the action grew out of concern that the president's office could become a focal point for demonstrations which were already occurring on campus. The president's secretary was back in her place in the office by 3 p.m. the same afternoon.

Contrary to published reports, armed guards were not employed from outside sources. Only campus security personnel were on site.

We were all saddened that Dr. Dilday did not accept early retirement. We now understand had we better informed our Southern Baptist family about the difficulty we were having, the shock of the dismissal would not have been so great. We apologize for the appearance of abruptness.

There were irreconcilable philosophical differences that led to our action. Typical examples are:

(1) An executive with the Cooperative Baptist Fellowship was to speak at the May Commencement. This was in violation of the direction of the board's clearly stated policies, which the president declined to correct. It is totally inappropriate to have a representative from a competing organization at such an important event.

(2) There has been a continuing difference of opinion on the kind of training ministers of music for our churches should receive at the seminary. The music curriculum is excellent but is often out of step with church music as revered and sung in most Southern Baptist congregations. The board had sought for years to maintain the core and add a broadened base that includes traditional, gospel and contemporary elements.

(3) An administrative reorganization plan was recommended that combined three vice presidential positions with the deanships of the three schools, adding a vice president for development. This plan was unacceptable to trustees.

The conflict between the president and the board has been described as grid-lock or logjam. The trustees tried to work cooperatively with the executive officer but efforts led to frustration and lack of confidence and trust. The executive officer forced the issue by his unwillingness to cooperate with the board as evidenced by the items listed above and by:

(1) Repeated criticism of the denominational leaders, members of the board and others.

(2) Failing to adhere to directives of the board not to be involved in the SBC controversy. The majority of the board members felt he was strongly sympathetic to the Cooperative Baptist Fellowship (CBF) agenda in direct opposition to the SBC, which he denies.

(3) At the heart of the controversy is a battle over the nature of Scripture. Using his high office in a denominational institution, Dr. Dilday, in his book *The Doctrine of Biblical Authority*, champions the position from one side of the debate over the nature of Scripture as he shifts the emphasis from the nature to the purpose of Scripture. Dr. Dilday demonstrates a commitment to the principles of higher criticism, which spawned theological liberalism (modernism), neo-orthodoxy, the death of God, situational ethics, etc. From a decidedly biased position, Dr. Dilday is dedicated to berate, misrepresent, and assail those who hold the Bible to be God's inerrant, infallible and authoritative Word.

(4) The relationship became one of constant confrontation, both individually and collectively.

In recent days the students and faculty members have expressed their loyalty to the former president. We understand their dilemma and think their concern is commendable.

The rumor that Dr. Dilday received a positive or favorable annual "Performance Review" from the Executive Committee of the trustees the night before the action is simply a misstatement of fact or it is his own interpretation of what happened. In fact, the committee challenged his actions and attitudes. This has been the case for the previous two years.

The purpose and mission of the Seminary as determined by the Southern Baptist Convention is very much intact. We are looking to the higher good and long term ministry of the school. We know this time has been painful for Dr. Dilday and the trustees. We regret this for both. Nevertheless, we are compelled to look beyond personalities and immediate reaction. The action of the trustees was based on a desire to look to the future of the seminary's ministry within the Southern Baptist Convention and to the vast unreached world.

We ask the students, faculty and Southern Baptist members everywhere to help us move on from this point to continue building upon the rich heritage of preparing men and women to serve Him faithfully in Christian ministry. We need your constant and continuing prayers and support and ask that you assist us with every opportunity the Lord gives you.

You will be interested to know that nine trustees from six states have been appointed as the President's Search Committee. A faculty member and a student will be added soon as advisory members. Rev. Miles Seaborn, Jr., a former SBC missionary to the Philippines who has been pastor of a Fort Worth church for over 26 years, is the chairman.

Committee members are in the process of determining criteria to be used and the process to follow in choosing a new president. The chairman has contacted each of the other five Southern Baptist seminary presidents for suggestions in drawing up this vital information. Please pray for them.

The officers and the members of the board of trustees are grateful for all Southern Baptists who have prayed and continue to pray for Dr. Dilday and the trustees. We have confidence that God has a ministry for the seminary which will foster harmony within the convention and bring honor and glory to our Lord Jesus Christ.

Cordially,

Ralph Pulley, Jr. Chairman
Lee Weaver, Vice Chairman
T. Bob Davis, Secretary

BOARD OF TRUSTEES
Southwestern Baptist Theological Seminary
Fort Worth, Texas

Letter from "Friends of Southwestern" in response to trustee letter: April 18, 1994

Dear SBC Pastor,

On March 9, 1994, the Board of Trustees of Southwestern Baptist Theological Seminary (SWBTS) in Fort Worth, fired Dr. Russell Dilday, president of Southwestern since 1978.

On April 1 the Board of Trustees (BOT)* mailed a letter to all pastors and associational directors of missions in the Southern Baptist Convention "explaining" the "reasons"—a list of charges and allegations the trustees managed to develop during the days after they fired the president of the world's largest theological seminary.

That four-page letter contains gross inaccuracies, distortions and misrepresentations. The printing and mailing of this collection of untruths cost more than $10,000 in Cooperative Program funds.

Friends of Southwestern believe these false charges cannot go unchallenged. The following pages, 2-4, contain summaries of the charges and allegations by the Board of Trustees (BOT). After each charge is the FACTS.

The funding for this response comes from private donations, and not from Cooperative Program funds. We regret the necessity of this letter, but feel it is important that Southern Baptists know the truth about the disgraceful events of March 9 and its effect on students, faculty, and staff of Southwestern, and Baptists around the world. Perhaps some action can be taken at the convention in Orlando, June 14-16, to correct this situation.

From Friends of Southwestern Seminary, including:

John McNaughton, Chair, Southwestern Council
Jeanne Grubbs, Former Member, Southwestern Council
Kenneth H. Cooper, M.D., Immediate Past Chair, Southwestern Council
Jerold McBride, President, Baptist General Convention of Texas, Pastor FBC San Angelo
Jerry W. Yowell, Past Chair, Southwestern Council
Phil Lineberger, Past President, Baptist General Convention of Texas, Pastor FBC Tyler

The Southwestern Council is the seminary's 38-year-old fund-raising and advisory group. It consists of 138 laypersons.

Whenever the "SWBTS Board of Trustees" or BOT is referred to on these pages, it applies to 80% of the board—those who voted to fire Russell Dilday on March 9.

*The following pages contain summaries of the charges and allegations the SWBTS Board of Trustees (BOT) * made against Russell Dilday. The minutes of the board meetings, as well as the contents of the annual appraisal forms, refute these allegations. Following each charge of the Board of Trustees (BOT) is the truth (FACT).*

"Doctrinal Differences"

BOT: "At the heart of the controversy is a battle over the nature of Scripture." ... "Dilday's doctrinal beliefs contradict basic scriptures." . . . "Dilday is dedicated to berate, misrepresent, and assail those who hold the Bible to be God's. . . authoritative Word."... "Using his high office in a denominational institution, Dr. Dilday, in his book, *The Doctrine of Biblical Authority*, champions the position from one side of the debate over the nature of Scripture as he shifts the emphasis from the nature to the purpose of Scripture. Dr. Dilday demonstrates a commitment to the principles of higher criticism, which spawned theological liberalism (modernism), neo-orthodoxy, the death of God, situational ethics, etc. From a decidedly biased position, Dr. Dilday is dedicated to berate, misrepresent, and assail those who hold the Bible to be God's inerrant, infallible, and authoritative Word."

FACT: Dilday's doctrinal beliefs have never been criticized as "contradicting basic scriptures." The board has never gone on record criticizing his personal doctrinal beliefs as unbiblical or contrary to sound Baptist theology.

Dilday's book presents the Bible as the perfect word of God, absolutely trustworthy. The TRUTH about this allegation is best summarized by a statement from the Faculty of the SWBTS School of Theology:

Statement from the Faculty of the School of Theology, Southwestern Baptist Theological Seminary (adopted April 2, 1994)

In their letter to pastors, SWBTS trustee officers implied that President Dilday holds liberal views of Scripture and uses "higher criticism" in destructive ways. Both charges are false. We respond not just to defend Dr. Dilday, but also to defend valid methods of Bible study among Southern Baptists.

In *The Doctrine of Biblical Authority*, published by Convention Press in 1982 and widely used for doctrinal study in Southern Baptist churches, Dilday strongly affirms traditional, conservative Southern Baptist views of the Scriptures. No careful reader should miss his repeated statements about his firm confidence in the full truth, inspiration, and authority of the Bible.

The book opens with Dilday's saying, "My own conviction is an unapologetic and unconditional commitment to biblical authority" (p. 10) and closes with an appeal to obey the teaching of the Bible (pp. 129-30).

Nothing in this book raises any question about the author's conservative views of the Scriptures. It is not true that Dr. Dilday is "dedicated to berate, misrepresent, and assail those who hold the Bible to be God's inerrant, infallible, and authoritative word." In fact, he has repeatedly urged us to avoid such practices. We are dismayed and offended by misrepresentations, distortions, and the use of guilt by association in the letter from the trustee officers.

We believe fully that "the Holy Bible was written by men divinely inspired and is the record of God's revelation of Himself to man" (SBC Statement of Baptist Faith and Message, 1963). Because the Bible is the inspired record of God's self-revelation, we affirm its authority. Inspired by God, the Bible was written by men and is a historical and literary document. Christians must remain free to use in a reverent way literary and historical tools of Bible study to understand what God is saying to us through the biblical authors.

In 1986 Dilday led the six SBC seminaries in adopting "The Glorieta Statement," which says, in part, that the Bible is "not errant in any area of reality." In 1987 he took the lead in planning the first national Inerrancy Conference.

"Disloyalty, Insubordination, Arrogance and Isolationism"

BOT: Dilday has repeatedly been cited for disloyalty and insubordination. He regularly refused to take direction given to him by those appointed to do so. He was arrogant, an isolationist, and disdained authority. He discouraged dissent and debate of issues important to students, faculty, trustees, and society. He mismanaged relationships with both conservative and liberal segments of Baptist life. The trustees tried to work cooperatively with the executive officer but efforts led to frustration and lack of confidence and trust. The executive officer forced the issue by his unwillingness to cooperate with the Board . . . .

FACT: Dilday carried out every one of the board's directives or policies. With only one or two exceptions, all recommendations Dilday brought to the board during the past 16 years were approved. He was never charged with disloyalty or insubordination by the board or anyone else—until after he was fired. Individual board members may make suggestions and express opinions, but the authority of the board is expressed only when the board acts officially, as a body. The minutes of the board meetings will show that not once has Dilday failed to carry out directives given by the board.

Keith Parks Invited to Commencement

BOT: "An executive with the Cooperative Baptist Fellowship was to speak at the May Commencement. This was in violation of the direction of the board's clearly stated policies, which the president declined to correct . . . ."

FACT: The faculty program committee's invitation to Dr. Keith Parks to speak at the 1994 commencement was extended in 1991 when Parks was with the Foreign Mission Board. The trustees were not aware of the invitation until Dilday announced it during his report to the board on March 9, 1994. The decision to dismiss Dilday was made before the board was even aware that Parks was to be the speaker. This could not have been a factor "that led to (the board's) action."

Church Music School

BOT: "There has been a continuing difference of opinion on the kind of training ministers of music for our churches should receive at the seminary. The .music curriculum is excellent but is often out of step with church music as revered and sung in most Southern Baptist congregations. The board had sought for years to maintain the core and add a broadened base that includes traditional, gospel and contemporary elements." Southwestern's approach is "far behind what is going on in churches today," said trustee T. Bob Davis. Trustees have' pushed for "a new approach to a broad based teaching of music," but have found the current music school faculty unresponsive to their concerns, said Davis, who is active in the music ministry at Prestonwood Church in Dallas. Surveys done by the seminary "overwhelmingly indicate a need for a balanced teaching in the music area" including "liturgical, traditional, gospel, contemporary, even seeker-service type music," Davis said . . . ." The trustees wanted another approach, but Russell and the entrenched old guard was bound and determined to foil any effort to succeed," Davis said.

FACT: Dilday never refused to carry out any policy or suggestion from the board regarding the music school. The minutes of the meetings of the board prove this. The faculty and administration, including President Dilday, have worked patiently and laboriously over the past few years to meet the expectations of some of the trustees within the limits of the academic requirements of a graduate music school. The TRUTH about this allegation is best summarized by a statement from the Dean (representing the faculty) of the SWBTS School of Music: *Statement from the Dean of the School of Music, Southwestern Baptist Theological Seminary (April 11, 1994)*

In response to the concerns of certain trustees about the music school, in 1987 the faculty began serious and open discussion of the issue. In 1988 a study committee was charged with the responsibility of determining how our training of church musicians was perceived by different-groups and what we might do to improve that training.

A survey was sent to a broad spectrum of people asking for their opinion. The results were overwhelmingly supportive of the church music work offered at Southwestern.

Serious consideration was given to all suggestions and eight special courses, conferences and seminars have been offered during the past three years.

In 1991 Dean James McKinney established the Advisory Council of Metroplex Ministers of Music to bring to the campus ministers of music from a wide spectrum of churches to discuss current practices in church music and ways the seminary might better relate to churches. The council meets each semester; 18 churches have participated.

The Field Education class our music students are required to take visits a number of different churches each year with the express purpose of exposing students to different forms and style of worship.

Three years ago, at the invitation of Dean McKinney members of the Music Ministry department faculty met with two trustees, T. Bob Davis and John McKay, for a discussion of trustee concerns. Davis and McKay were then invited to visit any music classes and speak to students or faculty. After the visits they made a favorable report to the full trustee body.

Almost half the church musicians enrolled at our six Southern Baptist seminaries are at SWBTS. Southwestern graduates are in great demand; alumni presently serve in many strategic church, college, and denominational positions in the United States and around the world. Enrollment in the School of Music at SWBTS is growing; many prospective students have expressed interest in attending Southwestern.

A summary report of what the School of Church Music has done since 1988 to meet trustee concerns, plus documentation for any of the information contained in this statement, is available upon request.

This is a summary of a statement made by James McKinney, Dean of the School of Church Music, SWBTS. The statement was made at the unanimous request of the music faculty.

Enrollment Decline

BOT: Dilday failed to strengthen and advance the growth of the school from 1985–93. The enrollment declined 20% while the administrative staff rose by 20%.

FACT: All six SBC seminaries declined 20% or more in enrollment since 1985–86. Factors in this decline include demographics and economics, as well as the ongoing denominational controversy which became widely public in 1985. Southwestern has increased in enrollment for the last five consecutive semesters. The school has advanced in the estimate of outside appraisers as well as denominational constituency. In an attempt to reduce administrative staff for a significant economic savings, Dilday proposed a bold realignment proposal (see below).

Realignment Plan

BOT: "An administrative reorganization plan was recommended that combined three vice presidential positions with the deanships of the three schools, adding a vice president for development. This plan was unacceptable to trustees."

FACT: Dilday proposed a realignment plan designed to drastically reduce the number of administrative personnel and save the seminary between $200,000-$300,000 a year. Board members looked with favor on the administrative restructuring plan in committee meetings; they did not reject it but deferred it to the executive committee for further study. Just recently the board added yet another new administrator when they hired John Seelig.

"Repeated Criticism of Denominational leaders"

DOT: Dilday was guilty of: "Repeated criticism of denominational leaders, members of the board, and others. Failure to adhere to directive of the Board not to be involved in the politics of the SBC controversy.

FACT: Dilday publicly and vigorously opposed the SBC takeover efforts from 1979 to 1989. However, after a covenant agreement with the board of trustees in 1989, he has not criticized denominational leaders. Dilday has not violated at any time the directive in the covenant agreement that neither board members nor the president would be involved in the SBC controversy.

"Sympathetic to CBF"

BOT: "The majority of the board members felt he (Dilday) was strongly sympathetic to the Cooperative Baptist Fellowship (CBF) agenda in direct opposition to the SBC, which he denies."

FACT: While Dilday sympathizes with disillusioned Baptists in the CBF, he has clearly not advocated CBF. Dilday has uncompromisingly given total support to the SBC and the Cooperative Program.

Performance Review

BOT: "The rumor that Dr. Dilday received a positive or favorable annual 'Performance Review' from the Executive Committee of the trustees the night before the action is simply a misstatement of fact or it is his own interpretation of what happened. In fact, the committee challenged his actions and attitudes. This has been the case for the previous two years."

FACT: The report of a favorable and positive performance review is not a rumor. Not once during the meeting "the night before the action" did the Executive Committee "challenge his actions and attitudes." While reviewing the 10 criteria by which the president's performance is appraised, the secretary of the board expressed the opinion, "Russell, we know you're doing a marvelous job in these areas." When board members began to discuss faculty members about whom they were "suspicious," Dilday told the board he had heard rumors that he was to be fired. The trustees denied that there was any basis for the rumors and dismissed the stories as untrue. These denials were made even though the plans were already in place, and news releases announcing the firing had been printed. At the conclusion of the evening session, Dilday escorted the Executive Committee out to meet the 200 students gathered in the hall outside the room. He said, "We have just had a frank and open appraisal review and, in spite of the rumors, there were no confrontations, and I am still your president." The group cheered and had a prayer of thanks for the committee and the good news. Dilday and the concerned students went home that evening "assured" there would be no effort to fire Dilday at this time.

More about the "Performance Review"

BOT: The executive committee of the board has challenged Dilday's actions and attitudes for the past two years.

FACT: The minutes of the March 1993 meeting of the board of trustees report the findings of the Executive Committee's appraisal: "The committee agreed

unanimously to commend President Dilday on his performance in all the categories on the formal appraisal form." The only negative criticism was brought by
trustee Damon Shook: "While faculty recommended in the past has been conservative biblically and theologically, efforts should be made to recommend faculty
who are also politically conservative . . ." (Minutes of March 7-10, 1993, meeting, page 8, signed by T. Bob Davis. secretary). ("Politically conservative" means
supportive of the fundamentalist takeover of the SBC.)

"Lack of Vision and Strategic Planning"
BOT: Dilday lacked vision and strategic planning skills necessary to solidify the
school s future.

FACT: Dilday's administration has been marked by a strong emphasis on long-
range and strategic planning. He enlisted a vice president, Dr. Scotty Gray, to
give fulltime attention to developing and monitoring a series of strategic plans
which were complimented by the recent accrediting team and are models for
other schools in the Association of Theological Schools and throughout the SBC.
The contents of the annual appraisal forms refute this charge.

Early Retirement or The "Golden Parachute"
BOT: "The (retirement) offer was so generous that it has been referred to as a
"golden parachute . . . included continuation of full salary and benefits until he
was 65 . . . secretarial assistance . . . access to a fund established in 1986 to
provide a home . . . The total package amounted to almost $400,000."

FACT: The "Golden Parachute" offered in a confrontational and threatening
spirit as a "buyout"—or even a bribe—does not calculate to $400,000. The
housing fund is a deferred compensation plan to provide $150,000 at age 65.
The plan was approved by another group of trustees (1986); it was not a provision from this current board. The money was deducted from Dilday's salary each
month and deferred to the special fund.

BOT: Dilday's refusal to accept early retirement brought embarrassment and
potential permanent injury to the seminary.

FACT: When Dilday refused to accept early retirement from the officers of the
board, he offered to announce to the board his retirement plans for age 67 or 68;
this offer was refused. Dilday was told to either accept the "golden parachute" or
be dismissed. The board's actions—not Dilday's refusal to retire—"brought
embarrassment and potential permanent injury to the seminary."